MARITIME STRATEGY
AND GLOBAL ORDER

MARITIME STRATEGY AND GLOBAL ORDER

Markets, Resources, Security

Daniel Moran and James A. Russell, Editors

Georgetown University Press / Washington, DC

Library of Congress Cataloging-in-Publication Data
Maritime strategy and global order : markets, resources, security / Daniel Moran and James A. Russell, editors.
      pages cm
  Includes bibliographical references and index.
  ISBN 978-1-62616-300-3 (hardcover : alk. paper) — ISBN 978-1-62616-072-9 (pbk. : alk. paper) — ISBN 978-1-62616-301-0 (ebook)
 1. Naval strategy. 2. Security, International. I. Moran, Daniel, editor. II. Russell, James A. (James Avery), 1958– editor.
  V163.M37 2016
  359'.03—dc23
                    2015024227

17 16   9 8 7 6 5 4 3 2 First printing

Printed in the United States of America

Cover design by Trudi Gershenov Design. Top cover image © National Maritime Museum, Greenwich, London; bottom cover image courtesy of US Navy/Mass Communication Specialist 3rd Class Dylan McCord.

Contents

Acknowledgments

It is a pleasure, in presenting this volume, to thank the US Navy's International Programs Office, which supported the conference where it was originally conceived; and the Department of War Studies at King's College of the University of London, which served as host for the event.

The contents of this book are entirely the responsibilities of the individual chapter authors. Nothing in it reflects official policy, nor has any of it been reviewed or approved by any agency of any government.

Daniel Moran
James A. Russell
Monterey, California

Introduction

DANIEL MORAN AND JAMES A. RUSSELL

For the purposes of this volume strategy means a course of action, conducted by a political community in its relations with others, in which the use of force is not ruled out. This is not to say that violence is strategy's only concern, nor its preferred instrument, merely that strategic interactions differ, in their psychological and moral characteristics, and sometimes in their logic, from dealings governed by the conventions of the marketplace, routine diplomatic practice, and so on. The ends of strategy are in principle those of policy, to which the use of forcible means, real or implied, may nevertheless add imponderable and even confounding features. To have politics at all, one must be willing to compromise, and to fight. Strategy is concerned with where and how this line is drawn, and the manner in which it is crossed. It is in the reconciliation of ends and means that strategy poses its most severe challenges, and achieves its most distinctive results.[1]

Our theme is the exercise of strategy on and from the sea. Maritime strategy, to borrow a phrase from Clausewitz (who paid it little mind), has long been recognized as having a "dual nature." Traditionally, as Nicholas Tracy has said, the term has been used to describe "the employment of naval forces to achieve political ends by their impact on international trade."[2] Trade is, in itself, a crucial source of political power, and of explicit or implicit strategic leverage, as the contents of this volume demonstrate. Yet it strains belief, or at any rate muddies the water, to conceive of trade as a weapon. The distinctive weapons of maritime strategy are navies, whose application is shaped by the fact that human beings do not live on the sea but on land. As a consequence, as Julian Corbett observed, "great issues between nations at war have always been decided—except in the rarest cases—either by what your army can do against your enemy's territory and national life, or else by the fear of what the fleet makes it possible for your army to do."[3] Navies on their own have limited value for controlling people and territory. Their strategic leverage lies in their capacity to secure or deny access to resources, to markets, to enemies, to allies, to battlefields, and to information.

In addressing these matters, our focus is less on the actions of navies in war than on their role in creating and sustaining global order, as reflected in the abundant, reliable, and generally nonviolent movement of goods, money, and people on the sea. When sailing navies mastered the oceans, they made the world a much bigger place for its human inhabitants, literally and figuratively; but they also made it a smaller one, lending impetus to a new and compelling idea: that the human prospect could be improved by increasing interaction among humanity's diverse communities, from which any and all might benefit. As Steven Haines observes in his chapter on international law, the great Dutch jurist Hugo Grotius first conceived of the sea as a natural zone of freedom because its ubiquity could only be understood as a providential sign that the many parts of the human family should come to know one another. Such an idea would not have been thinkable if the sea had not been transformed from a nearly impassable barrier into what Mahan would famously call "a great highway."

That the exercise of freedom is dependent on the establishment of order is as true at sea as on land, and explains why global order is a strategic achievement rather than a natural phenomenon. Order can take, and has taken, diverse forms; but none of them are value free.[4] There are always those who think they can profit from disorder, or that the workings of global markets or the system of nation-states are configured to do them harm. Such impressions are not necessarily misplaced. It is scarcely credible to argue that order, however constituted, is equivalent to equity.[5] Yet the consequences of global disorder for peace and prosperity remain, on balance, so foreseeably appalling that its avoidance can fairly be judged the preeminent goal of modern politics.

The preservation of peace at sea, and of free access to it, provides crucial ballast for the stability of the international system. This volume aims to shed light on how this is accomplished. Throughout, the emphasis falls on the longer and slower rhythms whereby the military, political, and economic uses of the sea contribute to the maintenance of peace, the integration of the world economy, and, when necessary, the conduct of war. We have thus sought to place the development, maintenance, and use of naval forces within the broader political and economic contexts that give them meaning.

Our goal in this volume is to draw attention to the exercise of maritime power in its diverse forms, and over the long run. The governing idea throughout is that the significance of maritime strategy becomes more clearly visible when viewed across significant stretches of time and space, and when the integration of military and nonmilitary elements is given full weight. In peace, as in war, the passage of time accrues to the benefit of those who have the means to employ the forms of strategic leverage that mastery of the sea affords. This process is easily obscured by the episodic drama and intense violence of naval combat. Periods of violent conflict at sea do not serve well as the baseline from which the general working of maritime strategy can be judged. We have tried to do these periods justice in the chapters that follow, and do not mean to diminish their consequence. Yet they are the exception rather than the rule at all times, and most certainly so recently, as the last great era of naval warfare fades from living memory.

Although this book is mainly concerned with contemporary conditions, all its contributors have sought to bring an appropriate depth of historical perspective to their work. The first three chapters, which constitute part I, are explicitly historical in character. They survey the exercise of maritime strategy from the dawn of the industrial era to the end of the Cold War, a period during which stretches of "long peace" and "long war" are equally in evidence. Andrew Lambert's account of the Pax Britannica reveals maritime strategy as the quintessential tool for the pursuit of empire, from which has sprung the globalization of the modern world economy. It was under the shelter of British naval supremacy that Europe's global influence reached its apogee, an achievement that did not prove sufficiently impressive to quell the rivalrous appetites of those who felt that their share was insufficient. The calamitous results are the subject of Daniel Moran's chapter on the "long war" that began in Europe in 1914 and had spread around the world by 1945, before extinguishing itself in a conflagration of unparalleled ferocity.

Whether Geoffrey Till's discussion of maritime strategy in the Cold War is a study of peace or war is doubtless a matter of opinion. But that the Cold War was long is one of its essential characteristics, and goes far toward explaining its outcome. Like the world wars that preceded it, the Cold War was ultimately won by the richer side, in the form of an alliance held together, for all intents and purposes, by water. It was across the water that crushing economic advantages gradually accrued, to which the Soviet Union, like Germany before it, could finally offer no convincing response. The navies of the United States and its Allies "held the ring" while all this unfolded, as Till says. Although the end seemed surprising when it came, it appears much less so in retrospect.

The last global challenger to the supremacy of the West's navies disappeared with the collapse of the Soviet Union. Since then, the exercise of maritime strategy has been devoted primarily to problems of regional security. Part II of this volume considers four examples. Each presents distinctive strategic challenges and opportunities, and the future of each will depend heavily on the successful management of competing interests that converge on the water. Collectively, they reflect the diversity of challenges that current conditions present at sea.

In the Mediterranean, as Giuseppe Schivardi argues, the central question is whether this sea, on whose shores Western Civilization was born, can regain its ancient role as a "bridge" among the diverse societies that surround it, or whether it remains a "fault" dividing North and South. The main challenge now facing Mediterranean navies is a humanitarian crisis, owing to the recurring upheavals of the Muslim societies on its southern and eastern shores, and the diverging economic development of Southern Europe and North Africa.

The South China Sea, in contrast, is an arena of increasingly open economic and geopolitical rivalry, driven above all by China's effort to regain what it regards as its natural regional preponderance. As Alessio Patalano's account shows, the stakes go far beyond control of the resources that lie beneath the seabed. In the final analysis, this region's strategic challenges are chiefly about prestige, from which more concrete forms of power may grow. That the region's states have profound motives for minimizing their differences is also true, however. The South China Sea defines a well-integrated economic space in whose prosperity all its littoral nations have a share, a common interest that has moderated their conduct up to now.

Klaus Dodds considers the Arctic, where the main strategic challenges are ecological. Until recently, the Arctic was no more than an icy planetary carapace, a refuge for submarines, and a magnet for scientists and adventurers. But now the gradual melting of the ice has stirred the interest of the Arctic's littoral states. In contrast to the South China Sea, which defines a region with hundreds of millions of inhabitants, the High North is a place where those who actually live there must struggle to be heard by the powerful. If the Arctic were to become more readily accessible to trade and the exploitation of its natural resources, it would present all its littoral states with a combination of economic opportunities and security concerns, none of which can yet be judged with real clarity—though none can safely be ignored, either. Even on its warmest day, the Arctic remains an extraordinarily challenging maritime environment, at once fragile and unforgiving. Russia, which has the longest Arctic coastline, has so far shown the greatest determination to make the most of it; but what "the most" might amount to remains to be seen.

Our fourth regional case centers on the Indian Ocean, around which a good deal of real but mostly indecisive fighting has raged for more than half a century. James Russell argues that, despite its unsettled surroundings, the Indian Ocean retains its long-standing role as a damper on regional conflict. This is partly because its size exceeds the grasp of any of the regional powers that might aspire to influence it. Yet it is also partly because, as in the South China Sea, even the region's most dissatisfied and aggressive littoral states could not expect to gain by disrupting the transoceanic trade on which its economy depends, and which flows under the effective protection of the United States.

Part III deals with some of the major structural elements of contemporary maritime strategy—its "architecture." Of these, the most fundamental is the warship, whose evolution in the aftermath of the Cold War is described by Larrie Ferreiro. His analysis shows how new strategic and operational imperatives have found expression in the design of warships. In the twenty years following the fall of the Berlin Wall, warships became less numerous but larger, more capable, more expensive, and more modular in their design—a fair reflection of an increasingly diversified and distributed strategic environment. These changes have, in turn, imposed themselves on the shipyards and logistical systems whereby warships are created and sustained, and on the budgets to pay for them. Because warships are by nature nodes in a complex system for distributing power, their design and employment always reveal how the world works.

The distribution of power at sea has always been embedded in a dense structure of legal norms, whose historical emergence and current condition are described by Steven Haines. He shows international law to be an essentially practical business, rooted in the real conduct of states, and serviceable to their needs. Generally speaking, international law has proven more significant in regulating the use of force at sea than on land, if only because so much of the sea is beyond the reach of national jurisdiction. Yet its power to resolve disputes and shape conduct at the strategic level remains more limited than a high regard for the interests of humanity might wish.

The contribution of maritime strategy to global order is owed in large part to the weight of economic interests that command of the sea creates, when this command is employed to facilitate the operation of global markets. These interests, if arrayed behind a common strategic purpose, normally weigh heavily on the side of peace. There is, of course, no guarantee that the weight will be sufficient, or reliably assembled. Michael Klare considers the modern world economy with an eye to identifying any structural features that might cause the weight to shift. He finds these features in the rising international competition for access to natural resources, above all oil. Whether such competition may someday break the market forces that currently contain it is impossible to say. But the fact remains that oil is simply the most important of a range of raw materials that are mostly consumed far from where they are produced. Sustaining the political relationships on which such trade depends, and defending the sea lanes over which it moves, are matters of supreme importance to the world's navies.

Our volume concludes by considering the role of information and intelligence in the exercise of maritime strategy. Navies, as John Ferris shows, are voracious consumers of both, and producers too. As the range of interests that navies must defend has expanded, so too has the range of types of information that they need. Navies in the past struggled to understand the sea, and other navies. Today, they are equally concerned to understand the political and social forces that determine how the sea is used, and where threats to its use may arise.

It goes without saying that a book of this kind is not intended to exhaust its subject, but to open a door to it. Our aim has been to highlight those aspects of maritime strategy that are of the greatest salience in circumstances when a major war at sea is unlikely, but when the orderly, productive, and militarily effective use of the sea is of paramount concern. We hope this book will be of value to both students and their teachers, and to anyone concerned with what is today called grand strategy, of which maritime strategy is the original example.

NOTES

1. There are, needless to say, many other ways to approach one of the most fungible concepts in the lexicon of modern politics. The value of insisting upon the use of force as an element of strategic behavior is analytical: It helps to bring the most distinctive and unnerving dimensions of strategic interaction to the fore. Other approaches have other virtues. Official definitions in the United States emphasize the breadth of

interests, organizations, and methods that strategy may encompass, a tendency coincident with the unparalleled expansion of the American national security state during the Cold War, but persisting to this day. The US National Security Strategy published in 2015 offered no definition at all, but described an array of interests that American strategy would pursue, ranging from territorial defense to the improvement of global health. White House, *National Security Strategy 2015* (Washington, DC: White House, 2015), whitehouse.gov/sites/default/files/docs/2015_national_security_strategy.pdf.

2. Nicholas Tracy, *Attack on Maritime Trade* (Toronto: University of Toronto Press, 1991), 1.

3. Julian Corbett, *Some Principles of Maritime Strategy* (London: Longmans, Green, 1911), 13.

4. An excellent brief summary of the theoretical literature on the normative character of global order is given by Rosemary Foot and Andrew Walter, *China, the United States, and Global Order* (New York: Cambridge University Press, 2011), 1–15.

5. This is easily forgotten even by those who should know better. Thus N. Gregory Mankiw, the chairman of Harvard University's economics department, has declared, in a newspaper column supporting trade liberalization, that the beneficial effects of free trade are a "no-brainer" on which modern economists have achieved "near unanimity"; see N. Gregory Mankiw, "Economists Actually Agree on This: The Wisdom of Free Trade," *New York Times*, April 24, 2015. Any number of commentators immediately noted the contrast between this lapidary claim and the discussion of trade in Mankiw's popular introductory textbook, where he explains that the net benefits of trade only exist because "the gains of the winners exceed the losses of the losers, so the winners could compensate the losers and still be better off." "But," he goes on to ask, "*will* trade make everyone better off? Probably not. In practice, compensation for the losers from international trade is rare" (emphasis in the original). N. Gregory Mankiw, *Principles of Economics*, 7th ed. (Stamford, CT: Cengage Learning, 2015), 177.

PART I

Long War—Long Peace

CHAPTER 1

The Pax Britannica and the Advent of Globalization

ANDREW LAMBERT

Between the downfall of Napoleon and the outbreak of World War I, Britain sustained and exploited unequaled naval and economic power that enabled it to build a world empire of profit. This last great maritime empire, like those that went before, was built on money and communications. As one contemporary observed, Britain had become "a world Venice."[1] The British expanded trade and provided ever-faster communications across secure oceans—entirely in their own interest, it should be stressed—creating the modern, globalized world in the process. Although other states profited from British activity, entering new markets without the costs of control, and expanding their economic horizons, few adopted the model. Without sea power to dominate the oceans, it would have been unwise to invest heavily in global economic activity when the outbreak of war would allow the British to seize those investments. Similarly, few understood the subtle, elegant way in which Britain harmonized public and private interests, employing critical assets for commerce and war, to keep down costs.

Yet this elegant construction disguised profound weaknesses and critical vulnerabilities. The primary threat to this unique, highly advantageous global position came from the one part of the world that Britain could not control: the continent of Europe. If Britain exerted significant influence in Europe, it was because its aims were essentially negative: the maintenance of an approximate equilibrium in which no hegemonic power dominated the western continent, while ensuring that the key invasion staging posts of the Rhine and the Schelde rivers remained in the hands of minor powers. Threats to this situation in 1815, 1830, and 1870 saw the British act quickly and effectively.

THE PAX BRITANNICA

Although Britain's bombastic self-justification in the late nineteenth century made a conscious connection with the Roman imperium, the reality of British power was strikingly different from the classical model. The British did not rule the known world, they were not a military power, and they avoided, whenever possible, the need to rule peoples and collect taxes. Yet there remains an element of truth; both the Romans and the British imposed peace for a purpose. The British Pax was a highly fluid system of global control that evolved to provide cheap security and expanding trade, to ensure low taxes and high employment at home, both to satisfy the increasingly powerful middle-class voters and to defuse domestic instability. Whatever late Victorian apologists might have implied, the British worked to sustain peace because peace was better for business, and they had no ambitions that required them to attack another major power. They did not so much impose peace as work to sustain it in defense of their interests.

The purpose of Pax Britannica was to avoid international activity that threatened British interests, European or imperial. Stability and peace were good for business, for capital exports, and for the vital flow of food and raw materials into the British Isles. And they could only be sustained by a maritime strategy that relied on industrial and technological leadership, and sustained economic commitment to secure long-term dominance. This required constant, sophisticated monitoring and low-level interventions, with occasional bursts of intense activity, deterrence, arms races, and colonial seizures in response to the most blatant threats.

In contrast to the detailed operational-level planning that underlay the emergence of the Prusso-German strategic concept for land warfare in the mid–nineteenth century, the British Pax evolved a more diversified, flexible, and responsive approach, the first recognizably modern grand strategy, relying on the integration of civil and military leadership. Not having the luxury of planning for predictable wars against its continental neighbors, Britain emphasized higher-level preparation based on intelligence gathering, information dominance, and technological superiority, while planning to mobilize reserves of seaman and ships from the private sector, along with industry and finance.

In the first half of the nineteenth century, strategy was determined by the cabinet, which included statesmen with experience giving higher direction to war between 1803 and 1815. In addition, the cabinet could call on the advice of senior officers and outside experts as required. After the death of Henry Palmerston in 1865, the cabinets gradually compensated for their lack of military expertise by evolving a formal civil–military coordinating body, which became the Committee of Imperial Defense in 1904, ensuring that Britain went to war in 1914 with a uniquely capable system for the higher direction of global conflict. The civilians retained control of the higher direction of war and the military planned strategy and operations, while commercial and industrial expertise could be co-opted to win the conflict. In 1914 Britain thought and fought on a global scale. Its rivals, which included its allies, did not. This outlook reflected the fact that British policymakers operated at the junction between commerce, capital, and strategy.

One of the key strengths of the British system was that it remained open to new, often informal, inputs. Connections between the state, commerce, shipping, engineering, banking, insurance, science, and geography were extensive, and often personal. Key individuals linked information, power, and application; for instance, John Barrow, for forty years permanent secretary to the Admiralty, was an expert on China, and a founder of the Royal Geographical Society—the informal strategic intelligence organization that served the Admiralty, the War Office and Foreign Office, and Indian and other colonial governments. Barrow's advice, and that of the opium merchants Jardine Matheson Company, provided Britain with an effective strategy to fight China in 1842. Steamships and hydrographers turned this intelligence into effectual action, enabling a small amphibious task force to seize the southern end of the Grand Canal. With London thus having denied Beijing its rice supply, China made peace the next day.[2]

SEA POWER

If sea power provided the core of the Pax Britannica, it must be understood as far more than the armed might of the Royal Navy. The sea was central to Britain's security, prosperity, and stability. Sea power was not a strategic option; it was an existential necessity that dominated every sphere of British life, from political calculation to popular culture. The Royal Navy may have been Britannia's right arm, but it was organically connected to every other sinew of the British body politic. Such total engagement between nation and ocean was not unique, but Britain would be the last maritime great power. Although the British chose a Roman metaphor to express their power, they understood that their sea-based economy and culture owed far more to Athens and Venice, empires that owed their very existence to the sea. Like those classical precursors, Britain's sea power reflected weakness, not strength. Its sea power enabled it to overcome its geographical limitations and lacks of natural resources through external trade, colonies, and an alternative strategy based on economic warfare. The English consciously chose to become a sea power in the early sixteenth century, and long before 1815 they had evolved a distinctive state that depended on the ocean. If Britain lost the ability to use the sea, it would be utterly destroyed. As Admiral John Fisher observed, "It's not invasion we have to fear, but starvation!" British sea power provided strategic defense for a maritime empire. By contrast, modern usage treats sea power as a power projection asset. At the turn of the twenty-first century, the United States is the dominant sea power in strategic terms, but no one would argue that it is dependent upon the ocean for its existence. For continental states, sea power is a matter of choice, not necessity.

The evolution of the British Constitution reflected the need to integrate commerce and landowning; in exchange for their taxes, wealthy merchants required a degree of political power. In 1688 the partnership between the aristocracy and the City of London imposed a constitutional settlement that took control of the Royal Navy from the king, and shared it between land and trade—the people who paid for it. Within twenty years the House of Commons would legislate to compel the navy to commit 25 percent of its ships to the defense of trade. The City of London loved the navy. It rewarded naval heroes handsomely, and it honored their sacrifice; it is no accident that Nelson is buried in Saint Paul's, the cathedral of the City of London, and not in Westminster Abbey. When British naval dominance was challenged in the late nineteenth century, it was the City that took control of big navy agitation, and unseated Prime Minister William Gladstone.[3]

THE CHERBOURG STRATEGY

Although Pax Britannica is normally associated with "gunboat diplomacy," the grand strategy of British power was both more complex and more potent. In the realm of great power relations, British policy relied on an effective sea-based deterrent. And though Britain lacked the military power to invade and defeat the other major powers, its naval power meant that it could not be invaded or defeated either. The economic implications of this sort of maritime power were obvious to all students of the Napoleonic conflict. Britain would outlast its enemies so that, in the end, even the greatest conflicts would be decided by economic strangulation. The British knew that this agonizingly slow form of war was best avoided, and posed great risks to itself; but even so, it was quite enough to deter its continental rivals from seeking any sort of direct confrontation. That said, however, it must be emphasized that the Pax was anything but peaceful in the wider world. Britain used the same strategic instruments with which it deterred other major powers to coerce and compel smaller and weaker ones. The ultimate symbol of the Pax, the colonial gunboat, was a by-product of deterrence.[4]

Between 1815 and 1914, Britain deployed major fleets to demonstrate its naval power in European waters, the Mediterranean, the Atlantic, and occasionally the Baltic. The appearance of such a fleet in the West Indies in the early 1860s protected Canada against Union threats during the American Civil War. Elsewhere, British naval power could be deployed in smaller units, which were made up of the cruisers and gunboats that represented British imperial interests wherever trade or investment warranted their presence. Occasionally, they had to use force to suppress piracy, pry open markets, or collect debts.

This much is clear from existing studies; yet there was also a third element required to sustain Pax Britannica. Technological development between 1815 and 1890 profoundly altered the relationship between land-and sea-based strategies, to Britain's advantage. Power projection capabilities, economic leverage, and communication speeds were enhanced, while steam warships, shell guns, and armor transformed the tactical balance between land and sea.[5] Armored steamships could pass existing shore defenses that had been built to resist sailing ships, whereas long-range heavy artillery could destroy forts, or more usefully the arsenals and cities that lay behind them. Merchant steamships, another sector in which Britain dominated construction and use, enabled ever-larger expeditionary forces to be moved and sustained by sea.[6] Land-based systems were unable to cope with this expanding power projection capability because of the sheer scale of the defensive task. It was economically impossible to defend the coasts of Russia, France, or the United States against British sea power. By contrast, the British could use the same force to threaten hostile ports and arsenals in any quarter of the globe.

British strategy had always emphasized the destruction of hostile warships and dockyards, a concept that guided the development of new technologies, and by the 1840s it was being used to counter the latest French naval challenge. The focal point would be the new fortress and arsenal complex at Cherbourg, which was only 200 miles from England and the only base from which France could stage an invasion. The Royal Navy—using steam, shell guns, cutting-edge tidal research, the latest charts, newly built steam bases, and mass-produced gunboats—intended to blockade, bombard, and destroy Cherbourg. And this intelligence-led concept was equally applicable elsewhere.[7] When the Crimean War broke out in March 1854, British planners simply transferred the focal point from Cherbourg to the Russian arsenals at Cronstadt and Sevastopol.[8] British industrial resources produced a massive gunboat flotilla for coastal offensive operations, and in August 1855 it destroyed the dockyard at Sweaborg (outside Helsinki), without the loss of a single man.[9] Subsequent British plans to attack Cronstadt and Saint Petersburg encouraged Russia to sue for peace in 1856. In order to ensure that the lesson was not lost on other powers, the gunboat armament built to attack Cronstadt was given a public demonstration at Spithead on Saint George's Day (April 23) in 1856. The *Times* declared: "A new system of naval warfare has been created. . . . We have now the means of waging really offensive war, not only against fleets, but harbours, fortresses, and rivers, not merely of blockading, but of invading and carrying the warfare of the sea to the very heart of the land."[10]

The deterrent effects of the Cherbourg strategy can be seen in the *Trent* crisis of 1861,[11] the war scares with Russia in 1878 and 1885,[12] the Fashoda crisis of 1898,[13] and the first Moroccan crisis of 1905.[14] On each occasion, the threat of an attack on a major naval base, fortress, or coastal city provided the focal point of British deterrence.

These positive developments have been ignored by the historians of British power, which is widely presumed to have been in decline even when the Pax Britannica was at its height. They argue that Britain would be starved into submission by a serious attack on its shipping.[15] This argument is unsustainable in the face of British dominance of global shipping, coal, insurance markets, and communications. Its preponderance in these critical areas of international life reduced, rather than increased, the threat to Britain's interests, much less its survival as a power. A tenfold increase in world trade between 1860 and 1900 translated into almost equal growth in the annual tonnage of shipping movements.[16] Furthermore, the increasing efficiency of the marine steam engine captured key trade from sailing ships, and channeled shipping into narrowly defined routes.[17] The argument that these developments harmed Britain was logically unsound. To restate it today requires an uncritical acceptance of the deliberately alarmist case made by the City of London and the Naval Intelligence Division in the late 1880s, solely to push up naval spending.[18]

In fact, the threat to oceanic shipping in that period was declining. Contemporary warships depended on frequent access to major bases for effective operation. Their complex, high-performance engines demanded extensive, skilled maintenance.[19] Speed and range were also influenced by underwater fouling, which could only be removed in a dry dock. Without a sheltered anchorage, steam-powered warships could not even refuel; and by 1890 even second-class navies could no longer rely on sails. Only Britain had a global network of naval bases and commercial harbors, linked by a unique communications network, from which well-maintained, fully fueled cruisers could sortie to meet any threat. Its rivals had few bases outside their metropolitan areas, and none approaching the size and quality of those under British control. During this period, any attack on British oceanic commerce, which had already been hamstrung by the abolition of privateering, would have been short-lived and ineffective. The failure of German oceanic cruiser warfare in 1914 is instructive in this regard.[20]

The cornerstone of British war-fighting strategy had long been the economic blockade, which worked hand in hand with some form of naval blockade to keep enemy warships in harbor, and to keep British commerce safe on the oceans while the economic life of the enemy was slowly annihilated. Throughout the Pax, Britain had the necessary naval power and intelligence assets to stop the shipping of any rivals, with serious implications for their ability to wage war. The ability to mount an economic blockade formed a component of the new wave of navalist writing that began to emerge in 1890.[21] Although Britain had always used its naval power to cripple the economic life of its rivals, the effectiveness of its blockades had been greatly enhanced by developments in naval and communications technologies between 1860 and 1890.

COMMUNICATIONS

In order to react effectively to unexpected events around the globe, the British, with a limited resource base, were uniquely dependent on information dominance and strategic mobility. Among the more obvious by-products of their sustained effort to maintain these critical advantages would be the creation of the communication system needed to establish a truly global economy, and a globalized world, through British government subsidies. Government support ensured that high-risk projects relying on cutting-edge technology could be capitalized by the City of London, and then run on a commercial basis.

Although the effective power of British forces, rather than their size, was growing, the key to using them effectively to secure British interests was improved control—what would today be called network-centric warfare. After 1815 Britain committed substantial financial resources to promote superior long-distance communications, with oceanic steamships, submarine telegraph cables, and finally wireless. After an initial, experimental phase, when Britain's government attempted to run steamships on the sailing packet route through the Mediterranean, commercial logic and government financial weakness made it imperative to transfer such operations to private concerns, using a state subsidy to ensure the strategic interests of the state were secured.[22]

These developments were at once commercial and strategic. Although the shipping and cable companies needed government subsidies to be commercially viable, they effected a radical reduction in state expenditures by operating their services on commercial lines, and by being open to competitive tenders. Sea powers, which generally possess small armies, depend on the agility provided by superior information flows for the conduct of statecraft, war, and trade. The partnership between the state and the commercial sector epitomized by competitive tenders meets the needs of both parties. The British deliberately managed their commercial engagement in long-distance overseas trade so as to enhance their ability to control the periphery from the center, and more significantly to move forces from the center or other parts of the periphery to meet emergent threats. In this way the empire, both formal and informal, was welded into a single strategic entity.[23] Britain controlled the sea, and almost all the submarine cables that ran beneath it. As a consequence, it possessed information dominance unlike that of any other power, which enabled it to project political and commercial influence and to move military forces around the globe, while denying communication and mobility to an enemy.[24]

The effect of this unique public–private partnership is well illustrated in the remarkable growth of the Peninsular and Oriental Mail Steamship Company, known to history as P&O. It began its life sending ships back and forth across the Irish Sea, and within thirty years it had become the dominant shipping provider between Suez, Hong Kong, and Sydney. In so doing, it also replaced the old, publicly chartered East India Company as the major provider of military transport shipping. "Within just ten years of the company's foundation," as one scholar has noted, "a situation of mutual dependence had been created. P&O could not survive without state support; but equally, the

British government relied on this great enterprise to support or further its ambitions. P&O provided the mails, specie, and employees that underpinned its interests. Always a means of 'power projection,' visible evidence of the British presence, in emergency they were a military resource."[25] Later, when the threat to oceanic shipping lanes became serious, the P&O fleet would provide a powerful reinforcement of armed merchant cruisers for global patrolling—the ships being built for the purpose, and entering naval service complete with most of their crew.[26]

The benefits of scheduled oceanic steam shipping routes were redoubled by the development of the submarine telegraph cable. Pioneered in the 1840s, it attracted immediate naval interest. After linking Dover and Calais in 1851, it spread rapidly, creating a global network. North America was connected by 1867, India by 1870, Australia and Japan by 1872, Brazil by 1873, and the rest of the world soon thereafter. As in the case of P&O, links between the dominant Eastern Telegraph Company and the government were close.[27] And in times of crisis, the company acted as an imperial agency.[28] Empire, however defined, was now defended as a single unit, rather than as a series of geographically and intellectually distinct areas. The cable network was also easily expandable in the face of new threats. In 1899, when war broke out in South Africa, it took only two months to lay 3,000 miles of cable from the Cape Verde Islands to Cape Town.[29] It is little wonder that the French considered the cable network more important to British power than the navy.[30]

However, the effective exploitation of these epochal technical developments for global trade and naval dominance relied on a relatively unnoticed element in the totality of imperial defense—the dry dock—which would be the pivot around which British imperial strategy was transformed between 1860 and 1890. Dry docks were the basic requirement for sustained local operations by iron-hulled ships, for war or communications. Although costly, docks were an invaluable force multiplier, even in the age of sail. The construction of docks at Bombay in the mid-eighteenth century was indispensable to Britain's command of the Indian Ocean.[31] Nevertheless, the great age of the dry dock was a product of the advent of steam propulsion. Screw-propeller steamships needed frequent docking to keep their hulls clean, and to maintain the propeller, an intricate piece of technology for that era. The construction of docks with adequate depth and width was a complex, costly task involving much specialized knowledge, and it was inevitably a business dominated by British engineering firms.[32]

Only fleets with adequate bases for supply, repair, and concentration could control the sea. Between 1815 and 1860, new bases were developed to meet the expanding demand for naval support from the aggressive, expansionist British commercial sector. These included the Falkland Islands, Aden, Hong Kong, and Sydney. Existing bases at Malta, Gibraltar, Bermuda, and Halifax were improved, while facilities at Esquimalt, Singapore, and Cape Town were useful, as were naval depots in foreign harbors like Rio de Janeiro, Valparaiso, Callao, and Honolulu. The expansion of support facilities was driven by the need for squadrons to follow economic activity, but was necessarily limited by cost.[33]

The rapid spread of docking accommodations between 1860 and 1890 reflected technical change, commercial pressure, and strategic need. Dry docks enabled the Royal Navy to send squadrons to any part of the globe. In areas of overwhelming strategic need, where economic activity would not support docks for commercial purposes, they were built by the British government. Elsewhere, the Navy encouraged the construction of commercial docks, providing financial assistance to ensure that they were configured to accommodate warships along with commercial vessels. The emergence of an effective policy followed a period of haphazard development at the outer reaches of the empire.

Before 1840 only Britain and Bombay had docks. After the Syrian crisis of 1840, a dock was begun at Malta, opening in 1848. It was extended in 1857, as the telegraph connection arrived. A second dock opened in 1871, and two more were added in the 1890s as battleships became deeper and broader.[34] The construction of a major base at Gibraltar provided additional docking accommodations at the turn of the twentieth century.[35]

Outside European waters, the British interests that required defense were oceanic trade and communications, rather than territory. These were best secured by naval control of the oceans. To this end, the first dry dock was built at Sydney, which was configured to take the latest Royal Navy steamships and was partly funded by an Admiralty subsidy. It opened in 1857. The dry dock acted as a force multiplier for Royal Navy units, enabling them to refit and repair more effectively, and more rapidly, than any rival force. And critically, the dock enabled the Royal Navy to operate steam warships in the region, a key advantage over any rival power. With a local base for steam warships, the Royal Navy would dominate the region, securing floating trade, imperial communications, and, by default, an entire continent. Because Sydney was first and foremost a thriving commercial port, situated in a colony with responsible government, there was no need for the full cost of the dock to be met by the government in London.

This example was followed at Hong Kong in the early 1860s, because the existing docks near Canton, built to support P&O liners, were too "scanty" and insecure for naval purposes.[36] Hong Kong merchants opened a dock on the island in 1860, a larger structure able to accommodate frigates opened in 1862, and finally a battleship dock opened in 1867.[37] Singapore opened a dry dock of modern proportions in 1859, and a second in 1890.[38]

In 1864 the House of Commons set up a Select Committee to consider the Admiralty's plans to increase the docking accommodations in Portsmouth and the other home dockyards. But within two months, the remit was extended to include docking accommodations in Malta and at all foreign stations.[39] Suitable commercial docks were under consideration in Cape Town, Vancouver, and the Falkland Islands, but the committee was struck by the lack of a suitable dock in the Americas. Admiral Alexander Milne, who commanded the Royal Navy's forces at the North American station and in the West Indies, advised building on Bermuda, the "key" to the United States. The need for heavy investment in docks had "become almost indispensable, in consequence of the conversion of the Navy into a Steam Navy."[40] The recommendation to create a dock on Bermuda was accepted by the government, while initiatives in Halifax, Singapore, and Vancouver would bear fruit in due course. On Bermuda, where strategic necessity far outweighed commercial demand, the Admiralty ordered an iron floating dry dock, which was towed out in 1869 by two of the largest battleships afloat. This innovative technology enabled the Royal Navy to operate first-class ironclad ships in the waters of the New World; however, such ships were rarely dispatched.[41] The first mastless capital ship, designed to operate from first-class bases, was HMS *Devastation*, laid down in 1869. First-class bases were heavily fortified imperial fortresses that combined dry-docking accommodations with cable communications and a regular garrison. They were funded by the Imperial Government. The best examples were Gibraltar, Malta, Bermuda, and Halifax. The threat posed by this new combination of floating docks and ironclad warships was not lost on the more acute observers in the United States.[42]

In other areas the relatively low level of threats allowed the government to wait until commercial needs required a private dock. When Admiral Fisher spoke of "five strategic keys that lock up the globe!" he was referring to Dover, Gibraltar, the Cape of Good Hope, Alexandria, and Singapore.[43] He might have added Bermuda, but the concept was correct. These bases either had, or were very close to, major dockyards; they were connected by cable; they were defensible by land and sea; and, in the hands of a superior navy, they secured global power.

MARKETS AND GLOBALIZATION

As an island nation unable to feed its own population, Britain depended on international trade. Although much of its earlier commercial success had been built on the control of markets and on high tariff barriers, the trend of nineteenth-century economic thinking ran in the opposite direction. The strength of the British economy after 1815 encouraged liberal economic ideas, notably free trade, to cut costs and reduce tax burdens. All these things contributed to the dominance of the City of London in global capital markets, insurance, and shipping. London became the hub of a new world economy.

The response of other developed nations to Britain's embrace of free trade was generally negative. Tariff barriers went up, to encourage and protect domestic industry against British competition, which also had the effect of reducing primary exports. This coincided with Britain's deliberate attempts to reduce its dependence on European suppliers, especially for strategically vital raw materials. The substitution of Canadian timber, naval stores, and grain for products of the vulnerable Baltic trade system transformed the economy of Atlantic Canada, and enabled the British to view the Baltic as a strategic avenue for attacking Russia, and later Germany, rather than as a region where they were obliged to compromise with regional players in order to secure critical resources. Across the empire, economic and scientific research found new resources to exploit, and substitute sources for older supplies. Here, the intimate connection between the government, the Royal Navy, and the Royal Geographical Society continued to pay dividends.[44] The integrated nature of national maritime strategy ensured that naval resources were deployed to support scientific research, often benefiting the wider maritime sector. Admiralty charts were an obvious example; they were sold for a profit, but created for war.

When high tariff barriers closed European and American markets, British exports were redirected to new markets, a form of commercial flexibility that was itself an expression of Britain's maritime dominance. Such practices sustained economic growth despite political obstruction from abroad. British capital, backed by naval power, secured control of key areas in South America, Asia, and Africa, largely as an informal empire, a system of economic control and strategic defense, but without the costs of administration or local government. In this respect India, far from being the jewel in the British crown, was an expensive anomaly in commercial terms, and could only be justified because it was the base for British strategic power east of Suez. But the system remained flexible, and in the late nineteenth century the British became active imperialists, to secure their strategic and economic interests against rival powers.

THE BRITISH ECONOMY 1860–90

By 1860 the British economy had adapted to the free trade policy that followed the repeal of the Corn and Navigation Laws in the 1840s. Any adverse effects were largely disguised by the tremendous expansion of the world economy, the beginning of a tenfold increase in trade between 1850 and 1910, and the introduction of iron steamships. This was not accidental. And this expansion was sustained by the impulse provided by American and Australian gold discoveries, the ability of railways to open formerly remote continental regions to long-distance trade, and falling long-distance freight rates. Britain's share of this expanding world trade was relatively stable, partly because its extensive formal and informal empire provided secure markets and key raw materials, while American and European markets were becoming more competitive, and subject to tariff barriers.

Although the empire was a valuable segment of the economy, it was never dominant, accounting for about 25 percent of national trade in most areas. The most dynamic sector of the British economy was the exporting of capital, which by 1890 amounted to almost £100 million annually, much of it invested outside the empire. This sector was intimately linked to the financial services and commercial support systems of the City of London. The preeminence of the City in finance and trade was reflected in British dominance of world shipping and related services. By 1900 Britain had more than £2,000 million invested overseas, which provided income to cover its balance-of-payments deficit on manufactured goods and food.[45]

The global liquidity provided by British capital markets, combined with free trade, made the world system fluid.[46] In this era of "gentlemanly capitalism," the City of London and financial services came to dominate the economy, with the links between the City and British governments growing ever closer. Agricultural values were in decline, while manufacturing remained provincial. The wealth generated by the City gave it enormous influence, and made it a vital source of state revenue. In turn, the City made certain governments recognize that the dominant roles of the pound sterling (the closest nineteenth-century equivalent to a reserve currency) and the City in global trade allowed for cheap government, low taxes, balanced budgets, and the maintenance of the gold standard (on which sterling itself rested)—all of which turned upon the security afforded to trade and investments by the Royal Navy. In balancing these qualities, in effect settling the premium to be paid on national wealth in the form of defense expenditures, successive governments tried to steer a fine line between running risks and overtaxing the national resource. In August 1857 Charles Wood, first lord of the Admiralty in the liberal government headed by Palmerston, and a one-time chancellor of the exchequer, defended the post–Crimean War retrenchment from royal criticism by referring to the unique staying power of the British economy. Although Russia and France had been effectively exhausted by two years of war, Britain was "more willing and more able to continue the war than at its commencement."[47] Most liberal economists believed that this long-term power had been created by low levels of taxation and expenditures in peacetime.

A major political benefit of economic success came in the collapse of mid-century political agitation, one of the key arguments used in favor of free trade. Limited political reform, domestic prosperity, and opportunities for emigration defused the kind of social unrest that would produce revolution across much of Europe in 1848.[48] Throughout the century, the aggressive expansion of trade into nonimperial areas was a key government task, notably for Palmerston, who was the outstanding figure among British liberals from the 1830s until his death in 1865. For Palmerston, the answer to economic distress at home was an ambitious foreign policy to open new markets.[49] After the Second Reform Act of 1867, British politics was dominated by domestic and economic concerns, which replaced foreign policy and defense as the key concerns of statesmen. The dominant figure of this latter era was William Gladstone, who was a liberal like Palmerston but was cut from a different sort of cloth. Gladstone served as chancellor of the exchequer (1852–55, 1859–66) and prime minister (1868–74, 1879–85, 1892–94). He took a less interventionist stance than Palmerston. Confident that British trade would always triumph, and taking British power as a given, he presided over a period of very low defense spending, as part of an overall small government stance.[50] He did not value the empire and ignored colonial defense scares, cutting both the defense budget and the colonial share of that budget. Gladstone's financial policies led to a marked fall in the cost of servicing the national debt, the legacy of previous wars, from 41 percent of government expenditures in 1860 to 27 percent in 1890.[51]

Although the Conservatives under Gladstone's great rival, Benjamin Disraeli, were less economically minded and became more avowedly imperialist in the mid-1870s, both men found their external policy influenced by economic issues, notably the acquisition of the Suez Canal shares in 1875, and the occupation of Egypt in 1882.[52] In 1888 the City shifted to a Unionist/

Conservative posture, and awarded the Conservatives the ultimate accolade, supporting a major conversion of the national debt that reduced interest on £500 million of stock by 0.5 percent.[53] This demonstrated the City's confidence in peace and stability. As Niall Ferguson has suggested, "the Victorians appeared to have achieved empire without overstretch."[54] Such optimism would not last, but the 1888 conversion could be seen as the high-water mark of Pax Britannica.

The financial elite knew that the British economy would only prosper if the world was open to trade, and the seas, the great common across which goods and services were exchanged, were safe for British shipping. In this context, the defense of the empire takes on a more expansive and diffuse meaning. The globalization of trade was the basis for British power, making the security of global trade, rather than imperial territory, the Royal Navy's core mission. The fact that Britain traded with the empire complicated the picture, but it did not affect the fundamentals.[55] The Pax Britannica, the strategic aspect of this program, served as a mechanism to stabilize the international capital market for the City. In essence, Britain could not function without international trade, and this allowed the City of London to defeat the challenge posed by domestic manufacturing and protectionist interests in the early twentieth century.[56]

The only serious threat to British power was Europe, a region of rapidly declining relative economic interest. British investment in Europe had fallen from 50 percent of total capital exports in 1854 to only 5 percent by 1900.[57] Unsurprisingly, trade followed the same pattern, although the decline was less marked. In an increasingly protectionist market, British trade suffered. However, the rest of the world took up the slack, and the British economy continued to grow strongly until 1914. As long as Europe was stable, balanced, and prosperous, British interests were secure. The wars of 1864, 1866, and 1870–71 did not threaten vital British strategic or commercial interests, although these were signaled to the belligerents, notably the need to maintain strategic access to the Baltic Sea and respect the independence of Belgium in 1870. Provided those conditions were met, Britain did not need to intervene. Only the threat of a potential hegemonic power occupying the region where the Rhine and Schelde met the sea (Belgium and the Netherlands) would force Britain to act.

Because Britain had no positive interests that would be served by taking part in a European war in this period, it used the ideology of free trade to position its all-powerful fleet as a world policeman. In this respect the Pax Britannica was an exogenous universal good, rather than the cutting edge of a national policy. The convergence of Britain's national interests and the preservation of global order was genuine, but there is no question that it was the defense of the former that mattered. Belief in the universal benevolence of British power, actively fostered by late Victorian publicists, continues to confuse the unwary. In reality, the link between trade and power was clear. The import duty on tea from China more than covered the cost of the Royal Navy in 1850, and still met half the cost in 1857.[58] By contrast, the self-governing colonies made a minimal contribution. Britain spent £1.14 per head per annum on defense, and the self-governing colonies spent 12 pence—amounting, respectively, to 37 percent and between 3 and 4 percent of central government spending.[59] Consequently, British governments were unimpressed by colonial alarmism, especially when it was linked to protectionist measures against British goods. With no serious threat in Europe, or the wider world, defense spending remained low until 1889.[60]

War threatened the British system in three related ways. First, it would reduce access to markets, calling into question the underlying economic foundations of British power. Second, it would raise expenditures and taxes, making Britain less attractive for investors. And third, it would reopen fundamental questions about the existing social system; during the Crimean War (1854–56), the middle class demanded greater political power. Therefore, when British access to markets was called into question, the City of London pushed for a major naval buildup, as an insurance premium on the existing order. The London Chamber of Commerce, which had been founded in 1882 as a City pressure group, persuaded the Conservative government of 1886–92 that the mutual interests of City and party required extra naval protection. In 1889, only one year after the spectacular conversion of the national debt to a new financial basis, which significantly reduced the cost of government borrowing, the government introduced the Naval Defense Act, which, as Prime Minister Robert Salisbury told the Chamber of Commerce, was intended to protect their trade.[61] It was thus little wonder that the City abandoned the Liberals, although any imperialist urge was tempered by a continuing preference for investing outside the formal empire. The City's interests requiring protection were global; they were not restricted to the formal and informal empires. And the only effective defense of these interests would be based on naval mastery, preferably secured through the deterrent effects of superior armament rather than war.

However, the naval buildup that began in 1889 should not be seen as a negative, defensive response. Under the aegis of a renewed Royal Navy, Britain secured control of South African gold and diamonds and much of Sub-Saharan Africa, and improved its control of nonimperial markets like South America.[62] Britain recognized that trade and investments might have to be protected by war; but economic, social, and political concerns made fighting the policy of last resort. Instead, Britain used its financial power to secure markets and to create the naval might to back up its careful diplomacy. It was for this deterrent role against other major powers that the Royal Navy was maintained at a high level, not for the defense of outlying imperial assets. The fleet created by the Naval Defense Act was designed to win battles in European waters, not patrol the colonies. The empire, however defined, would continue to be secured by maintaining the peace and stability of Europe. If war broke out, rival fleets would be blockaded in port or destroyed in battle. Only as a last resort would ships be dispatched to the distant corners of the globe. They could be sent quickly, and operated effectively anywhere in the world, because Britain alone had the steamships, cables, coal stations, and dry docks to direct, maintain, and support them.

Much of the infrastructure that sustained and extended the economic dominance of the City of London was also used to maintain Britain's global power. Between 1860 and 1890, the globe was effectively encircled by London-centered and British-owned, -laid, and -operated submarine telegraph cables, which were largely paid for by revenue from everyday economic use. The cable generated new types of business and internationalized the financial world, increasing the primacy of London.[63] By 1890 the City of London controlled "an expanding world economy knit together by instant communications," dominated the British economy, and ensured that governments understood and supported its concerns.[64]

The prime mover of globalization, British-built iron steamships, depended on the cable for market information, and on supplies of British coal for motive power and a guaranteed export cargo. Along with the London insurance and shipping markets, these assets gave Britain the ability to monitor the cable traffic and shipping movements of rival powers. The intimate relationship between economic activity and imperial strategy limited the government's role, and government expenditures, to providing subsidies for cable companies, defending coal harbors, and occasionally pushing specific projects like the "all-red" cable routes—British-owned, -laid, and -controlled submarine cables that circled the globe and gave the British Empire information dominance. Overall, the main economic burden was borne by the private sector.

INTERNATIONAL LAW

Viewed in isolation British attitudes toward Maritime International Law appear to be at best haphazard. The British gradually liberalized their legal outlook between 1815 and 1911, only to make a swift reverse march in 1914. Yet the underlying rationale was strikingly simple and essentially consistent. The basic interests of the British state—peace, stability, and trade—required an agreed-on legal framework that would protect British trade during wars between third parties. This meant limiting the rights of belligerents to interfere with neutral shipping. Because peace was the normal condition for most of the century, a liberal interpretation of the position was adopted, even during the Crimean War, when a legally recognized close blockade was used to wage economic warfare, rather than the older, and far more permissive, methods of trade interdiction employed during the Napoleonic Wars, when both belligerent and neutral ships anywhere in the world were liable to be stopped, searched, and (if legally permitted) seized by British warships. The 1856 Declaration of Paris enshrined a new system of neutral rights in international law, above all through the abolition of privateering. Privateering, the state-licensed predation by private ships, was the only real threat to British maritime commerce in war. It was also a key element in the national strategies of Britain's only dangerous maritime rivals, the United States and France. In 1856 the United States refused to sign the declaration because the abolition of privateering would have disarmed that nation in a war with Britain. Consequently, the 1856 conditions would not apply in an Anglo-American war, and Prime Minister Palmerston was confident that France and Russia would soon violate the terms if they went to war with Britain. He expected, in effect, that the declaration would be a dead letter if Britain became involved in a major war. In any other conflict, however, the 1856 rules would help Britain.

Growing pressure to establish the immunity of private property from capture at sea, driven by liberal internationalists of the Cobden school, and taken up with rather less sincerity by states that feared the effects of a British blockade, reached an apogee with the 1911 Declaration of London.[65] The great maritime strategists Mahan and Corbett demonstrated that granting immunity to private property at sea would disarm sea powers, to the enormous advantage of land powers.[66] In essence, it would play into the hands of Imperial Germany. Consequently, the British government never ratified the 1911 declaration, and in 1914 it began a highly effective economic blockade, conducted on terms that displayed scant regard for the sanctity of private property.

The British understood that international law was a tool of statecraft, one that was only enforceable by the strong, and that it had to reflect the realities of the world. With a legal system based on precedent and open to interpretation, they were able to adapt their position with relative ease.

In the process of expanding trade and control across the oceans, the British used their maritime power to suppress piracy, from Algiers to Shanghai. Not only were pirates a hindrance to oceanic trade, but piracy was also usually associated with weak or failed states, which were poor trading partners. Although the Navy could restore order at sea, only shore-based initiatives, good governance, the rule of law, and economic growth offered any hope of ending the problem.[67] Security at sea lowered insurance rates, reduced crews, and ended the need to carry defensive armaments. The sustained campaign against the Atlantic Ocean and then Indian Ocean slave trade had both moral and economic objects. Slavery, most Britons concluded, was bad in itself, and bad for economic growth. However, this moral purpose was tempered by the economic imperatives of free trade, and not infrequently suspended to secure diplomatic or strategic needs. Only when the demand for slaves collapsed, and the supply dried up, was the trade finally eradicated. The maritime trafficking in slaves, like piracy, could only be fully resolved by action on land.[68] Julian Corbett's analysis of the effects of command of the sea in war is equally applicable to these constabulary functions.

LEARNING

If the prevailing image of Pax Britannica was one of comfortable complacency, the reality was very different. Throughout the century that separated Waterloo from World War I, British intellectuals and policymakers grappled with the nature and antecedents of their success. Nor was this a novel line of inquiry. The debate between maritime and continental schools was already lively in the early fifteenth century, and did not let up thereafter. Although much of the debate was conducted through historical analogy and case studies, nineteenth-century authors—including George Grote, John Ruskin, James Anthony Froude, and John Seeley—took it into mainstream culture and the universities. They ensured that sea power had entered the British lexicon long before Alfred Thayer Mahan provided it with systematic validation. The problem facing the British pioneers was relevance. They used classical, sixteenth- and eighteenth-century examples at a time when steam, iron, armor, and shells, not to mention mines and torpedoes, seemed to have changed everything. In this context of rapid technological change, Mahan's argument about eternal principles proved useful, an American endorsement of British practice that proved priceless as naval spending steadily ramped up during the 1890s.

Mahan's other contribution was to link naval education with strategic thinking. His work had been generated for use at the US Naval War College, which became the model, suitably adjusted, for the Royal Navy's War Course (later the War College), in 1902. Naval strategy had been taught at the Royal Naval College Greenwich since the late 1880s. Admiral Philip Colomb provided six lectures a year there between 1887 and 1895, which formed the basis for his 1891 book *Naval Warfare: Its Ruling Principles and Practice Historically Treated.*[69] Starting in 1898, the college's captain, Henry May, delivered similar lectures. In June 1900 the Admiralty directed the admiral president of Greenwich to arrange "for the formation of a Naval Strategy course at the [Royal Naval College Greenwich]."[70] The broad lines on which the course was started were those of the American Naval War College, but were altered to suit the different conditions under which the work was to be carried out.[71]

The Naval War Course provided midcareer and senior naval officers with access to naval, military, and maritime expertise; shipping, insurance, cable communications, and international law were featured, alongside naval technology and strategy. The course, which was attended by every significant senior officer of World War I (except John Jellicoe), transformed a battle-oriented force dominated by gunnery into one attuned to the needs of a total maritime conflict. A War Staff Course, added in 1912, ensured that the new doctrine was spread across the service. Finally, the Naval War Course became the locus for the development of the first exposition of maritime strategy, Julian Corbett's 1911 book *Some Principles of Maritime Strategy.* Although it appeared at a time when the Royal Navy needed an effective defense of its position against the continentalist strategic visions of the army, the underlying analysis of the "British way of war" has stood the test of time.

This was no accident. Corbett occupied a central place in the course, as the longest-serving and most consistently used external expert. His close relationship with John Fisher, successive course directors, other staff, and students connected him with contemporary war planning, and ensured that he remained inside naval command until his death in 1922, as strategist, educator, historian, and author of key memoranda. He developed maritime strategy in response to the latest iteration of the age-old debate between maritime and continental strategies. The new Army General Staff had seized upon the strategic ideas of Imperial Germany and France in order to generate a strategy that privileged soldiers over sailors. To combat this unusually sophisticated (if utterly irrelevant) case, the navy needed to start thinking about strategy in a far more coherent and professional manner. It could no longer assume that everyone understood, while pointing to Trafalgar Square for validation. The job required all the subtle, incisive analytical rigor and public advocacy that were the defining features of Corbett's legal mind. That said, the great majority of his students picked up the arguments and turned them to profit, not least David Beatty.

Having reduced the British past to order, Corbett used the Russo–Japanese War of 1904–5 to bring maritime strategy into the modern age, complementing his Clausewitzian study of Britain's most successful maritime conflict, which was published in 1907 as *England in the Seven Years' War: A Study of Combined Strategy*. This was "history on the large scale with military principles guiding the selection."[72] His study of "the British Way" at its zenith consciously harmonized political, diplomatic, naval, and military elements as a template for contemporary strategy. Fisher approved.

In *Some Principles*, Corbett produced a sophisticated, nuanced handling of Clausewitz, using his theoretical framework to create a British strategy based on naval history.[73] He developed Clausewitz's concept of limited war, a prominent feature of *England in the Seven Years' War*, by removing it from the difficult context of a European war and elevating it into the master principle of "the British Way."[74] Britain could wage limited war, using the sea to isolate enemy territory, thereby limiting the amount of force required to capture it, as the ideal strategy in a war waged for limited political aims. Limited aims and the strategic use of the sea had been critical in the Russo–Japanese War. Corbett proved a far abler student of Clausewitz than the contemporary German General Staff, which perverted his lessons on the political nature of war, creating a military solution to complex political problems. In addition, he demonstrated that a decisive battle victory could only be secured under favorable conditions by forcing the enemy to fight. The best example was to cut the enemy's vital trade routes. Like Fisher, he believed that German dependence on Swedish iron ore made the Baltic the key theater if the High Seas Fleet was to be brought into battle.

Like Clausewitz, Corbett wrote his strategy book as a result of, rather than as a key to, historical study.[75] He reduced naval history to order, rendered the strategic issues clear for his students, and pointed up the critical fact that without professional historical research, the work of strategists was inevitably flawed. Although *Some Principles* was developed from War College lectures, and owed its public appearance to Fisher's anxiety to sustain his policy after 1910, by 1914 Corbett's work was the basis for British strategy.

If the core strategy of 1914 differed little at a fundamental level from that envisaged in 1815, the intervening century had witnessed a remarkable transformation in the way these ideas were transmitted. In 1815 statesmen knew from experience, and consulted naval experts on operational issues. By 1914 the Committee of Imperial Defense, established ten years earlier as an advisory committee to the government, provided a structured forum for civil–military coordination, with a strategically educated secretariat generating extensive intelligence-based briefings. The British had a grand strategy, conceived in global, maritime terms. This was essential because the British needed to react to events, using a conceptual framework to deter great power conflict by effective signaling and diplomacy.

However, the process of mastering maritime strategy remained incomplete in July 1914. Key decision makers missed the underlying deterrent imperative, and fatally misused the most potent deterrent symbol on Earth, the Grand Fleet, during the crisis that led to war. In their anxiety to prepare for war, the naval leadership hid the fleet at Scapa Flow, its designated war station, when it should have been used to warn Germany that Britain would fight for the independence of Belgium and to preserve the European balance of power. Given the experience of 1815, when Prussian soldiers, including Clausewitz, found themselves fighting in Belgium to uphold these very principles, and of 1870, when Britain sent a very clear warning to Berlin that it would not tolerate the violation of Belgian neutrality, this should have been clear. Yet the British cabinet, more concerned with Irish issues and preservation of consensus, proved inattentive, leaving the foreign secretary to put his trust in German promises. The dispatch of the fleet into the Baltic Sea, as in 1905, would have presented the German government with a clear and unmistakable signal of British intent.

Corbett's work, for all its historical depth and incisiveness, was more concerned with waging war than preventing it, and as a consequence it significantly underrepresented the experience gained during the Pax Britannica. Like Mahan's work, it had more to say about an era when Britain was aggressively creating global power than the subsequent period, when global order was sustained without war. The tragedy of 1914 is that Britain had already defeated Imperial Germany in a naval arms race, and it could anticipate ending the temporary continental Ententes that linked its interests to those of its long-term rivals, France and Russia. Once France and Russia were strong enough to counter Germany and Austria, British interest would have required it to disengage in any case, for fear that its support of the Franco-Russian partnership would encourage them to start a war. Maritime strategy requires constant, subtle oversight.

The cost of failure in 1914 was catastrophic. A strong, dynamic economy was crippled by the human and economic cost of war; the first casualty was the principle of maintaining naval dominance, without which the last maritime empire would be doomed. It is instructive that American delegates at the Paris Peace Conference—and subsequently at Washington, Geneva, and London—never understood the difference between Britain's comprehensive dependence on the sea and America's desire to project power over and across it.[76]

CONCLUSION

In pursuing their economic agendas, the British developed a maritime strategy that linked naval power to the economic activity it served. The system was constantly upgraded to exploit new technologies and meet changing political realities. Between 1856 and 1868, the strategy shifted from permanently stationed forces overseas to a centrally controlled expeditionary strategy, a shift made possible by a carefully matured public–private partnership that provided the necessary combination of British-controlled steam shipping, cables, coal, and dry docks. These enabled a small country with low levels of defense spending to control, if not the whole world, then the connective structures and system that, over the course of the nineteenth century, had given the expression "the whole world" real meaning. The same assets that created new forms of global order created the global economy. The two were indissolubly intertwined, and they would stand or fall as one.

When tension in Europe began to rise, in part prompted by rivalries over the non-European world, the British increased their defense spending, improved their cable network, built new dry docks, and redeployed their forces. Many historians have drawn negative conclusions from the movement of British ships and squadrons from the periphery to the center after 1900, seemingly unaware of the fundamental strategic mobility of naval power.[77] The key indicators of imperial strategy were the fixed assets: communications, docks, and fortifications, along with the mechanics of maintaining peace, arms races, and deterrence.

The main threat to Britain's unique and highly advantageous situation came from the one area that it could not control: the continent of Europe. However, Britain was able to exert significant influence even here, because its aims were essentially negative, the maintenance of an approximate equilibrium, in which no one power dominated the western continent, and the key invasion staging posts of the Rhine and the Schelde remained in the hands of a minor power. British policy in Europe was carefully calculated to avoid war and, failing that, to employ whatever force was required to avert the creation of a hegemonic state on the continent.

By 1890 Britain's epoch of unchallenged imperial dominance was ending. The growing economies of the United States and Germany, and the imperial expansion of France and Russia, were inexorably raising the stakes, forcing Britain to increase its defense spending and to reconsider the physical and intellectual basis of its strategy. Within little more than a decade, Britain felt compelled to enter alliances and ententes with other major powers. However, the underlying policy remained identical: to preserve peace and stability in the medium to long term at the lowest cost. Until 1914 British global power still depended on sound strategy, cheap government, and maximizing technological opportunity to sustain the unique global economy that drove the entire process.[78]

The sea power at the heart of the Pax Britannica was at once strikingly potent and alarmingly fragile. Only maritime powers possessed a mixed political system, and therefore the long-term commitment to sustain key instruments like navies, communications, and infrastructure that extended economic activity. Continental states, some of which have built impressive military navies, have generally failed to sustain their naval activity in the long term. Mahan recognized and feared this truth. His sea power trilogy focused on France and America, continental states that had been defeated by British sea power.[79]

Ultimately, the Pax Britannica created the conditions for globalization because those conditions favored British interests. However, we must not overstate the issue of choice. Maritime strategy was a necessity, not an option. Britain could not choose isolationism, or protectionism, because the home islands were not self-sufficient in food or raw materials. Britain had to be global to survive. If the combination of a positive, expansionist global maritime approach with the maintenance of European stability shaped the elegant, economic *Pax Britannica*, it relied on sustained, sophisticated management. The overriding requirement was to avoid a major war by diplomacy or deterrence. Although Britain had enormous reserves of power, which could be mobilized to wage total war against French or German attempts to dominate Europe, the human and economic costs proved all but catastrophic in World War I. A second total war two decades later completed the process. Changing from a maritime to a continental strategy cost Britain its empire. This had also been the case for other maritime empires. Athens, Carthage, Venice, and Holland had all perished on land.

NOTES

1. J. R. Seeley, *The Expansion of England* (London: Macmillan, 1883), 291–92.

2. For an overview of this campaign, see A. D. Lambert, *Admirals* (London: Faber & Faber, 2008), 223–33.

3. S. R. B. Smith, "Public Opinion, the Navy and the City of London: The Drive for British Naval Expansion in the Late Nineteenth Century," *War & Society* 9, no.1 (May 1991): 29–50.

4. A. D. Lambert, "Foreword," in *Send a Gunboat! The Victorian Navy and Supremacy at Sea, 1854–1904*, 2nd edition, ed. A. Preston and J. Major (Annapolis, MD: Naval Institute Press, 2007), 7–12.

5. Robert Gardiner and A. D. Lambert, eds. *Steam, Steel and Shellfire: The Steam Warship 1815–1890* (London: Conway Maritime Press, 1991).

6. The Crimean War (1854–56) and the American Civil War (1861–65) were the key demonstrations of this enhanced power.

7. The British vice consul at Archangel provided a rich haul of cartographic and other intelligence, which ensured that the squadron sent to the White Sea in 1854 had superb charts, useful sailing directions, and a clear concept of operations.

8. A. D. Lambert, *The Crimean War: British Grand Strategy against Russia 1853–1856* (Manchester: Manchester University Press, 1990), 73–74.

9. A. D. Lambert, "Under the Heel of Britannia: The Bombardment of Sweaborg, August 1855," in *Seapower Ashore: 200 Years of Royal Navy Operations on Land*, ed. Peter Hore (London: Chatham, 2001).

10. Editorial, April 24, 1856, in *The War Correspondents: The Crimean War*, ed. A. D. Lambert and Stephen Badsey (Gloucester, UK: Sutton, 1994), 304—5.

11. In 1861 an American warship illegally detained the British Royal Mail steamer *Trent* in intentional waters and removed two Confederate envoys. The British demanded an apology and full restitution, and when they began to mobilize their coast assault fleet, the Lincoln administration backed down. See A. D. Lambert, "Winning without Fighting; British Grand Strategy and Its Application to the United States, 1815–1865," in *Strategic Logic and Political Rationality: Essays in Honor of Michael I. Handel*, ed. Bradford A. Lee and Karl F. Walling (London: Frank Cass, 2003).

12. In 1878 and 1885 Russian attacks on Turkey and Afghanistan, respectively, were stopped and repelled by the mobilization of a British fleet to attack Saint Petersburg, then the Russian capital city, on the Baltic coast.

13. In 1898 British and French forces met on the headwaters of the Nile, and it appeared war was likely. Well aware that they could not defeat the British fleet in a war over Africa, the French gave way.

14. In 1904–5 Germany attempted to provoke a war with France over the recent French occupation of Morocco. Britain backed France and sent a fleet into the Baltic to remind Germany that it would not stand aside in a conflict, and Germany backed down.

15. For a discussion of this thesis, see A. D. Lambert, "The Royal Navy, 1856–1914: Deterrence and the Strategy of World Power," in *Navies and Global Defence: Theories and Strategies*, ed. Keith Neilson and E. J. Errington (Westport, CT: Praeger, 1995), 69–92, esp. 71–74.

16. The key indicator here would be the tons carried per mile per annum, not the size of the shipping pool. Steam ships make more voyages than sailing ships, and fast ships make more voyages than slow ones.

17. Denis Griffiths, *Steam at Sea: Two Centuries of Steam-Powered Ships* (London: Conway Maritime Press, 1997).

18. R. Mullins, "Sharpening the Trident: The Decisions of 1889 and the Creation of Modern Seapower" (PhD diss., University of London, 2000).

19. A three-quarter-power crossing of the Atlantic by a cruiser with triple expansion engines would end with a visit to the dockyard and weeks of maintenance.

20. For the legal and strategic issues, see A. D. Lambert, "Great Britain and Maritime Law from the Declaration of Paris to the Era of Total War," in *Navies in Northern Waters*, ed. Rolf Hobson and Tom Kristiansen (London: Frank Cass, 2004), 11–38.

21. The key text is by Alfred Thayer Mahan, *The Influence of Sea Power upon the French Revolution and Empire* (Boston: Little, Brown, 1892).

22. For an overview of the relationship between the British state and subsidized mail steamship companies across the globe, see Howard Robinson, *Carrying British Mails Overseas* (London: George Allen & Unwin, 1964), 105–271.

23. For an example of smaller imperial works, see S. J. Earle, *A Question of Defence: The Story of Green Hill Fort, Thursday Island* (Thursday Island, Australia: Torres Strait Historical Society, 1993). This fort covered the cable relay, the key shipping route and a major coal depot in the Torres Straits. It was built by the Colony of Queensland, but the British Imperial government provided the guns.

24. J. Winkler, *Nexus: Strategic Communications and American Security in World War I* (Cambridge, MA: Harvard University Press, 2008); D. R. Headrick, *The Invisible Weapon: Telecommunications and International Politics, 1851–1945* (Oxford: Oxford University Press, 1991); Paul Kennedy, "Imperial Cable Communications and Strategy, 1870–1914," *English Historical Review* 86 (1971): 728–52.

25. S. Palmer, "Afterword," in *Flagships of Imperialism: The P&O Company and the Politics of Empire from Its Origins to 1867*, ed. F. Harcourt (Manchester: Manchester University Press, 2006), 229.

26. Richard Osborne, Harry Spong, and Tom Grover, *Armed Merchant Cruisers, 1878–1945* (Windsor, UK: World Ship Society, 2007).

27. For the links between Lord Stanley, later the fifteenth earl of Derby, and Eastern chairman John Pender, see J. R. Vincent, ed., *Disraeli, Derby, and the Conservative Party: The Political Journals of Lord Stanley, 1849–1869* (London: Hassocks, 1978); and J. R. Vincent, ed., *The Derby Diaries, 1869–1878: A Selection from the Diaries of Edward Henry Stanley, 15th Earl of Derby, between September 1869 and March 1878* (Cambridge: Cambridge University Press, 1996), 117.

28. Hugh Barty-King, *Girdle Round the Earth: History of "Cable and Wireless"* (London: William Heinemann, 1980), 73–74. Eastern Telegraph was one of the constituent parts of the modern company.

29. Ibid., 126.

30. Kennedy, "Imperial Cable Communications," 748.

31. M. Duffy, "Devon and the Naval Strategy of the French Wars, 1689–1815," in *The New Maritime History of Devon, Volume 1: From Early Times to the Late Eighteenth Century* (London: Conway Maritime Press, 1992), 182–84; A. D. Lambert, "Strategy, Policy and Ship-Building: The Bombay Dockyard, the Indian Navy, and Imperial Security in

Eastern Seas, 1784–1869," in *The Worlds of the East India Company*, ed. H. V. Bowen, Margarette Lincoln, and Nigel Rigby (Woodbridge, UK: Boydell Press, 2002), 137–52, esp. 150–51.

32. Charles Colson, *Notes on Docks and Dock Construction* (London: Longmans, Green, 1894). Colson was assistant director of works at the Admiralty.

33. Gerald S. Graham, *Great Britain in the Indian Ocean: A Study of Maritime Enterprise, 1810–1850* (Oxford: Oxford University Press, 1967), 305–28.

34. Joseph Bonnici and Michael Caesar, *The Malta Grand Harbour and Its Dockyard* (Malta, 1994), 38–122.

35. Thomas Allnutt Brassey, *The Naval Annual, 1886* (Portsmouth: J. Griffin, 1886), 100.

36. Report of the Select Committee on the Dock and Basin Accommodation Available for the Repair of Her Majesty's Ships, House of Commons Papers 8 (1864), 45.

37. A. Coates, *Whampoa: Ships on the Shore* (Hong Kong: South China Morning Post, 1980), 7–85.

38. Port of Singapore Authority, *Singapore: Portrait of a Port—A Pictorial History of the Port and Harbour of Singapore, 1819–1984* (Singapore: Port of Singapore Authority, 1984).

39. House of Commons Papers 8 (1864), 87, 91, 94, 161, 203, 222, 324, 428.

40. Ibid., 14.

41. For a brief survey of earlier dock projects, see http://www.bermuda-online.org /rnd.htm.

42. See John Ericsson's contemporary opinion, cited by Stanley Sandler, *The Emergence of the Modern Capital Ship* (Newark: University of Delaware Press, 1979), 243.

43. Paul M. Kennedy, *The Rise and Fall of British Naval Mastery* (London: Allen Lane, 1976), 206.

44. The Royal Society of London was founded by Joseph Banks in 1660 and granted a royal charter by King Charles II. It has served ever since as principal scientific adviser to the British government.

45. The standard account of this process is by P. J. Cain and A. G. Hopkins, *British Imperialism: Innovation and Expansion 1688–1914* (London: Longman, 1993), 125–77.

46. P. J. Cain, "Economics and Empire: The Metropolitan Context," in *The Oxford History of the British Empire, Volume 3: The Nineteenth Century*, ed. A. Porter (Oxford: Oxford University Press, 1999), 42–50.

47. Wood Memorandum of August 1857, Royal Archives, E 49 f.30.

48. A. H. Imlah, *Economic Aspects of the Pax Britannica* (Cambridge, MA: Harvard University Press, 1958), 186–88.

49. M. Lynn, "British Policy, Trade, and Informal Empire in the Mid–Nineteenth Century," in *Oxford History of the British Empire*, 3:101–21. J. Y. Wong, *Deadly Dreams: Opium and the Arrow War (1856–1860) in China* (Cambridge: Cambridge University Press, 1998), 470–78, argues that British imperialism was complex, and included key economic elements, in which Palmerston took a leading role.

50. Cain and Hopkins, *British Imperialism*, 204–5.

51. Niall Ferguson, *The World's Banker: The History of the House of Rothschild* (London: Weidenfeld & Nicolson, 1998), 819.

52. David Kynaston, *The City of London, Volume 1: A World of Its Own 1815–1890* (London: Pimlico, 1994), 335–40; and Ferguson, *World's Banker*, 817–26. For the links

between government and finance, and the City's bellicose attitude toward securing investments, see Cain and Hopkins, *British Imperialism*, 206–8.

53. Ferguson, *World's Banker*, 853.

54. J. H. Clapham, *The Bank of England*, 2 vols. (Cambridge: Cambridge University Press, 1944), 1:318; Ferguson, *World's Banker*, 863.

55. A. Porter, ed. *The Oxford History of the British Empire, Volume 3: The Nineteenth Century*. The importance of nonempire areas, capital exports, and global trade in sustaining British power is debated in this volume.

56. Particularly notable is Joseph Chamberlain's Tariff Reform and Imperial Preference movement of 1904–6.

57. Ferguson, *World's Banker*, 680.

58. Wong, *Deadly Dreams*, 350–55.

59. Cain and Hopkins, *British Imperialism*, 239.

60. Ferguson, *World's Banker*, 812.

61. Kynaston, *City of London*, 1:377–78.

62. Cain and Hopkins, *British Imperialism*, 315.

63. Kynaston, *City of London*, 1:175, 226, 258, 260, 306, 348–49.

64. Ibid., 400; and see 430–36 on the 1890 Baring Crisis.

65. Lambert, "Great Britain and Maritime Law," 11–40.

66. Corbett's brilliant essay "The Capture of Private Property at Sea" was published in *Some Neglected Aspects of War*, ed. Alfred Thayer Mahan (London: Sampson Low, Marston & Company, 1907).

67. A. D. Lambert, "The Limits of Naval Power: The Merchant Brig *Three Sisters*, Riff Pirates and British Battteships," in *Piracy and Maritime Crime: Historical and Modern Case Studies*, Newport Paper 35, ed. Bruce A. Elleman, Andrew Forbes, and David Rosenberg (Newport, RI: Naval War College Press, 2010), 173–90.

68. A. D. Lambert, "Slavery, Free Trade and Naval Strategy, 1840–1860," in *Slavery, Diplomacy and Empire: Britain and the Suppression of the Slave Trade, 1807–1975*, ed. Keith Hamilton and Patrick Salmon (Eastbourne: Sussex Academic Press, 2009), 65–80.

69. This is a work of similar purpose to Mahan's better-known *Influence of Sea Power* of 1890. Like all serious naval educators, Colomb created a synthesis between naval history and strategic ideas.

70. A. J. Marder, *The Anatomy of British Sea Power: A History of British Naval Policy in the Pre-Dreadnought Era, 1880–1905* (New York: Alfred A. Knopf, 1940), 389.

71. Slade to Corbett, May 20, 1906, RNC Greenwich CBT 13/2/1, Slade's Notes on the origins of the Course.

72. D. M. Schurman, *Education of a Navy: The Development of British Naval Strategic Thought, 1867–1914* (Chicago: University of Chicago Press, 1965), 164.

73. J. S. Corbett, *Some Principles of Maritime Strategy* (London: Longmans, Green, 1911), 1–8.

74. Ibid., 54–55.

75. Schurman, *Education of a Navy*, 182.

76. For a recent overview, see J. W. Jones, "The Naval Battle of Paris," *Naval War College Review* 62, no. 2 (2009): 77–90.

77. See, e.g., A. L. Friedberg, *The Weary Titan: Britain and the Experience of Relative Decline 1895–1905* (Princeton, NJ: Princeton University Press, 1988).

78. The US Navy's *Cooperative Strategy for the 21st Century* (October 2007) declares that "our Nation's interests are best served by fostering a peaceful global system comprised of interdependent networks of trade, finance, life, law, people and governance" (p. 4), a statement that encapsulates much of what the British thought, while "we believe that preventing wars is as important as winning wars" (p. 5) shows that the United States is still moving toward the British position, where deterrence and suasion are more important than war fighting. US Navy mission statements start with winning wars, before moving on to deterring aggression and maintaining the freedom of the seas. The British start with the word "deter."

79. Alfred Thayer Mahan, *The Influence of Sea Power upon History 1660–1783* (Boston: Little, Brown, 1890), 67, 88. Also focusing on this linkage is Peter Padfield, *Maritime Dominion and the Triumph of the Free World: Naval Campaigns That Shaped the Modern World, 1852–2001* (London: John Murray, 2007).

CHAPTER 2

The Great Disorder

Maritime Strategy in the World Wars, 1914–1945

DANIEL MORAN

This chapter surveys the conduct of maritime strategy during a period when the forces sustaining global order were at full stretch. As far as possible, it treats the twentieth century's two world wars, and what Marshal Ferdinand Foch called the "twenty-year truce" that separated them, as a unified historical episode. The point in doing so is not to minimize the tactical and technological changes that distinguish the two conflicts, some of which loom large, as does the changing ideological framing, which gave World War II its unique scale and ferocity. Two important maritime powers—Italy and Japan—also changed sides from one war to the next. Yet it is worth recalling that, from the point of view of those involved, the sense of continuity was strong. One British officer, who joined the Royal Navy as a sublieutenant during World War I and finished World War II as an admiral, recalled afterward that in 1939 "it was as if time had stood still. A lot of the ships were even the same, too. Ruddy uncanny, I can tell you."[1]

The naval history of the world wars has been so thoroughly studied that there can be no excuse for attempting to add to it in this brief chapter. The goal instead is to consider how far war on the high seas—and the continued movement of goods, soldiers, information, and money across them—determined the overall result of the world wars taken as a whole. With that in mind, it may be helpful to state the obvious at the start: Both wars were won by coalitions of powers that were much richer, collectively, than those they defeated. Their superior wealth was heavily dependent on transoceanic trade, just as their capacity to cooperate militarily depended on their control of the water that separated them. Their superior wealth only mattered, however, because both wars lasted long enough for the underlying economies of the winners to adapt to the requirements of war as an industrial enterprise, a development whose implications were only dimly foreshadowed by even the most violent conflicts of the preceding century. The essential achievement of maritime strategy in the world wars was to buy the time necessary for the economic superiority of the eventual winners to make itself felt, in the form of armies, navies, and air forces capable of defeating those of the other side.

Anxiety about the consequences of protracted war under industrial conditions goes a long way toward explaining the strategic outlook of the period's major aggressors, Germany and Japan. They recognized that they stood at a disadvantage in relation to their prospective opponents; but they calculated that by achieving sufficiently stunning success at the outset of the war, they could shift the strategic balance in their favor. Tactical proficiency might thus triumph over the foreseeably crushing strategic advantages that would accrue to those powers able to retain their connection to the world economy. This calculation proved incorrect, but it was a close-run thing.

The influence exerted by maritime strategy in the world wars was linked to economic and political conditions that were unusual, if not unique. "In both world wars," as Stephen Broadberry and Mark Harrison have shown, "the main combatants were able to devote more than half of their national income to the war effort."[2] This had not been possible in the past because neither the organizing power of the still-emergent modern state nor the productive capacity of pre- and proto-industrial societies had been capable of generating such enormous resources, or of eliciting (or imposing) such enormous sacrifices on their populations. Now, for good or ill, they were. Given roughly comparable state capacity, social cohesion, and military competence, the passage of time favored those belligerents who were best able to retain their connection to distant trading partners and critical resources areas. Those connections allowed them to accumulate superior military power. They also allowed their economies to continue operating at a level helpful to sustaining the morale of the civil population.

This analysis, as simple and even self-evident as it seems, is more or less the opposite of what proponents of sea power expected when the twentieth century began. The phrase, or at any rate its ubiquity, it owed to the American naval officer and theorist Alfred Thayer Mahan, whose writings were widely if tendentiously interpreted as showing that command of the sea by powerful naval forces would reduce other forms of fighting to secondary importance. But this is not what happened. It is more accurate to say that command of the sea made other forms of fighting possible. It did not ensure success, but it afforded crucial advantages in a setting where violence itself had become an industrial commodity. Global order was fractured by the world wars, but it was not dissolved. Victory went to those best able to reassemble the pieces to their advantage.

EMPIRE, ARMAMENTS, AND THE COMING OF WAR

At the turn of the twentieth century, when hindsight shows the Pax Britannica on its way to unraveling, plenty of intelligent observers thought it might last forever. A central promise of market theorists, dating back to Adam Smith, had been that market expansion and integration would create all sorts of mutually beneficial relationships that would cut against the inherent bellicosity of states, whose natural relations embodied mere anarchy and ceaseless, violent competition.[3] To this day, this seminal proposition of modern social theory remains central to the strategic outlook of commercial democracies like the United States. This is all the more reason, then, to note carefully what is being claimed: not that free markets and rising prosperity will make people more benevolent or complacent, but that market expansion will increase the self-evident costs of war to the point where even the most blinkered militarist will think twice before taking up arms.[4] When Mahan declared that "the commercial interest of the sea powers lies in the preservation of peace," he was not speaking as a humanitarian or as a man of business, but as someone who understood how much additional risk had been added to the calculations of the strategist by the ongoing transformation of the world economy.[5] For him, maritime strategy was about managing the new sources of risk on which modern life had come to depend.

Not everyone conceived of this risk in the same way. Many on the left believed that the risk could not be managed at all, because it embodied the hand of fate. From their perspective, the pursuit of empire, which was the practical manifestation of untrammeled market expansion, could only end by multiplying the sources of conflict among states, which were merely the armed expressions of underlying economic interests. Even if the interests changed, what the American social critic Randolph Bourne called "the war system" would continue to function as it always had.[6]

An analogous skepticism can be found among conservatives, who considered that, if Mahan was right about the natural interests of sea powers, the natural interests of other kinds of powers might be different. It was apparent, after all, that the fruits of empire were not accruing evenly among the great powers, and that those less well positioned would try to protect themselves from forms of competition that the average citizen might regard as unfair, even if economic theorists claimed they were not. The spread of protectionist tariffs in Europe during the twenty years preceding the outbreak of World War I was a reflection of this concern, and of another: that, in the event that war did come despite the weight of economic interests arrayed against it, it would be better if one's own defense was not unduly dependent on access to remote markets. The embrace of free trade was, in strategic terms, a gigantic bet on the power of modern navies to defend the intricate global supply chains on which advanced societies were becoming dependent. Not everyone was equally prepared to make this bet.

More precisely, continental states—Germany, most consequentially—were strongly inclined to hedge their bet, because in the end some version of the bet could not avoided. Industrialization necessarily creates more goods than can be consumed locally. Protectionist tariffs might moderate this development on the margins, but no more. On the eve of World War I, Germany was importing 19 percent of the calories its population consumed every day from overseas, a reflection of the reallocation of labor from farm to factory that industrialization had required.[7] This ratio would only grow worse in wartime, as the demands of the army for manpower would be added to those of industry, whose production would also accelerate. By any reckoning, the requirements for managing an industrial society at war gave ample cause for concern, and weighed heavily in favor of operational methods that promised a quick result, before the corrosive effects of modern war could eat into what was imagined to be the fragile fabric of modern life.

At the end of the 1890s Germany also embarked upon a second form of strategic hedging: a program of naval building that, when complete, was supposed to secure British neutrality during the next European war. The resulting "arms race"—this expression comes from journalistic accounts of the period—has always counted among the harbingers of the war, though the exact nature of its influence needs careful characterization. Germany's decision to challenge Britain at sea, and Britain's defiant response, were conditioned by economic rivalry, including the shared knowledge that Britain's preeminent position in overseas markets and international finance would make it a dangerous adversary for Germany, if it chose to become one. German naval building was designed to influence Britain's choice. Germany could not build a fleet capable of competing with the Royal Navy in the pursuit of empire, a contest that had basically already been decided. The idea was rather to build a fleet sufficiently dangerous to cause Britain to stand aside during a war between Germany and its neighbors, rather than risk a clash at sea that might prove so damaging that Britain's grip on its empire might slip.

The great fleets in which Britain and Germany invested so heavily were made up of giant battleships that would be of no use in policing the far corners of the world. Their only purpose was to sink each other. German planners were not so naive as to imagine their actions would not inspire a competitive response. But they calculated, wrongly, that Britain could not bear the expense of maintaining a large fleet to fight in the North Sea while simultaneously sustaining the naval presence required to support its global empire. In the end, however, it was the German public whose appetite for naval expenditures proved limited. In 1909 the government of German chancellor Heinrich von Bülow fell because it was unable to levy the taxes required to continue what had become an unsustainably expensive building program. This failure marked the de facto finish line of the arms race, from which Britain emerged the winner.[8] But this outcome did nothing to moderate what had by then become entrenched hostility between the competitors.

There is no way to know whether, absent Germany's challenge to British maritime supremacy, Britain would have supported Germany's continental opponents so unflinchingly during the crisis that brought on the war. If, in 1900, a British statesman had been asked to describe the main threat to Britain's global position, he would have pointed to his country's rivalry with France and Russia, which had recently signed a treaty of mutual defense calculated to foster cooperation against Britain's overweening global presence. The least one can say about German navalism is that it provided a powerful incentive for Britain to resolve its differences with its imperial rivals, in order to concentrate its attention closer to home.

There is no question that the onset of the Great War was rooted in the stresses and strains of a rapidly globalizing economy, whose social and political consequences proved unmanageable for Europe's traditional elites. Yet however the influence of those deeper forces may be weighed, it remains the case that war did not break out owing to the rising friction of imperial competition or global capitalism. It arose from "some damn foolish thing in the Balkans," as Bismarck famously foresaw. In all the years since Waterloo, such a war would not have been one in which Britain would necessarily have felt compelled to fight. It did feel compelled in 1914 because its leaders had come to regard German ambitions as dangerously uncertain in direction and scope, an outlook that Berlin's naval building program reinforced in no uncertain terms.

THE GREAT WAR AT SEA

When war broke out in August 1914, Germany possessed twenty-two modern capital ships, plus five under construction. Britain had thirty-four, and another dozen being built. Given that Germany's High Seas Fleet had already failed in its original purpose, which was to deter Britain's entry into the war, there was no immediate reason to risk its destruction. If Germany's opening offensive against France had succeeded, the existence of a powerful fleet would certainly have mattered in whatever negotiations might have followed. Once the war on land devolved into a grinding attritional struggle, however, the question of what the fleet might do about it had to be faced. The answer was not obvious.

The same can be said on the British side. Great fleets do not come within weapons range of each other by chance. Major naval battles arise from a limited set of circumstances: attacks against the enemy's coast by gunfire or seaborne troops; attacks against trade via commerce raiding or blockade; or, in the rarest case, if the stronger fleet imposes battle on a weaker opponent in its own anchorage, a feat the Royal Navy accomplished twice in the long war against Napoleonic France.

In the hundred years since, however, long-range guns, naval mines, and torpedoes had made it exceedingly dangerous for warships to approach the enemy's coast. Prewar apprehensions on this score were vindicated in 1915, when British warships failed to force their way through the guns and minefields guarding the Dardanelles, with a view to bombarding Istanbul if the Ottoman Empire did not abandon the war. As a strategic conception the attack on the Dardanelles, and the subsequent landing of armed forces on the Gallipoli Peninsula, exemplified maritime power projection in classic form, by which the superior mobility afforded by the sea was exploited to attack the enemy coalition at what was believed to be its weakest point. Yet in execution the prospect of success proved illusory.[9] Even on the most charitable reckoning, the net effect was merely to extend the carnage of the Western Front rather than to outflank it, as intended.

Britain also sought to suppress its enemies' trade from the first day of the war to the final conclusion of peace. In the past such an exercise would have involved a "close blockade" by warships operating directly off enemy ports. Neutral vessels were expected to avoid contact with a blockading force, and were liable to be stopped or seized if they did not. Yet the very expression "close blockade" reflected the difficulty of doing any such thing, given the presence of the same new weapons that had rendered amphibious operations so perilous. Instead, Britain was forced to rely on a "distant blockade," conducted hundreds of miles from enemy ports by ships patrolling off Gibraltar and to the north and east of Scotland.

This distant blockade, apart from being more porous than the close kind, raised awkward questions about the rights of neutral states, a number of which were on the wrong side the line that Britain was determined to hold.[10] Their maritime trade became subject to comprehensive regulation by a belligerent power, a procedure that, then as now, was not in accord with international law. Britain's success in finessing the legal and diplomatic pitfalls created by its prosecution of the war at sea was crucial to its strategic success. The Entente could not have prevailed if Britain had been forestalled in its effort to curtail the Central Powers' access to the material and financial resources of the larger world. But insufficient regard for the rights and interests of this larger world might have limited the Entente's access to these same resources, and in the worst case would have converted neutrals into adversaries.

This was not a problem that could be solved by superior naval power as such. It also depended on the development of a complex financial and administrative infrastructure, much of which operated ashore in the neutral ports themselves. These arrangements allowed Britain to continue borrowing money overseas, and to use it to purchase the neutral goods that its naval blockade was meant to interdict; which goods ultimately became fuel for the Entente's own war effort. That a formidable bill would come due for all this was true; but given that the alternative was defeat, and that the bill could only be paid if the war was won, there was really no choice. Analogous considerations also weighed on neutral powers. In the final analysis even the strongest among them did not wish to confront the Royal Navy directly. As a consequence they found themselves becoming de facto financiers of the Entente. Not the least of the reasons why the United States entered the war against Germany was that it had developed a long list of accounts receivable from Britain and its allies, which would be subject to fierce discounting if the Entente were defeated.

Britain's distant blockade was not a measure calculated to bring about a naval battle, and it did not do so, except in the sense that, by conceding the southern half of the North Sea as a "naval no-mans land," it invited Germany's

High Seas Fleet to try its luck there from time to time.[11] Given German material inferiority, the point of such an exercise could only be to improve the long-term odds by drawing out Britain's forces piecemeal, and engaging them on favorable terms. It was the misfiring of just such a scheme that brought about the only major fleet action of the war, fought off Jutland in 1916.

The battle arose from a German plan to sortie its forces as if to mount a raid on the coast of England, taking pains to create the impression that the raid would only be conducted with a portion of its fleet, whereas the entire High Seas Fleet would be committed. The British, it was hoped, would respond using only that portion of its naval forces based at Rosyth, near the apparent point of attack, while the main body, farther north at Scapa Flow, would remain idle and unaware. In the event, however, the British learned in good time that the entirety of Germany's fleet had put to sea, and dispatched the entirety of theirs to meet it.

That the High Seas Fleet should have escaped destruction on this occasion has been the subject of much critical comment ever since.[12] Yet the outstanding question is not how the Germans got away, but why it mattered so little that they did. The British, disappointed in their hopes for a Trafalgar-like affirmation of their supremacy at sea, were eager for a rematch: the Grand Fleet signaled its readiness to put to sea the day after it returned to port. The German commander, Vice Admiral Reinhard Scheer, saw things differently. His ships, ostensibly the victors by virtue of having inflicted more damage than they sustained, would nevertheless remain out of action until mid-August. In the meantime, he was obliged to report to the kaiser that, even in the best case, there was no reason to think that defeat in a fleet action would affect Britain's capacity to carry on the war.[13]

In Scheer's view such a diminishment of capacity could only be accomplished by a stepped-up attack on British commerce, in which Germany had been engaged since the first weeks of the war, and which now entered its decisive phase. War against trade has been a central feature of maritime strategy since the Age of Sail. Battle fleets were originally created to protect (or attack) the vessels of the trading companies chartered to secure the riches of the Indies and the New World.[14] Even Mahan, the apostle of fleet action as the highest expression of naval supremacy, was emphatic that "navies . . . exist for the protection of commerce," and that it was scarcely possible "to conceive what broad military use they can subserve that at all compares with the protection and destruction of trade."[15] Neither, however, was it easy to foresee how economic and technological change would combine to lend *guerre de course*—"war of the pirate"—a desperate lethality it had not previously possessed.

In the Age of Sail commerce raiding had been the natural recourse of the weaker navy. A belligerent unable to sustain a blockade of the enemy's ports might nevertheless attack his trade in transit, by deploying individual ships and small squadrons to prowl the world's shipping lanes. Modern theorists like Mahan, while accepting that the leverage of sea power ultimately lay with its impact on trade, nevertheless doubted that such tactics would be practicable for steam ships, whose dependence on a shore-based infrastructure for fuel and maintenance would limit their range, and make their movements too predictable. In the decades preceding the outbreak of the war, however, a new weapon and a new form of warship had reached sufficient maturity to render this calculation irrelevant.

The weapon was the torpedo, an improved form of naval mine that could move under its own power. The torpedo was originally intended to be used for coastal and harbor defense, a role for which its slow speed and limited range suited it. As its speed and range improved, however, its revolutionary potential became apparent. Since the advent of gunpowder weapons, the laws of physics had ensured that, with few exceptions, only big ships could mount big guns, and that only big guns could sink big ships. This harmonious architecture had survived the advent of steel hulls, steam propulsion, and rifled shell guns; but it could not survive the coming of torpedoes, which could be launched from vessels of almost any size and sink the largest ships afloat.

Worries about the operational implications of torpedoes were widespread before the war. In particular it was feared that smaller vessels armed with torpedoes might interpose themselves between battle fleets, preventing the decisive engagement that was every sailor's highest aspiration. These concerns were not misplaced—it was fusillades of torpedoes fired by German destroyers that kept the British and German dreadnoughts from coming to grips at Jutland—but they were incomplete. Torpedoes also proved admirably suited to the destruction of commerce, once they were married to a vessel capable of surviving alone and undetected on the high seas.

This vessel was the submarine, which had been a pipedream since the days of Da Vinci, and which had visited watery death on any number of daredevil inventors. The new materials and techniques thrown up by the Industrial Revolution had turned the pipedream into a reality, albeit one whose military application did not seem especially promising. A typical submarine in the Great War displaced something over 500 tons, and was too slow to operate in conjunction with surface warships. It did have the almost magical property of being able to operate under water for half a day at a time, however, and that plus its small size meant that it might lurk in the offing for extended periods, awaiting the enemy's approach.

The natural prey of submarines was expected to be warships that strayed too close to a hostile shore. In February 1915, however, Germany declared the waters around the British Isles to be a war zone, and dispatched submarines to enforce it. This extemporized counterblockade was without basis in international law, but Germany believed it to be justified by British conduct, which also contravened the laws of war.[16] It almost goes without saying that Germany's action was not part of any deeply laid plan. Its motives seem to have been compounded of a desire to appease domestic opinion by striking back against Britain's "hunger blockade," and to mobilize neutral opinion in favor of enforcing traditional norms by dramatizing what could be expected if they were not.[17]

The tactical characteristics of submarines put all these subtleties in the shade. Submarines take no prisoners. In the first weeks of their operations, German submariners tried to adhere to what were called cruiser rules, which require that the crew of a merchantman destined to be sunk be removed to a place of safety first. A submarine can honor this requirement only in gestural terms, offering a targeted ship sufficient warning to get its personnel into lifeboats, assuming they were available. Even this limited accommodation soon proved infeasible, however. German submarines that afforded merchant ships a chance to save their crews soon came under fire from their intended victims, which began to mount deck guns to defend themselves. From the German perspective, this practice eliminated all doubt as to the legitimacy of merchantmen as targets, and permitted them to be sunk without warning. From the perspective of non-German public opinion, however, the wanton destruction of ships manned by civilians became another example of the Hun's beastliness, most especially following the sinking of the Cunard liner *Lusitania* in May 1915, an action that killed more than 1,100 people, including 128 Americans.[18]

The sinking was not an accident. *Lusitania* was listed as an auxiliary vessel of the Royal Navy, and the German Embassy in Washington ostentatiously warned prospective passengers that it was liable to be sunk once it entered the waters around the British Isles. But the sinking was a miscalculation just the same, and produced a stern warning from the Wilson administration that any similar action in the future would be regarded as a deliberately unfriendly act. Afterward, German submarine captains took more pains to avoid sinking passenger ships, and to ensure that their targets were national vessels of

Great Britain and its allies. As the war in Europe wore on, however, and as the deprivations of the British blockade began to wear on German society, the submarine war began to look like an unworthy half-measure. By the end of 1916 Germany's leadership had concluded that only a comprehensive effort to destroy British economic life made sense under the circumstances, and to that end it declared that, starting on February 1, 1917, German submarines would operate without restriction as to their targets.

It is widely accepted that America's declaration of war against Germany, which came three months later, was largely owed to official and public outrage over German conduct of the war at sea. This is fair enough, though American belligerency might equally be regarded as a decisive expression of British naval supremacy. The Germans justified the submarine war as a response to the British blockade, which they portrayed as illegal in form and tactics, and as a calculated effort to starve civilians. There is some truth to this, just not enough to overcome the shock inflicted by Germany's willingness, by way of reprisal, to wreak indiscriminate havoc at sea. The new technologies of the industrial era made this possible, and the new global economy made it desirable; but neither could make it morally or politically acceptable—at least not immediately.[19] Britain's ability to transgress neutral rights and get away with it was a provocation to the Germans, and arguably a fatal one; but in the final analysis it was simply a reflection of Britain's superiority as a maritime power. Germany's indiscriminate brutality was in turn a reflection of its weakness.

It must be admitted, however, that it did not suggest weakness at the time. The onset of unrestricted submarine warfare came as a shock to the Royal Navy, not to mention the Americans, who imagined they were joining the winning side in a war that had nearly run its course.[20] In the first two months of the unrestricted campaign, five hundred ships displacing over 1 million tons had gone to the bottom. When America's senior naval liaison officer, Rear Admiral William Sims, reached London in April, he was astonished to learn from Britain's first sea lord, Admiral John Jellicoe, that "it is impossible for us to go on with the war if losses like this continue."[21]

But the losses did not continue, thanks to the introduction of convoys for oceangoing trade. The use of warships to escort merchantmen is the foundation on which the integration of global commerce and naval power was originally built. The Royal Navy had rejected this time-honored remedy during the early stages of the submarine war because its leaders feared that, under modern conditions, the risks and costs would outweigh the benefits. The primary risk was that the bundling together of large groups of merchantmen, all steaming as one at a speed dictated by the slowest among them, would present the submarine with something like an ideal target. The main cost came from the organizational burdens the convoys would impose on production and consumption ashore. The training of merchant crews; the scheduling and management of convoy movements; the loading and unloading of masses of vessels, all arriving and departing together—all this would impose delays on the normal movement of goods, to be paid for in the form of spoiled cargoes, the disruption of industrial supply chains, and constraints on domestic consumption.

Convoys became acceptable because the unrestricted submarine campaign altered the cost calculation: More ships were being sunk, and a great deal of neutral shipping had ceased to move altogether.[22] The introduction of convoys did in fact impose a severe burden on British industry and consumers, and can fairly be counted as a victory for the U-boat. But it was not sufficient to alter the course of the war, because the fear that convoyed trade would make easy prey turned out to be misplaced.[23] "The size of the sea is so vast," Winston Churchill wrote in his account of the war, "that the difference between the size of a convoy and the size of a single ship shrinks to insignificance. There was in fact very nearly as good a chance of a convoy of forty ships in close order slipping unperceived between the patrolling U-boats as there was for a single ship; and each time this happened, forty ships escaped instead of one."[24]

Far from presenting the submarine with ideal targets, convoys "emptied the sea."[25] They did not empty it of submarines, however. The introduction of convoys deprived the U-boats of their targets, but this was a problem for which a remedy might one day be found. In the fall of 1918, as the fighting in Europe neared its bitter end, there were more operational German submarines afloat than there had been when the unrestricted campaign began.[26] Their day was not done.

HITLER'S WAR

In July 1917 the American ambassador to Great Britain, Walter Page, declared the submarine "the most formidable thing the war has produced—by far—and it gives the German the only earthly chance he has to win."[27] Adolf Hitler, who viewed the war from the trenches in Flanders, and ended it temporarily blinded by a British gas attack, might have felt that other formidable things were also in play. But he undoubtedly accepted the view that the Royal Navy had been the war-winning weapon, whose unbridled attack on German civilian morale had finally cast the valor of an unvanquished army into the abyss.[28] His policy as chancellor was aimed at reversing this defeat, while postponing a confrontation with Britain until Germany's position on the continent had been made secure. This policy collapsed when the Hitler–Stalin pact failed to dissuade Britain from making good its guarantee to Poland; whereupon what Churchill would call the Battle of the Atlantic resumed, more or less where it had left off twenty years earlier.[29]

Strategically, the stakes were what they had always been: to sever (or secure) the maritime communications that connected Britain and its allies to their suppliers, financiers, friends, and partners in the Western Hemisphere. The terms on which the second round of the struggle would be fought were different, however, owing to the achievements of the German army. Its stunning descent upon Norway, followed by the overrunning of France, meant that the British Isles no longer stood between the U-boats and the Atlantic. The scale of Germany's initial conquests in Europe also meant that there would be no hunger blockade this time. From the point of view of the Royal Navy, the Battle of the Atlantic had become an overwhelmingly defensive struggle.

The tactical picture also changed, thanks to a dramatic increase in submarines' operational range, which had more than doubled since 1918. The vast majority of ships sunk in World War I had gone down within 100 miles of the British coast. Twenty years later, German U-boats could operate for extended periods in the mid-Atlantic or in American waters. This allowed the development of new tactics designed to counter the convoys that Britain reintroduced immediately after the war broke out.

The essential advantage of convoys, as already described, was that they allowed U-boats to be avoided; only a small fraction of Atlantic convoys were even sighted by German submarines in 1917–18. Twenty years later, U-boats were no longer obliged by their mechanical limitations to position themselves like goalkeepers guarding a net. Many were deployed as pickets in mid-ocean, with a view to detecting potential targets days out from port. The first U-boat to locate a convoy would shadow it, while relaying its position so that other submarines could converge against it. If successful, the result would be a concentration of submarines capable of engaging a convoy's escorts on even terms while harrying its merchantmen for days on end.

The best defense against what were called wolf-pack tactics remained evasion. The chances of accomplishing this were improved by Britain's breaking of Germany's naval cipher, an achievement sufficiently remarkable that it remained a secret until 1974.[30] Even more decisive was the employment of long-range, land-based aircraft to patrol the Atlantic shipping lanes, supplemented by small escort carriers to provide close-in air cover. The effectiveness of aircraft as antisubmarine weapons can scarcely be exaggerated. More than half of all U-boats sunk during the war were destroyed by aircraft alone, or in combination with surface vessels. Aircraft also offered the advantage that their mere appearance would force a submarine to submerge, markedly reducing its speed and range, not to mention the situational awareness of its captain.[31] To which must also be added a gradual improvement in the capacity of surface vessels to detect submerged submarines, a near impossibility in World War I, but not in World War II.[32]

These technical and tactical influences matured in their own time, waxing and waning so as to produce some periods when the tide of battle favored the U-boat, while at other times those hunting them had the upper hand. The war on land also exerted a significant influence. Until the spring of 1941, when the German Army was deployed to attack the Soviet Union, the Royal Navy was hard pressed to provide escorts for Atlantic shipping because it needed to guard against a cross-channel invasion. In 1942 the British temporarily lost their ability to read German ciphers, a development whose effect was obscured because America's entry into the war made its unescorted coastal trade a magnet for U-boats. These periods were known to German submariners as "happy times." They did not last.

The tipping point came in the spring of 1943. By then American industry was producing more new hulls than the U-boats could sink; the air gap over the mid-Atlantic had finally been closed by long-range aircraft operating from the United Kingdom; and convoys, far from emptying the sea, were now filling it up with men and matériel to prepare for the invasion of northwestern Europe, agreed to at the Casablanca Conference in January and destined to unfold on the beaches of Normandy in June 1944. The result was a series of what can fairly be described as pitched battles, in which dozens of submarines converged against scores of cargo ships and their escorts. It was the submarines that emerged the losers. In May 1943 forty-one U-Boats were sunk, amounting to 30 percent of Germany's effective strength in the Atlantic. Such losses could not be allowed to continue, and the wolf-packs were withdrawn. No one dared say so at the time, but the Battle of the Atlantic was over.[33]

German submarines carried on until the end, operating against unescorted vessels, coastal trade, and other targets of opportunity. But the odds against them only grew steeper, as both sea and sky came under the unambiguous control of the Allies. By 1945, 74 percent of U-boats had gone to the bottom, an outcome sufficiently calamitous to invite the question whether something might have been done to improve their chances.

In terms of tactical efficiency, German submarines in World War II fell short of the record established in World War I. Their efforts took a toll on the British economy, but it is hard to imagine a British admiral in World War II sharing John Jellicoe's anxiety, in the spring of 1917, that Britain had been pushed within sight of surrender.[34] Might they have done better with a better start? Germany had fifty-seven submarines when the war began in 1939. If they had possessed, say, three times that many—a number comparable to the force still afloat in 1918—perhaps they could have fallen upon British trade with greater effect, before the technical and material advantages of their enemies had time to mature. This is an unanswerable question, but one that draws attention to the ambivalence of German prewar planning, which reflected the goals of Hitler's policy.

Hitler believed that it had been a fatal error for Germany to go to war with Britain while simultaneously grappling with a major continental opponent.[35] This insight shaped his policy. Before attacking Poland, Hitler's aim had been to isolate Eastern Europe so as to demonstrate to the Western powers that intervention in the East would be pointless. That he envisioned some future war against those Western powers is of course true. It was in preparation for that climactic struggle that he sought to restructure the German economy in order to reduce its dependency on overseas markets, finance, and resources, an autarkic policy that the near collapse of international trade in the 1930s reinforced. But war with Britain was not the war he was looking to start in 1939.

German naval planning reflected Hitler's vision. Naval building was pegged to a war at sea beginning sometime in the mid-1940s, and took a back seat to the rearmament of German land and air forces. This conceptual scheme also helps explain why, in the years leading up to the war, Germany's naval leadership was so committed to the production of "pocket battleships," which were heavily armed surface raiders of about 19,000 tons, together with traditional battleships, which were twice as large.[36] Such vessels would have posed a formidable threat to convoyed trade, assuming they could have survived.

In the war as actually fought, they could not have done so for long. All of Germany's heavy warships were eventually sunk or scuttled, often after extended refuge in well-protected anchorages. The most powerful among them, *Bismarck* (41,000 tons), survived on the open sea for only eight days before being disabled by a torpedo plane. How such vessels would have fared under the conditions envisioned by Hitler's policy is hard to say. In the best case Germany would have possessed many more heavy warships, while the Royal Navy's capital ships would have been pinned close to home to guard against invasion from an opponent with the full resources of Europe at its disposal. In such circumstances, reliance on *guerre de course* by surface raiders makes at least a modicum of sense, given the prevailing belief that only heavy surface ships could defeat the convoys, against which the submarine was judged to have failed.

Like the *Blitzkrieg*, the wolf-pack was a wartime discovery, in which tactical resourcefulness combined with new technical capacities to produce results beyond what was anticipated by prewar doctrine.[37] At sea, however, just as on land, early success proved transient, and once effective countermeasures had been developed, fighting devolved into precisely the sort of attritional struggle that German leaders had labored to avoid since the days of Frederick the Great. By the time the wolf-packs were withdrawn in 1943, no part of the German Navy was in a position to attack the productive capacity of the Allies, only to absorb it by drawing resources away from the war on land.[38]

The fundamental rhythms of the Allied war effort were defined by the struggle to control the seas. This was true even for the Soviet Union, which bore the brunt of the fighting on land and inflicted 70 percent of the casualties suffered by the German army. The Soviets were not ideologically disposed to cooperate with their allies beyond what was necessary for survival, an outlook that their isolated geography and autarkic economy reinforced. Even so, something on the order of 15 percent of the food and war matériel consumed by the Red Army originated overseas. This scale of assistance has proven just sufficient to inspire unresolvable arguments about whether it constituted the margin of victory on the Eastern Front. The most one can say is that there were moments when it seemed to in the eyes of the Soviet leadership.[39]

What the Soviets wanted most was for their allies to get their own armies to grips with Germany's. They found it difficult to accept that this could not be done until control of the North Atlantic had been assured. So did most of the senior officers of the US Army, who were dismayed to find themselves leading American troops ashore in North Africa in November 1942. The resulting campaign has been widely deprecated for having diverted Allied forces into a theater where the war could not be decided. Others have argued that, even as a diversion, prosecuting the war in the Mediterranean made sense, because the Axis could less easily afford to expend more limited resources there.[40]

On the military merits the issue is ultimately a narrow one, on which judgments will inevitably divide. Strategically, however, the decision to carry the war into the Mediterranean offered two decisive advantages. The first was that fighting there reassured the Soviets that, despite the logistical impossibility of an immediate cross-channel attack, the Western powers were eager to grapple with the Germans on any terms that were not obviously suicidal. The second was that, even if the Mediterranean was not on the main line to Berlin, committing American forces there reassured the British about the primacy of America's commitment to Europe, at a time when the psychological pull of the Pacific was overwhelming for the United States.[41]

It must be emphasized, moreover, that in naval terms the Mediterranean was not peripheral. It was part of the connective tissue of the British Empire, and integral to the same global supply networks whose survival was at stake in the Atlantic. The Mediterranean was the scene of fierce naval combat in both world wars. Its shallow waters and narrow straits proved friendly to submarines, whose ferocity was increased by the fact that there was less neutral shipping to worry about (above all, less American shipping). Whatever doubts attach to the value of the Mediterranean as a theater of war can only refer to the land campaigns fought there.

But this raises an issue that is both obvious and easily overlooked: that command of the sea may expand one's strategic opportunities but offers no guarantee as to the results. However harshly one may judge the execution of Britain's effort to force the Dardanelles in 1915, it is hard to say that the underlying conception, which was purely naval in character, was not worth trying. The subsequent commitment of land forces on the Gallipoli Peninsula is a different matter. It was inspired less by expectations of strategic leverage than by fear that abandoning the naval campaign would undermine British prestige—a consideration that might have been foreseen, but was not. When that attack also failed, the bet was raised again. The forces withdrawn from Gallipoli were committed against Bulgaria, which had entered the war seeking to profit at Serbia's expense. By 1918 the Entente had upward of 700,000 soldiers fighting along a static front stretching from the Adriatic to the Aegean. Bulgaria eventually became the first of the Central Powers to sue for peace, but this does not fully answer the charge that such an enormous commitment of resources would have been better employed against Germany itself.

A similar dynamic was evident after 1940, when Italian belligerency made its colonial position in North Africa fair game, and fighting there became a compelling option once the British were driven out of Northern Europe. That Germany deployed its own forces in reply shows that this judgment was not misguided. The fighting there in turn provided an opportunity for early American engagement against Germany, the politics of which have just been described.

Up to that point it was difficult to deny that war in the Mediterranean made sense. Control of the North African shore, and of the air over the

Mediterranean itself, would have sufficed to secure the most important strategic prize on offer, however, which was the restoration of maritime communications between Gibraltar and Suez. Once that was accomplished, the further expansion of operations to the Italian Peninsula can only be judged in terms of the correlation of forces involved: which side could least afford the fight. Given that any German forces not beaten in the Mediterranean would need to have been beaten somewhere else, it is perhaps vain to wonder whether the whole business might have been managed more efficiently.

Nevertheless, it should by then have become obvious that the Mediterranean's appearance as an open flank was an illusion. In both wars there were moments when it seemed possible that a blow delivered there might have such resonance as to allow the bitter cup of industrialized warfare to pass by. But it was not to be. Fighting in the Mediterranean afforded no special leverage to the maritime powers, except to extend the line along which the attritional effects of Allied material superiority could be applied.

The culmination of the war at sea did not come in the Mediterranean but in northern France, where the Germans had always expected it. Operation Overlord, the greatest amphibious assault ever attempted, can fairly be regarded as the exploitation phase of the Battle of the Atlantic—which is not in any way to diminish the extraordinary effort required for Anglo-American land and air forces to fight their way to final victory, merely to acknowledge the principle that for maritime powers, armies are projectiles fired by navies.[42]

Overlord's slow gestation has sometimes been held to diminish its military significance—the German army having been severely diminished by the time Western armies came ashore in force. Yet the fact remains that the timing of Overlord was dictated by the pace at which the U-boats could be mastered, and by the speed of American economic mobilization. Those who wish to argue that it could have happened sooner should devote themselves to considering how those two foundational processes could have been accelerated.

It is also worth emphasizing, finally, that Operation Overlord's significance is not confined to its part in the overthrow of Hitler's Germany. The campaign that it inaugurated also ensured that, when that overthrow was accomplished, a large American army would be present in the middle of Europe. Viewed in light of the Cold War already brewing on the horizon, the consequences of victory in the Battle of the Atlantic, without which that army would not have been there, can hardly be overstated. The leverage afforded by command of the sea may be slow to emerge, but it can last a long time.

THE PACIFIC

The Western Pacific saw no significant fighting in World War I because nearly all the states and territories there were colonies or protectorates of the Entente powers, or of important neutrals like the Netherlands and the United States. The only important exceptions were Germany's treaty ports and leaseholds in China, and its dispersed colonial holdings in the South Pacific. Once Germany went to war with Great Britain there was no chance that it could protect these far-flung possessions, and all of them were swept up by Australia and Japan.

Japan and Britain had become allies in 1902. Their treaty required each to adopt a stance of benevolent neutrality if the other were to become involved in war with a great power, and to enter such a war directly if a third power were to intervene. From the British perspective, the merits of such an arrangement were straightforward: The treaty would disconcert Russia, an imperial rival; and it would allow Britain to pull some naval forces out of the Pacific and into home waters, by way of responding to Germany's naval buildup.

Japan had more aggressive ends in view. Toward the end of the nineteenth century, it had become involved in a bruising competition for influence on the mainland of Asia, leading to war with China, which it won. This victory virtually assured Japan's eventual confrontation with Russia, against which a connection with Britain would provide a complex but effective form of insurance. The Japanese did not expect Britain to involve itself in such a war. They merely wished to ensure that, when the clash came (as it did, in 1904), Japan would not need to fight Russia's most important ally, France, which had a significant naval position in the Far East. The Japanese calculated that an alliance with Britain would deter the French from aiding Russia, whose main fleet would in fact be destroyed by the Japanese in the war's climactic battle.

Japan's victory confirmed it on a course of imperial expansion, whereby it hoped to supersede the Western powers in Asia. The coming of World War I further encouraged this ambition. Japan's alliance with Britain made it a belligerent in the war, and provided an occasion to seize German-controlled territory in China and elsewhere. For the most part, however, Japan's contribution to the Allied victory was logistical and financial. Like the United States, Japan was a beneficiary of the Royal Navy's success in preserving the Entente's access to trade and finance. Its economy (and self-esteem) benefited handsomely as a consequence.[43]

To these points must be added the observation that, in contrast to the United States, Japan expected to gain from the war regardless of which side won, because it judged the war itself to be a blow against European prestige.

This outlook underpinned the highly prejudicial demands for political and economic concessions that Japan presented to China in January 1915, long before Germany's defeat could have been foreseen. China, which was neutral as regards Europe but had been in the throes of an incipient civil war since the collapse of the Qing Dynasty in 1912, was in no position to resist. Britain and the United States were bitterly opposed, however: The British were opposed because they feared for their own favored position if China were to become a client of Japan; and the Americans were opposed because Japan's demands contradicted its preference for free trade and the Open Door.

Postwar international relations in Asia were dominated by Japan's efforts to capitalize on Chinese weakness, and by the desire of Britain and the United States to prevent it from doing so. Japan's scheme for coping with these two antagonists resembled the strategy that had brought it success against Russia. Japan had defeated Russia, an inherently stronger opponent, because it was able to exploit conditions in Europe to its advantage. Japan's treaty with Britain was crucial, but so too was its estimate that Russia's military strength would always be committed primarily to the defense of its western frontiers, which meant that the true centers of Russian strength were so far away that, by the time its forces reached the Far East, they would be sufficiently degraded that Japan would be able to cope with them. The Russian fleet that the Japanese destroyed transiting the Tsushima Strait had sailed more than half way around the world before it even laid eyes on a Japanese ship, a grinding journey whose wear and tear went a long way toward sealing its fate. Similar problems seemed certain to afflict any British or American fleet that attempted to approach Japan's home islands.

Japan hoped to get its way versus the British and the Americans because it was separated from each of them by nine time zones worth of water, and because the instability of postwar Europe would make it too dangerous for either of them to make a major strategic commitment in Asia. This approach succeeded versus Great Britain. The resurgence of German power under Hitler made it impossible for Britain to maintain its military presence in the Pacific. When war came in 1941, British strategy had been reduced to the defense of a single bastion—Singapore—3,000 miles from Tokyo, and easily overrun even so. Although Britain would eventually claim a share of the Allied victory in Asia, its achievements were circumscribed by the effort required to hold off the Nazis. Absent American belligerency it is barely possible that Britain and the Soviet Union might together have defeated the Axis powers in Europe. But it is hard to imagine that either of them would have emerged afterward with the will and wherewithal to roll back the gains

Japan would still have made by sweeping up the broken bits of European empires in the Far East.

These gains were reversed because Japan's strategy did not succeed versus the United States. The United States had regarded Japan as a potential rival in Asia since it took the Philippines away from Spain in 1898. But it also viewed Japan as a potential partner in an effort to replace European imperial hegemony with arrangements based on self-determination and free trade.[44] The Washington Treaties of 1921–22 were intended to set this transformation in motion, by limiting naval armaments, guaranteeing the territorial status quo in Asia, and securing international endorsement for the Open Door. Japan was a reluctant party to these agreements, which required it to accept a lower limit than the major Western powers on its future construction of capital ships. It was also obliged to return what territory it had taken from China during the Great War, and to abandon its alliance with Britain, in which it set great store as a symbol of its status as a power of the first rank. It received significant advantages in return, however, above all in avoiding a potentially ruinous naval arms race with the United States. It also obtained a general prohibition against new fortifications in the western Pacific, a provision that assured Japan of naval preeminence in its own region.

The Washington Treaties stoked long-standing Japanese resentment that they remained second-class citizens within a world order in which they aspired to a leading role. Such feelings do not, in themselves, contain the seeds of war. Japan in the 1920s was a country with few natural resources and a rising population, which had experienced two decades of rapid economic growth that it had every reason to expect would continue, provided it retained cordial relations with its overseas trading partners. The dramatic contraction of the world economy in the 1930s caused this expectation to be cast aside, and to be replaced with a policy of militarized expansionism aimed at economic self-sufficiency and regional supremacy.[45]

China remained the immediate object of Japanese ambition. It had passed the 1920s in a state of incipient dissolution, and was in no position to offer an effective defense. Neither was anyone else. The United States was nevertheless prepared to employ its dominant position in global commodity and financial markets to compel Japan to abandon its aggressive policies. And here it must be observed that Mahan's claim that the natural interest of maritime powers is in peace incorporated an important subtext: that trade rather than war should play the preponderant role in relations among states. This had been an aspirational feature of American foreign policy since the founding of the republic.[46] It was fully on display in the American effort to contain Japan following its invasion of China in 1937, after which each major Japanese move was met by increasingly onerous restrictions on access to American goods.[47] Both sides recognized that economic leverage was being employed in lieu of military force, to achieve a military result—the withdrawal of Japanese forces from China. Even so, both sides were surprised when the outcome proved to be war. When the Pacific War began, Japan was still America's largest trading partner in Asia.

Japanese and American planners shared a common picture of how war between them would unfold, a problem defined by the enormous size of the ocean that separated them. For the Americans war with Japan would require the systematic advance of its forces across thousands of miles of open sea, a formidable logistical challenge that would need to be managed so that each phase of the advance would capture new forward bases to sustain the next one. The climax would be the culminating defeat of Japan's main naval forces in Japanese waters, after which the home islands would be beaten into submission. Japanese planners saw things the same way, except for the outcome. They envisioned the long American advance as an extended opportunity to wear down American strength, so that the climactic battle in Japanese waters would be one they would win.[48]

Against this background, the Japanese offensive of December 1941, whose centerpiece was the attack on the US Pacific Fleet at Pearl Harbor, stands out as the first step in a process that would gradually derange Japan's strategic conception. The decision to move against the United States had been set in motion in July, when the Americans had stepped up their campaign of economic sanctions by freezing Japanese dollar-denominated assets in the United States. This action was motivated by Japanese encroachment in Southeast Asia, a region that Germany's conquest of Western Europe had rendered indefensible by its erstwhile colonial overlords. From the Japanese perspective, the asset freeze would make it impossible to continue purchasing oil from the United States, their largest supplier. Absent a reliable supply of oil, Japan's position in China could not be sustained.[49]

There was a further Japanese calculation: that Europe, and not Asia, would be the focus of the American strategic effort as long as Hitler's regime survived. This assessment was fully consistent with American conduct.[50] In the summer of 1941, at precisely the time when America was ratcheting up its economic pressure in the Pacific, 25 percent of its Pacific Fleet was being transferred to the Atlantic, to support the enforcement of a maritime security zone stretching from North America to Iceland. A few months earlier the passage of the Lend-Lease Act had provided an unlimited line of credit with which war against Germany could be financed. The fact that American politics required all this to be done under the aegis of de jure neutrality and "hemispheric defense" did not alter its obvious meaning: Even America was losing its balance in the face of Germany's inexorable advance. The result was an increasingly conspicuous vacuum of power in Asia. Japan's attack on the United States was calculated to drive the United States back long enough for Japan to seize the opportunity that these conditions presented.

Pearl Harbor was by any reckoning a feat of arms, but it was no substitute for the climactic battle toward which Japanese strategic thinking was oriented. On the contrary, by transforming the United States from engaged neutral to enraged belligerent, Japan had set in motion a process of unstinting economic mobilization that virtually guaranteed that, however long it might take American forces to make their way to Japanese waters, they would be invincible when they arrived. The measures best suited to obstruct an eventual American advance—the seizure of the Hawaiian Islands or the occupation of Australia—were ruled out as logistically infeasible and as requiring military forces Japan did not possess. There remained, however, the possibility of bringing about a second great battle sooner rather than later, on terms favorable to the attrition of the American navy.

To this end, Japanese naval planners conceived the idea of seizing Midway Atoll.[51] Midway, among the westernmost of the Hawaiian Islands, was of no great significance in itself. But it was still US territory, hence a place the Japanese believed the Americans would feel morally bound to recover. By the time the Americans could attempt to do so, however, Japanese forces would be in a position to fight a well-prepared defensive battle on favorable terms.

It is probably idle to consider whether the Japanese vision of what they might accomplish by seizing Midway made any sense. The least one can say is that it is a bad sign when the margin of strategic success is entirely dependent on the psychological response of the enemy. As it happened, the real Battle of Midway, fought on June 3–7, 1942, was nothing like what the Japanese had hoped for, owing to the discovery of their plans by American naval intelligence. As a result a task force of American carriers was in position to surprise and destroy the leading elements of the advancing Japanese fleet, the remainder of which turned away in confusion.[52]

Midway is universally regarded as the decisive battle of the Pacific War, which makes sense, provided one is careful about what got decided. The loss of four Japanese fleet carriers was a severe material and emotional blow, but they scarcely represent the margin of America's eventual victory. Midway was not a battle preceding which the United States was losing the war, and afterward winning it. There is more truth to the claim that after Midway the Japanese lost the initiative, meaning their capacity to dictate the pace, location, and character of operations; but this does not mean that such initiative passed directly to the Americans. Two years after Pearl Harbor, fighting in the Pacific was still concentrated around the defensive perimeter established in Japan's opening offensive.[53] It was only toward the end of 1943 that Japan's initial conquests began to fall from its grasp, after which the weight of American power became progressively more crushing.

When viewed against this background, what Midway decided is both clear and simple: The American victory there ensured that the war in Asia would be won or lost in the Pacific. The alternative, in the minds of Western planners, was a Japanese move into the Indian Ocean, where its forces had already begun operating in the spring of 1942. British intelligence feared for the security of the British base in Cairo, and by extension for the entire campaign in North Africa. In the worst case, India itself might have broken away, into neutrality or even revolution. But like all roads not taken, it is not easy to see where this one might have led. There can be no certainty that the Japanese would have grasped how profoundly such a move might have reshaped the entire war. But their chances of doing so would surely have increased if they had managed to win a significant respite in their war against the Americans. After Midway there was no chance of that.

The series of naval and amphibious campaigns that finally brought Japan down is unique in the history of war: a two-pronged advance by naval, land, and air forces, conducted on and from the sea, but in the manner of a great army advancing over land. In the Atlantic maritime strategy was concerned with the military and economic synergy to be obtained by connecting the two sides. In the Pacific the problem was simply how to project power from one side to the other. There were no neutral interests to consider there. Although the indiscriminate use of submarines against commercial shipping was part of the picture, the campaign was conducted by the Allies, whose scruples in the matter were overcome from the moment the first shot was fired.[54] In the Pacific, *guerre de course* was just an aspect of total war.

The culminating act of the Pacific War was a bombing campaign of unmatched ferocity against the home islands of Japan. Like the climactic advance of the Anglo-American armies in northwestern Europe, the air campaign was also expressive of the possibilities that command of the sea created. Interwar theorists of strategic bombing had imagined that such operations would be the opening act of war in the future, preparing the way for the advance of other forces, perhaps even making them superfluous. This view failed to consider the extraordinary industrial and logistical preparation required to create and sustain the necessary air forces; also, in the particular conditions of the Pacific, it failed to consider the enormous distances involved. The operational radius of the American B-29, the most capable bomber of the war and workhorse of the air campaign against Japan, was about 1,600 miles. An awful lot of water had to pass under the keels of the US Navy before such weapons could be used.

The bombing of Japan has contributed to the reputation of the Pacific War as epitomizing merciless violence. Without disputing this description, it must still be observed that it could have been much worse, and would have been, if the war had not been conducted primarily on and from the sea. In proportional terms Japanese military and civilian casualties were far below those suffered by Germany, because such a large share of Japan's army was marooned in China, or simply bypassed in the so-called island-hopping campaign whereby the American forces made their way forward.[55] Many lives were also spared because Japan surrendered before suffering invasion, whose consequences would almost certainly have been terrible.[56]

It must be observed, finally, that the exercise of maritime strategy in the Pacific produced different long-term results than in the Atlantic. In Europe command of the sea created conditions under which the maritime powers were eventually able to share in the postwar governance of the continent, to facilitate its economic recovery, and ultimately to see off the Soviet Union. In the Pacific it enabled the United States to defeat Japan far more efficiently than is commonly recognized; but it did not, and could not, put the victors in a position to fill the political vacuum the Pacific War created. Except for Japan, every country touched by the war in Asia would find itself at war again within five years. In Asia as in Europe, the means by which the world wars were won defined the terms on which the Cold War would be conducted. But the terms would be very different.

NOTES

1. A comment by Admiral William Tennant, June 18, 1961, reported by Richard Hough, *The Longest Battle: The War at Sea, 1939–45* (New York: William Morrow, 1986), 3.

2. Stephen Broadberry and Mark Harrison, eds., *The Economics of World War I* (Cambridge: Cambridge University Press, 2005), 36. See also an earlier volume: Mark Harrison, ed., *The Economics of World War II: Six Great Powers in International Comparison* (Cambridge: Cambridge University Press, 1998).

3. See Edmund Silberner, *The Problem of War in Nineteenth-Century Economic Thought*, trans. Alexander H. Krappe (Princeton, NJ: Princeton University Press, 1946).

4. The best-known prewar statement of this argument is by Norman Angell, *The Great Illusion: A Study of the Relation of Military Power in Nations to Their Economic and Social Advantage* (New York: G. P. Putnam's Sons, 1910).

5. Alfred Thayer Mahan, *The Problem of Asia and Its Effects upon International Policies* (Boston: Little, Brown, 1900), 99.

6. Randolph Bourne, "The War and the Intellectuals," *Seven Arts* 2 (1917): 133–46.

7. Avner Offer, *The First World War: An Agrarian Interpretation* (Oxford: Oxford University Press, 1989), 25. Ratios were worse for protein (27 percent) and fats (42 percent).

8. V. R. Berghahn, *Germany and the Approach of War in 1914*, 2nd. rev. ed. (New York: St. Martin's Press, 1993), 97–135.

9. On the failure of the naval attack on the Dardanelles and the genesis of the amphibious assault that followed, see Tim Travers, *Gallipoli 1915* (Stroud, UK: Tempus, 2001), 20–36.

10. Martin Gilbert, *Atlas of the First World War* (New York: Oxford University Press, 1994), 76.

11. Geoffrey Till, *Sea-Power: A Guide for the Twenty-First Century* (New York: Routledge, 2013), 180.

12. See, e.g., Andrew Gordon, *The Rules of the Game: Jutland and British Naval Command* (London: John Murray, 1996).

13. See Scheer's after-action report to William II, as given by V. E. Tarrant, *Jutland: The German Perspective* (Annapolis, MD: Naval Institute Press, 1995), 250. Scheer does not say it in his report, but the real results of Jutland—six major British ships sunk, six more ships badly damaged, and six thousand British seamen dead—are close to what might have been expected if his original plan of ambush had actually succeeded. Jutland was celebrated as a victory by the German navy until the end of World War II; but that it was an empty one was obvious to the man most entitled to take credit.

14. See Richard Harding, *Sea Power and Naval Warfare, 1650–1830* (Annapolis, MD: Naval Institute Press, 1999).

15. Alfred Thayer Mahan, *The Interest of America in Sea Power, Present and Future* (Boston: Little, Brown, 1897), 128.

16. George Politakis, *Modern Aspects of the Laws of Naval Warfare and Maritime Neutrality* (New York: Routledge, 1997), 35–45.

17. Germany began rationing food and regulating agricultural prices at the start of 1915; Offer, *First World War*, 26.

18. German cruelty toward civilians became established in the public mind because of widespread reports of atrocities committed during the occupation of Belgium in 1914. The same moral and iconographic framing was applied to the submarine war, as can be seen in the US Navy's recruiting poster shown at http://www.loc.gov/pictures/item/2001700444/. Until recently, accounts of German barbarity in Belgium were wrongly regarded as exaggerated, on which see John Horne and Alan Kramer, *German Atrocities 1914: A History of Denial* (New Haven, CT: Yale University Press, 2001).

19. As discussed below, unrestricted submarine warfare was the norm for all belligerents in World War II.

20. On the day Congress declared war, a representative of the US Army staff testified before the Senate Finance Committee that "we may have to have an army in France," a prospect that caused the committee chairman to cry out in dismay. See Thomas Fleming, "Illusions and Realities in World War I," *Historically Speaking* 6, no. 1 (September–October 2004): 7–9.

21. W. S. Sims, *The Victory at Sea* (London: John Murray, 1920), 6.

22. The latter effect far outweighed the number of ships actually sunk. See Nicholas Tracy, *Attack on Maritime Trade* (Toronto: University of Toronto Press, 1991), 139–43.

23. A similar assessment might be made of the Entente's blockade of Germany, which suffered economic disruption and social deprivation, but not the point where it considered abandoning the war. Offer, *First World War*, is a comprehensive analysis of Germany's efforts to cope with its most critical shortage, which was of food. See also Tracy, *Attack on Maritime Trade*, 143–48.

24. Winston S. Churchill, *The World Crisis, 1911–1918*, abridged and rev. ed. (New York: Charles Scribner's Sons, 1931), 745.

25. David Stevenson, *With Our Backs to the Wall: Victory and Defeat in 1918* (Cambridge, MA: Harvard University Press, 2011), 313.

26. V. E. Tarrant, *The U-Boat Offensive, 1914–1945* (Annapolis, MD: Naval Institute Press, 1989), 68.

27. John Terraine, *Business in Great Waters: The U-Boat Wars 1916–1945* (Barnsley, UK: Pen & Sword, 2009), 673.

28. The linkage of the British blockade to the "stab in the back" legend promulgated by the German right has caused some historians to underestimate its effect, if only to avoid the implication that the German army was not really defeated. On the incongruity of separating the performance of the army from the deterioration of the German economy, see Offer, *First World War*, 69–78; to which add that, as bad as things were at the end, collapsing civilian morale did not compel Germany's surrender. See Michael Geyer, "People's War: The German Debate about a *Levée en masse* in October 1918," in *The People in Arms: Military Myth and National Mobilization since the French Revolution*, ed. Daniel Moran and Arthur Waldron (Cambridge: Cambridge University Press, 2003), 124–58.

29. See Adolf Hitler, *Mein Kampf*, trans. Ralph Manheim (New York: Houghton Mifflin, 1998), 143.

30. An informative account, by one of those responsible, is by Peter Calvocoressi, *Top Secret Ultra* (Kidderminster, UK: M. & M. Baldwin, 1980).

31. On the causes of loss for German U-boats, see Tarrant, *U-Boat Offensive*, 242. The commitment of aircraft to the submarine war was hampered by the reluctance of the Royal Air Force to divert forces from the pursuit of victory via the bombing of German cities, on which see Correlli Barnett, *Engage the Enemy More Closely: The Royal Navy in the Second World War* (New York: W. W. Norton, 1991), 458–90. This misjudgment has been seen as a serious blot on Churchill's record as war leader. It was serious, but so too were the considerations that underlay it, on which see Christopher M. Bell, *Churchill and Sea Power* (Oxford: Oxford University Press, 2013), 254–82.

32. Terraine, *Business in Great Waters*, 29–31.

33. Ibid., 108–19.

34. In the war of 1914–18, the Entente lost 62,500 tons of shipping for every German submarine sunk. In World War II, every U-boat lost accounted for only 17,700 tons of Allied shipping. These figures were compiled from Tennant, *The U-Boat Offensive*, passim. On the impact of the submarine campaign on the British economy and war effort see Tracy, *Attack*, 192–208.

35. Hitler, *Mein Kampf*, 143.

36. On German naval planning before the war, see Wilhelm Deist, Manfred Messerschmidt, Hans-Erich Volkmann, and Wolfram Wette, *Germany and the Second World War, Volume I: The Build-Up of German Aggression*, trans. P. S. Falla, Dean S. McMurry, and Edwald Osers (Oxford: Oxford University Press, 1990), 456–80.

37. See Karl-Heinz Frieser, *Blitzkrieg-Legende: Der Westfeldzug 1940* (Munich: R. Oldenbourg, 1996).

38. Hitler made this point in his instructions to the navy leadership when the wolf-packs were withdrawn. See his remarks of May 30, 1943, in the collection of captured documents published by the British Admiralty, *Fuehrer Conferences on Naval Affairs*, 2 vols. (London, 1947), 2:46.

39. Although the majority of Western aid reached the USSR after 1943, it probably mattered most early on, when the Soviet economy was reeling from the initial German attack. See Roger Munting, "Lend-Lease and the Soviet War Effort," *Journal of Contemporary History* 19, no. 3 (July 1984): 495–510; and Alexander Hill, "British Lend-Lease Aide and the Soviet War Effort, June 1941–June 1942," *Journal of Military History* 71, no. 3 (July 2007): 773–808.

40. Cf. Douglas Porch, *The Path to Victory: The Mediterranean Theater in World War II* (New York: Farrar, Straus & Giroux, 2004); and the more dyspeptic analysis by Simon Ball, *The Bitter Sea: The Struggle for Mastery in the Mediterranean, 1935–1949* (New York: Harper Press, 2009).

41. The most incisive account of why the Allies carried the war into the Mediterranean Sea region is still that by Michael Howard, *The Mediterranean Strategy in the Second World War* (New York: Frederick A. Praeger, 1968).

42. This famous proposition is usually attributed to Britain's Admiral John Fisher, though Fisher himself attributed it to Edward Grey; see Ruddock F. Mackay, *Fisher of Kilverstone* (Oxford: Oxford University Press, 1973), 382. Julian Corbett, *Some Principles of Maritime Strategy* (London: Longmans, Green, 1911), does not repeat the phrase, but his work is an exploration of its theoretical implications.

43. See Frederick R. Dickinson, *War and National Reinvention: Japan in the Great War, 1914–19* (Cambridge, MA: Harvard University Press, 1999). Japanese gold reserves increased sixfold over the course of the war; Edward S. Miller, *Bankrupting the Enemy: The US Financial Siege of Japan before Pearl Harbor* (Newport, RI: Naval Institute Press, 2007), 56–57.

44. See Akira Iriye, *After Imperialism: The Search for a New Order in the Far East, 1921–31* (Cambridge, MA: Harvard University Press, 1965).

45. Michael Barnhart, *Japan Prepares for Total War: The Search for Economic Security, 1919–1941* (Ithaca, NY: Cornell University Press, 1987), 22–63. Barnhart notes (p. 50) that American self-sufficiency in food and energy was an inspiration for Japanese policy.

46. See Felix Gilbert, *To the Farewell Address: Ideas of Early American Foreign Policy* (Princeton, NJ: Princeton University Press, 1961); and William H. Becker and Samuel F.

Wells, Jr., eds., *Economics and World Power: An Assessment of American Diplomacy since 1789* (New York: Columbia University Press, 1984).

47. See Walter LeFeber, *The Clash: US–Japanese Relations throughout History* (W. W. Norton, 1997), 160–213.

48. See Edward S. Miller, *War Plan Orange: The US Strategy to Defeat Japan, 1897–1945* (Annapolis, MD: Naval Institute Press, 1991); and H. P. Willmott, *Empires in the Balance: Japanese and Allied Pacific Strategies to April 1942* (Annapolis, MD: Naval Institute Press, 1982), 67–129.

49. The details of this crucial episode are difficult to interpret. The United States might have chosen to embargo oil sales to Japan, but expressly rejected the idea in the same meeting in which the asset freeze was ordered. The Japanese could have applied for permission to continue purchasing oil, which would have required that their initial payments be made in dollars that were beyond the reach of American policy. The Japanese rejected this because it would only heighten their future susceptibility to American pressure; which must surely have been the American goal. Secretary of the Interior Harold Ickes recalled President Roosevelt declaring that the basic idea was not to force a confrontation, but to "slip the noose around Japan's neck and give it a jerk now and then"; *The Secret Diaries of Harold L. Ickes,* 3 vols. (New York: Simon & Schuster, 1954–55), 3:588. Many historians have concluded that the American oil embargo was either inadvertent or executed by subordinate officials in disregard of Roosevelt's intentions. Be that as it may, it is apparent that Japanese–American relations had reached an impasse such that war could be averted only if one or the other abandoned policies on which each had staked its national prestige.

50. It is also consistent with American strategic planning. One of the best-known documents of the war is a memorandum prepared in November 1940 by the American chief of naval operations, Harold Stark, in which Stark laid out the reasons why the United States should adopt a defensive attitude in the Pacific while seeking to take the offensive in Europe. This is the fourth option ("D") that Stark considers; hence, "Plan Dog," which proved to be a crucial step in the development of American strategy, for which the byword would become "Europe First." The memo can be found in facsimile at http://tinyurl.com/p5zvta4.

51. On the genesis of the Midway plan, see Jonathan Parshall and Anthony Tully, *Shattered Sword: The Untold Story of the Battle of Midway* (Washington, DC: Potomac Books, 2005), 19–37; and H. P. Willmott, *The Barrier and the Javelin: Japanese and Allied Pacific Strategies to June 1942* (Annapolis, MD: Naval Institute Press, 1983), 3–80.

52. The authoritative account of the tactical battle is now that by Parshall and Tully, *Shattered Sword.* Willmott, *Barrier and the Javelin,* 291–523, remains compelling on the bigger picture.

53. This is well illustrated by the map of the Pacific Theater given by Peter Calvocoressi, Guy Wint, and John Pritchard, *The Penguin History of the Second World War,* rev. ed. (New York: Penguin Books, 1999), 1170–71.

54. A general order to "execute against Japan unrestricted air and submarine warfare" was issued to American forces on the afternoon of the Pearl Harbor attack. The resulting air campaign has been very well studied, the submarine war much less so; but see Joel Ira Holwitt, *Execute against Japan: The US Decision to Conduct Unrestricted Submarine Warfare* (College Station: Texas A&M University Press, 2009). The Japanese

also employed their submarines against Allied merchantmen to the extent possible. But targets were few.

55. The online *West Point Atlas* includes an instructive map showing the areas still under Japanese control at the end of the war, at http://tinyurl.com/Asia-1945.

56. Germany was a country of about 78 million when World War II began, and it suffered about 4.2 million military and civilian deaths. Japan's population was 73 million, and its death toll was about 2 million. It goes without saying that casualty estimates in modern war are subject to dispute, but in this instance inevitable uncertainty does not alter the basic picture. These figures are from the *Encyclopedia Britannica*. An extensive compilation of published casualty estimates may be found at http://tinyurl.com /Necrometerics-WWII. On the likely consequences of an Allied invasion of the Japanese home islands, see Richard B. Frank, *Downfall: The End of the Imperial Japanese Empire* (New York: Random House, 1999).

CHAPTER 3

The Cold War at Sea

GEOFFREY TILL

THE MAHANIAN NARRATIVE

For latter-day Mahanians, the victory of the West over the Soviet Union in the long Cold War may seem to be a classic example of the inevitable triumph of the sea powers over yet another land-bound and constrained continental adversary. The Soviets had gone the way of Napoleon, Wilhelmine Germany, and Hitler. NATO, an alliance centered on an ocean, had been able to bring the full resources of the West's global maritime power against an adversary constantly having to worry about its territorial borders, the inevitable inefficiencies of its economy, the political reliability of its allies, and the moral resilience of its own people.[1] In the long run, the maritime West was bound to win. Or at least that is what Alfred Thayer Mahan would probably have thought, if he had been around at the time.

But that is not how it appeared to Western politicians and analysts, or to the soldiers, sailors, and airmen of the time—nor to their adversaries in the Soviet Politburo or on the General Staff. At that time and since then, the "terrible simplicities" of the Mahanian narrative could easily be discounted as largely irrelevant in the strategic circumstances of the mid–twentieth century, for three basic reasons:

- The sea power of a continental state can prove strategically decisive.
- Transformational military technology had changed the terms of the debate.
- The force of history could determine different outcomes.

Let us consider, in turn, each of these challenges to the Mahanian explanation for the victory of the West in the Cold War.

The Sea Power of the Continental State

Russia, it could well be argued, was a sea power and had always been one, but a different kind of sea power with a different approach. As Admiral Sergei Gorshkov, commander in chief of the Soviet Navy from 1956 to 1985, claimed, "The fleet wrote into the history of our homeland many remarkable heroic pages and played an important role in the history of the development of Russia," hostile propaganda and endless difficulties notwithstanding.[2] Russia has the longest coastline in the world—one washed by two oceans and twelve seas. As Fred T. Jane reminded his readers at the beginning of the twentieth century, the Russians have a longer seafaring tradition than the British. They were keen explorers, and were often surprisingly innovative in developing naval technology.[3] Accepting that the navy's history in the Tsarist era was not always exemplary, some Russian navalists—like Admiral Nikolai Klado and, seventy years later, Gorshkov himself—disputed the relevance of the Tsarist legacy, good or bad. Russia, they said, had been allowed to become a nonmaritime country through centuries of uneven development and often plain neglect, much of which could be ascribed to the deficiencies of the Tsarist system rather than to the characteristics of the Russian nation. In the Soviet period, things would not be the same.[4] Moreover, this distinctive Russian approach to sea power looked to be particularly valid in the circumstances of the mid–twentieth century.

All this challenges the common—and quite often, notably patronizing—Western view that the Russian approach to maritime strategy was simply a pale and uncomprehending copy of Western concepts that the Russians never really understood or properly implemented. This view has been challenged by academics like William C. Fuller, who argued that "Russia became a great power not so much by emulating the West as by inventing a new style of fighting" that capitalized on the unique set of characteristics that constituted its strategic environment.[5] Indeed, many in the Soviet Navy advocated this. In their view, instead of slavishly adhering to inappropriate foreign concepts of maritime warfare, Russia should substantiate its own. Thus, the commissar of the Naval Forces of the Red Army explained:

> We often . . . identify with the classical sea powers and try to operate like they do. The battle of Jutland is our model which we study and attempt to imitate. Admirals Beatty and Spee—they are our role models. That which we learn from foreigners is good. . . . But to try to transplant all that directly into our conditions is not correct. We have other forces, other means, and we operate under different conditions. Consequently, it is necessary to work out the tactics for a small navy which acts together with the army according to a single strategic plan.[6]

The Soviet Union's land-power orientation—its "socialist principles" and societal approach and, in the early days, the poor state of its naval infrastructure—shaped this particular example of Russian exceptionalism.[7] But the point here is that in the circumstances of the mid–twentieth century, this approach conferred particular advantages as far as Soviet observers were concerned. Three stand out.

First, there were the advantages of land power. In campaigns as various as the Crimean War and a putative war of the atomic age, Russia's geography arguably reduced its vulnerability to external attack. In 1945 one US report concluded: "In contrast to our concentrations of industry and population and our exposure to attack by bombs launched from the sea, Russia is inaccessible from the sea, and its industry and population are widely dispersed over vast areas."

Two years later, the members of the US Air Policy Board were warned: "You can see quite readily how deep in her interior Russia's vitals are. . . . They have developed their industrial sinews roughly along the median line of the earth's broadest land mass."[8] This institutional, geographic, and cultural setting had considerable consequences for the way in which Soviet naval officers approached their tasks at both the tactical and operational levels—not least in how they influenced the Soviet understanding of such terms as "sea control," "antisubmarine warfare" (ASW), and "maritime borders." The resulting abstruse and theoretical debates that often took place about issues like this frequently proved crucial to operational and procurement outcomes in a way that was less true in the more pragmatic West.[9]

The second advantage of the distinctively Soviet approach was the benefit to be gained from the Leninist stress upon the unity of forces. Gorshkov's successor, Admiral Vladimir Chernavin, put it like this: "Today . . . there is no purely specific realm of warfare. Victory is achieved by the combined efforts of all [branches of the armed services], which brings about the need to integrate all knowledge of warfare within the framework of a united military science."[10]

A good case can indeed be made that the principle of combined arms invigorated Soviet naval development throughout the period. As Jacob Kipp remarked, "Cooperation between the army and the navy in the struggle for access became the hallmark of Russian naval history and gave that history a distinctly un-Mahanian cast."[11]

Russia's pragmatic approach, combined with its strictly limited resources, introduced a healthy realism into naval planning. Naval procurement could be tailored to Russia's particular requirements and not to some idealized perception of what a navy should be.[12] The fact that its naval forces were frequently put under the control of the generals during World War II was frequently portrayed at the time by Western analysts and historians as a grave source of weakness, and it quite often was.[13] But it could also be helpful. Successful army operations could capture coastlines and ports for the navy to use. Air and missile forces could be projected deep into the ocean, thereby providing much power at sea. That this focus on combined operations was in fact a strategic advantage may be inferred from the fact that "jointness" has since become the mantra for military forces around the world.

The third, and perhaps the biggest, maritime advantage that the Soviet Union enjoyed was a corollary of a factor mentioned above, namely, the fact that its principal adversary was maritime. Although navalists like Mahan claimed that sea power was a source of strength, it could also sometimes be a source of weakness. During the Cold War era, for example, NATO's maritime dependence on secure sea lines of communication (SLOCs) across the Atlantic and its vulnerability to attack from possibly quite small numbers of modern submarines provided a permanent leitmotif of strategic anxiety among analysts and practitioners alike. As Gorshkov noticed, a glance at the disproportion between the Allies' efforts to defend their shipping in World War II and the Germans' efforts to attack it seemed to prove a point foreseen by the British geographer Halford Mackinder, among others: Western maritime vulnerabilities and, even more, sensitivities, could be regarded as a source of Soviet sea power.

The immense size of the Red Army dominated the strategic calculus. In the early days of the Cold War it was thought to be capable of sweeping quickly through much of Western Europe. US strategic plans, like Makefast and Offtackle, were designed to redress the balance by recourse to atomic weapons and a long countercampaign of sea-based conventional attacks, especially from the south.[14] Soviet land power continued to dominate Western strategic thinking about the employment of naval forces, even when the threat was not seen in quite such apocalyptic terms. In the Jimmy Carter era, for example, it forced a significant downgrading of the US Navy's perceived strategic importance, except as a means of conveying reinforcements and supplies across the Atlantic. If transatlantic resupply could not be assured, NATO could only revert to the use of nuclear weapons, and thus risk destroying Western Europe in order to liberate it. Hence NATO's defensive fixation on the safety of its SLOCs.[15]

For all the notional advantages of the Soviet approach, the Soviet Navy increasingly reverted to classical Mahanian thinking as the Cold War went on. In this, the navy of Admiral Gorshkov in fact followed the pattern set by his prewar predecessors.[16] After the heady days of the Soviet New School, starting in 1936, the Soviet Navy slowly reverted to orthodoxy, under the tutelage, especially, of Vladimir Belli, who argued that a more ambitious interpretation of homeland defense justified a larger navy. Stalin was by then sympathetic to this approach, the ruler's caprice once more working to at least the short-term benefit of the navy. Thus naval commissar P. I. Smirnov noted in 1938: "We need a still more powerful navy, a more modern sea and ocean navy. So decided the party. So decided the government. The whole Soviet people so decided."[17]

Opponents were accordingly purged, and the right-thinking Nikolay Kuznetsov took over as commander in chief. Shortly afterward, the Soviet army moved into Finland, the Baltic Sea republics, and Poland, hugely improving Russia's maritime geography. It seemed that the Soviet Union was once more on the road to becoming a great sea power in the orthodox mold. But these plans were put on hold—interrupted by the urgent necessities of the Great Patriotic War, as World War II was known—then revived by Stalin in the postwar period; were then put on hold again, owing to the skepticism about sea power that marked the period of the "atomic shock"; and were then slowly revived once more. Even at the worst time, however, the navy nonetheless flourished. In 1957 the Soviet navy, displacing 1.8 millions tons, was more than three times bigger than it had been in 1917, and twenty times its 1923 size.[18]

The contemporary salience of traditional thought was also warily rehabilitated. "Our navy is 300 years old this year," one officer wrote. "The history of its formation and development and also its contribution to Russia's transformation into a world power, offer a key to understanding important principles that must be correctly applied in today's conditions rather than rejected as outdated. The future usually takes revenge for such arrogance."[19] When he was once charged by an American admiral with sounding very Mahanian, Gorshkov apparently replied "And why not? The man was eminently sensible."[20]

The Soviet Navy's exercises grew steadily more ambitious. Its total ship-days-out-of-area mounted. The size and quality of the fleet expanded. Battle cruisers were built, fleet carriers were planned, and amphibious forces expanded. Even Gorshkov's ambition of creating a properly "balanced fleet," peaking at about 2.5 million tons by the early 1980s, was achieved. It was the Soviet Navy's golden age, and the maritime West grew steadily more alarmed. Nor was this maritime expansion confined to the navy; there were also huge and beneficial expansions of the merchant, fishing, and oceanographic fleets. Unsurprisingly, this extraordinary phenomenon raised the issue of what all this naval expansion was for, and what the West's reaction to it should be.

The Soviet Navy's top priority at this final stage of the Cold War was the custodianship of an increasing share of Russia's nuclear deterrent. This mission attracted huge resources and resulted in a level of technological achievement comparable, and in some ways superior, to that of the West. The main task of the surface fleet was the defense of the submarines performing this duty. The Soviet Navy planned to harass Western nuclear-missile-firing submarines, and pushed its defensive perimeter down to the Greenland–Iceland–United Kingdom (GIUK) gap and out into the northwestern Pacific, a much broader concept of sea control than the Russian Navy had had since the eighteenth century. The Soviet Navy's presence in more distant seas—such as the Mediterranean, the Indian Ocean, and, most provocatively of all, the Caribbean—for the first time made it a global actor. Russia, it seemed, had finally arrived as a global sea power.

However, for the navy's critics, these were not rubles well spent, if only because, as could be predicted, the maritime West reacted strongly. And the Soviet Navy's expansion provoked a particularly furious response from the United States. And so in the 1980s the Reagan administration countered the Soviet challenge with a program to produce a navy of six hundred ships, and a much more assertive approach, which became known as the maritime strategy.[21]

Thus the Soviet Union can be seen as always responding—usually from a position of weakness—to the orthodox strategic maritime challenges posed by the United States and its navy. The US Navy of the 1980s could play on such weakness quite deliberately—for example, in the battleship *Iowa*'s voyage into the Baltic Sea, the Crimean freedom-of-navigation exercises in the mid-1980s, and the American attack on Libya. These were part of a whole series of interactions that ranged from spying to competitive exercises to real confrontations, such as those that took place during the Cuban Missile Crisis of 1962.[22] The extent to which the Soviet Union was concerned about the strategic advantages conferred by Western maritime supremacy may be deduced from the vigor with which the Soviet Navy pursued the notion of naval arms control in the 1980s, and by the determination with which the US Navy "just said no."

Transformational Technology

Soviet naval leaders hoped, indeed expected, that the Western advantage in accumulated naval power would be negated by technological advances, in two ways. First, and particularly during the Khrushchev era from 1956 to 1964, nuclear weaponry would render much of the West's naval arsenal obsolete at the level of grand strategy.[23] A Soviet Navy able to operate a sea-based nuclear deterrent force would strategically "equalize" the two fleets. Tactically and operationally, what would later be called asymmetric technologies in the shape of anti-ship missiles and fast torpedoes, possibly armed with nuclear warheads, would prove a means for keeping Western striking fleets well away from the Soviet coast. The air was thick with epithets to the effect that in this new missile era, large surface ships—and especially American ones, though the point was also relevant to the Soviet fleet—were expensive "metal-eaters" and "floating coffins."

These concerns mirrored Western conclusions in ways that worried naval-ists. In 1953 the Eisenhower administration challenged traditional thinking with the introduction of the concept of massive retaliation, and the British government followed suit in 1957. By this time the prospective scale and dev-astation of an initial nuclear exchange had been clearly demonstrated by such exercises as Fallex/Strikeback 1957, in which hundreds of air-delivered atomic strikes had been simulated against Orange forces attacking Blue forces in Nor-way and Denmark; at the same time, NATO's Striking Fleet and land-based air forces were likewise subjected to severe atomic attack by Orange forces.[24] This represented a considerable challenge to Mahanian ways of thinking.

The scenarios of Western naval exercises reflected a growing preoccupa-tion with how this nuclear technology would require the opposing navies to take on new missions involving the use of nuclear weapons both offensively and defensively. The capacity to maintain a deterrent force of submarines at sea, and to negate as much as possible the adversary's equivalent forces in "the deep Cold War," became a major preoccupation for both sides. For both protagonists, nuclear deterrence became the core strategic mission, but the putative tactical and operational use of nuclear weapons alongside conventional operations was also important. In the 1957 power projection exercises in Europe's northern waters, hundreds of atomic strikes were made on targets in Norway and the Kola Peninsula. One of the clearest lessons to emerge was the need to deconflict the large-scale atomic strike plans of the carrier force and "external air forces."[25]

For Russia, however, the point was that all this new technology proved not to be to its benefit after all—certainly, not to the extent of simply being a force equalizer. And even worse, there was the growing view, in both the West and the East, that early recourse to nuclear weapons was not to anyone's benefit. In consequence, there was a reversion to a more conventional approach to the conduct of large-scale interstate war between the two.

The Western navies had all along remained unconvinced of the extent to which nuclear weapons had transformed the nature of war in practical terms. For the British, at least, the prevailing notion in the late 1940s and early 1950s was of "broken-backed warfare," in which an initial nuclear exchange did not in fact decide the outcome but was instead followed by a long period of conventional military operations. These operations would be aimed at supporting NATO forces ashore, especially on the flanks, and providing the conditions for US and Canadian reinforcements from across the Atlantic.[26] This conception was tried out in Exercise Mainbrace in September 1952. This large-scale and very successful exercise established the structure of Supreme Allied Command Atlantic (SACLANT), under Admiral Lynder McCormick, and operationalized the whole concept of the Striking Fleet. It assumed that Germany had already fallen and that Orange forces were now seeking to conquer Norway and Denmark. This was no artificial contrivance designed simply to preserve traditional forms of naval power. The Western allies really believed it, and based their maritime preparations on the expectation that many of the ancient verities of maritime strategy would still hold true.[27]

Starting in the late 1950s, moreover, under the impetus of Britain's controversial director of naval intelligence, Rear Admiral Anthony Buzzard, the Royal Navy moved away from the crude and common expectations of massive retaliation, by arguing for a concept of graduated deterrence, which emphasized the naval role before rather than after a nuclear exchange, and which put a much greater emphasis on the deterrence of major attack. Crisis management was an increasingly important aspect of exercises through the

1960s. The first Teamwork exercise in 1964 involved 160 ships from seven nations, centered on the deterrent effect of a large-scale maritime reinforcement of Norway. Reservations about the practicality of massive retaliation grew throughout the 1960s, until flexible response was formally adopted by NATO in 1967. This had major implications for all the major navies involved in the Cold War.

By the mid-1960s there was more stress on conventional maritime power projection. Operation Straight-Laced in 1966, for example, was a follow-up to the Rip Tide series and involved a high-speed run-in by a carrier striking force to a launch area, from which conventional air strikes were launched on D-Day to D+3, with an escalation to nuclear strikes on D+4 if necessary. The carrier force comprised the USS *Newport News* and HMS *Ark Royal*. There was particular interest in gauging the force's capacity to handle a submarine attack by Orange forces—in this case, represented by British, Dutch, Norwegian, French, and American submarines.

The Russians, by and large, followed suit. Their thinking on the impact of nuclear technology gradually converged with the developing thoughts of the West. Khrushchev's departure from office was followed by a long and confusing period that culminated in Communist Party general secretary Leonid Brezhnev's historic speech at Tula in 1970, in which he declared that nuclear warfare of any sort would be an irrational act.[28] Nuclear war had "negated itself." During this period, in the view of the Soviet General Staff, both the relative likelihood and anticipated length of the conventional nonnuclear phase of a systemic war with the West gradually increased. At the same time, the prospect of a nonsystemic conflict in defense of Soviet interests outside Europe was also taken more seriously.

In effect, then, the technological challenge to Mahanian orthodoxies seemed to fall by the wayside, taking hoped-for Soviet advantages with it. As Mahan himself had argued, technology may change the tactical and operational details, but it does not alter the broad principles or the importance of maritime strategy.[29]

The Force of History

Good Marxists might hope, finally, for the determinant effects of history. Soviet leaders should be able to take comfort from the fact that history was on their side, and that, as a result, the Soviet Union would in the long run prevail. They could also be encouraged by the observations of the geopolitics school of analysis. In 1904, for instance, Halford Mackinder had warned that "the great industrial strength of Siberia and European Russia and a conquest of some of the marginal regions would give the basis for a fleet necessary to found the world empire."[30] In many ways, this proved true.

The long-delayed maturation of Soviet industrial capacity gradually put significant resources at the disposal of the navy, despite its relatively low status in the strategic pecking order. For example, the Soviet Ministry of Shipbuilding Industry constructed about fifty significant shipyards during the Cold War, thirty of them very large indeed. Despite the frigid climate, the construction yard at Severodvinsk on the White Sea (a southern inlet of the Barents Sea located on Russia's northwestern coast) produced more submarines than the rest of the world put together. The Soviet Union also took control of about seventy percent of the shipbuilding capacity of Eastern Europe and Finland. Nor was this merely a question of quantity. In those fields where the Soviet leadership chose to concentrate resources, achievements were impressive. For example, by the 1970s the Soviet Union was producing about seven thousand naval architects a year. And the graduates of its prestigious Institute of Welding were contributing expertise in critical aspects of construction—such as welding titanium hulls for submarines—that were highly advantageous, and perhaps ten years ahead of comparable American techniques.[31]

Furthermore, the resources available for naval purposes were as much a matter of political will as of technological capability. In the past, Russia's intrinsic industrial and economic limitations had often proved less constraining than outside observers had expected. Some analysts have found no particular chronological correlation between Russian naval expansion and the state's broader economic or industrial success—the first has often not been dependent on the second. They have thus concluded that the Russians have always been able to overcome any industrial-technological deficiency with a mixture of technical and tactical ingenuity, plus sheer determination.[32] The Russians could hope to prevail, in other words, simply because they were Russians, and so favored by history.

According to the Soviet ideological narrative, the general trend of world development, particularly in the shape of global decolonization and the growth of socialism and nationalism in the developing world, seemed likely to doom Western hegemony.[33] From Khrushchev's time onward the Soviet Navy was seen as a way of transforming the potentially deadly East/West confrontation over Europe into a politico-military competition for the support of the developing world. Only the navy could provide Russia with the geographic reach it needed to achieve its ideological destiny.

In contrast, the West appeared divided and fragmented. Defense spending was unpopular in Western nations, and domestic support for NATO and all its works seemed fragile. This translated into real naval weaknesses—a point frequently if inadvertently demonstrated in naval exercises. For example, the arcane imperatives of NATO's Nordic members put a Scandinavian twist on defense cooperation: no permanent deployment of foreign troops, no nuclear weapons, and pre-positioned equipment at Trondheim (rather than Tromso, where it was really needed). In 1968, during Exercise Silver Tower, there were pained comments that "Norwegian airfields generally only operate during normal working hours [0800–1600]. On two occasions, an awkward situation arose when these fields were used outside these hours and on a Sunday."[34]

The French were the most marked in maintaining the cultural and strategic distinctiveness that they called "*la difference.*" The need to recover national greatness and maintain specifically French interests inside and outside Europe, along with a prevailing skepticism that the United States really would risk New York to save Paris, led France to withdraw from the NATO command structure.

The Europeans were particularly intent on not provoking the Russians, as was made clear from the start. The instructions for Exercise Mariner, for example, said that Soviet units had a perfect right to be within the exercise area. Operations to "shake them off" should be undertaken to minimize their capacity to gain useful intelligence, but these should not be aggressive or provocative: "Normal international courtesies are to be observed. . . . In the event of an attempt by Soviet or Soviet-controlled forces to interfere with units participating, evasive action is to be taken and no offensive action in defence of forces under command is to be taken unless directly attacked."[35]

Rightly or wrongly, there were also those in Europe who felt that the US Navy was less inclined than many of its partners to follow this long-standing requirement to reassure, as well as deter, the Soviet Navy. American rules of engagement were likewise criticized by the Europeans for being overly aggressive.[36] This contributed to caveats about the role of US naval forces in Europe's northern waters: "To guarantee security and stability in the northwestern corner of Europe, and to preserve the state of low tension in the area, it is important to Norway that allied naval forces are present in the Norwegian Sea with reasonable regularity, but without indicating any wish for permanent presence."[37]

The 1970s were difficult times for NATO. There was some concern that neutralist/isolationist opinion was gaining ground in Scandinavia, a concern that was apparently confirmed when Norway rejected membership in the

Common Market in 1972, during the Icelandic Cod War. Moreover, in 1972 the US Navy also had its global distractions—most obviously, the Vietnam War—and NATO was plagued by the difficulties common to all coalitions. Most obviously, the Europeans were not a homogenous group, and their maritime perspectives were diverse. Although they all acknowledged the centrality of their Atlantic connection, they each naturally tended to focus on the specific threat closest to them: Thus the Southern European nations worried about the situation in the Mediterranean. The Greeks and Turks worried about each other. And the northwestern Europeans were mainly concerned about the Baltic, North, and Norwegian seas; about their relative proximity to Soviet land and air forces; and about the continental rather than maritime threat that these seemed to pose, which helped shape their maritime priorities. As a consequence of these variations, NATO's maritime strength could be less than the sum of its parts.

As Soviet submarine and air capacity steadily grew, this became more of a problem. In the 1968 Exercise Silver Tower, for example, "analysis has shown that by the end of the second day of Strike Fleet operations, two carriers and several ships of the URG [underway replenishment group] would have been lost for two Orange submarines sunk." The steady fall in the number of ASW escorts, especially from the Europeans; Britain's decision to radically reduce its carrier force in the future; and the fact that Canada had paid off its last carrier, HMCS *Bonaventure*—all were worrying portents that might undermine the political and operational feasibility of NATO's forward operations north of the GIUK gap. The Brosio Study (named for NATO's then–secretary-general, Manilo Brosio), which was conducted by SACLANT in 1969, came to pessimistic conclusions about the Alliance's capacity to handle the Soviet Navy in northern waters by the mid 1970s.[38] These concerns were also echoed by many leading figures in the US Navy. A major disconnect emerged between the Alliance's focus on the strategy of flexible response and its access to the conventional forces needed to put such a strategy into effect. European reductions were also replicated in the US Navy, with more emphasis on sea control and ASW, operating largely in the gaps, rather than forward in the Norwegian Sea. There was discussion about "pre-inforcement" before hostilities began, rather than reinforcement afterward. The Norwegians became increasingly concerned about their potential isolation, seeing it as a consequence of NATO's apparent inability to keep up with the challenges posed by the growing capacity of the Soviet Navy. The initiative seemed to be lost, not least in the Mediterranean,[39] where in a 1972 exercise Soviet submarines "defeated" an allied group of ships, further illustrating the scale of the problem.[40]

Worse still, Western navies seemed to be facing multiple threats. In addition to the conventional standoff with the Soviet Union at both ends of the Eurasian landmass, other problems also had to be tackled, which often demanded very different types of naval forces. The extent to which Admiral Elmo Zumwalt's US Navy was affected by the unexpected lessons of estuarine/riverine operations in the Vietnam War (Market Time and Sea Dragon, most notably) shows how the sheer diversity of the strategic environment complicated matters and made the maintenance of conventional superiority challenging even for the United States.[41] As late as 1985 the Europeans were responding to the apparent distractions of the US Navy by calling for greater capacities of their own. As the British defense white paper of the time put it, "it must be assumed that only limited US Navy forces would be available in the Eastern Atlantic at the outbreak of hostilities. European Navies, and in particular the Royal Navy, must therefore be ready to play a leading role in initial operations."[42]

European navies would need to maintain a significant presence in the north to act as a deterrent to the Soviet Navy and to provide the time and the conditions for the "heavy mob" to arrive—in the shape of the Strike Fleet led by the US Navy.[43] There was also a greater emphasis on monitoring the movements of the Soviet fleet, and developing the technologies to do so, in order to reduce the prospects of such dire strategic surprises and of losing the all-important "battle for the first salvo."[44]

It was therefore easy for observers to conclude from all this that the Soviet Union was indeed benefiting from being better able to make the most of its political, economic, and military advantages—in contrast to a divided if potentially stronger West that was apparently unable to do likewise. Yet in the end, despite all these worries, history did not prove to be on the Soviet side after all. It was the Soviet Union, not the maritime West, that collapsed into economic disaster, social division, and imperial disintegration. So one must ask: To what extent can this be explained, after all, by a Mahanian narrative?

HOW MAHAN WON THE COLD WAR

At the time of the introduction the US maritime strategy and NATO's Concept of Maritime Operations in the 1980s, there was much talk of the advantages of knowing one's adversary, defining its weaknesses, and then specifically targeting them in a competitive strategy. On this basis, Western sea power could be said to have made four important contributions to the West's winning the Cold War.

Subverting the Soviet System

First, Western maritime strategy both exemplified and contributed to the greater resilience of Western society. It is no coincidence that the West proved better able to sustain the economical, social, and political, as well as military, effort required to prevail over its communist rivals. Navalist writers argue that navies tend to reflect the kind of society that produces them—but by their actions, their requirements, their failures, and their successes they also help to shape those societies. In the West navies have long been associated with the defense of their country's trading interests, and they became especially strong in those countries where the merchant classes were able to wield significant political interest. For this reason, many have argued that sea power and liberal democracy go together and are mutually supportive.[45] Social enterprise and successful trading depend on free information, open and responsive government, and fair taxation. Such attributes of liberal democracy encourage the accumulation of wealth, which in turn provides the resources that produce great navies: a permanently supportive government, financial infrastructure providing the necessary investment, industrial capacity, dockyards, ports, and educated and innovative seafarers.[46] Further, such navalists argue, this sets in motion a virtuous circle in which navies provide their countries with the capacity to "trade with advantage" and thus provide, in due course, still more resources for naval development. In effect, the navies of the West were able to "hold the ring" and to provide the conditions for the natural advantages of the societies they defended to prevail.

The contrast is stark between this vision of an ideal state–navy relationship and the realities confronting the Soviet Union and its Navy, as it had been for the USSR's Tsarist predecessors. Russia had never been a "natural" sea power in which maritime consciousness welled up from the mercantile nature of civil society, as it had in England or the Netherlands. Instead, in the Tsarist era the prominence of the navy at any particular time was the product of an imperial ukase, which usually was issued in response to some immediate military, dynastic, or political need. All too often, the navy was seen as little more than an imperial caprice. Much the same was true over the whole Soviet era, during which the navy waxed and waned according to the prejudices of its rulers to an extent rarely encountered in the West. These systemic limits were particularly evident in the Great Patriotic War.

The Stalinist purges of the 1930s and their operational consequences in the early days of the war were a grisly reminder of the impact that the nature of a regime can have on the conduct of its navy. The depressing effect of the *zampolits* (political officers) throughout the Cold War period produced systemic constraints on military initiative. The tendency for the Soviets to avoid concepts of mission command, to obey orders, and to "go by the book," so often remarked upon by their opponents, helps explain the sometimes-disappointing levels of performance.[47]

For all its virtues and determination, the Soviet Navy revealed the fatal flaws of its origins. In comparison with the outward-looking, commerce-driven economies of the maritime West, the Soviet Union's economy was essentially autarchic. The navy had little Soviet trade to defend, and so was able to derive little institutional benefit from it. Although making heavy demands on the resources of the state, it could make little contribution, ether direct or indirect, to the production of a free and economically successful society.

All this encouraged Western strategists to come to a paradoxically Marxist conclusion: that the more Western navies pushed scientific and industrial investment and innovation, the more socioeconomic pressure they would put on the USSR. But this was no illusion. By the mid-1980s looming economic and social crisis forced Soviet Communist Party general secretary Mikhail Gorbachev to instigate an overdue, and overheated, campaign of *perestroika* (restructuring) that, perhaps inevitably, ran out of control. There is little doubt that this crisis had severe and immediate effects on the efficiency of the Soviet Navy. The more interesting issue, however, is the reverse of this: To what extent did the USSR's attempt to meet the military challenges it faced actually cause the crisis? This is indeed a contentious matter.[48]

Some doubt the confrontation was a major cause, pointing instead to the intrinsic domestic limitations of the Soviet Union that were discussed earlier in the chapter. In an interesting inversion of Soviet thinking, they concluded that those historic limitations meant that the West was bound to win in the end and, echoing George Kennan's famous telegram, all the West needed to do was contain the Soviet Union until it finally collapsed. At the very least, however, the West's major military-technical challenge severely aggravated Gorbachev's problem. In the 1980s President Ronald Reagan forced the Soviet Union into an arms race with important naval characteristics, which it could not afford. Thus Robert Love noted: "By this time, the enormous economic and political pressure imposed on the Soviet Union by John Lehman's 600-ship navy and the US maritime strategy was convincing Moscow's leaders that their nation had lost the Cold War."[49]

What made this maritime challenge so unendurable was that it came as part of a much bigger threat, because a thoroughly aroused West was posing a variety of highly sophisticated and demanding technological challenges.[50] Reflecting on the implications of the West's Strategic Defense Initiative, air- and sea-launched cruise missiles, microprocessors, electronic warfare, particle beam research, and so on, Marshal Nikolai Ogarkov warned grimly that future war would be waged on the basis of "new physical principles" and that the Soviet Union was falling behind technologically. Only by spending even more on conventional defense could it hope to compete, at sea as elsewhere.[51]

Soviet political leaders also took this new maritime-technical threat very seriously indeed, and began to feel even more insecure than they had before. They came to conclusions diametrically opposed to Orgakov's. Starting in 1985, the new leadership under Gorbachev concluded that the Soviet Union simply could not further increase its defense expenditures. Only by immediately making drastic cutbacks in defense and, it was increasingly recognized, by remodeling the structure of the state itself, could the Soviet Union hope to reform its economy and secure its future as a superpower. Thus did Gorbachev feel forced to initiate a policy that led inexorably to the end of the Cold War, the collapse of the Soviet Union, and his own political demise.

Western naval forces could therefore be said to have sparked and legitimized the expansion of the navy within Soviet circles and seduced the Soviet Union into a naval arms race that it could not win. Far from confirming the fears of navalists in the West, the expansion of the Soviet Navy could therefore be seen as strategically counterproductive.

Holding NATO Together

Second, NATO was not in the end divided. There was never any doubt that maritime supremacy was crucial to the West's survival and success, not least in helping to hold the geographically divided West together strategically until its superior industrial potential decided the issue. The Atlantic Ocean could have divided NATO. Instead, it united it. The centrality of "Atlantic" in the Alliance's name was more than merely presentational—it determined its nature. One of the clearest statements of this effect came in the midst of the German defense white paper of 1983, and is worth quoting at length:

NATO is an alliance of maritime orientation, much more so than seen in the Central European perspective. It is an alliance spanning the North Atlantic. Its leading power, the United States, is both an Atlantic and a Pacific power. Owing to the situation of the North American continent between two oceans, the weight and prestige of the United States depend on its determination and ability to bridge oceans and to protect its overseas allies.

This implies an essential geostrategic disadvantage for the West; Western Europe is separated from the strategic reserves of NATO's leading power, the United States, by some 6,000 kilometers of Atlantic Ocean.

But European NATO territory as such also has a strongly maritime orientation. West Europe is a heavily broken peninsula-like appendix to the European land mass, bordering on maritime areas in the North, West and South. In this general topography, numerous individual countries in turn are of peninsular character. In fact, almost all the European NATO countries border on seas, some of them having coastlines of considerable length. A number of these countries are by tradition sea powers operating and recognised as such worldwide.[52]

This Atlantic perspective plainly required the West to protect the Atlantic Ocean "bridge" in both peace and war. Failure to do so would split and doom NATO. Success, conversely, meant that NATO would probably prevail in the end, given its far greater social and economic resources, except in the cataclysmic circumstances of nuclear war.

Maintaining that bridge required both political and military action. Throughout the period, NATO needed a diplomatic coalition-maintenance effort expressly intended to deal with the political divisions and factionalism described above. At sea, this took the form of a series of large-scale cooperative exercises, and the formation of standing multinational naval forces and headquarters.[53] Keeping the coalition together was a two-way street, in which the British, rightly or wrongly, considered themselves particularly important. One abiding aspect of their approach was a very strong sense that the United States needed to be guided by wiser (i.e., by British) heads. It was all summed up back in 1944 by one UK Foreign Office official: "If we go about our business in the right way, we can help to steer this great unwieldy barge, the United States of America, into the right harbour. If we don't, it is likely to continue to wallow in the ocean, an isolated menace to navigation."[54]

Holding NATO together required action across the strategic spectrum, and was a constant struggle, especially in the 1970s. Western navies had an important role to play in both demonstrating and fostering the Alliance's unity and professionalism. This political strategy was advanced through the conduct of innumerable naval exercises, which symbolized Western togetherness, enhanced naval proficiencies, and, hopefully, helped deter the Soviet Union while reassuring allied and neutral opinion. It also reassured domestic opinion in the United States that Europe was neither a lost cause nor a free rider. From the Europeans' point of view, simply being there was a crucial requirement—right from the days of their extraordinarily high level of combatants in early NATO exercises, such as Exercise Mainbrace in 1952 and Exercise Mariner in 1953. These efforts satisfied the Americans' need to not "[march] alone. . . . If our effort is not joined by all who are threatened, we could lose at home the critical public support for which we have labored long and hard."[55]

For NATO, two benefits flowed from this. First, the notional but crucial Atlantic bridge was maintained, to the strategic benefit of both the Americans and their allies. The Europeans preserved the United States' guarantee of their freedom, and the Americans kept the sense that they were not alone and that their allies had something to offer in the common defense. Second, with much operational and material help from the United States, the Europeans remodeled their navies in varying degrees, away from strictly national preoccupations and toward the creation of a contributory, coalition force that made the most sense when its various national components were fitted together.

The result of this effort in coalition maintenance was a significant accretion of Western naval power, because within the limits of their resources most of the navies of Europe did have significant things to offer. The British, for example, were the first to apply "vertical envelopment" through helicopter assault during the Suez Campaign. Despite their owing much to American technical help in the 1950s and 1960s in the provision of nuclear-powered attack submarines, known as SSNs, and of nuclear-powered missile submarines, known as SSBNs, the British demonstrated real capability to design, build, and operate nuclear submarines and weapons. Indeed, in some areas— such as sea-keeping, quiet running, and submarine hull construction—the British claimed to be ahead of their American mentors.[56]

The Dutch produced a small but highly competent navy concentrating on the provision of ASW and mine countermeasures (MCM) for operations in the North Sea, the English Channel, and the Eastern Atlantic. Later, the US Marine Corps was earmarked for operations on the Northern Flank.

In many cases this process of reconfiguration led to a kind of informal region-specific specialization, with countries like Belgium concentrating on MCM in the English Channel, and Norway, Denmark, and West Germany developing effective means of asserting control of the coastal waters and narrow seas of Northern Europe. In their own coastal disciplines, moreover, the Norwegians, Danes, and Germans were first class. They knew the distinctive challenges of their own waters much better than anyone else. This took some of the pressure off the US Navy, which could afford to concentrate on high-intensity operations on the open ocean. And of course it also significantly complicated the Soviet planners' task by multiplying the challenges and requirements facing the Soviet Navy. The French, under General Charles de Gaulle, made confounding the Soviet General Staff's search for certainty a major philosophical plank of their strategic policy of determined independence, even if in a manner more appreciated by their allies in retrospect than at the time.

In this way the Soviet Navy was confronted not just by an accretion of the numbers and skills of its putative adversaries, but also by an extension of the range of situations in which it would need to counter them. And along-side, and as part of, this campaign of demonstrated togetherness, there was the military need to rehearse the defense of the SLOCs along which the all-important forces of North America would travel in a crisis. SLOC defense was always a high priority—even when concerns about nuclear weapons and the sustainability of NATO forces on the Central Front were at their most acute.

From the start in Operation Broiler of 1948 and the first Western Union exercise, Operation Verity, in July 1949, the Europeans recognized the threat posed to Atlantic shipping by the Soviet submarine force, which had been enhanced by its postwar access to German technology. Operation Verity saw 109 British, French, Dutch, and Belgian vessels engaged in a large-scale convoy defense exercise fought from off the Dutch Coast, through the English Channel, and deep into the Bay of Biscay, being subjected to repeated attacks by submarines, mines, land-based bombers, motor patrol boats, and destroyers.[57] The Dutch and French, respectively, commanded its 1950 and 1951 successors.[58]

Exercise Mariner likewise had a substantial component dedicated to the exploration of the defense of SLOCs across the Atlantic and was followed by a series of similar large-scale exercises that rehearsed all aspects of the problem. Exercise Silver Tower was held in 1968, involving American, Canadian, Dutch, Norwegian, Belgian, German, and British forces. The exercise showed that although safe routing and sanitized lane routing should be seriously considered, this task demanded more escorts.

The effective protection of short-haul convoys can only be ensured by preventing enemy forces—in particular, small, fast surface craft equipped with missiles—from getting within weapon range. Therefore, it was considered best for area and distant support operations to take priority over close support operations, particularly because a shortage of escorts in a future war might prevent the use of both distant and close support.

Maritime patrol aircraft had not prevented any submarine from firing its missiles, and if this could not be achieved by conventional convoy-and-escort means, then nuclear weapons might need to be used, assuming release had been agreed on. Overall, "the vulnerability of convoys and task forces to submarine surface-to-surface missile attacks was again clearly demonstrated"—and thus ASW techniques and capacities needed to be radically improved.[59]

In 1975 the Ocean Safari exercise series began. Ten years later, one of these exercises, which involved the Striking Fleet, did move into the Arctic Ocean, taking the battle to the adversary. This exercise thus illustrated an important feature of the NATO response to the Soviet threat to shipping—namely, that an attack on the source of the threat would offer an *indirect* defense of the all-important shipping routes across the Atlantic. In this way, forward allies like Norway and Iceland and notional neutrals like Sweden and Finland might be reassured at the same time the Soviet Union was being dissuaded from risky enterprises. Equivalent efforts in the Mediterranean Sea region, it was hoped, would have the same consequence for Greece and Turkey.

Taking Back the Strategic Initiative

The Ocean Safari exercise series also led logically to a new, more confident strategy explicitly intended to change the rules in the naval competition with the Soviet Union, and to seize the advantages that maritime supremacy could confer. In 1980 NATO produced its Concept of Maritime Operations. In parallel the "Maritime Strategy" white paper was issued in the United States. Both were intended to rescue the notion of substantial operations forward of the GIUK gap. This intention was exemplified by the Teamwork series of exercises, which grew steadily more ambitious in their aspirations to go north and to secure the operational initiative by launching attacks on Soviet forces, both onshore and afloat. This trend culminated in the closing days of the Cold War with Teamwork 88, when carriers for the first time made positive use of the sheltering possibilities of Norway's northern fjords. This possibility had been suggested by the Falklands War of 1982, and by the experience of a number of earlier amphibious operations on the northern flank starting in the late 1970s. The idea seemed to work.[60]

The purpose of the US maritime strategy, as described by George Baer, "was to establish an internal consensus on the offensive value of the forward-deployed, big fleet, triphibious Navy and, with Mahan's admonitions ever present, to engage public as well as professional support."[61] It was an unashamedly offensive plan to seize the initiative by taking on the Soviet fleet in Europe's northern waters and the northwestern Pacific. This action was intended to create favorable conditions for the defense of NATO's SLOCs across the Atlantic; for strikes on the opponent's home territory; and for the support of forward allies like Norway, South Korea, and Japan. The strategic aim was to improve the "correlation of forces" on the central front, by posing an outflanking threat to the north and by threatening the Soviet Union's all-important ballistic missile submarines.[62]

The strategy had [and for that matter still has] its critics in the West. The US Navy was accused of a perversely Mahanian pursuit of a battle that was operationally infeasible and/or strategically destabilizing. Some wondered about the contribution it would make to holding the central front.[63] Whatever the validity of these charges, the Soviet Union showed deep alarm at this strategy, both in its responsive preparations and in its pursuit of naval arms control. This new danger, plus a new assertiveness in US operations, such as its freedom of navigation activities off the Crimean coast,[64] reinforced the general trend of Soviet strategic thinking to fall back onto the defensive.[65] But after all, this was the aim of the exercise.

The resulting contrast between Exercise Strong Express in 1972 and Exercise Teamwork sixteen years later in 1988 showed that real progress had been made, even against potentially much more sophisticated opposition.[66] The navies of northwestern Europe played a full part in the precursor operations in the gaps through which the Striking Fleet would have to pass, and in the local defense of the US carriers when they arrived in Norwegian waters. Getting forces ashore and effectively integrated into the land campaign in the difficult conditions to be found in Northern Norway was now a familiar and well-rehearsed requirement. Of course, problems were still legion—especially in logistics, in command and control, and increasingly in mustering the number of merchant ships and crew that the exercise required—but NATO's togetherness had been demonstrated, and the Soviets had become properly depressed.[67]

Controlling the Outer Oceans

Finally, Western sea power rescued the West from the prospect of being so preoccupied with the defense of Europe that it ignored the fate of the outer world, where, in Khrushchev's opinion, the decisive struggle between socialism and capitalism was really going to be played out—not least because of the developing world's importance as a market and a source of oil and other strategic materials. This prognosis seemed all too believable, in the slow and sometimes very painful process of decolonization and readjustment after the searing experiences of World War II.

The reality, however, turned out to be much less apocalyptic, and Western maritime forces deserve some of the credit for this. The American fleet, while meeting its more obvious Cold War commitments, was able to help secure American interests around the world while becoming in many cases the president's first resort when crises flared.[68] American naval power was able to help secure American interests around the world; and the Europeans, especially the British and the French, did not quite abandon the waters of the outer ocean, even in the dark days of the 1970s.[69]

In Britain, for example, from the start and whatever the politicians might apparently say, there was a clear desire to chip away at the more egregious aspects of the historic decision of January 16, 1968, to terminate the country's role east of Suez and to reconfigure the Royal Navy into an ASW specialist force. Less than four weeks afterward, the Assistant Chief of the Naval Staff (Policy), Rear Admiral Terence Lewin, was publicly talking about the "continuing capability to go to the assistance of our friends anywhere in the world if we are required to do so." He added, "I hope that in the future the navy will have an opportunity to range the oceans and seas of the world. . . . One of the most important parts which we have played in NATO is to persuade the Europeans that there are important countries and important things going on in the world outside Europe."[70]

Lewin instituted a growing series of "global deployments" to ensure that the Royal Navy would continue to "range the oceans of the world." And in fact, the next couple of decades saw a steady increase in naval activity outside European waters.[71] The Dutch, Italians, and Spanish likewise maintained a modest but continuing watching brief over the outer oceans; for their part, the French had never said they would abandon them in the first place, and so maintained a considerable capacity for "external action" throughout the Cold War period.[72] Commitments outside the NATO area, therefore, continued to be a significant determinant of the size and shape of

European fleets, allowing them to play their part in preventing Khrushchev's prophecy from coming to pass.

CONCLUSIONS?

Assessing the role of Western sea power in the winning of the Cold War is immensely complex, and thus such analyses are unlikely to produce clear-cut answers for a while. But at the very least, the defensive and potentially offensive naval capabilities of NATO, which was essentially a maritime alliance, helped prevent the West from *losing* the Cold War's strategic competition with the Soviet Union, a constrained land power that had resolved to go to sea. By that very fact of not losing, NATO was likely to prevail in the end, given its economic and industrial advantages, provided of course that the competition did not end in a nuclear holocaust. The only surprise is the limited extent to which this was understood at the time.

NOTES

1. For an interesting review of resilience and the problems of estimating the power of nations, see Dhruva Jaishankar, "Resilience and the Future Balance of Power," *Survival*, June–July 2014.

2. Sergei Gorshkov, *The Sea Power of the State* (London: Pergamon Press, 1979), 68–69, 70–71.

3. Fred T. Jane, *The Imperial Russian Navy: Past Present and Future* (London: W. Thacker, 1904), 23.

4. Gorshkov, *Sea Power*, 68.

5. William C. Fuller, *Strategy and Power in Russia 1600–1914* (New York: Free Press, 1992), xix.

6. Quoted by Robert Herrick, *Soviet Naval Theory and Policy* (Washington, DC: US Government Printing Office, 1988), 10.

7. For the all-important evolution of thinking in the interwar period, see also Gunnar Aselius, *The Rise and Fall of the Soviet Navy in the Baltic, 1921–1941* (London: Frank Cass, 2005).

8. J. G. Barlow, *Revolt of the Admirals: The Fight for Naval Aviation 1945–1950* (Washington, DC: Naval Historical Center, 1994), 65, 96.

9. P. Gillette and Willard C. Frank Jr., eds., *The Sources of Soviet Naval Conduct* (Lexington, MA: Lexington Books, 1990). For more on this, see Herrick, *Soviet Naval Theory*; and J. N. Westwood, *Russian Naval Construction 1905–45* (London: Macmillan, 1994), esp. 1–34, 218–28.

10. Admiral V. Chernavin, "On Naval Theory," *Morskoi sbornik*, no. 1 (January 1982).

11. Jacob Kipp, "The Second Arm and the Problem of Combined Operations" in *The Sources of Soviet Naval Conduct*, ed. P. Gillette and Willard C. Frank Jr. (Lexington, MA: Lexington Books, 1990), 121. Arguably, it also performed best in this role; see Westwood, *Russian Naval Construction*, 220.

12. Michael MccGwire, *Military Objectives in Soviet Foreign Policy* (Washington, DC: Brookings Institution Press, 1987), 123–24.

13. For examples of failure, see Aselius, *Rise and Fall*, 198–217, 224–32.

14. Barlow, *Revolt*, 72.

15. Julian Lewis, *Changing Direction: British Military Planning for Post-war Strategic Defence, 1942–47* (London: Sherwood Press, 1988), 242–339.

16. Aselius, *Rise and Fall*, esp. chaps. 7,10, 13.

17. Quoted by Donald W. Mitchell, *A History of Russian and Soviet Sea Power* (London: Andre Deutsch, 1974), 374.

18. Bradford Dismukes and James McConnell, eds., *Soviet Naval Diplomacy* (New York: Pergamon Press, 1979), 15–16.

19. Captain First Rank Boris Usvyatov, professor candidate in military sciences, "Navy in Crisis," *Krasnaya Zvezda*, July 18, 1996.

20. Bryan McL. Ranft and Geoffrey Till, *The Sea in Soviet Strategy* (London: Macmillan, 1989), 163–71; John Hattendorf, *The Influence of History on Mahan* (Newport, RI: Naval War College Press, 1991), 4.

21. Admiral James Watkins, "The Maritime Strategy," special supplement to *Proceedings of the US Naval Institute*, January 1986.

22. M. MccGwire, *Perestroika and Soviet National Security* (Washington, DC: Brookings Institution Press, 1991), 46, 120–24; Raymond L. Garthoff, *The Great Transition: American–Soviet Relations and the End of the Cold War* (Washington, DC: Brookings Institution Press, 1994), 211, 231, 269, 343.

23. James J Tritten, *Soviet Naval Forces and Nuclear Warfare* (Boulder, CO: Westview Press, 1986), 215–22.

24. Ibid., 141; "Fallex/Strikeback 1957," exercise report, Naval Historical Branch, Portsmouth (hereafter, NHB). I am very grateful to Captain Chris Page, Kate Tilney, and all their colleagues for their help in preparing this chapter.

25. Eric Grove, *Battle for the Fjords: NATO's Forward Maritime Strategy in Action* (Annapolis, MD: Naval Institute Press, 1991), 10–12; "Exercise Mariner," Exercise Reports, NHB.

26. Richard Moore, *The Royal Navy and Nuclear Weapons* (London: Frank Cass, 2001), 65, 144–45.

27. Grove, *Battle for the Fjords*, 6–9; Sean Maloney, *Securing Command of the Sea* (Annapolis, MD: Naval Institute Press, 1995), 157.

28. J. M. McConnell, *The Soviet Shift toward and away from Nuclear War Waging*, Working Paper (Arlington, VA: Center for Naval Analyses, 1984).

29. A. T. Mahan, *The Influence of Sea Power upon History* (London: Sampson Low, Marston & Co., 1890), 1–23.

30. Halford Mackinder, "The Geographic Pivot of History," *Geographic Journal* 23, no. 4 (1904).

31. Boris S. Butman, *Soviet Ship-Building and Ship Repair: An Overview* (Arlington, VA: Spectrum Associates, 1986). See also *Understanding Soviet Naval Developments*

(Washington, DC: Office of the Chief of Naval Operations of the Department of the Navy, 1985), 79.

32. Paul Olkhovsky, *Russia's Navy from Peter to Stalin: Themes, Trends, and Debates*, Report CRM 92–40 (Washington, DC: Center for Naval Analyses, 1992); Fuller, *Strategy*, 452–64.

33. For early British strategic worries about this, see Lewis, *Changing Direction*, 295–305.

34. "Exercise Silver Tower," Report II-C-2-2, NHB.

35. "Exercise Mariner, General Instructions," p. P Q-2, NHB.

36. For evidence, see Francis J. West et al., *Naval Forces and Western Security* (Washington, DC: Pergamon-Brasseys, 1986), 45–49.

37. J. J. Holst, "Nordic Security Perspectives," address to the Oxford University Strategic Studies Group, March 10, 1987.

38. Joel J. Sokolsky, *Seapower in the Nuclear Age* (London: Routledge, 1991), 177–84.

39. George W. Baer, *The US Navy 1890–1990: One Hundred Years of Sea Power* (Stanford, CA: Stanford University Press, 1994), 400–415.

40. David F. Winkler, *Cold War at Sea* (Annapolis, MD: Naval Institute Press, 2000), 1.

41. S. Howarth, *To Shining Sea: A History of the US Navy 1775–1991* (London: Weidenfeld & Nicolson, 1991), 518.

42. UK Ministry of Defence, *Statement of Defence Estimates, 1985*, Cmd 9430 (London: Her Majesty's Stationery Office, 1985), 53.

43. See the British, German, and Norwegian comments given by Geoffrey Till, *Britain and NATO's Northern Flank* (New York: Macmillan, 1988), 70, 105, 112, 118; and "Statement of the Danish Minister of Foreign Affairs, in Parliament," Danish Ministry of Defence, December 9, 1987.

44. N. Friedman, *Seapower and Space* (London: Chatham Publishing, 2000), 52, 82, 175, 189.

45. Not least, Peter Padfield, *Maritime Supremacy and the Opening of the Western Mind* (Woodstock, NY: Overlook Press, 1999); and Richard Harding *Seapower and Naval Warfare 1650–1830* (London: University College Press, 1999).

46. N. A. M. Rodger, *The Safeguard of the Sea: A Naval History of Britain, Volume I: 660–1649* (London: HarperCollins, 1997), 432–33.

47. For an especially hostile review, see Friedrich Ruge, *The Soviets as Naval Opponents 1941–45* (Annapolis, MD: Naval Institute Press, 1979); and Aselius, *Rise and Fall*, 224–32.

48. See Colin Gray, "Sea Power for Containment: The US Navy in the Cold War," in *Navies and Global Defense: Theories and Strategy*, ed. Keith Neilson and Elizabeth Jane Errington (Westport, CT: Praeger, 1995), 181–207.

49. Robert W. Love Jr., *History of the US Navy 1942–1991* (Hamburg, PA: Stackpole Books, 1992), 715. The alternative proposition is extensively argued by Garthoff, *Great Transition*; and MccGwire, *Perestroika*.

50. Gordon S. Barrass, *The Great Cold War: A Journey through the Hall of Mirrors* (Stanford, CA: Stanford University Press, 2009); Vladimir Kuzin and Sergie Chernyavskii, "Russian Reactions to Reagan's 'Maritime Strategy,'" *Journal of Strategic Studies*, April 2005.

51. Christopher Donnelly, "Planning Parameters for the Soviet General Staff," in *East–West Relations in the 1990s: The Naval Dimension*, ed. J. Pay and G. Till (London: Pinter, 1990), 64.

52. Federal Ministry of Defence, *Defence White Paper of the Federal Republic of Germany* (Bonn: Federal Ministry of Defence, 1983), 40.

53. These were started in 1964, with the appropriately named *Matchmaker* exercises.

54. Memo of 21st March 1944, FO 371/38523, National Archives, London. I am grateful to my colleague Jon Robb-Webb for drawing my attention to this minute.

55. Secretary of Defense Caspar Weinberger at Nuclear Planning Group, Bonn, April 1981; quoted by E. F Gueritz et al., *NATO's Maritime Strategy: Issues and Developments* (Washington, DC: Pergamon-Brassey's, 1987), 1.

56. For evidence of this with regard to the cowling of propellers, the rafting of machinery, and sound-deadening tiles in submarines, see Jim Ring, *We Come Unseen: The Untold Story of Britain's Cold War Submariners* (London: John Murray, 2001), 97; also see Gary E. Weir and Walter J. Boyne, *Rising Tide: The Untold Story of the Russian Submarines That Fought the Cold War* (New York: Perseus Books, 2003), 4; David K. Brown and George Moore, *Rebuilding the Royal Navy* (Annapolis, MD: Naval Institute Press, 1993), 120, 187.

57. "Western Union Naval Exercises," July 1949; in the author's possession.

58. Eric Grove, *Vanguard to Trident: British Naval Policy since World War II* (London: Bodley Head, 1987), 165–66.

59. See exercise reports for Lifeline in 1955, Stand Firm in 1957, and Silver Tower in 1968, NHB.

60. Grove, *Battle for the Fjords*, 24–25.

61. A good introduction to the US maritime strategy is by Norman Friedman, *Seapower as Strategy: Navies and National Interests* (Annapolis, MD: Naval Institute Press, 2001), 219ff. For a variety of competing views, see James Goldrick and John B. Hattendorf, eds., *Mahan Is Not Enough* (Newport, RI: Naval War College Press, 1993), 185–86, 202; and Stephen E. Miller and Stephen Van Evera, *Naval Strategy and National Security* (Princeton, NJ: Princeton University Press, 1988), 16–170. Also see Baer, *US Navy*, 429 ff. The definitive history of the development of the Maritime Strategy is by Peter Swartz, "The Maritime Strategy of the 1980s: Threads, Strands, and Line," manuscript, Center for Naval Analyses.

62. Christopher A. Ford and David A. Rosenberg, "The Naval Intelligence Underpinnings of Reagan's Maritime Strategy," *Journal of Strategic Studies*, April 2005, 392–402.

63. Robert F. Komer, *Maritime Strategy or Coalition Defense?* (Cambridge MA: ABT, 1984).

64. Garthoff, *Great Transition*, 269.

65. Andrei A Kokoshin, *Soviet Strategic Thought 1917–91* (Cambridge, MA: MIT Press, 1998), 184–92.

66. Dr. Luns, *The Times*, September 18, 1972; exercise commentary, *Daily Telegraph*, September 18, 1972. See press briefings for Exercise Strong Express, London, September 16, 1972, NHB.

67. Grove, *Battle for the Fjords*, 119 ff.

68. See Philip D. Zelikow, "Force without War, 1975–1982," *Journal of Strategic Studies*, March 1984.

69. Baer, *US Navy*, 344–46, 361–64, 384–93, 440–42.

70. Rear Admiral T. T. Lewin, "The Royal Navy in the Next Decade," *Journal of the RUSI*, May 1968, 207, 209.

71. See G. Till, "Return to Globalism," in *The Royal Navy East of Suez*, ed. G. K. Kennedy (London: Frank Cass, 2004).

72. Marcel Duval, "French Naval Forces and the Defense of Western Europe," in *NATO's Maritime Flanks: Problems and Prospects*, ed. H. F. Zeiner-Gundersen et al. (Washington, DC: Pergamon-Brassey's, 1987), 31–34.

PART II

Regional Security

CHAPTER 4

Middle Sea

The Mediterranean

GIUSEPPE SCHIVARDI

A SEA BETWEEN LANDS

The Mediterranean Sea region is today a theater of substantial strategic complexity. In the aftermath of the Cold War, the lines separating friends from foes, and strong powers from weak, have become difficult to draw. In other maritime theaters, like Southeast Asia and the Indian Ocean, the presence of players with competing strategic objectives committed to maintain military forces to protect national interests facilitates the identification of a firm strategic framework. But in the Mediterranean, strategic priorities are more fluid. Relationships and links among nations on opposite sides of this basin have lately grown stronger, and coastal countries entertain regular commercial exchanges along a north–south line. Thus, the divide between the two sides of this theater pertains more to differences in political, economic, religious, and social systems, which are, for this reason, at the core of the theater's strategic problems.

The complexities of maritime strategy in the Mediterranean arise less from any straightforward competition of interests than from the need to bridge or ameliorate multiple forms of diversity, in order to meet common challenges and achieve integrated prosperity. Some analysts today regard the Mediterranean as a natural strategic singularity, which brings together North and South, and East and West, in a virtuous circle of mutually supportive purposes. This is an optimistic perspective. The reality is more complex and disjointed, and needs a systematic analysis. As has been noted by the French historian Fernand Braudel, the Mediterranean is "a thousand worlds at once, not one but a thousand landscapes," and for this reason, it forms a geographical context that is easier to think of as a "crossroad where, for thousands of years, everything flowed, enriching its history."[1] The British strategist Julian Corbett similarly captured the essence of the Mediterranean as a fabric made of different realities, one that "for centuries . . . was like the heart of the world; and even the barbarians as they surged forward in their wandering seemed ever to be pressing from the ends of the Earth towards the same shining goal, as though their thirsting lips would find there the fountain of dominion."[2]

This chapter details how different levels of analysis—drawing together geographic, historical, economic, political, and social factors—inform national strategies and diplomatic agendas. Seen from above, the Mediterranean Sea appears to be nothing more than a crack on the Earth's crust, a great lake among mountains compared with the vast oceans that surround it. Yet it has long been seen by the West as the "cradle of civilization"—indeed, of more than one civilization. Understanding the Mediterranean today entails making sense of the words of the Lebanese analyst Joseph Maila, who argued that Mediterranean societies are "the owners of a legacy in which the alphabet was Phoenician, the concept Greek, the science Arabic, the power Ottoman, the idea of coexistence Andalusian, the sensitivity Italian, the freedom French, and the eternity Egyptian."[3]

The richness and complexity of the Mediterranean region are among its greatest strengths and, for naval strategists and political analysts, an important opportunity to seize. An integrated approach to security issues at the regional level is not a matter of if, but of how. Finding the best pathways to bridge differences is the main challenge. For the Romans the Mediterranean was *mare nostrum*, an expression introduced by Caesar in the fifth book of his *Gallic Wars* to describe a maritime area where Roman ships had no enemies. *Mare nostrum* meant a single geopolitical space realized by means of uncontested command of the sea. Today, the same expression has a different connotation, whereby ethnic and cultural differences are not subordinated under a single imperial ruler but rather are bound together by common interests in an integrated economic and security system.

GEOGRAPHIC AND LEGAL DIMENSIONS

Approximately 5 million years ago, the Mediterranean was not a sea but a deep and dry valley dividing what later became the continents of Europe, Africa, and Asia. A major earthquake opened a gap in the western part near Gibraltar, and the waters of the Atlantic filled the basin, creating a "lake between mountains," as today we know it. The Mediterranean is not only a closed sea. It is also compartmented. Taking as a landmark the longitudinal line connecting the Italian Peninsula with the African coast, it can be divided into two separate basins, the western and the eastern Mediterranean. Both, in turn, are composed of several subbasins or, as the geographers say, seas—the Alboran, Tyrrhenian, Ionian, Aegean, Adriatic, and so on, each with its own peculiarities.

This compartmentalization has consequences for the partition of its maritime space. For example, in contrast to the coastal states of other closed or semiclosed seas, the Mediterranean states have not fully taken part in the process of extension of the exclusive economic zones (EEZs), as defined by the UN Convention on the Law of the Sea (UNCLOS). The very nature of the Mediterranean prevents the integral application of regulations originated in oceanic states whose geography is quite different. The difficulty of determining Mediterranean maritime boundaries essentially rests on its geomorphologic characteristics. Attempts to apply new principles of maritime law in such a limited area have already caused several controversies. Approximately 50 percent of Mediterranean waters are deeper than 2,000 meters, and only 20 percent are shallower than 200 meters; yet the continental shelf (shared by Europe, Asia, and Africa) covers all of it, with direct consequences for the application of the definitions adopted by UNCLOS and customary international law. The relative poverty of the Mediterranean seabed and surface, in terms of mineral and fish resources, is another obstacle to the application of the EEZ concept. The vulnerability of a geographically enclosed marine environment, with limited exchange of water via Gibraltar and the Bosporus, emphasizes the interdependence of littoral states and the need for close regional cooperation to safeguard it. The indented nature of the coasts, with frequent bays and gulfs, the underwater morphology, and the limited access to oceanic waters, all act to create a slow biological renewal cycle and accelerate the evaporation of seawater.

In this restricted setting, any agreement, arbitration, or legal regulation concerning maritime boundaries, both between neighboring countries and states on opposite shores, will have inevitable repercussions for interstate relations. Conflicting definitions of coastlines often complicate the achievement of equity and proportionality. The fact that the northern and southern shores of the Mediterranean are less than 400 miles apart has, in general, prevented the definition of demarcation lines up to the 200-mile limit that defines the EEZ. At the ratification of UNCLOS, only Egypt included a statement regarding the EEZ, while vague formulations were made by Tunisia and Morocco. Subsequently, a number of states issued more limited documents regarding functional zones.[4]

In recent years Spain and France have also declared their own EEZs, extending outward from their own, nationally defined ecological and fisheries protection zones.[5] These declarations may signal the future institutionalization of EEZs in the Mediterranean, which could lead to a sea exclusively made up of such zones—through which an enormous amount of international trade would nevertheless need to pass. To date, ad hoc agreements have been the prevalent means of defining Mediterranean marine spaces. It is possible that in the future, due to more advanced technologies for the exploitation of sea depths, the states that have hitherto refused the institution of EEZs could in the end decide to resort to them. This, in turn, would mean a shift toward a more uncooperative regional system.

SEAPOWER IN THE MEDITERRANEAN

Comprehension of the Mediterranean Sea region requires an analysis of its history and the roles played by the powers that have successively built their fortunes around its waters. For almost two thousand years (500 BC–AD 1500), the limited technological evolution of rowed warships assured continuity in the evolution of the ways in which regional states exercised naval power. Byzantines, Arabs, Venetians, and Ottomans faced the same strategic, tactical, and technological questions that the Persians, Athenians, Spartans, Romans, and Carthaginians had to address before them. The era of oar propulsion was characterized by repeated confrontation between maritime and continental powers. In this period, however, the continental powers generally prevailed, as long as they could build up and maintain naval forces, as exemplified by Sparta against Athens and Rome against Carthage. Throughout these centuries, naval assets spent relatively short periods at sea, had limited endurance, and relied on a network of bases that made maritime power ancillary to land power.

Starting in the ninth century BC, Hellenic commercial expansionism eventually led to the establishment of several colonies on the coasts of Anatolia. The position of the Greek Peninsula proved decisive in this process, and thus the profits obtained through the Greeks' burgeoning maritime trade allowed them to expand their geographic horizons in the Mediterranean. Economic development brought improved standards of living and favored demographic increases, which in turn constituted the main motive for a wave of colonial expansion. In the sixth century BC, these growing Greek colonies came into contact with Persian expansionism. The Persian Empire twice invaded Greece, in AD 490 and in AD 479–80, but the fierce resistance put up by the Greeks thwarted these attempts. One of the most famous events in the Greco-Persian Wars was the naval battle of Salamis, in which 300 to 400 Greek triremes (i.e., galleys) defeated between 700 and 1,400 enemy units. Sea power was pivotal to turn the tide in Greece's favor.

After defeating the Persians, Athens promoted the creation of the Delio-Attic League (477 BC) to prevent a possible Persian comeback.[6] Athens came to directly control about 170 cities that encompassed approximately 2 million people, and its political and economic influence extended over a population ten times that number. Economic rivalry was the main cause of the outbreak of the Peloponnesian War, the fateful clash between Athens and Sparta for Greek supremacy that occurred from 431 to 404 BC. Sparta won, thanks to its alliance with Persia. As a consequence, a period of Persian influence over Greece followed, at least until the ascendance of Macedonia and the subsequent campaigns waged by Alexander the Great. Alexander defeated the Persian Empire after neutralizing its naval potential by conquering its bases by land.

The rise of Greek maritime city-states like Athens rested on the wider economic order they had built throughout the region. Merchant ships transported the lifeblood of this system, while Greek triremes defended it from external interruptions. The limited political influence of the individual city-states and the fragmentation of Greece represented a vulnerability that subsequently was systematically exploited by more powerful military land powers.

Roman Naval Power

Imperial Rome transformed the Mediterranean into a stronger, more integrated political and economic system—a system supported by maritime power. The Romans were able to impose a monopoly over the Mediterranean after the conquest of Greece and the rest of the Mediterranean coast. Rome became a naval power starting in the third century BC after defeating Carthage, the main mercantile power of the period.[7] Its victory was due to superior tactical organization, better material and human resources, and a stronger political determination in pursuing victory.

Under imperial rule, Rome continued to be a continental power that sought to prevent attacks against its frontiers. As the Roman Empire stretched to the furthest corners of the Mediterranean region, the Romans needed maritime security. Maritime communications sustained the imperial system, linking seaborne transportation with road networks. It was for this reason that piracy was eradicated in the last years of the Roman Republic, following a massive military campaign by Pompeus. Keeping their enemies far from the sea was essential for the Romans, and the use of the Mediterranean and of rivers like the Rhine and the Danube proved an invaluable means of support in repulsing the Persians and other enemies.

Byzantium at Sea

The Roman Empire in the West fell in the fifth century AD. Its successor regime in the Eastern Mediterranean, Byzantium, was obliged to view the Mediterranean as a defensive frontier rather than as a means of connection. The Byzantines represented the principal bulwark of Christian Europe against invasions coming from the East. Constantinople, founded by Constantine on the site of the Greek colony Byzantium, was a natural link between Asia (Anatolia) and Europe (the Balkans) and a choke point between the Mediterranean and the Black Sea.[8] For its protection, Byzantium maintained considerable naval power. Over a millennium, the Avars, Arabs, and Turks—all continental powers—had to learn how to master the sea if they were to contend with Constantinople. The Byzantines were able to adapt their naval power to the needs of the moment. At the beginning of the sixth century AD, the empire built a force suited for power projection. During the seventh and eighth centuries, the navy was employed in a defensive role; but in the ninth and tenth centuries, it was used again offensively to conquer safe bases for the protection of maritime trade—including Cyprus, Crete, Rhodes, and Sicily. In the eleventh and twelfth centuries, the Byzantine Navy was almost the only defense against Norman incursions from Southern Italy, and the only naval support for the Crusaders.

Venice

In the eleventh century, however, the Byzantine Empire started to face the growing power of one of its vassals, Venice, which in 1082 was granted a "Golden Bull" by the emperor Alexios I Komnenos, according it special trade privileges in the Eastern Mediterranean. Venice was able to create a vast mercantile empire thanks to its privileged strategic position between East and West. It proved resourceful in opening new markets through war and skilled diplomacy. Control of the Adriatic gave it invaluable strategic depth, offering good bases for offensive operations and the possibility to concentrate its forces while exploiting shorter SLOCs and maintaining close ties with its Aegean colonies.

After the disastrous Byzantine defeat by the Turks in 1071, Venice became the principal agent of Constantinople in the West—effectively, its heir. Not unlike Britain in centuries to come, Venice created a series of bases and trade stations comprising island and coastal enclaves progressively taken away from Byzantine control. In 1204 Venetian forces embarking on the Fourth Crusade occupied Constantinople, in order to reassert its trade privileges. For the next two centuries, Venice maintained and expanded its commercial empire and ensured its ascendancy over Genoa, which was the principal threat to its regional supremacy. This success marked the military and commercial apogee for Venice in the fifteenth century. The end of that same century, however, saw the rise of Ottoman naval power, which posed a mortal threat to Venetian economic interests. Starting in the sixteenth century, Venice was also attacked on land by a series of Italian and European coalitions. Despite the odds, Venice managed constantly to concentrate its resources to good effect. The War of Cyprus, of which Lepanto (1571) is the most illustrious episode, and the Cretan War (1644–69) are great examples of the determination, coupled with diplomatic dexterity, which enabled Venice to sustain its naval supremacy and defend its SLOCs. In the seventeenth century, however, the regional order the Venetians had created succumbed to the growing weight of Dutch and English political power and commercial enterprises. The loss of Crete in 1669 symbolically marked the moment when the Republic of Venice surrendered the trident of the Mediterranean and was reduced to the rank of an Adriatic power.

The Atlantic Powers

At the end of the fifteenth century, an extraordinary combination of moral energies and technological advancements in seamanship and armaments propelled an unprecedented European expansion at sea. Portugal was the first nation to build a commercial empire based on trade in high-value goods. Its naval power, however, was seriously undermined by its reliance on foreign-produced artillery imported from Germany and the Low Countries.When this flow of technology waned, Portuguese maritime power was compromised. The empire of Charles V depended heavily on imported artillery, but Spain nevertheless maintained an effective maritime power in the Mediterranean through the seventeenth century. Its center was based in the Tyrrhenian Sea, at the intersection of the interior lines of communication between the Spanish and German territories, while the financial center was Genoa. The empire remained under constant threat from the Ottomans, then in their rising phase, and the Barbary pirates, a serious menace remembered now mainly for having caused the first appearance of the US Navy in the Mediterranean, early in the nineteenth century.[9] By then Spanish and Venetian power in the Mediterranean had been replaced by that of the Dutch and, more decisively, the English, whose preeminence was secured by the defeat of the French at Aboukir (1798) and Trafalgar (1805).

THE GEOPOLITICS OF THE MEDITERRANEAN

The Mediterranean Sea today is surrounded by twenty littoral states.[10] These are inhabited by nearly 465 million people, 40 percent of whom live in the European Union. Another 17 percent live in countries aspiring to become EU members, Turkey most significantly. Mediterranean geopolitics continue to be shaped by a north/south divide extending from Gibraltar to the Turkish straits, an imaginary line based above all on cultural and religious distinction; to the north are countries of Christian heritage, to the south states of Muslim tradition. The Muslim successor states of the former Yugoslavia—including Bosnia, Macedonia, Montenegro, Kosovo, and Albania, which include about 10 million Muslims—are modest exceptions to what is now a very old rule.

Among the states of the Mediterranean littoral, Turkey deserves particular attention, having served for so long as a cultural and strategic link between Christian Europe and the Muslim South and East. Its location was the main reason for its admission into NATO in 1952. With the drawing of the iron curtain, the United States intended to keep the Soviet Black Sea Fleet in check by controlling the Turkish straits. Turkey retains its strategic importance today, a fact that has made the question of Turkish admission into the EU especially delicate. If it were to be admitted, it would constitute the most populous country in the EU, with important consequences for the balance between the member states. Turkey's strategic value, furthermore, rests on its position at the receiving end of several gas and oil pipelines coming from Central Asia and the Middle East. From Turkey originate also the Tigris and the Euphrates rivers, the fundamental sources of water for Syria and Iraq. Equally, Turkey connects the Black Sea with the countries looking onto it, a Mediterranean appendix if not quite part of the Mediterranean itself. If one accepts Samuel Huntington's view of the Mediterranean as a fault line dividing civilizations, it is one that Turkey surely straddles.[11]

Other elements responsible for the Mediterranean's complex strategic geography are the three huge peninsulas, the Iberian, the Italian, and the Balkan. Each gives birth to other spaces characterized by distinctive features. The western basin, dominated by the choke point near Gibraltar, is marked by delicate Spanish–Moroccan bilateral relations, owing to illegal migration from the African continent and the significant commercial relations between the states. Morocco, despite a long history of relative stability, is now threatened by the radical Sunni Jihadism that plagues its African neighbors.

On the European side of the strait, the British enclave of Gibraltar remains a point of contention between England and Spain. To the south lies the port of Tangiers, a potentially critical, though currently undeveloped, hub for economic, political, and commercial interactions between Europe and North Africa. Nearby are the two Spanish enclaves of Ceuta and Melilla, European outposts in North Africa. Politically, the fate of Western Sahara is the crux of Moroccan foreign policy, and generates frictions with neighboring Algeria, which openly supports the nationalist Saharawi movement against Moroccan occupation.[12] The tension between these two states has a distinct maritime aspect, illustrated by Morocco's recent acquisition of two Sigma-class corvettes and a FREMM-class frigate, and by Algeria's purchase of a major amphibious ship and three MEKO-class frigates.[13] This jump in quality could be a prelude to a more muscular maritime confrontation in the future.

France and Italy possess the strongest navies in the western Mediterranean. Both have important commercial ties with the Maghreb: France by virtue of its colonial past, and Italy due to its historic links and geographic proximity. The cooperation between north and south in this area is significant, as is the migratory flow of refugees, which has increased exponentially since the collapse of the Gadhafi regime in Libya in 2011, followed by the ongoing destabilization of all governmental institutions there.[14] In recent years thousands have died trying to reach Europe from Africa.

At the eastern end of the Mediterranean, the politics of the Arab/Israeli dispute represents the most important issue shaping maritime security. This subregional theater has an impact on intra-Mediterranean relations and also draws in global actors. Israel's maritime spaces, including those of the Gaza Strip in the south and off the Lebanon border in the north, are rich in natural gas and petroleum, in addition to their obvious importance from a security perspective.

Following Hamas's electoral victory in the Gaza Strip in 2006, Israel contested the right of the Palestinian Authority to continue the exploitation of Gaza's offshore gasfield, which had begun in 2000 under Yasser Arafat. Although Hamas has declared its sovereign right to exploit the fields, Israel has intensified its patrolling of these waters, and has reinforced the blockade it imposed on Gaza following Hamas's seizure of power there.

It was this blockade that led to the so-called Freedom Flotilla episode in May 2010, when Israel intercepted a Turkish-flagged cargo ship vessel bound for the Gaza Strip with humanitarian aid. Ten of the humanitarian activists were killed, resulting in a serious crisis between Israel and Turkey, two states with historically good relations. An additional source of potential conflict may arise owing to the discovery of enormous natural gas and petroleum fields, called Leviathan, opposite the Israeli/Lebanese border, whose extension into the Mediterranean has not been fixed. Israel's discovery of Leviathan off its coast immediately created a new geopolitical conflict as soon as Lebanon affirmed its territorial rights under its EEZ. Israel effectively controls these waters, beneath which lie sufficient petroleum reserves to afford it energy independence in the future, for the first time in its history.[15]

Also shaping the maritime environment in the Eastern Mediterranean is the persistent conflict between Greece and Turkey, which have long disagreed over the definition of Hellenic territorial waters in the Aegean, and over the delicate question of Cyprus. The island remains divided between the Republic of Cyprus, which controls two-thirds of its territory and is a member of the EU, and the Turkish Republic of Northern Cyprus (TRNC), self-proclaimed in 1974 after Turkish military intervention. Here too, long-standing (and somewhat "normalized") disputes could worsen with added economic interests, owing to the discovery of natural gas off the coasts of Cyprus.

The Balkan–Adriatic subtheater displays a similarly delicate equilibrium, afflicted by interstate disputes over boundaries and wider diplomatic issues connected with the admission to the European Union of Bosnia and Herzegovina, Serbia, Croatia, and Macedonia. Here, too, the control of prospective new energy reserves is the crucial consideration.

By any measure, the geopolitics in the Mediterranean region are complex and are characterized by a variety of interstate tensions. However natural it may be to think of the Mediterranean as a single theater, within which goods and ideas move along many axes, maritime security is dominated by problems of a localized, isolated character. This means that the Mediterranean presents a double geopolitical dimension: the first as an integrated region, the second as a blend of diverse (and more divisive) subregional segments. However insistent the problems of the latter may be, it is the first dimension, which has given rise to wide-ranging diplomatic initiatives seeking the creation of common denominators, that may be more significant in the long run.

ECONOMY BEYOND DIVISIONS

The concept of the Wider Mediterranean Community has become popular among Euro-Mediterranean diplomats, who increasingly wish to see the region as one whose interests and influence extend beyond Gibraltar, the Dardanelles, and Suez—east to the Caucasus and Central Asia, and south toward the Red Sea and the Persian Gulf.[16] The foundation for the concept of the Wider Mediterranean is obviously aspirational, and essentially historical: that global order would be well served if the Mediterranean were to regain the integrative role it played in ancient times. This is surely a worthy goal, however formidable the obstacles in its way.

Historians and ethnographers debate the concept of the existence of a shared Mediterranean identity. It is often easier to think that the littoral states of its major subregions share more with their immediate neighbors than with the countries on the opposite side of the sea. Indeed, it was said in the past that the Mediterranean is characterized more by differences than similarities.

The most important divide, across the region as a whole, is demographic; the European countries on the northern side have very low rates of population growth (Italy's has been close to zero for many years now), whereas the states on the southern shore have a strong positive trend. In general, the North African countries have on average younger populations, even if their mortality rates are higher than the European ones. The higher fertility and rapid urbanization rates of the North African countries may exercise an important influence in the short and medium terms on the volume of South–North migration flows, linking the poor South to the rich North. From an economic point of view, considering the average per capita gross domestic product, there is a significant difference between South and North. In recent decades the most advanced countries have become roughly eight times richer than the least developed ones.[17] Moving on to social indicators, the divide remains huge; unemployment and poverty rates are higher in the states of the Southern Mediterranean, where serious inflation and other forms of financial instability are virtually endemic. Differences are also serious in the fields of welfare, education, health, and environmental policies, in which the countries on the southern shore invest less. The latter element is also an important consideration for foreign direct investors, who tend to turn to the more prosperous Mediterranean countries, where profit opportunities are higher.

The Role of Energy Resources

The chief economic advantage of the southern shore lies in the availability of natural resources, especially petroleum. Southern Mediterranean states generally have deposits of natural gas and oil, which they export to Northern Mediterranean states. By contrast, the northern states have highly industrialized, export-oriented economies, but they lack the energy resources that would be essential for their optimal economic performance—the major exception being France, owing to its reliance on nuclear power.

For the European countries, energy dependency on Russian gas can be politically problematic. As a consequence, these governments have sought alternatives in the North African countries, especially Algeria, which is already supplying the EU through the Trans-Mediterranean Pipeline. Libya is another important natural gas supplier to the EU, thanks to the GreenStream Pipeline, which is linked to Sicily through a submarine route. New projects are under development: a pipeline that should bring Algerian natural gas to Spain; another linking the Algerian coast to Sardinia, with the consequence of increasing the volume of gas imported by Italy; and additional projects that involve Niger and Nigeria, countries building a connection with Europe via an Algerian infrastructure called the Trans-Saharan Gas Line. Finally, there is the Arab Gas Pipeline, which should provide Europe with Egyptian gas. This pipeline, moreover, should also link Egypt with Syria, Jordan, Lebanon, and Turkey, where it would be integrated in the Nabucco Pipeline to supply Eastern Europe through Bulgaria, Romania, Hungary, and Austria.

Turkey, a traditional terminus for North African gas, is destined to become a hub for energy pipelines coming from Central Asia and directed to the EU. The latter is interested in diversifying its energy purchasing as much as possible, in order to avoid a dangerous dependency on Russia. The fact that Turkey can receive natural gas from five different production areas (Russia, the Caspian Sea, Iraq, Iran, and Egypt) represents an important strategic advantage to be used in the negotiations for its admittance into the EU, assuming this remains a priority for Ankara.

It almost goes without saying that, under current conditions, it is easy to imagine strategic scenarios for the Mediterranean in which energy is the decisive issue. There, as elsewhere, particular attention must be paid to the actions of the major European energy companies, which are principally interested in countering any moves by Russia or Iran to create cartels with the North African countries. Viewed in the broadest terms, the Wider Mediterranean appears increasingly to be an extension of the international rivalries for the control of the energy resources of Central Asia and the Caucasus.

Commerce and Trade

Maritime commerce is another key factor that will help determine the future of the Mediterranean region. About a third of global commerce passes through the Mediterranean, including 30 percent of the world's oil and two-thirds of European energy supplies. As the globalization of trade has increased the demand for standardized practices and infrastructure, world shipping has responded by developing a hub-and-spokes system: Enormous container cargo ships unload their cargo in ports with the appropriate infrastructures to receive them, called hubs, from which smaller ships, called feeders, transport them to minor ports using different routes from the ones occupied by the main flow of world trade.

It is especially on the trans-Indian route that the creation of gigantic hubs has proceeded most rapidly in recent years, thanks to the investments made by shipping companies and European financial groups, but also to Chinese and Arab investors. The importance of the Mediterranean has grown accordingly, due to the expansion of manufacturing centers in Asia and the enlargement of the Suez Canal. The consequence has been a whirling infrastructural development of Mediterranean ports, which have struggled (successfully for the most part) to keep up with the volume of trade destined for Europe. Shipping companies, rather than governments, are the main actors, participating directly in the management of ports through amalgamations and deals with sea terminal operators. Alongside European companies, the Chinese are very active in this sector, displaying aggressiveness in the acquisition of growing slices of the market, while Arab investors are more concentrated on

North African outlets. European ports, once the epicenter of Mediterranean traffics, are facing problems in coping with the growing size of container ships, which could consequently instead shift to the Maghrebine ports. Thus, along with Gioia Tauro (Italy), Valencia, Algeciras, and Barcelona, Tangiers is expanding rapidly. According to the project for its development, Tangiers aims to become the most important port in terms of containers handled, although the economic crisis of 2008 slowed the construction of a second terminal, called Tanger Med II. Other hubs with up-to-date facilities and capacity are being developed in Tunisia, at Enfidha in the Gulf of Hammamet; and in Egypt, at Damietta, 70 kilometers from Port Said, the northern terminus of the Suez Canal.

Even in the face of this rapid development, however, the last few years have seen a relative decrease in the growth of container traffic in the Mediterranean compared with the always-competitive ports of Northern Europe. The main cause is the lack of an infrastructural network connecting the ports with the ultimate markets for which the goods are destined (Gioia Tauro in Italy is a clear example of this). Northern European ports are closer and better connected to the final consumers of the goods they handle, so it is often more efficient to spend three more days at sea, in lieu of longer overland drives from Southern Europe. The most desirable solution would be to create the necessary infrastructural network, both on land and at sea, in order to make the Mediterranean more competitive. But the competitiveness of maritime commercial hubs is not necessarily the main concern of Mediterranean littoral states, compared with the problems of security that may accompany the increasing flow of trade. This was highlighted by the attack in November 2014, which was carried out by three small terrorist craft against a small Egyptian patrol boat 40 miles from the port of Damietta. This was a minor incident on its face, but was widely regarded as a potential turning point for the expansion of Islamist terrorism at sea. At a minimum, this event illustrates the vulnerability of SLOCs in the vicinity of Mediterranean ports, where there are the major concentrations of trade close to major concentrations of political unrest.

DIPLOMACY

The political attention paid to the Mediterranean by Europe has increased markedly since the creation of the European Community, and especially since the end of the Cold War. The failed attempts to create regular "Mediterranean dialogues" during the Cold War found new impulse after the collapse of the Soviet Union. The realization of the importance of cooperation to guarantee stability in the Mediterranean was the basic driver behind the Declaration of Barcelona in 1995. This declaration created the Euro-Mediterranean Partnership, which includes the EU countries and twelve states on the Mediterranean's southern shore (the only exception being Libya). The activities of the partnership have been oriented around three pillars: ensuring security and stability in the region; promoting economic and commercial cooperation, which led to the creation of a free trade zone in 2010; and encouraging intercultural and social dialogue.

Fifteen years after its creation, it is still premature to judge the partnership an outright failure, though it is evident that the process has reached a stalemate. During the French presidential campaign of 2007, candidate and later president Nicolas Sarkozy attempted to reinvigorate the cooperative project by proposing the idea of a Mediterranean Union, which should include the coastal countries of Europe, the Southern Mediterranean, and the Middle East. The intent was to overcome the inertia that increasingly threatened to overcome efforts to promote regional cooperation by raising France to a position of leadership. Despite initial enthusiasm, however, this new initiative inherited all the obstacles and the errors of the past. The apprehension of the Northern European countries (especially Germany) about being left out of the agreement caused the idea behind the project to be watered down and given a new name: Union for the Mediterranean. And the recurring violence between Israel and the Hamas authorities in Gaza in 2008–9 and 2014 caused the union's Arab members to veto most development programs in their infancy. To date, the dialogue has produced few tangible results.

Why, even today, is it so difficult to advance dialogue and cooperation between the Mediterranean countries? The main obstacle is surely represented by the conflicts and the tensions that afflict the entire basin; with the exception of the European bloc of Spain, France, and Italy, the Mediterranean coastline is marked by crises and tensions of various magnitudes. This leads us to a critical consideration about the policies adopted by the EU: In recent years, because it has perhaps been too occupied by its eastern enlargement or, more simply, has still not been able to cope unanimously with questions of inter-national relevance, it has not managed to impose its diplomatic weight in order to sustain its Mediterranean ambitions and an active role in the Israeli–Palestinian question. To promote Mediterranean cooperation, it is necessary to assume an active role in the dynamics of the basin, and to be a recognized actor in order to acquire respect and credibility.

A further problem is represented by the positions assumed in this context by the countries on the southern shore of the Mediterranean. The entrenched economic and political elites of the Maghrebine countries tend naturally to defend themselves against sudden economic, social, and cultural changes, which could prove fatal for their very existence. In particular, what seems to be lacking among the countries of Saharan Africa is a common will, as demonstrated by the failure of integration policies strongly sponsored by the EU. Throughout the Barcelona Process, the Maghrebine countries have displayed a limited cooperative attitude, one dominated by strong concerns for their national interests, which have often entailed efforts to carve out preferential roles for themselves, in agreements with the EU, inevitably at the expense of their immediate neighbors.

This North–South dialogue remains extremely complicated because it is characterized by a combination of fragmented and contrasting interests, which have prevented the emergence of an effective southern counterpart to the EU. The Arab Spring further complicated an already-difficult situation, which turned the North African geopolitical panorama upside down, starting from Tunisia and extending to Egypt—with inevitable reverberations in the region's other states, such as Libya, Algeria, Syria, and Yemen.

Each revolt was particular to each state and its peoples, involving in many cases the replacement of the heads of government (as in Tunisia, Libya, Egypt, and Yemen). All these countries continue to experience difficulty in reconstructing their sociopolitical fabric, which has been lacerated by internal strife. Three of them, Libya, Syria, and Yemen, have broken down into civil war. Even if these conditions were to improve, the general perception of insecurity and instability is likely to inhibit any concrete cooperation between the various Mediterranean states, notwithstanding the good intentions of many of them.

THE MEDITERRANEAN DIALOGUE AND THE 5+5 DEFENSE INITIATIVE

Against this background, it is perhaps unsurprising that it has been in the realm of security that regional cooperation has been most determined and effective. In this realm, the broader regional outlook is one of stability. Leaving aside the subregional quarrels discussed above, the main concerns in this area focus on threats to the freedom of maritime trade, drug trafficking and other forms of smuggling (including weapons), and clandestine migration. The last is perhaps most important because it undermines confidence building between Europe and the countries on the southern shore. It is also a security issue, however, because its destabilizing effects could fit into the plans of Islamist radical groups. The problem therefore requires a common effort, as claimed by Italy and Spain, the two countries that are being directly affected by clandestine migration, which are pushing for a more decisive European approach and more equal burden sharing. A subsequent step would involve a wider Mediterranean approach, whereby all the countries looking onto the Mediterranean would be involved in a common effort, rather than signing bilateral agreements of limited effect.

Two examples of security initiatives informed by determined multilateralism are NATO's Mediterranean Dialogue and the 5+5 Defense Initiative. The Mediterranean Dialogue—which includes Algeria, Morocco, Tunisia, Mauritania, Egypt, Jordan, and Israel—was created in 1994 with the aim of promoting security and stability in the region and fostering understanding of NATO's objectives and policies following the collapse of the Soviet Union. The initiative was at first viewed with skepticism by the Arab countries, but it has nonetheless evolved toward genuine active collaboration, sanctioned by the Istanbul Cooperative Initiative (2004), and involving participation in Partnership for Peace exercises, cooperation on maritime surveillance, and measures against the proliferation of weapons of mass destruction.

The key factor in the success of the initiative is the possibility it gives to each participant to choose the degree of cooperation and the level of military capabilities it intends to provide to common missions. For example, in the operation Active Endeavor, Moroccan and Algerian units have been deployed in order to contribute to NATO's wider effort in the fields of maritime surveillance and security.

NATO's Mediterranean Dialogue has been designed to showcase new forms of regional cooperation between the European Union and the United States. The importance of doing so has been reaffirmed in NATO's current Strategic Concept, which was adopted at the Lisbon Summit in November 2010. The rise of the so-called Islamic State on the shores of the eastern Mediterranean has made synergy between the Mediterranean countries and NATO more necessary than ever. The NATO secretary-general, Jens Stoltenberg, at the North Atlantic Council–Mediterranean Dialogue Seminar celebrating the dialogue's twentieth anniversary, has pointed out that any bilateral contacts between NATO and each dialogue partner individually will remain important, as will all the multilateral consultations, in order to deepen mutual understanding of the region's key security challenges. The goal is to have a better conceptual basis for any practical work that NATO and the dialogue partners might undertake together.[18]

Of even greater significance is the 5+5 Defense Initiative. This project, launched in 1990, was proposed by the Italian and Spanish foreign ministers and gained the participation of Portugal, Spain, France, Italy, and Malta on one side and Mauretania, Morocco, Algeria, Tunisia, and Libya on the other side, thus assuming a Western Mediterranean character.[19] In 2004 Italy proposed expanding the project in three areas of collaboration: maritime surveillance, aerospace security, and environmental management. There have been exercises intended to increase interoperability and mutual understanding, plans for common vocational colleges, and the development of specific areas of cooperation. One of the core actions at the heart of the 5+5's success is the project to develop the Virtual-Regional Maritime Traffic Centre (V-RMTC), a joint maritime surveillance capability in whose development and promotion the Italian Navy has played a leading role. The 5+5 initiative may fairly be said to set the standard for similar projects, because it displays the key principles for a successful Mediterranean dialogue: mutual respect and trust, realism, and perseverance. It must also be admitted, however, that the initiative's limited membership has facilitated success; the participating countries have more freedom and can choose the level of collaboration, decisions are more easily reached, and possible tensions arising from the Israeli/Palestinian conflict have been avoided.

SEA CONTROL AND SURVEILLANCE

The Mediterranean can be described as a "regional maritime security complex" because it fits perfectly into Buzan and Weaver's definition of a security complex as "a group of states whose primary security concerns link together sufficiently closely that their national securities cannot realistically be considered apart from one another."[20] As such, controlling the Mediterranean means emphasizing the integrated surveillance of maritime spaces, which consists of patrolling and monitoring the waters of interest in cooperation with all the forces operating at sea. Navies and coast guards collaborate by committing their units to common security policies like the European Patrol Network, the European Agency for the Control of External Frontiers (known as FRONTEX), and NATO's program of maritime surveillance and fighting against international terrorism. The Mediterranean security complex is characterized by the integration of all the actors responsible for maritime security into a common network of regional maritime surveillance based on a comprehensive approach, which allows an operational effectiveness not possible through traditional means.

An Export Model

A national example of a surveillance system responding to the requirements of operational need and efficiency is the above-mentioned V-RMTC, created by the Italian Navy. In October 2002, during the Fourth Regional Seapower Symposium of the Mediterranean and Black Sea Navies, the regional navies agreed on the need to reinforce the security of Mediterranean maritime trade.[21] Building on this momentum, the Italian Navy sponsored a project that gave adhering navies the possibility to choose their level of participation in a common network of information on maritime traffic within the region, to be shared by all members. In 2003 the navies that had been approached responded favorably, and in October 2004 the Italian Navy presented the pilot V-RMTC to general approval. The operational phase started in October 2006 with a system based on a virtual network linking the operational headquarters of the navies involved, on which nonclassified information on maritime traffic is shared through software developed by the Italian Navy. It also has the responsibility for storing the data in a hub at its Fleet Command. The system, using internet and commercial platforms, is cheap, easy to run, and highly accurate, because the information has a certified provenance from the participating navies, which at the moment is a peculiarity of the V-RMTC.[22] The flexibility of the system has permitted the creation of networks based on the V-RMTC in different configurations adaptable to security initiatives like the 5+5 or the 8+6 (the latter involving the countries of the Persian Gulf).

Since its presentation, the V-RMTC has also met with a favorable response outside the Mediterranean. In 2006, during the conference for the development of the Wider Mediterranean Community, countries like India, Singapore, Ireland, and Mexico started to explore the possibility of reproducing the V-RMTC model in their geographic areas. This interest has led Italy to contemplate the expansion of the project to a transregional dimension, even beyond the Wider Mediterranean; of great importance in this regard are experiments with Brazil and Singapore, which began in 2008. Thanks to the flexibility of the model, and without additional costs, it has been possible, with the assent of the other countries, to exchange data between the V-RMTC and the Brazilian system, which is called SISTRAM. The platform thus provides a clear picture of maritime traffic in and between the two regions. A similar experiment will soon connect Singapore's OASIS with the V-RMTC and the Gulf states.

This experience prompted the Italian Navy to sponsor the creation of a database management system for the control of national maritime traffic. The resulting System for Inter-Agency Integrated Maritime Surveillance is part of an interagency network through which data are exchanged between the national agencies involved in homeland defense and security. The investment made is significant. Italy, at the heart of the Mediterranean, is deeply committed to its security, and it is possible that other countries will soon decide to integrate their systems with the one under development in Italy.

Any effective surveillance system requires the capability to acquire information from both national and foreign contexts, and to properly integrate this information in a way that creates a complete and coherent picture to distribute in time. Maritime security is being built through surveillance and awareness, a complex and costly process. In the Mediterranean its realization is at present unequally balanced; the producers and suppliers of information (Italy, France, and Spain) are few, but its users are many. Time will show whether the architecture of integrated systems for Mediterranean maritime surveillance is really effective, or if the overlap of competences and agencies is an obstacle to operational efficiency. Doubtless, however, these experiences are highly valuable for confidence building, an element of considerable value in itself.

THE UNITED STATES AND NATO

The US Navy first operated in the Mediterranean in 1801, when it defended American commerce against pirates based along the Barbary Coast (modern-day Tunisia, Algeria, and Libya). Since World War II, the US Navy's role has been that of a superpower, with forward bases and troops in Italy, Greece, and Turkey. For decades the Sixth Fleet represented US defense interests in the Mediterranean, and contributed decisively to shaping the identities and doctrines of the navies of its regional allies. Even at the height of the Vietnam War, the Mediterranean remained sufficiently important for the US Navy that it did not reduce its presence there, notwithstanding the pressing needs in Southeast Asia.

The end of the Cold War eroded the foundation of US policies in the Mediterranean but did not mean its abandonment; although US strategic interests are no longer as focused on Europe and the Mediterranean as they once were, the basin remains important by virtue of its proximity to key conflict areas. Its role is twofold: It serves as a valuable logistical platform for the wider Middle East, and as a monitoring station for potential terrorist threats in the region. US interests in the Mediterranean no longer require a massive naval presence, but they can be effectively pursued through NATO activities intended to ensure regional stability and cooperation with the countries on the southern shore.

The Mediterranean is closely linked to the Persian Gulf. More than just an important energy corridor, it also allows privileged access to areas of potential conflict. Notwithstanding the recent differences between the United States and Israel over Iran, Israel remains a fundamental ally in the region, and the Arab/Israeli dispute is going to remain an important item on the agenda of any US president for the foreseeable future. In comparison with the Cold War, the United States and the other Western countries seem more interested in implementing effective forms of maritime surveillance, especially for counterterrorism purposes, than traditional forms of sea control. In the Mediterranean the United States can reasonably assume European capability to play a key role in the area, by reason of proximity. As a consequence, it is possible to delegate the security of the region to the EU, at least up to a point. In this respect, the reintegration of France into the military structure of NATO, and the reconciliation between Paris and Washington after the frictions created by the US invasion of Iraq in 2003, are of great importance, anticipating future cooperation on Mediterranean maritime security.

THE MEDITERRANEAN NAVIES

This section addresses the roles played by the different navies to verify the extent to which maritime policies and global strategic ambitions are matched by actions on the water. It must be noted that the division between North and South, already discussed in more general political and economic terms, also retains its significance from a naval point of view. It reflects a difference in operating concepts, numerical strength, investments, and doctrines between the navies on the northern shore of the Mediterranean, which belong to the European bloc, and the navies of North Africa and the Middle East.

From a naval perspective, France, Italy, and Spain are the most important countries, followed by Turkey and Greece. The North African and Middle Eastern navies are sufficiently advanced technologically; but numerically, they are of little significance, and thus almost exclusively perform only coastal tasks, without any power projection capability.[23] Their mission is to protect their respective territorial waters, for which purpose they have no need for the range and sustainability required to conduct operations far from their home ports. In contrast, the navies of the larger European littoral states are characterized by expeditionary and power projection capabilities. Spain and Italy are best suited to operate in the context of multinational coalitions. France is able to conduct significant operations independently, and also possesses ballistic missile submarines.

The Adriatic and the Aegean

Surveillance and the safeguarding of national interests within territorial waters are the only tasks assigned to the Adriatic navies. Slovenia, Croatia, and Albania, as members of NATO, also wish to maintain the capacity to operate in cooperation with their larger alliance partners. In this regard, Italy's presence and support in the area are important. The Greek and Turkish navies, largely as a result of the confrontation between the two countries over Cyprus and in the Aegean, have developed their forces with reference to each other. The deep-sea component of the Greek Navy is efficient and its ships are relatively new, but on the whole its power projection capabilities are limited. Procurement problems arising from its ongoing financial crisis are liable to weigh heavily for some time. The prospects for the Turkish Navy appear to be more optimistic. It is undergoing an extensive modernization program, with the parallel objective to increase the capabilities of its national industry. If economic forecasts are confirmed and Turkey experiences a period of steady growth, the construction of a modern and balanced naval force would become a realistic objective.

The Middle East

Israel possesses the only navy of significance in the Levant. Since the 2006 war, Lebanon has been slowly developing a naval force intended to control its territorial waters. The Syrian Navy consists of missile boats with a limited capability of sea denial. The Israeli Navy, in contrast, is able to participate in joint operations with other regional navies. Its fundamental task is to guarantee the security of SLOCs in both the Mediterranean and the Gulf of Aqaba.

The increasing need to safeguard its sovereignty in the EEZ will probably lead to a significantly enhanced role for the navy in order to protect the rich fields of natural gas and petroleum that have recently been discovered off its shores. This in turn will lead to greater procurement of naval hardware.

Apart from the United States, one other external actor demands consideration in the Eastern Mediterranean: Russia. Its leadership has more than once declared, and has recently demonstrated, its intention to utilize the base at Tartus, in Syria, to deploy a naval group in the Mediterranean. Russian naval authorities, as well as President Vladimir Putin, have confirmed that the return to the Mediterranean is driven by the need to defend Russian interests in the area; however, definition of what these interests amount to remains elusive. Nonetheless, they would appear to be both political and economic in nature. Politically, a Russian naval presence in the Mediterranean will help nurture existing ties with Syria. Economically, a Russian naval presence in the Mediterranean would serve the ambitions of the energy giant Gazprom, which has designs on the natural gas and oil fields off Cyprus. In this respect the return of the Russian Navy to the Mediterranean on an almost permanent basis recalls the atmosphere, if not the perils, of the Cold War, when interactions with Soviet warships were a daily routine.

North Africa

The North African navies are generally characterized by heterogeneous equipment, which consists of mainly older vessels acquired from both former Soviet and Western countries. North African countries generally lack both the technical skills and the industries to build their own ships. Their navies are oriented toward territorial defense, ranging from the protection of offshore facilities to the surveillance of exclusive fishing zones and the control of choke points. The main problems are the difficulty of keeping their vessels operational, due in part to deficiencies of training and doctrine. Egypt has benefited from its good relations with the United States, and has built a credible force consisting of four *Perry*-class frigates. The Libyan Navy was practically neutralized during the NATO-led intervention in March 2011, and is currently unable to patrol Libyan territorial waters. The Tunisian Navy is suited only for the surveillance of its coasts and fishing zones. In contrast, the interest shown by Algeria and Morocco in obtaining modern European frigates may prefigure an intention to acquire creditable forces, with a view to future collaboration within the region, and with NATO.

Western Europe

In spite of the constant constraints on military expenditures resulting from economic difficulties, the Spanish, French, and Italian Navies have managed to modernize themselves, remaining the only regional forces able to project naval power throughout the Mediterranean. These three countries mostly share strategic objectives: fostering Mediterranean dialogue to guarantee mutual security, the safeguard of SLOCs, the diversification of energy procurement, and the promotion of Mediterranean issues as a major focus of EU policies. The result is the development of an instrument that is able to integrate itself into multinational operations, that is flexible and projectable, and that is made up of multifunctional units with command-and-control capabilities, without neglecting patrolling and surveillance units. All three countries have subscribed to the concept that Europe must guarantee its own security.

Spain made a considerable effort with the construction of the new, 30,000-ton multipurpose vessel, *Rey Juan Carlos*, and a new supply ship, which have partly closed the gap separating it from the French and Italian navies. The French, having shelved the construction of a new aircraft carrier, have developed their amphibious component with the entry into service of the two *Mistral*-class assault ships and the announcement of a third. The Italian Navy is already testing the capabilities and the range of missions of the new *Cavour* carrier. Italy, without Atlantic or overseas commitments, has the advantage of being able to concentrate its energies in the Mediterranean alone, and in recent operations it has played a prominent role; examples are Operation Leonte (2006), the commands of the United Nations Interim Force in Lebanon (2014) and of Operation Atalanta (2014),[24] and the continuing cooperation and dialogue with the other Mediterranean navies.[25]

Italy's strenuous engagement in Operation Mare Nostrum, begun in October 2013 to confront the humanitarian emergency presented by massive immigration from Africa across the Straits of Sicily, is a typical example of the employment of today's Mediterranean navies in a combination of constabulary and humanitarian missions.[26] Italy's subsequent abandonment of this operation also underscores the difficulty of addressing maritime security needs in the face of a persistent economic crisis. It remains to be seen whether the efforts of the Italian Navy to obtain budgetary support for additional ships, capable of coping with the rising security needs of the Mediterranean basin, will bear fruit.

It is apparent that a significant imbalance has arisen in recent years between the capacities of regional navies and the challenges of regional security, which have become significantly worse owing to the rise of Islamist violence, and the persistent instability that has followed the so-called Arab Spring. The main responsibility for maritime surveillance and security in the Mediterranean falls upon European navies, employed in Maritime Interdiction Operations (MIOs), as exemplified by NATO's Operation Active Endeavor, and also in support of the Proliferation Security Initiative.[27] Mediterranean navies represent the front line of a highly articulated system of surveillance, involving a multitude of governmental institutions from all the Mediterranean countries. Many naval missions now involve tasks more typically entrusted to coast guards. The latter, as a consequence, have seen a rise in their importance (mainly in France, Italy, and Spain), and participate in the numerous activities of cooperation at all levels among the Mediterranean countries. These initiatives, moreover, are the main instrument for a more equal sharing of the burden imposed by virtually continuous sea control operations.

Given the high costs of maritime surveillance, the long and unpredictable duration of the effort required, and the resulting effect on training for other missions, the navies of Europe's Mediterranean states are accepting a reasonable reduction in their capabilities in return for the security of their sea. These navies are adapting themselves as best they can, trying to maintain a balanced force, with the bigger ones preserving their power projection capability. In this context they have also cooperated to reduce research-and-development costs, by sharing requirements and industrial synergies. If the process of confidence building between the two shores of the Mediterranean proves successful in the end, it will be due to the work done by these navies in recent years.

FAULT OR BRIDGE?

Whether the Mediterranean Sea will serve as a bridge connecting the states of its northern and southern littorals, or as a fault line that divides them, is at present difficult to judge. So, too, is the prospect for serious conflict in the region, a seemingly remote possibility at present, but not one that can be ruled out indefinitely. Much depends on the consequences of the social movements currently unfolding in North Africa. One of the side effects of the Arab Spring has been increasing distrust of the new state institutions emerging from the overthrow of previous regimes, particularly in Egypt and Libya. This is largely due to the perceived collapse of the new states' policing functions and their relative inability to control organized crime, both nationally and transnationally. The most dramatic expression of this failure is the massive flow of migrants seeking to cross the Mediterranean from Africa to Europe, thousands of whom have died in the process. This migratory flux is not merely composed of people from North Africa. It encompasses people from a much wider area, stretching from the Middle East to the Maghreb. This development is not merely a humanitarian crisis. It poses a significant security challenge, to the extent that it may enable and encourage a wide range of illegal activities, ranging from smuggling and human trafficking to terrorism and the proliferation of weapons of mass destruction. In response, the Italian Navy has begun integrating border control activities within its standard portfolio of missions, a move that will certainly detract from more traditional military activities. Conversely, the scale and complexity of the challenge have led to stronger interagency coordination. The terrorist dimension of the migratory issue, in particular, should not be underestimated—as proved by the attack on the Egyptian patrol vessels in Damietta, discussed above. This act would suggest that the Islamic State's capacity to extend its influence out to sea cannot be dismissed. As a consequence, trade, commerce, and offshore natural gas and oil fields—all crucial for European economies—are at risk, and their protection will require increasing commitments from the region's navies. The need for increased maritime security—at sea as well as in ports—is putting a tremendous strain on European naval resources; but as a shared security issue, it should also be regarded as a useful driver toward economic and strategic cooperation.

In addition, it is possible that the Mediterranean may be about to resume its traditional role as an arena of confrontation between the world's great navies—in the present case, those of Russia and the United States. Recent developments do not compare with the large Soviet deployments in the area during the Cold War; yet they clearly reflect Russia's desire to flex its naval muscles in support of its aggressive policies in Georgia, Crimea, and Ukraine. The EU's response to these developments will go a long way toward determining whether the chill of the Cold War is again felt in the Mediterranean.

One factor brings these threads together: the global economic crisis and its impact on the stability of the Mediterranean region. The prospect that Greece may default on its government debt, and as a consequence be forced out of the European monetary union, has raised widespread apprehensions about the future of Europe's weaker economies, a disproportionate number of which are Mediterranean states: Greece, Spain, Italy, and even France. It is difficult to predict how quickly these countries will come out of recession, and also whether their recovery efforts can remain consistent with the monetary requirements of the euro zone. However these issues ultimately play out, the current situation is already having an impact on the policies of openness and outreach that have distinguished European foreign and security interactions. Economic crises, declining investment, and decreasing government capacity along the Mediterranean's northern shore can only exacerbate the social crises brewing to the south.

Among the first victims of these crises will be the elaborate system of cooperative maritime surveillance that is now at the center of the European approach to security in the Mediterranean. Such a deterioration would ensure the Mediterranean's reemergence as fault line stretching from Gibraltar to the Dardanelles—an outcome well worth avoiding.

NOTES

1. Fernand Braudel, *La Méditerranée et le monde méditerranéen à l'époque de Philippe II* (Paris: Armand Colin, 1990).

2. J. S. Corbett, *England in the Mediterranean* (London: Longmans, Green, 1904), 1:4.

3. J. Maila is a professor of political sociology of Lebanese origin who migrated to France during the civil war that devastated the country at the end of the 1970s. An expert on the Middle East, he was appointed adviser for interreligious dialogue, through the Ministry of Foreign Affairs, to then–French president Nicolas Sarkozy. His words are reported by the Lebanese journalist Antoine Sfeir, "Sécuriser le développement durable de la méditerranée: Actes du colloque, Union pour la Méditerranée, École Militaire, 17 et 18 avril 2008," *Cahier du Centre d'Etudes et de Recherche de l'Ecole Militaire*, no. 6 (September 2008): 30–31.

4. E.g., the contiguous zone, the fisheries zones, or the ecological protection zones.

5. The dimensions of such zones are reduced in comparison with the fixed limits for the EEZ (200 miles) defined by UNCLOS.

6. The very nature of the Delio-Attic League favored Athenian hegemony: The contracting parties could choose between direct military participation (warships) or economic support in return for military protection by those with greater military capacity. Most of the parties chose the latter option, so that the league, formally without a supreme authority, was controlled by Athens.

7. Carthage was among the numerous colonies founded by the Phoenicians in their trading journeys westwards from present-day Lebanon.

8. The geographic position of Constantinople was particularly favorable, so that only a force of considerable size, that was able to organize both land and naval operations, could hope to conquer it.

9. In the sixteenth century the Barbary states in North Africa became a naval power in the Mediterranean, and they subjected the coasts of Italy and Spain to constant raiding. As many as 1 million Europeans may have been captured and sold as slaves in North Africa and the Ottoman Empire between the sixteenth and nineteenth

centuries. See Robert C. Davis, *Christian Slaves, Muslim Masters: White Slavery in the Mediterranean, the Barbary Coast and Italy, 1500–1800* (Houndmills, UK: Palgrave Macmillan, 2004).

10. The littoral states of the Mediterranean Sea are Italy, France, Spain, Albania, Algeria, Tunisia, Slovenia, Morocco, Libya, Egypt, Israel, Lebanon, Syria, Turkey, Greece, Malta, Croatia, Montenegro, Bosnia, and Cyprus.

11. Samuel P. Huntington, *The Clash of Civilizations and the Remaking of World Order* (New York, Simon & Schuster, 1996).

12. Western Sahara is a former Spanish colony that was occupied in 1975 by the Moroccan army after the Spanish withdrew. There followed a war in which the nationalist front fought against the Moroccan occupants and the Mauritanians, who were also interested in exercising some influence over the region. Morocco still occupies the country, mainly owing to its interest in the exploitation of natural resources both on land and offshore in the correspondent EEZ. The international community is monitoring the situation through the United Nations Mission for the Referendum in Western Sahara.

13. FREMM-class frigates (*frégates européennes multimission*) are produced by a joint program between France and Italy. Sigma-class corvettes are frigate-like, Dutch-built vessels capable of operating on the open ocean. Algeria's new amphibious vessel, displacing 9,000 tons, is a "landing platform dock" of Italian construction. The MEKO-class frigates (from *MEhrzweck-KOmbination*, meaning multipurpose), to be delivered in 2016, have capabilities similar to the FREMMs and are of German construction.

14. In response to the resulting humanitarian emergency, in October 2013 the Italian Navy embarked on Operation Mare Nostrum, a large-scale search and rescue effort intended to avert loss of life among those seeking to cross from Africa to Europe. The operation ended in October 2014, and has been replaced by a reduced effort under the auspices of the European Union.

15. For a map showing the location of the fields, see US Energy Information Agency, "Overview of Oil and Natural Gas in the Eastern Mediterranean Region," August 15, 2013, http://www.eia.gov/beta/international/analysis_includes/regions_of_interest /Eastern_Mediterranean/eastern-mediterranean.pdf.

16. The concept of a "wider" Mediterranean was used by the French historian Fernand Braudel in his path-breaking work on the "Mediterranean world"; see Braudel, *La Méditerranée*. Since the winding down of the Cold War in the 1980s, this concept has been employed by the Institute of Maritime Warfare of the Italian Navy to define the theater of operation where Italy would seek to project power and exercise influence through naval and diplomatic means.

17. Paolo Malanima, *Rapporto sulle economie del Mediterraneo: Edizione 2009* (Bologna: Il Mulino), 8–13.

18. This is as was reported in the keynote address by NATO secretary-general Jens Stoltenberg at the North Atlantic Council–Mediterranean Dialogue Seminar celebrating the twentieth anniversary of the Mediterranean Dialogue, December 9, 2014, http://www.nato.int/cps/en/natohq/opinions_115773.htm.

19. The scheme thus favored the reintegration of Libya into the Mediterranean community.

20. Barry Buzan and Ole Weaver, *Regions and Powers: The Structure of International Security* (Cambridge: Cambridge University Press, 2003), 44.

21. These symposiums are a series of biennial meetings, convened in Venice and organized by the Italian Navy, that are attended by representatives of the principal NATO navies and others from as far away as Brazil and India.

22. In parallel with the V-RMTC's technical development, a legal framework for the V-RMTC has also been formulated in the "Operational Arrangement" document, to which seventeen countries have now adhered: Portugal, Spain, France, Italy, Slovenia, Croatia, Montenegro, Albania, Greece, Turkey, Cyprus, Malta, Jordan, Israel, Romania, the United Kingdom, and the United States. Subsequently, Germany and Bulgaria have also begun to participate in the Wider Mediterranean Community. The original statement of the Operational Agreement is at http://www.5plus5defence.org/EN /VRMTC%20DocLib/V_RMTC%20Operational%20Arrangement.pdf.

23. Israel is the obvious exception to this observation. Algeria's recent acquisition of a major amphibious warship would also equip it to conduct wider-ranging operations. Whether it will do so is unknown.

24. EU NAVFOR Somalia–Operation Atalanta is an EU military diplomatic mission to prevent and neutralize piracy off the coasts of the Horn of Africa in support of UN Security Council resolutions 1814, 1816, 1838, and 1846, which were adopted in 2008.

25. Operation Leonte was a naval operation conducted under the auspices of the UNIFIL to observe the implementation of the cease-fire following the 2006 war between Israel and Hezbollah. Atalanta is a multinational EU counterpiracy operation off the Horn of Africa, in which overall command rotates among the contributing navies.

26. Mare Nostrum was a highly demanding humanitarian and rescue operation begun in October 2013 in response to the exceptional flow of immigrants from Africa. The operation ended in October 2014, and has been replaced by Operation Triton under the EU's FRONTEX initiative.

27. Operation Active Endeavour is NATO's only Article 5 operation devoted to counterterrorism since the attacks of September 2001. It aims to prevent the movement of terrorists and of weapons of mass destruction, and it employs a balanced fleet of submarines, surface vessels, and patrol aircraft. It is run out of the Allied Maritime Component Command in Naples. The Proliferation Security Initiative is a global effort that aims to stop trafficking in weapons of mass destruction, their delivery systems, and related materials.

CHAPTER 5

Maritime Strategy in the South China Sea

ALESSIO PATALANO

> The boundary is thus not only a line of demarcation between legal systems but also a point of contact of territorial power structures. From the long-term point of view, the position of that line may become an index to the power relations of the contending forces. Stability then suggests an approximation to balanced power, and shifts indicate changes in the relative strength of the neighbors, either through the accretion of power by one or through a decline in the resistance of the other.
>
> —Nicholas John Spykman, "Frontiers, Security, and International Organization"[1]

The South China Sea (SCS) is an area of shifting forces and power relationships, and two different phenomena are contributing to its present evolution. Throughout the two decades following the end of the Cold War, the development of Asian countries contributed to a steady increase in the circulation of goods and primary resources across its waters, reshaping the place of the SCS within the global economic order. The increasing influence of international regimes and norms, conversely, oversaw contested processes of territorialization over its maritime space, paving the way for phases of intraregional competition among coastal states. Emblematically, the staggering economic and military modernization and the territorial claims set forth by its most influential littoral state, the People's Republic of China, well encapsulate the shifting forces at work in the SCS.

The SCS is the sixth-largest body of water on the planet, and the strategic balance in the region it defines affects the international order in two important ways. First, as an area of dense maritime traffic and transportation at sea, the SCS is at the heart of global trade. It is located at the center of the sea lanes connecting the Middle East to Southeast and Northeast Asia and, with almost three-quarters of the world's oil and natural gas transiting its waters, it provides a crucial economic lifeline to the world's leading economies in Asia, Europe, and North America. Second, as a marine environment, the SCS is rich in primary resources and fertile and diverse in its flora and fauna. These unique geological and biological features make it a locus of potential strategic competition resources, as well as a basin requiring coordinated action to avoid the depletion and destruction of its ecosystem.

This chapter examines the strategic complexity of the SCS, arguing that sea power is indispensable to face the multidimensional challenges to its stability and security. Environmental pollution, fishery protection, piracy, maritime terrorism, territorial disputes, and energy security are all crucial features of a complex security picture, one in which the missions of naval forces—with their diplomatic, constabulary, and military potential—can find full application. Four main sections address issues of geopolitics and maritime strategy in the region. The first sets the stage by providing an analysis of the SCS's geography. The second section examines how its geophysical features have affected its evolution as a strategic and operational theater, with specific reference to operations in World War II. The final two sections detail the considerations underpinning the approaches to security of the SCS's main players and the nature of the maritime operations in the area.

This chapter also contends that external naval powers with major interests in maritime trade and commerce, such as the United States and Japan, have a potentially significant role to play vis-à-vis the SCS. By employing their maritime capabilities, these actors can take the lead in stimulating regional cooperation and responsible state behavior. In particular, in the face of a shifting regional power balance, the transnational character of some of the core challenges ahead should be regarded as an important opportunity to facilitate these external naval powers' proactive engagement with China, the state most eager to force a reconfiguration of power in the region.

GEOGRAPHY: THE COMPLEXITIES
OF NATURE'S ORDER

The geography of the SCS is an exquisite expression of the rich complexity of nature and of the choices it imposes on humankind's attempts to order its space and control its resources. As an independent body of water, the SCS presents itself as a semi-enclosed sea encompassing an area of approximately 3.5 million square kilometers, with identifiable geophysical limits separating it from the rest of the world's oceans. It is delimited at its northeast end by the Philippine Islands, and at its southwest extremity by the Indonesian Archipelago and the Thai-Malay Peninsula. There are six primary points of entry and egress. The Straits of Luzon and Taiwan represent the main gateways to Northeast Asian maritime space, while the straits of Sunda, Lombok, Malacca, and Singapore connect the SCS to the Indian Ocean. At the eastern edges of the Philippines, from north to south, and running from west to east, the straits of San Bernardino and Surigao offer two additional points of passage for traffic transiting to the Pacific Ocean through the Philippine Sea.

Maritime space within the SCS is less easily delineated. This is the result of the land formations that define it—a bewildering constellation of islands, rocks, reefs, coral cays, low-tide elevations, and shoals—with the distinction among many of these features being highly problematic.[2] The paramount source of geographical complexity in the SCS is provided by two groups of island features, the Paracel Islands in the northwest and the Spratly Islands in the south. Not the least of the issues related to them is that it is difficult to establish the exact number of "islands" present. In the case of the Spratlys, the larger of the two archipelagos, estimates vary between 500 and (more realistically) 150. The discrepancy rests on the fact that, according to the relevant provisions of the United Nations Convention on the Law of the Sea (UNCLOS), most of the Spratlys should be considered as either low-tide elevations or submerged banks. The largest insular feature of the archipelago, Itu Aba Island, is just 1.4 kilometers long and 400 meters wide, while Spratly Island itself measures 750 meters long and just 350 meters wide at its widest point. The total land area of the entire island group, as defined by the highest astronomic tide, is less than 8 square kilometers.[3] The status of these varied geographic and geological formations has crucial consequences for the maritime territorial claims set forth by coastal states. If considered "islands," they afford territorial rights to their claimants in accordance with UNCLOS. If not, they are simply hazards to navigation.[4]

This factor is directly related to two other geographical characteristics that contribute to explaining the territorial ambitions of the area's littoral states. The SCS is often regarded by media analysts and political scientists as an oil-rich area. Chinese commentators have not hesitated to define it as the new Persian Gulf, estimating the presence of oil resources equal to a value between 105 and 213 billion barrels.[5] But these opinions are far from being universally accepted. Data from the US Energy Information Administration suggest much more conservative figures, with the total oil resources available estimated at about 7 billion barrels.

What is certain is that a large part of the seabed of the SCS, particularly to the south and west, consists of a continental shelf (the Sunda Shelf) in relatively shallow waters, a factor that should facilitate access to whatever hydrocarbon reserves are present. The Reed Bank and associated banks in the Spratlys include approximately 10,350 square kilometers of seabed at similar or lower depths. Currently, the Reed Bank and the Vanguard Bank are considered promising areas with significant quantities of oil and natural gas. Nonetheless, as one expert has observed, the lack of sufficient exploration seems to be the main reason for so much persisting uncertainty.[6]

A third distinctive feature of this area concerns its marine environment, "which supports a number of unique habitats and ecosystems that are amongst the most biologically diverse shallow water marine ecosystems globally."[7] The SCS is very rich in marine flora and fauna. It contains forty-five of the fifty-one mangrove species in the world, encompassing approximately 30 percent of all the mangroves on the planet, and 18 of the 60 known species of sea grass. Southeast Asia is also home to the single largest concentration of coral reefs across all the Australasian seas—a third of the Earth's total.[8] These formations include the Spratly Islands, the Tung-Sha Reefs, and the Paracel Islands, all of which are considered to play a critical role in the maintenance and replenishment of regional biodiversity.[9]

As one recent study summarized it, geology and local weather patterns are key to explaining the area's biological diversity and richness in marine resources. Geologically, the SCS is distinguished by a large number of archipelagos, reefs, islands, and peninsulas, which create large areas of shallow, relatively temperate waters that support numerous species of organisms. Reefs also buffer wave impact, naturally protecting beaches and limiting erosion. Climatically, seasonal monsoon winds and underwater currents grant to this semi-enclosed sea the ideal conditions for a fertile marine environment, a richness that is further enhanced by the 125 rivers draining into it.[10] In particular, the Spratly Islands are considered by scientists as a reef habitat of irreplaceable value representing prolific breeding grounds for fisheries.[11]

Similarly, data from the UN Food and Agriculture Organization (FAO) on the state of world fisheries and aquaculture indicate that the Pacific West Central Region, which includes the SCS, is "the most productive fishing area of the tropical regions," with highly diverse and multispecies fisheries.[12] The SCS is highly exemplary of such prosperous marine fauna. In its waters, there are as many as 3,500 species of finfish and invertebrates, and at least 182 of them are listed by the FAO as supporting major harvests. In particular, catches from the Gulf of Thailand and the SCS are estimated to contribute to approximately 10 percent of yearly global fisheries production.[13] The populations of the SCS's littoral states (nearly 300 million people) rely on the fish catch for almost half their total protein intake. Tuna and tuna-like species are the most valuable fish in the area, making up 24 percent of the total catch in the Pacific West Central Region.[14] In the SCS alone, more than 1,500,000 tons of tuna were caught in 1999, marking a sharp 350 percent increase compared with figures from 1979. Anchovies and sardines ranked second among the most sought-after species of fish, with a total of 925,000 tons of catch. Shrimps, prawns, and other types of crustaceans proved to be equally important, accounting altogether to an amount of 380,000 tons.[15] In all, the geography of the SCS has favored the growth of a wealth of natural resources, making its maritime spaces essential contributors to the survival and economic development of the communities living along its contours.

HISTORY

The peculiarities of the geography of the SCS have had a considerable impact on its evolution as a maritime and naval theater. The navigational challenges that it has historically posed to seafarers have not prevented the SCS from becoming a perennial arena of imperial competition.[16]

By the fourteenth century, the SCS was a vibrant component of the economic system of Imperial China—in effect, a "Chinese lake." This does not mean that Chinese emperors ruled the waves of the SCS. Rather, its confines had long been part of trade patterns connecting merchants from Southeast Asia and the west coast of the Malay Peninsula with traders in India, Persia, Arabia, and East Africa.[17] These cross-regional exchanges played an important role in the initial development of the maritime sector in South China, where naval and riverine forces contributed to the emergence of the Ming Dynasty

(1368–1644).[18] It was this maritime power base that, though never fully under state control, progressively established local operators along coastal areas in the SCS as significant contributors to the national economy.[19] By 1415 the reopening of the Grand Canal provided further impulse to south–north trade, strengthening a coastal and riverine network that was already highly developed. This system of inner waterways became key to the distribution of bulk items such as grain, and to the transportation of tax revenues, making it affordable and more easily defendable against pirate activities.[20] Fishing, maritime trade, and piracy became the currencies that linked this area with the economic, social, and political life of the rest of the country.[21] Maritime affairs were an important aspect of the economic life of Imperial China, but naval policies struggled to gain priority in the Ming's national security agenda, especially after the 1430s, when a Mongol threat emerged on the country's northern land frontiers. Ming China did not disregard the sea, as it is often assumed. Rather, the Ming followed a largely laissez-faire economic approach, with state intervention limited to ensure the functionality of the rivers and coastal routes that distributed the nation's goods.[22]

The junk was the primary naval asset of the era.[23] Junks were multipurpose vessels by design and purpose. They could be used for commerce as well as for military and expeditionary missions, and in riverine, coastal, or oceanic waters—flexibility that nicely met the largely constabulary missions of the navy.[24] National enterprises such as the 1405–33 oceanic voyages under Admiral Zheng He and the 1575 naval expeditions to Luzon to hunt the pirate Lin Feng were symptomatic of a lively southern Chinese maritime sector, but sea power as it came to be understood in the West was not important for the state's survival. As a result, the need for specialized seagoing warships remained irregular, and the central authorities outsourced the maintenance of fleets to local commercial operators and facilities.[25] Under both the Ming and their successors, the Qing, naval forces operating in the SCS were designed to provide maritime security in coastal and riverine trade defense.[26]

The period between the late sixteenth and late nineteenth centuries witnessed the transformation of the SCS into a focal point for the transit of international commerce, its primary users being the Dutch, Spanish, Portuguese, French, and, above all, the British. By the second half of the nineteenth century, the SCS had a core strategic value within the wider context of the shipping routes connecting London, Singapore, and Hong Kong. One study underscored the magnitude of this trade, noting that by the 1820s "Britain was drinking some thirty million pounds of tea a year," most of which was ferried across these Asian waters.[27] In this new, global economic order, the SCS was no longer a Chinese lake. This became apparent on August 23, 1884, when, in a little more than a quarter of an hour, French naval forces destroyed most of the modern Fuzhou fleet in port, in what became the opening salvos of the Sino-French War of 1884–85.[28] By the time the century reached its close, most of the countries surrounding the SCS had become colonies or protectorates of Western powers.

With the consolidation of Western imperialism in the region, the relationship between the SCS and the world economy changed, but the main missions of naval forces there had not. Mutatis mutandis, warships operating in the SCS had to possess considerable flexibility in order to cover the large array of duties involving riverine, coastal, and "blue water" operations. At the beginning of the twentieth century, Britain's vice admiral, Cyprian Bridge, drew planners' attention in London to this subject. As commanding officer of the China Station, Bridge pointed out that it was not necessary for warships serving in Chinese waters to be of "great size and very high speed." Rather, he thought that "6 or 7 steamers like those which trade regularly to Tientsin and even to Ichang—real seagoing vessels drawing less than 11 feet, with an effective ocean speed of more than 10 knots, . . . should be in a better position to meet almost certain requirements than we are now."[29] Cruisers of large size, he added, represented British military power and strategic commitment vis-à-vis other powers, and therefore needed to appear in those waters on a regular basis. Nonetheless, conventional war in the SCS would be unlikely to put their qualities to maximum use.[30] This logic remained sound into the twentieth century, when it was undermined by a new Asian challenger against the established order.

From Lifeline to Battle Line

Throughout the first half of the twentieth century, the SCS slowly entered a new imperial order. In the aftermath of the first Sino-Japanese War (1894–95), Japan had emerged as a prominent naval power in Asian waters, and it had established a presence in the SCS with the annexation of Taiwan (Formosa). The SCS soon became part of Japan's economic network as well as a theater of potentially significant strategic value.[31] Economically, Japanese companies in Taiwan expanded their activities in the area, exploiting primary resources such as guano in the Paracels and Spratlys. From a strategic viewpoint, expansion toward the resource-rich areas of Southeast Asia, known as a "southern advance" (nanshin-ron), was originally understood as way of facilitating the economic penetration of the area. Eventually, it became the navy's alternative to the army's preferred "northern advance" (*hokushin-ron*) on the Asian mainland.[32]

Expansion to the south gained momentum as the vulnerability of Japan's energy supplies became more apparent. In 1939 the Japanese took advantage of the changing political balance in Europe to secure a firmer foothold in the SCS, seizing Hainan and, subsequently, Pratas Island and several of the Paracels and Spratlys. By July 1941, the navy's strategic vision had turned into a national strategy, and naval air bases were beefed up in territories in Indochina (with air groups based in Saigon) and Taiwan (especially Takao, Tainan, and Bako) to be used as staging platforms for a wider military conquest of the region.[33] The initial phase of Japanese expansion in Southeast Asia proved that, operationally, a blend of land-based air power and carrier-based naval task forces could dominate the SCS. Once Malaya, Singapore, and coastal Vietnam were under Japanese control, they enabled its navy to transform the SCS itself into a de facto " Japanese lake," whose island features provided local logistical support.

As the war ground on, the SCS assumed crucial significance as a source of energy resources. In 1942 Japan managed to recover 70 percent of the East Indies' prewar production rate of 180,000 barrels per day. Between 1942 and 1943, Japanese oil imports increased from 29,000 barrels per day to 40,000. In 1943 oil stood more than ever at the heart of Japan's military (and especially naval) war machine, and Southeast Asia was a pivotal artery.[34] By the end of 1943, however, Japan had already lost more than 2 million tons of shipping, resulting in a 3 million-ton shortfall in bulk commodities compared with the previous year. The situation worsened dramatically in 1944 and 1945, with just 9 percent of oil shipments from Southeast Asia reaching their final destination in Japan in 1945.[35] The ability of Allied forces to reach the sea lanes passing through the SCS and Southeast Asia transformed the area from a Japanese lake to a graveyard of critical raw materials. From November 1943 to the end of 1944, losses in the region accounted for the majority of total of Japanese shipping sunk, with severe consequences for Japan's ability to supply arms and ammunition to its armed forces.[36]

American submarines had a devastating impact. By the summer of 1944, they were sinking some twenty ships a month, totaling approximately 60,000 tons.[37] The tonnage of Japanese shipping sent to the bottom of the ocean doubled in the subsequent period, September–October 1944 (a little less than 130,000 tons), and reached the pinnacle in the months from November 1944 to August 1945, when fifty-eight ships, including naval and merchant vessels, totaling 178,230 tons were sunk.[38] The geography of the SCS favored submarine warfare, especially as Japanese land-based air power became overstretched and antisubmarine warfare capabilities were not particularly effective.

As Japan's air and naval war machine in the SCS weakened, carrier strikes completed the task. In January 1945, Admiral William Halsey's Third Fleet entered the SCS to hunt the Japanese battle force led by the hybrid battleships *Ise* and *Hyuga*, in order to support General Douglas MacArthur's landings in the Lingayan Gulf. During the ten days of the raid, Halsey's carriers failed to make contact with the Japanese battle group, which had withdrawn to Singapore. Nonetheless, in the sorties of January 12 alone, the thirteen fast carriers of the task force sank forty-six Japanese vessels plus the French cruiser *La Motte-Piquet*, and destroyed eighty-seven aircraft, effectively neutralizing the naval base in Camranh Bay.[39] The operational tempo was intense, with available planes flying an average of 1.7 sorties per day, almost 1,500 altogether.[40] In the following days, further attacks were conducted against port installations and airfields around Hong Kong, the Liuchow Peninsula, and Hainan, with mixed results.[41] In all, carrier-based air power showed itself capable of delivering killing blows to Japanese maritime and air assets in the SCS, though such effectiveness rested on the very limited opposition.

During the Cold War the SCS ceased to be part of any imperial system, and became a frontier region dividing the Communist and Western blocs in Asia. American military involvement in Vietnam is a case in point. During the war the SCS became a base for active carrier air operations, and the terminus for a gigantic maritime logistical chain, which carried "over 70% of the [US] fleet's ship fuel, 95% of its jet fuel, virtually all its aviation gasoline, more than 95% of its ammunition, 97% of its provisions, and over 70% of its other stores."[42]

Nevertheless, geography had not changed. In the Vietnam War, the US Navy faced dilemmas similar to those of the Royal Navy and Imperial China. At the beginning of the century, Admiral Bridge had stressed how any navy aspiring to maintain an effective presence in the region had to perform its duties at sea and also inland along rivers. Similarly, in the 1960s, the ability to control regional waters in order to cut North Vietnam's seaborne supply lines meant that the navy had to establish a series of interdiction activities along the coast of Vietnam and the Mekong Delta, reaching well into the dense network of inland rivers.[43] The challenges of riverine, coastal, and open-sea operations required a blend of air assets for routine patrols and precision strikes; warships, submarines, and coast guard cutters for a naval blockade; inshore coast guard cutters; and small, fast patrol boats to support special operations. In time, the navy brought together the different campaigns at sea and along the rivers and transformed them into one integrated and multilayered interdiction program, later known as SEALORDS (Southeast Asia Lake, Ocean, River, and Delta Strategy). By the time the United States withdrew from Vietnam, the SCS was entering a new phase, in which its fate and geostrategic role would be defined by global economic expansion and by the interests of the new states that had risen from the ashes of Western and Japanese imperialism.

GEOPOLITICS IN THE SOUTH CHINA SEA

The decades of peace that have followed the end of the Vietnam War have seen the SCS resume the twin roles of resource producer and transit area that it played in earlier times. Both roles have been crucial to sustaining the growth of the surrounding Asian economies, and of the larger world. One analyst has described the SCS as the "world's most important region of constrained navigation."[44] Through its primary entry point, the Strait of Malacca, approximately 60,000 ships deliver annually 80 percent of the oil transported to Northeast Asia. The traffic volume transiting through the strait amounts to 525 million metric tons, for a total of $390 billion. Shipping traffic through Malacca is several times greater than the traffic through the Panama or Suez canals, a trend that is likely to continue. An analysis of figures from 1999 to 2004 showed an increase in the traffic through the Strait of Malacca of 45 percent within the six-year period.[45]

Container traffic is a sizable component of the volume of goods annually ferried in the SCS and, more broadly, in Southeast Asia. Singapore, Prot Klang and Tanjung Pelepas in Malaysia, and Tanjung Priod in Indonesia are major transhipment hubs, with Singapore handling 27.9 million twenty-foot equivalent units.[46] One of the reasons for the vital role of shipping in this region is the presence of two of the world's largest archipelagic nations, the Philippines and Indonesia. Composed of thousands of islands, these countries depend on seaborne transportation of personnel and matériel to sustain their domestic economies, political and social unity, and military defense.[47] As in the past, global trade has continued to interact with local requirements to create an increasingly intricate and interdependent network of economic and political relationships.

Growing Asian energy imports are the most important reason for the sharp rise in regional traffic. Japan, South Korea, China, and other countries in Southeast Asia, including Australia and New Zealand, account altogether for more than a quarter of the world's oil demand. A total of 94 percent of that demand is satisfied by imports from the rest of the world.[48] Within the region, China is by far the largest energy consumer. In 2003 it overtook Japan as the largest Asian oil importer. It is now the largest in the world, having passed the United States in 2014. In China's oil importing strategy, the sea lanes passing through the SCS encompass its two main routes. Approximately 80 percent of China's imported oil passes through the Strait of Malacca, with most of the remainder imported from Southeast Asia and Australia.[49]

The intensity of maritime traffic throughout the SCS has raised a number of environmental challenges. A lack of sufficient safety of shipping has been conducive to oil spills, a by-product of the SCS's emergence as a maritime silk road that is cause for concern. This is a challenge of considerable significance, as it is leading to the rapid decline in quality of the region's marine and coastal waters. The region has already been exposed to numerous oil spill incidents along international shipping routes or in areas with large-scale exploitation activities. In particular, recent statistics suggested that the incidence of oil spills in Chinese waters has increased substantially.[50]

The increased use of the SCS as a medium for the circulation of goods has also highlighted a second general problem: the need for a more effective management plan for the maritime space. Arrangements for the safety of the environment are critical steps in this direction, but not the only ones. There is also a need for effective search-and-rescue services, good hydrographical surveys, and reliable meteorological forecasts. In this respect a security alert system introduced with the International Ship and Port Facility Security Code to signal emergencies on board of ships transiting across the SCS is a first example of the cooperative actions to improve regional security at sea.[51]

Rivalries and Maritime Territorial Disputes

Although economic interdependence has underlined the connectivity of the SCS, the disappearance of foreign colonial rule has left behind ill-defined maritime boundaries that have sometimes failed to provide adequate "physical and cultural separation of one sovereign state from another."[52] Competition for territorial ownership and favorable boundary delimitations of the SCS have become a form of political self-assertion, and each line drawn is seen as a way to legitimate a nation's status. Within this context, the exploitation of natural resources in the regional seabed has come to be seen as a measure of each coastal state's ability to secure territorial integrity, assert national power in regional politics, and exercise control over vital natural resources. In national discourses, maritime border disputes gauge crucial political ambitions and perceived security vulnerabilities. As such, their negotiation stands as a source of rivalry in itself, one in which national agendas are prioritized vis-à-vis potential benefits from cooperative initiatives.

Island features in the Spratly, Paracel, and Natuna archipelagos are at the center of multiple disputes among different regional claimant states. Among these, the most consequential revolve around the legal status of the Paracels and Spratlys, where the competing claims of China, Taiwan, Brunei, Malaysia, Vietnam, and the Philippines all converge. China and Taiwan have set forth historical claims for a large U-shaped area comprising almost 80 percent of the SCS, which first appeared on a map produced by the Nationalist Kuomintang in 1947.[53] Vietnam, too, has made large claims in the area, based on the historical ties established by the Nguyen Dynasty from the sixteenth to the nineteenth centuries, and by the French incorporation of the Spratlys into Cochin China in 1929. In particular, Vietnam claimed the right of succession for the entire SCS from French colonial rule. In contrast, other littoral states claim only contiguous zones based on the legal framework established by UNCLOS.[54] Chinese and Vietnamese historical claims have thus far been judged insufficient, because they require corroborating evidence of "continuous and effective occupation" in order to legally validate them. In this respect, the judgments by the Permanent Court of Arbitration between 1928 and 1931 in the cases of Palmas Island, Clipperton Island, and Greenland constituted important precedents in favor of the principle of effective occupation. Emphasis on physical occupation over historical claims has had a significant impact, especially on China's sense of injustice for what have been later regarded as "lost territories," an open scar left by the "century of humiliation."

The contest between historical claims and physical occupation has gained momentum in recent years, especially as the different claimants have resorted to taking possession of island features in the archipelagos to support their positions. Between the late 1950s and the end of the 1980s, the Philippines, Vietnam, and Malaysia pursued assertive policies with the goal of forcing a new status quo that would limit the options of other neighboring countries. Other states in the region have followed suit. With the exception of Brunei, all claimant states now occupy island features in the Paracels and Spratlys. Vietnam occupies twenty-one features; the Philippines, nine; China, seven; Malaysia, five; and Taiwan, one.[55] By the time UNCLOS was signed, the occupants of the islands had already created a fait accompli, whereby "their removal by anything short of military force (became) unlikely."[56] This process of confounding legal norms by creating new facts on the ground (or, more precisely, in the water) has continued apace.

Occupations by Southeast Asian states provided China with a strong incentive to rebalance the equations of territorial ownership in the SCS. Beijing did so by maintaining a two-pronged approach to the territorial disputes. Diplomatically, the country sought to reassure coastal states of its peaceful intent. Militarily, it began extending its footprint by moving into the Spratlys in the summer of 1987, with two islands subsequently occupied in January 1988. In March of the same year, Chinese naval forces clashed with the Vietnamese military over Johnson Reef and consolidated their position. By 1992 China had effectively occupied a number of strategically located island features, predicating a peaceful advance in the area while sending clear signals about the willpower and capabilities to safeguard its interests. The passing in February 1992 of legislation declaring the maritime space encompassing the Paracels, the Spratlys, Pratas Reef, Macclesfield Bank, Scarborough Shoal, Diaoyutai (or Senkaku in Japanese), Penghu, and Dongsha Islands as part of China's territorial waters, and the subsequent occupation and building of fortifications on Mischief Reef—inside the Philippine-claimed Exclusive Economic Zone, as defined by the UN Convention on the Law of the Sea—further reinforced this point.

Throughout the subsequent decade, mindful of growing regional concerns about Chinese ambitions, the authorities in Beijing decided to adopt a less muscular posture, setting forth more conciliatory political actions. The renewed tones of the dialogue with the Southeast Asian counterparts sought to build on the appeal to create a positive climate to solve the disputes set forth by the Association of Southeast Asian Nations (ASEAN) Declaration on the South China Sea of July 1992. The negotiations that followed culminated in the November 2002 Declaration on the Conduct of Parties in the SCS. The declaration was hailed as an important shift, for two reasons. First, China agreed to tackle the management of SCS stability multilaterally (and not bilaterally, as in the past). Second, the different parties committed to promote self-restraint when conducting activities in the area, and to work toward the implementation of cooperative confidence-building measures. Although the implementation of the declaration has proved complex, a sense of confidence was perceived in the communiqués released after the Sixteenth ASEAN Summit in April 2010 and in the Forty-Third ASEAN Ministers' Meeting in July 2010, where a consensus seems to be growing toward the need to reach an agreement over a Regional Code of Conduct in the South China Sea. These communiqués stressed that all parties must continue "to respect the freedom of navigation in and overflight above the South China Sea as provided for by the universally recognised principles of international law."[57]

The circumstances that have surrounded these latest statements suggest, however, that little fundamental change has occurred and that national ambitions are still the force underpinning regional negotiations. In November 2007 the National People's Congress reportedly passed a legislation to elevate Hainan Province's Xisha (Paracel) Islands to a county-level city named "Sansha City" with the responsibility to administer the Paracels and Spratlys. Between 2007 and 2010 China imposed temporary fishing bans and arrested foreign fishermen operating in the disputed areas. Both episodes prompted strong protests, particularly in Vietnam. In addition, between April and May 2009 Vietnam (independently, and jointly with Malaysia), the Philippines, Malaysia (jointly with Vietnam), China, and Brunei all made submissions to the Commission on the Limits of the Continental Shelf in order to extend their "outer" continental shelf in the south-central SCS. The joint Malaysian–Vietnamese submission in particular was met by strong opposition from Chinese authorities because it implied that the disputed islands in the Spratlys are in reality simply rocks that are incapable of generating rights for an exclusive economic zone and rights for a continental shelf. This notion is regarded as unacceptable by Chinese diplomacy, infringing on the country's "sovereignty, sovereign rights and jurisdiction in the South China Sea."[58]

Beginning in 2014, China also started intense reclamation work that has resulted in the creation of almost 12 kilometers of artificial land in the Spratley Islands, almost doubling the islands' total land area. What is remarkable about this activity is that, in fewer than two years, the Chinese authorities have managed to create seventeen times more land than all other claimants have created in the past forty years. Much of this new construction has features that suggest both civilian and military applications.[59]

The Role of Outside Naval Powers

The centrality of the SCS for global trade has inevitably placed it near the heart of a wide range security issues, whose management has afforded outside naval powers great scope for action. This is true for the United States. In addition to formal bilateral security ties with coastal countries like the Philippines and Thailand, Washington has declared a general, threefold strategic interest in the SCS. The ability to guarantee the free flow of trade and raw materials is at the foundations of Washington's attention to the region. In 1995 this prompted the then–US assistant secretary of defense, Joseph Nye, to state that, if conflict occurred in the Spratlys, Washington was prepared to provide escorts to ensure freedom of navigation.[60] At the July 2010 ASEAN Regional Forum meeting, Secretary of State Hillary Clinton restated the United States' position, and also declared its commitment to establish a legal process to resolve the disputes.[61] The involvement of American energy corporations in exploration and exploitation projects in the SCS is an additional source of American interest to the region.[62] Finally, free access to the sea lanes of the SCS represents an indispensable condition for the operational flexibility of the US Navy (USN), which must be able to transit the SCS at will if it is to deploy military power effectively in the Western Pacific and the Indian Ocean. In the words of the latest maritime strategic concept, the sea is a "vast maneuver space," one in which the use of sea lanes in theaters such as the SCS empowers the United States with the "asymmetric advantage of enlarging and contracting its military footprint in areas where access is denied or limited."[63]

In the SCS, the primary instrument of American naval power is the Seventh Fleet, which is composed, on average, of 60 to 70 warships, 200 to 300 aircraft, and 40,000 navy and marine corps personnel, with forward bases in Japan and Guam. At the heart of the fleet is its forward-deployed nucleus, which is composed of carrier and expeditionary strike groups based in Japan. These are centered on a nuclear-powered aircraft carrier (in 2015, the USS *Ronald Reagan*) and an amphibious assault ship (in 2015, the USS *Essex*). Between them, these groups include on average 21 surface warships and submarines. In addition to this forward-deployed force, the USN regularly deploys assets from other operational commands and theaters in Asian waters. In particular, as the world's trade and transport shift toward the Pacific, so have the capabilities of the USN, which envisions gradually adjusting its force posture to provide six operationally available carriers and 60 percent of its submarine force to support engagement, presence, and deterrence in the region.[64] The intention to continue pursuing this objective has been further restated in the latest Asia-Pacific maritime security strategy document.[65]

Although the USN's firepower and capabilities are the most evident guarantor of American interests in the SCS, one of the most important roles undertaken by the USN centers on constabulary activities that are designed to foster the capacity building of the maritime forces of coastal states. In a fashion reminiscent of the British posture in the area at the beginning of the twentieth century, high-level defense policy dialogues, official visits, bilateral and multilateral joint exercises, and training initiatives constitute prominent features of American defense policy in the SCS. They build confidence and reciprocal understanding among professionals operating in regional waters, and they help to overcome "long-standing historical and cultural barriers that inhibit multilateral cooperation."[66] Such initiatives also help allay anxieties among coastal states about the uneven distribution of military power in the region. An American presence emphasizing local capacity building and constabulary activities enhances the ability of regional navies to suppress piracy, organized crime, and terrorism.

Japan is a second potentially significant outside contributor to security in the SCS.[67] As an island country poor in primary resources, the Japanese archipelago relies heavily on maritime trade for its economic survival.[68] In the SCS its economic interests center on maritime trade, direct investments in Southeast Asian economies, and access to energy resources transported from the Middle East, accounting for about 90 percent of Japan's yearly crude oil imports.[69] Strategic interests in the area are supported by significant naval capabilities. At the end of the twentieth century, the Japan Maritime Self-Defense Force and the Japan Coast Guard had evolved, respectively, into well-balanced and capable naval and constabulary forces.[70] The latest Japanese maritime strategy, published in November 2008, made clear that Japan envisions a basic "commitment strategy" with wider international responsibilities.[71] In the SCS and Southeast Asia, the commitment strategy is identified as one of providing support for multilateral efforts against threats to the disruption of trade and of terrorist activities in formats such as the Proliferation Security Initiative. Equal emphasis is put on the capacity building of regional naval forces.[72] In this respect, the Japan Coast Guard led the way, enjoying considerable success in providing training, equipment, and funding to coastal states, notwithstanding initial suspicion from Indonesian and Malaysian authorities regarding "Japanese flags" in the area, recalling Japan's wartime past.[73]

The Royal Australian Navy is another naval actor with the potential to see greater involvement in regional maritime affairs, especially in light of the release in 2009 of *Force 2030*, Australia's latest defense white paper. The document championed a shift toward national strategy with a significant maritime flavor.[74] This would enable Australia to capitalize on its efforts to strengthen ties with coastal states of the SCS, including the Philippines and Indonesia. In May 2007 Australia and the Philippines signed the Status of Visiting Forces Agreement, which for the Philippines is its second most important security agreement, after that with the United States. Within this framework, Australia established an important legal basis for assisting the Philippines in its capacity for port security and border control, and the two navies engaged in a series of exercises, the first of which was held in

2007 (Exercise LUMBAS 2007), which enabled both countries to identify operational issues and challenges.[75] Similarly, in April 2010, Australia and Indonesia inaugurated a coordinated maritime security patrol, whereby air and naval assets from both navies coordinated enforcement operations, shared information, and conducted search and rescue exercises to build mutual confidence and improve combined operational performance.[76]

The Roles of Regional Navies

The roles of regional navies in the SCS have weighed increasingly heavy in defining strategic relationships in the region in recent years, during which the states of Southeast Asia have "dramatically" stepped up military purchases.[77] Investments in new military hardware are judged by some to constitute a regional arms race, in the sense that "one country buys something and others react to it, then the first one may itself react in turn."[78] Yet the wave of modernizing purchases is not merely a sign of persisting regional rivalries, but also a reflection of recovery from the economic crises that afflicted the region in the 1990s, and again after 2008.[79]

A good deal of interest throughout the region has fallen on the procurement of submarine platforms and, simultaneously, on the development of antisubmarine warfare (ASW) capabilities for sea denial purposes. Malaysia is a case in point. Partly in reaction to Singapore's parallel modernization efforts, and partly to renewed rivalry with Indonesia over the resource-rich area in the Celebes Sea called the Ambalat Block, the Royal Malaysian Navy has acquired two *Scorpene*-class submarines, and is now eyeing the acquisition of additional boats of the *Andrasta* class, specifically suited for operations in coastal waters.[80] The Malaysian Navy also plans to procure patrol vessels configured for ASW operations. Indonesia, for its part, has sought to improve its sea denial capabilities. Its two older, East German Type 209 submarines were both refurbished in 2006 by South Korea's Daewoo Shipbuilding and Marine Engineering. To these, the Indonesian Navy expect to add a dozen new, modern boats by 2024. In the words of senior Indonesian naval officers, submarines "will display our naval strength and allow us to be ready for any armed conflict," thus contributing to "maintain a regional balance of power to secure peace."[81]

Vietnam's long dispute with China over the Spratlys is still a source of major concern for the country, which is pursuing a wide range of capabilities to defend its interests in the occupied islands. Reportedly, the authorities in Hanoi have been in negotiation with Israel to purchase a new short-range ballistic missile system, which would include munitions with a range in excess of 150 kilometers and be capable of carrying a 125-kilogram warhead.[82] This system is regarded as very precise and would substantially enhance the potential of Vietnam's naval infantry force. This new addition, coupled with a recent order for six *Kilo*-class submarines and twelve Sukhoi SU-30MKK fighters from Russia, and another for three Canadian DHC-6 Series 400 amphibious aircraft, represent a serious step to deter operations against the Spratly Islands.

Except for Singapore and Taiwan—both of which maintain balanced, well-manned, and well-funded armed forces—one of the key questions surrounding the procurement programs and force structures of coastal states in the SCS is the extent to which the kind of rapid, procurement-driven modernization process that has been under way in recent years will produce significant operational improvements. This is particularly true in naval affairs, where constant training, adequate maintenance, and logistical infrastructures are crucial to overall efficiency and effectiveness.

Among the regional naval forces operating in the SCS, China stands out as by far the most capable, and as having undergone the fastest military modernization process.[83] This is because Chinese naval power serves wider national interests. It is supported by a new "naval nationalism" that has gained traction with Chinese public opinion, and reflects China's steadily increasing reliance on seaborne trade and overseas energy resources. China has also repeatedly expressed its uncompromising willingness to defend its territorial integrity, all factors that have created a consensus in favor of naval modernization.[84] Some authors have gone so far as to compare China's connection to the SCS with that of the United States to the Caribbean at the turn of the twentieth century, where it exercised unchallenged sway as the dominant sea power.[85]

Like other regional states, China is investing heavily in its submarine fleet. The silent service is fast evolving and today fields sixty-five boats, including twelve Russian-produced *Kilos*, featuring advanced Russian technology with stated performances comparable to those of equivalent platforms in Western navies. Other conventionally powered submarines, like the domestically produced *Yuan* class, could be fitted with air-independent propulsion systems, which would enable them to operate with reduced noise and greater endurance.[86]

Antisurface warfare is another area in which the Chinese People's Liberation Army Navy (PLAN) has been conducting advanced research. The navy's antiship cruise missile (ASCM) programs are reported to have focused on designs intended to increase both range and the ability to maneuver so as to penetrate ship defenses. The number of PLAN submarines deploying ASCMs has quadrupled over the past decade and a half, and these systems are now also a standard feature of surface combatants, land-based aircraft, and coastal defense sites. The breadth with which this system has been deployed testifies to a high degree of confidence in its effectiveness. ASCMs such as the Russian-procured SS-N-27 *Sizzler* and the domestically developed YJ-62 and YJ-83 are central to a multilayered strike capability intended to sink or disable warships.

A potentially more crucial asset to China's antisurface warfare effort is its program for the development of antiship ballistic missiles. Equipped with maneuverable reentry vehicles and combined with adequate broad-area maritime targeting systems, these ballistic missiles would be capable of hitting warships at sea. If operational, China could shield the maritime spaces of the SCS against attempts at power projection from outside, a capability on display in the form of the missiles featured in military parades in September 2015. Admiral Robert Willard, head of US Pacific Command, had voiced his concern some years before. As he put it, China is "developing and testing a conventional antiship ballistic missile based on the DF-21/CSS-5 MRBM designed specifically to target aircraft carriers."[87]

Shipboard area air defense is a third area where the PLAN has made impressive progress. Modern guided-missile destroyers have been commissioned, including four *Sovremenny*-class ships from Russia, and the domestically built Type 051C *Luzhou* and Type 052C *Luyang II*, the latter being equipped with a sophisticated phased-array radar system with claimed performance similar to the American Aegis. These platforms are complemented by a well-maintained fleet of more than 200 patrol and costal combatants, a critical asset in a strategy denying access to the waters of the SCS. In particular, the *Houbei* class of guided missile patrol craft, a wave-piercing catamaran that can exceed 36 knots and is equipped with four YJ-8A ASCM missiles and a 30-millimeter Gatling gun, exemplify China's determination to make its presence felt in the littorals. This class is relatively inexpensive to produce, and it includes approximately 60 units, with more planned for construction. Fleet air defense could also receive a boost from the use of carrier aircraft. The former Soviet aircraft carrier *Kuznetsov* was recommissioned by the PLAN as the *Liaoning* in 2012. A domestically produced carrier is expected to make its appearance in due course.

China is also pursuing the development of a large fleet of paramilitary vessels, which, both in displacement and in armament, can play a significant role in allowing the authorities in Beijing to pursue their political agenda. These assets, including a new 12,000-ton ship capable of ramming a 5,000-ton ship and "sink[ing] it to the sea floor," are designed to enforce maritime territorial claims while keeping the threshold of violence within a seemingly nonmilitary context.[88]

CURRENT MARITIME OPERATIONS AND ISSUES

The current process of the naval buildup in the SCS is impressive, but it does not fully convey the range of maritime operations being conducted by the regional navies involved in its waters. These can be divided in two main categories: those pertaining to constabulary and capacity-building activities, and actions best described as fostering "soft" deterrence and dissuasion.

The SCS and Southeast Asia generally have been described in the past as safe havens for piracy and other illegal activities, which have tended to increase sharply in the aftermath of economic crises. Even in the worst of times, however, the number of actual attacks has remained relatively low in relation to the enormous volume of shipping transiting the SCS sea lanes. Until recently maritime security has received quite limited attention from coastal states: the first joint patrols conducted by Malaysia and Thailand occurred in 2003, and in Singapore, Malaysia, and Indonesia in 2004.[89] Negative assessments of the area by shipping companies—coupled with the United States' increased concern with piracy as close kin to terrorism—prompted regional navies to take stronger action. In September 2005 the Eyes in the Sky initiative marked the beginning of coordinated air patrols over the Strait of Malacca by the three coastal states, which, together with the Malacca Strait Sea Patrols that began in 2004, came to be known as the Malacca Strait Patrol. By 2007 these patrols had led to a marked reduction of the actual attacks and the subsequent removal of the strait from the list of war risk areas.[90] Other joint initiatives included the information-sharing platform called Malacca Strait Patrol Info-System, which includes Thailand as a partner, and the Regional Maritime Information Exchange, an internet-based platform sponsored by the Republic of Singapore's Navy that was aimed at facilitating real-time information sharing and collaboration.

Bilateral and multilateral exercises to increase interoperability and effectiveness constitute an important dimension of maritime operations in the SCS. Such exercises often involve regional navies in combination with outside powers. One example is Cooperation Afloat and Readiness Training (CARAT), a series of bilateral exercises promoted by the US Pacific Fleet to enhance operational readiness, interoperability, and mutual understanding. The year 2015 will see the twenty-first exercise in the series, which has expanded beyond the original six partners—Brunei, Indonesia, Malaysia, the Philippines, Singapore, and Thailand—to include Cambodia, Bangladesh, and East Timor. The CARAT process has been supplemented, since 2002, by Southeast Asia Cooperation Against Terrorism, which was organized by Singapore as a means for the CARAT partners to train with the USN in maritime interception scenarios against criminal and terrorist threats.

At the opposite end of the spectrum, maritime interactions among SCS states have been characterized by operations with a less cooperative flavor. Patrolling activities, with the consequent seizing of fishing boats and detention of fishermen found in contested spaces, have become a primary tool to assert national jurisdictional rights. In this regard, China has been particularly prominent in stepping up its patrolling activities and the frequency with which it has seized fishing vessels, a sign of growing confidence in its naval capabilities and its ability to deter other claimant states. It has similarly deployed its forces "to restrict and put pressure" on other coastal states, notably Vietnam and the Philippines, and to prevent them from accessing disputed island features or other areas claimed by Beijing as part of its maritime territory.[91]

Similar considerations were also in play in the March 2009 incident that saw the surveillance ship USNS *Impeccable* harassed by a group of five Chinese patrol vessels. The maneuvers of the Chinese vessels were reported to be conducted in dangerously close proximity to the American ship, in violation of the International Regulations for Preventing Collisions at Sea.[92] As one senior American officer pointed out, the incident involving the *Impeccable* underlined how China, "particularly in the South China Sea, is behaving in an aggressive, troublesome manner and is not willing to abide by acceptable standards of behavior or 'rules of the road.'"[93]

CONCLUSION

As a maritime theater, the resource-rich SCS has always been at the heart of a wider economic system. It has operated as a web of waterways connecting the countries of the region with each other and with the larger world to which they have become increasingly bound. Its geography has favored maritime connectivity not only among the region's littoral states but also, crucially, with the surrounding continental land mass. Notwithstanding limitations on oceanic navigation imposed by the many groups of islands that dot the SCS, the numerous rivers flowing into it have bound riverine and coastal communities together, and have strengthened the influence of the maritime south on the continental north. Multipurpose assets capable of sea and riverine patrolling were crucial to both Chinese and European imperial systems in the region. Similarly, in more recent times, American operations in the Vietnam War reinforced the notion that, in the SCS, naval power has the potential to exert influence far inland. Conversely, as the early years of World War II demonstrated, land-based air power, whether in the form of aircraft or, as would be the case today, missiles, has proven its ability to limit maritime operations in this theater.

In the SCS, prospects for stability and cooperation are linked to its integration with today's global economy and the international legal order, with initiatives on environmental protection, the safety of navigation, and resource exploration at the forefront of regional confidence building. Between 2005 and 2008, the signing of a Joint Marine Seismic Undertaking represented a first attempt to cooperate on marine scientific research that brought together China, the Philippines, and Vietnam. Similarly, in the field of antipiracy, China, the ASEAN states, and five other partners (Japan, South Korea, India, Bangladesh, and Sri Lanka) have joined forces via their Regional Cooperation Agreement on Combating Piracy and Armed Robbery against Ships in Asia. This agreement, which was concluded in 2004, encompasses information sharing, capacity building, and cooperative exercises. The joint exploration of oil resources has been regarded as another potential catalyst for stability. The 2006 agreement between China and Vietnam for their joint exploration in the Gulf of Tonkin/Beibu is a case in point. Progress has thus far been limited to preliminary phases of research and study, and there has been little agreement among the parties concerning actual production sharing. Yet, taken together, such initiatives seem to have set the foundations for a more constructive atmosphere.

Outside powers like the United States and Japan are undoubtedly interested in promoting maritime security cooperation and capacity building in the SCS. Programs like the Pacific Partnership, which focuses on humanitarian and civic assistance as well as disaster relief for the Southeast Asian countries, both embody shared interests and encourage cooperative action.[94] Non-warfighting uses of naval power have a direct impact on local populations and can create wider support for the beneficial presence of outside naval forces in the theater. Such activities are not confined to the United States. In June 2010 JDS *Kunisaki*, one of the amphibious ships of the Japanese Maritime Self-Defense

Force, joined the USN in providing medical assistance to more than eight hundred locals in Cambodia, marking Japan's contribution as one of the most significant among those of the program's partner nations, and confirming its potential as a responsible partner in security. Recent talks between Japan and Indonesia to enhance security cooperation in antipiracy activities further suggest Japan's growing military maturity and political willingness to be involved in Southeast Asia. There can be no doubt of this theater's importance to Japan, or of its potential economic and military role there.

Although economic interdependence has established a basic framework for cooperation, competing nationalisms have tended to cut the other way. This tension has been exacerbated by the uneven distribution of economic and military power in the region, and by China's declared determination to recover from "a century of humiliation" and to resume what many Chinese clearly regard as its rightful regional preeminence. Rivalries, in turn, fuel competition over territorial ownership, with a few groups of islands becoming the battle line where political legitimacy, territorial sovereignty, and national prestige are decided. In this complex power game, naval power offers the means to impose political will and the strategic flexibility to enforce diplomatic solutions. The January 1974 Battle of the Paracel Islands and the March 1988 Johnson South Reef Skirmish in the Spratlys, both of which involved China and Vietnam, were early harbingers of how far naval power would contribute to shaping territorial claims and national rivalries. In the first clash, China's superior navy allowed it to seize the initiative, take the Vietnamese off balance, and also prevent any confrontation from escalating out of proportion. In the second clash, the Chinese decision to take possession of a reef within an established Vietnamese-controlled area constituted a carefully crafted political message to that effect, "a deliberate challenge of *teaching them a lesson*" (emphasis in the original).[95]

The current naval buildup in the region, coupled with China's recent behavior, add to the notion that naval power is likely to be crucial in determining how shifting political balances and rivalries will be decided. In the face of preponderant Chinese naval power, other coastal states are beefing up their sea denial capabilities, and are investing in submarines and platforms for ASW operations. The PLAN is also poised to acquire considerable sea-based as well as land-based access-denial assets. The emergence of China as a major regional military player is only part of its wider ascendancy on the international stage. As such, the strategic calculation of Chinese advantages on a regional scale cannot be disentangled from considerations of the country's ever-growing dependence on global trade and remote sources of energy. On balance, it seems obvious that no country has a greater interest than China in the continued flow of commerce across the SCS. What remains unclear is the extent to which the country's muscular enforcement of legally unconfirmed territorial claims will undermine cooperation and instead fuel fears and conflict.

In the South China Sea, national strategy and maritime strategy are so inextricably linked as to be almost indistinguishable. In terms of strategic posture, it remains essential for outside powers such as the United States to have access to the region as a staging area for operations centering on carrier-based air power, precision strikes, and submarine actions. This is a political statement of force, power, and will, whose principal object must be to deter and dissuade those that might seek to profit from regional disorder. Conversely, the United States' employment of its naval forces in a constabulary role, in cooperation with its regional partners, will contribute to securing American political influence and help ensure the stability of world trade, for which the South China Sea seems certain to remain a vital artery.

NOTES

1. Nicholas John Spykman, "Frontiers, Security, and International Organization," *American Geographical Society* 32, no. 3 (1942): 437.

2. Insular features dominate the national landscapes of many of the states facing the SCS. Indonesia is a case in point. It is the world's largest island nation, with approximately 17,500 islands, fewer than half of which are inhabited.

3. Victor Prescott and Clive Schofield, *Undelimited Maritime Boundaries of the Asian Rim in the Pacific Ocean*, Maritime Briefing 3, no.1 (Durham: International Boundaries Research Unit, 2001), 58.

4. All littoral states in the SCS are parties to UNCLOS, with the exception of non-UN member Taiwan. UNCLOS empowers littoral states with maritime jurisdiction over the 12-nautical-mile breadth of territorial waters from their baseline along the coast, with an exclusive economic zone out to 200 nautical miles as well as continental shelf rights. The text of the convention can be accessed at www.un.org/Depts/los/convention _agreements/texts/unclos/UNCLOS-TOC.htm.

5. Clive Schofield and Ian Storey, *The South China Sea Dispute: Increasing Stakes and Rising Tensions* (Washington, DC: Jamestown Foundation, 2009), 8.

6. Clive Schofield, "Dangerous Ground: A Geopolitical Overview of the South China Sea," in *Security and International Politics in the South China Sea*, ed. Sam Bateman and Ralf Emmers (Abingdon, UK: Routledge, 2009), 15–16.

7. UNEP/GEF South China Sea Project, *Strategic Action Programme for the South China Sea* (New York: United Nations Environment Program and Global Environment Facility, 2008), 1; www.unepscs.org/.

8. UNEP Coordinating Body on the Seas of East Asia, *State of the Maritime Environment Report for the East Asian Seas 2009* (New York: United Nations

Environment Program Coordinating Body on the Seas of East Asia, 2010), 41; www
.cobsea.org/publications.html.

9. UNEP/GEF South China Sea Project, *Strategic Action Programme*, 3, 9, 19.

10. David Rosenberg, "Fisheries Management in the South China Sea," in *Security and International Politics*, ed. Bateman and Emmers, 61–62.

11. Schofield, "Dangerous Ground," 17.

12. FAO Fisheries and Aquaculture Department, *The State of World Fisheries and Aquaculture 2008* (New York: Food and Agriculture Organization of the United Nations, 2009), 34, www.fao.org/docrep/011/i0250e/i0250e00.htm.

13. UNEP/GEF South China Sea Project, *Strategic Action Programme*, 35.

14. FAO, *World Fisheries*, 34.

15. Rosenberg, "Fisheries Management," 62–3.

16. Mention of the navigational risks posed by the Paracel and Spratly Islands can be found in ancient Chinese written sources. Cf. Marwyn S. Samuels, *Contest for the South China Sea* (New York: Methuen, 1982), 10–12; and Stein Tønnenson, "The History of the Dispute," in *War or Peace in the South China Sea?* ed. Timo Kivimäki (Copenhagen: Nordic Institute of Asian Studies Press, 2002), 7.

17. The evolution of the SCS as a wider trading area before the fourteenth century is thoroughly examined by Pierre-Yves Manguin, "Trading Ships of the South China Sea: Shipbuilding Techniques and Their Role in the History of the Development of Asian Trade Networks," *Journal of the Economic and Social History of the Orient* 36, no. 3 (1993): 255–64.

18. Andrew R. Wilson, "The Maritime Transformation of Ming China," in *China Goes to Sea: Maritime Transformation in Comparative Historical Perspective*, ed. Andrew S. Erikson, Lyle J. Goldstein, and Carnes Lord (Annapolis, MD: Naval Institute Press, 2009), 243.

19. Wilson, "Maritime Transformation." See also Jacques Dars, *La Marine Chinoise du Xe Siècle au XIVe Siècle* (Paris: Etudes d'histoire maritime, 1992), 37–49; John K. Fairbank, "Maritime and Continental in China's History," in *The Cambridge History of China, Volume 12: Republican China: 1912–1949*, ed. J. K. Fairbank and Dennis Twitchett (Cambridge: Cambridge University Press, 1983), part 1, 14–17; Bernard D. Cole, *The Great Wall at Sea: China's Navy Enters the 21st Century* (Annapolis, MD: Naval Institute Press, 2001), 2–6; and Samuels, *Contest*, 13–22.

20. Fairbank, "Maritime," 12–13.

21. The dynamic yet local nature of maritime trade meant that piracy remained a recurrent problem in the SCS. By the beginning of the nineteenth century, pirate families had organized themselves into associations commanding several hundred ships. See Wilson, "Maritime Transformation," 260–64; Robert J. Anthony, "Piracy in the South China Coast through Modern Times," in *Piracy and Maritime Crime: Historical and Modern Case Studies*, ed. Bruce A. Ellman, Andrew Forbes, and David Rosenberg, Newport Paper 35 (Newport, RI: Naval War College Press, 2010), 35–50.

22. This was the case with the institution in 1370–71 of regional naval commands, or *wei*, which were responsible for constabulary-like missions along rivers and on the coast. See Wilson, "Maritime Transformation," 247–55.

23. Fairbank, "Maritime," 14.

24. Dars, *La Marine Chinoise*, 80–112.

25. This seems to be true even during the period of oceanic expansion under the Ming Dynasty. Dars, *La Marine Chinoise*, 181.

26. Ibid., 272–352. Also see Bruce E. Elleman, "The Neglect and Nadir of Chinese Maritime Policy under the Qing," in *China Goes to Sea*, ed. Erikson, Goldstein, and Lord, 290–301.

27. Gerald S. Graham, *The China Station. War and Diplomacy, 1830–1860* (Oxford: Oxford University Press, 1978), 5–6.

28. Samuels, *Contest*, 45; Elleman, "Neglect and Nadir," 311–12.

29. Vice Admiral Cyprian Bridge, "Duties and Classes of Ships on the China Station," draft memorandum, China Station, 1902 (Printed Memorandum, Cawdor Papers, box 294, Carmarthenshire Service). The author wishes to thank Hiraku Yabuki for kindly providing a typewritten copy of this memorandum.

30. Ibid.

31. Euan Graham, *Japan's Sea Lane Security, 1940–2004: A Matter of Life and Death?* (Abingdon, UK: Routledge, 2006), 71–76.

32. David C. Evans and Mark R. Peattie, *Kaigun: Strategy, Tactics, and Technology in the Imperial Japanese Navy, 1887–1941* (Annapolis, MD: Naval Institute Press, 1997), 140.

33. Mark R. Peattie, *Sunburst: The Rise of Japanese Air Power, 1909–1941* (London: Chatham House, 2001), 167–69. On Japanese preparations for the air war in the Pacific and in Southeast Asia, see Koichi Shimada, "The Opening Air Offensive against the Philippines," in *The Japanese Navy in World War II: In the Words of Former Japanese Naval Officers*, 2nd rev. edition, ed. David C. Evans (Annapolis, MD: Naval Institute Press, 1986), 71–104.

34. During the period 1942–44, the Japanese Navy fought three major battles: Midway, the Philippine Sea, and Leyte Gulf. These three alone consumed more than 1 million tons of oil. Mark P. Parillo, *The Japanese Merchant Marine in World War II* (Annapolis, MD: Naval Institute Press, 1993), 28.

35. Ibid., 247, 215.

36. See H. P. Willmott, *The Second World War in the Far East* (London: Cassell, 2002), 204–5.

37. Data on submarine war patrols in the Pacific are from the Joint Army–Navy Assessment Committee, reported by Clay Blair Jr., *Silent Victory: The US Submarine War against Japan* (Annapolis, MD: Naval Institute Press, 2001), appendix F, 900–983.

38. Ibid., 966–75.

39. Samuel E. Morison, *History of the United States Naval Operations in World War II, Volume 13: The Liberation of the Philippines—Luzon, Mindanao, the Visayas, 1944–1945* (Oxford: Oxford University Press, 1959), 168–69.

40. Norman Polmar, *Aircraft Carriers: A History of Carrier Aviation and Its Influence on World Events, Volume 1: 1909–1945* (Washington, DC: Potomac Books, 2006), 457.

41. Morison, *United States Naval Operations*, 171.

42. George W. Baer, *One Hundred Years of Seapower: The US Navy, 1890–1990* (Stanford, CA: Stanford University Press, 1996), 392.

43. Ibid., 388–91.

44. Bernard B. Cole, *Sea Lanes and Pipelines: Energy Security in Asia* (Westport, CT: Preager Security International, 2008), 122.

45. These data are reported by Joshua H. Ho, "The Security of Sea Lanes in Southeast Asia," in *Asian Energy Security: The Maritime Dimension*, ed. Hongyi Lai (New York: Palgrave Macmillan, 2009), 206–7.

46. Ibid., 208.

47. Cole, *Sea Lanes*, 122–23.

48. Hongyi Lai, "Introduction," in *Asian Energy Security*, ed. Lai, 3–5.

49. Hongyi Lai, "Security of China's Energy Imports," in *Asian Energy Security*, ed. Lai, 51.

50. United Nations Environment Program Coordinating Body on the Seas of East Asia, "State of the Maritime Environment Report for the East Asian Seas 2009," 34–35; http://www.unep.org/pdf/StateMarineEnvEastAsia2009.pdf.

51. Sam Bateman, "Conclusion: The Prospect for a Cooperative Management Regime," in *Security and International Politics*, ed. Bateman and Emmers, 237.

52. Klaus Dodds, *Geopolitics in a Changing World* (Harlow, UK: Pearson Education, 2000), 32.

53. In this regard, one scholar noted how, between November 2009 and March 2010, China and Taiwan increased their academic and political dialogues concerning the possibility to cooperate to protect their common interests in the SCS. The overlapping nature of their claims would be a primary pillar underpinning such developments. Li Mingjiang, "South China Sea: Emerging China–Taiwan Cooperation," *RSIS Commentaries*, April 19, 2010, https://www.rsis.edu.sg/rsis-publication/rsis/1331-south -china-sea-emerging-chin/#.VVecW2Aki68. The Kuomintang's 1947 map can be found at https://upload.wikimedia.org/wikipedia/commons/4/43/1947_Nanhai_Zhudao.png.

54. All littoral states in the SCS are parties to UNCLOS, with the exception of non-UN member Taiwan. UNCLOS defines a state's territorial sea as extending 12 nautical miles from a baseline (normally coinciding with the high-tide mark) along the coast. The exclusive economic zone extends 200 miles from the same line. UNCLOS also affords rights of economic exploitation and environmental protection for the continental shelf. The text of the convention can be accessed at www.un.org/Depts/los/convention _agreements/texts/unclos/UNCLOS-TOC.htm.

55. This is according to data developed by Rommel Banlaoi, reproduced by Schofield and Storey, *South China Sea Dispute*, 10.

56. Leszek Buszynski and Iskandar Sazlan, "Maritime Claims and Energy Cooperation in the South China Sea," *Contemporary Southeast Asia: A Journal of International and Strategic Affairs* 29, no. 1 (2007): 143–71, at 147.

57. The text of the July communiqué is at www.aseansec.org/24899.htmQ1.

58. Permanent Mission of the People's Republic of China, "Note to the Secretary General of the United Nations," May 7, 2009, www.un.org/Depts/los/clcs_new/submis sions_files/vnm37_09/chn_2009re_vnm.pdf.

59. Andrew S. Erickson and Kevin Bond, "Dredging under the Radar: China Expands South Sea Foothold," *The National Interest*, August 26, 2015, http://www .nationalinterest.org/feature/dredging-under-the-radar-china-expands-south-sea -foothold-13701?page=show.

60. Lee Lai To, "China, the USA and the South China Sea Conflicts," *Security Dialogue* 34, no. 1 (2003): 34.

61. Jay Solomon, "China Rejects US Efforts in Maritime Spats," *Wall Street Journal*, July 25, 2010, http://www.wsj.com/articles/SB100014240527487039589045753882623711 73300.

62. A number of senior US officials have voiced growing American concerns over Chinese pressures on foreign companies, notably British Petroleum and Exxon Mobil, to suspend work on projects off the Vietnamese coast. See Schofield and Storey, *South China Sea Dispute*, 39–40.

63. James T. Conway, Gary Roughead, and Thad D. Allen, "A Cooperative Strategy for the 21st Century," *Naval War College Review* 61, no. 2 (2008): 10.

64. US Department of Defense, *Quadrennial Defense Review Report* (Washington, DC: US Government Printing Office, 2006), 47.

65. US Department of Defense, *The Asia-Pacific Maritime Security Strategy: Achieving US National Security Objectives in a Changing Environment* (Washington, DC: US Government Printing Office, 2015), 22–23.

66. Testimony of Deputy Assistant Secretary of Defense Robert Scher, Asian and Pacific Security Affairs, Office of the Secretary of Defense, before the US–China Economic and Security Review Commission, February 4, 2010, 36, www.uscc.gov /hearings/2010hearings/transcripts/10_02_04_trans/10_02_04_trans.pdf.

67. Alessio Patalano, "Japan's Contemporary Naval Power and Regional Maritime Cooperation," in *Australia and Its Maritime Interests: At Home and in the Region*, ed. Andrew Forbes (Canberra: Royal Australian Navy Sea Power Centre, 2008), 131–40.

68. This subject is thoroughly examined by Graham, *Japan's Sea Lane Security.*

69. David Rosenberg and Christopher Chung, "Maritime Security in the South China Sea: Coordinating Coastal and User State Priorities," *Ocean Development and International Law* 39, no. 1 (2008): 55–56. In November 2009 Japan hosted the first-ever Japan–Mekong summit, at which it pledged $5 billion in development assistance. Testimony of Scher before US–China Economic and Security Review Commission, 22, http://origin.www.uscc.gov/sites/default/files/transcripts/2.4.10HearingTranscript.pdf.

70. Patalano, "Japan's Contemporary Naval Power," 135.

71. Tomohisa Takei, "Kaiyō Shinkindai ni okeru Kaijōjieitai" [The JMSDF in the New Maritime Era], *Hatō* 11 (2008): 16–18.

72. Ibid., 20–21.

73. Rosenberg and Chung, "Maritime Security," 56.

74. Albert Palazzo, Antony Trentini, Jonathan Hawkins, and Malcolm Brailey, *Projecting Force: The Australian Army and Maritime Strategy,* Study Paper 317 (Canberra: Land Warfare Studies Centre, 2010), 5–15.

75. Cf. Rommel Banlaoi, "Philippines–Australia Maritime Security Cooperation and the Status of Visiting Forces Agreement," in *Australia,* ed. Forbes, 181–92.

76. "Australian–Indonesia Coordinated Patrol," April 27, 2010 http://indonesia .embassy.gov.au/jakt/MR10_038.html.

77. Kathrin Hille and Tim Johnston, "SE Asia Arms Purchases Fuel Fears of Clashes," *Financial Times,* March 14, 2010.

78. Robert Karniol, "Arms Resurgence in South-East Asia," *Straits Times,* March 15, 2010.

79. For Thailand, see International Institute for Strategic Studies, *The Military Balance 2010* (London: Routledge, 2010), 390. For Malaysia, see National Institute for Defense Studies, "Southeast Asia: Signs of a Changing Myanmar Problem," *East Asian Strategic Review 2010* (Tokyo: Japan Times, 2010), 162.

80. National Institute for Defense Studies, "Southeast Asia," 163.

81. Quoted in ibid., 164.

82. Robert Karniol, "Vietnam Bolstering Spratly Firepower," *Straits Times,* May 10, 2010.

83. There is a substantial literature looking at China's growing naval power and strategy. See, e.g., Bernard D. Cole, *The Great Wall at Sea: China Enters the Twenty-First*

Century (Annapolis, MD: Naval Institute Press, 2001); Thomas M. Kane, *Chinese Grand Strategy and Maritime Power* (London: Frank Cass, 2002); John Wilson Lewis and Xue Litai, *Imagined Enemies: China Prepares for Uncertain War* (Stanford, CA: Stanford University Press, 2006); Peter Howarth, *China's Rising Sea Power: The PLA Navy's Submarine Challenge* (London: Routledge, 2006); James R. Holmes and Toshi Yoshihara, *Chinese Naval Strategy in the 21st Century: The Turn to Mahan* (London: Routledge, 2007); and Toshi Yoshihara and James R. Holmes, *Red Star over the Pacific: China's Rise and the Challenge to US Maritime Strategy* (Annapolis, MD: Naval Institute Press, 2010).

84. Robert S. Ross, "China's Naval Nationalism: Sources, Prospects, and the US Response," *International Security* 34, no. 2 (2009): 46–81; Xu Qi, "Maritime Geostrategy and the Development of the Chinese Navy in the Early Twenty-First Century," *Naval War College Review* 59, no. 4 (2006): 47–67.

85. James R. Holmes and Toshi Yoshihara, "China's 'Caribbean' in the South China Sea," *SAIS Review* 26, no. 1 (2006): 85.

86. US Office of Naval Intelligence, "The People's Liberation Army Navy: A Modern Navy with Chinese Characteristics," 2009, 21–23, http://fas.org/irp/agency/oni /pla-navy.pdf.

87. Quoted by Ronald O'Rourke, *China Naval Modernization: Implications for US Navy Capabilities: Background and Issues for Congress* (Washington, DC: Congressional Research Service, 2010), 57.

88. Jiaxin Li, "China's New Generation of Coast Guard Ship Is Powerful," *People's China Daily*, July 29, 2015, http://en.people.cn/n/2015/0729/c90000-8927696.html.

89. Rosenberg and Chung, "Maritime Security," 60.

90. Chew Men Leong, "Operationalizing Cooperative Regional Maritime Security," in *Australia*, ed. Forbes, 158.

91. US Department of Defense, *Asia-Pacific Maritime Security Strategy*, 14.

92. See the legal argument presented by Jonathan G. Odom, "The True ''Lies' of the Impeccable Incident: What Really Happened, Who Disregarded International Law, and Why Every Nation (outside China) Should be Concerned," *Michigan State Journal of International Law* 18, no. 3 (2010): 1–42.

93. Admiral Timothy Keating, US Navy, quoted by Odom, "True 'Lies,'" 17.

94. E.g., in the four-month-long 2008 edition of the program, 90,000 patients were treated by medical teams onboard the hospital ship USNS *Mercy*, including 1,300 surgery patients and 14,000 dental patients.

95. Jou Ji, "The PLA Navy in the Changing World Order: The South China Sea Theatre," in *Maritime Power in the China Seas*, ed. Dick Sherwood (Canberra: Australian Defence Studies Centre, 1994), 97.

CHAPTER 6

The Arctic

From Frozen Desert to Open Polar Sea?

KLAUS DODDS

> Global climate change has catapulted the Arctic into the centre of geopolitics, as melting ice transforms the region from one of primarily scientific interest into a maelstrom of competing commercial, national security and environmental concerns, with profound implications for the international legal and political system.
>
> —C. Ebinger and E. Zametakis, "The Geopolitics of Arctic Melt"[1]

Since the European Renaissance, geographers and explorers have speculated about the state of the Arctic, and in particular that this frigid region might one day be ice free (not literally free from ice but rather, in contemporary parlance, as being a state of affairs where the Arctic Ocean is covered by less than 1 million square kilometers in any given season). Cartographers such as Mercator envisaged such a scenario, and represented both polar regions as open and ice-free zones, enticing men and their ships to explore these remote, at least from a European perspective, and alluring domains.[2] From the seventeenth century onward, reports were received from British and Russian sailors claiming to have traveled through open seas, as they sought various shipping routes north of European and North American continental spaces. The existence of an open polar sea was to become more than simply a geographical curiosity in the mid–nineteenth century, when a feverish series of searches were launched in search of an expedition organized by John Franklin to search for the fabled Northwest Passage.[3] Convinced that Franklin's missing men might be stranded in an open polar sea, explorers such as Elisha Kent Kane participated in several rescue expeditions in the vain hope that Franklin and his comrades might have survived the long polar nights and austere living conditions. The search activities for Franklin and his men did help to generate an extraordinary boost to the mapping and surveying of the Canadian Arctic.

Although Franklin and his expeditionary members were never found, the debate about the status of the high Arctic was an important one, and Kane was not the only explorer to be fascinated by the specter of ice-free seas. The American explorer Isaac Hayes contended that there were "thermometric gateways to the Pole," enabling relatively frictionless travel to the top of the world.[4] By the end of the nineteenth century, the prospect of finding, let alone navigating, this open polar sea appeared to be receding, as a whole series of expeditions failed to substantiate these claims. Subsequent expeditions involving ships such as the *Jeannette* were crushed by pack ice, and the survivors returned home with tales of monstrous ice-consuming objects caught within its grasp.

Although the open polar sea theory diminished in popularity by the end of the nineteenth century, recent events have drawn attention once again to the physical geographies of the High Arctic. Satellite imagery, in conjunction with scientific research pertaining to climate change, revealed new patterns of sea ice thickness and distribution. It appears to be a very real prospect that in the near future the Arctic Ocean may become ice free, at least for a limited period in the summer season.[5] Although the Arctic was transited in the twentieth century, there is a real possibility of expanding maritime traffic via the Northwest Passage and the Northern Sea Route (NSR).[6] Rising volumes of sea traffic within the Arctic region itself will also be witnessed. In the case of the NSR, journey times between Europe and Asia could be dramatically reduced, because ships would no longer need to travel via the Suez Canal.[7] The shipping potential of the Northwest Passage is considered to be rather more marginal, given prevailing weather and sea ice conditions.

This chapter explores how recent debates about the Arctic Ocean have centered on questions pertaining to accessibility, resource potential, governance, and maritime security.[8] Climate change is clearly the major geopolitical driver, because most analysts concur that the Arctic is a region on the cusp of substantial change. This chapter considers a series of vectors, such as the geographies of the maritime Arctic, historical context, current geopolitical circumstances, current maritime operations and issues, and, finally, implications for maritime strategy. Navigating between those critics who foresee a new era of enhanced geopolitical competition and others who suggest greater cooperation and governance sharing, I conclude with a sober assessment of a region that is attracting ever-greater resource and territorial pressures including the exploitation of fish and hydrocarbons, the mapping of the seabed, and the militarization of the High North.

THE PHYSICAL GEOGRAPHY
OF THE MARITIME ARCTIC

The Arctic region has been defined in a variety of ways, including all land and sea at or beyond the 66.5° northern latitude. The Arctic Ocean is, as the American geophysicist Henry Pollack records,

> a roughly circular ocean with the geographic North Pole at its center. The diameter of the ocean is about 2,800 miles, with North America and Greenland sitting on one side, and Europe and Asia on the other. The entire ocean lies north of the Arctic Circle, and thus experiences the annual extremes of solar illumination—including some days of around-the-clock darkness in the winter and unending daylight in summer. For as long as people have been paying attention, much of the ocean has remained frozen year-round in a vast sheet of sea ice.[9]

The Arctic Ocean is about five times the size of the Mediterranean Sea, with large continental shelves originating from continental landmasses. The central Arctic Ocean is approximately 2 nautical miles in depth.

The distribution and thickness of the sea ice has been subject to considerable academic study, and a number of seasonal and longer-term characteristics are noteworthy. As with the Southern Ocean, the short summer season acts as a catalyst for sea ice breakup, and subsequent melting exposes open water. This is a critical factor in shaping navigational accessibility. In the winter the sea ice freezes again. During the first half of the twentieth century, Pollack notes,

> about one-third of the sea ice melted and refroze each year, leaving two-thirds of the ocean with older ice, up to about five years old in places. The older ice is also thicker, occasionally reaching a thickness of fifteen feet or more. . . . Because sea ice is always on the move—drifting from the Far East, over the North Pole, on toward Scandinavia, and exiting the Atlantic—no extensive region of the Arctic Ocean has ice much older than five years old.[10]

The study of the basic processes of sea ice formation, melting, and movement has progressed considerably in the last fifty years, helped by the existence of scientific stations, aerial photography, and submarines equipped with radar. All these sources have contributed to a pool of knowledge about ice distribution and thickness. In the last two decades, thanks in large part to the existence of Earth-orbiting satellites, a synoptic overview has been possible, and this in turn has confirmed the attenuation of Arctic sea ice. Specifically, the thinning of polar sea ice is accelerating, sea ice coverage as a percentage of the Arctic Ocean basin is diminishing, and the number of ice-free navigation days is increasing. Although there are unquestionably local and regional variations in these generalized claims, the Arctic as a whole shows a clear trend toward diminishing ice cover. There is also a clear trend in favor of young sea ice, as older sea ice is subject to melting. In August 2007 it was announced that the Northwest Passage was free of ice, when the distribution of summer sea ice was recorded at what was then an all-time low. In 2008 the Northwest Passage and the NSR were opened for a limited period in the Arctic summer season. As Pollack concludes, "By the end of the twentieth century, the summer sea ice had diminished by some 25 percent from its mid-century extent. And as the older sea ice was replaced by younger ice, the average thickness of the sea ice diminished, to about half its mid-century measurement."[11] It is not uncommon to read that scientists believe that in the next two to three decades, the Arctic Ocean might well be ice free for much of the summer season. This would be an extraordinary change to an environment that has experienced ice for 50 million years.

The implications for an ice-free Arctic are considered throughout this chapter, but here it is worth noting some of the immediate issues at stake. Enhanced accessibility of the Arctic Ocean, especially via major transit routes such as the NSR, will facilitate long-distance trade, and may also make human activities such as fishing, mining, and tourism easier or more viable economically. Sea ice loss may also have an adverse impact on indigenous and northern communities that have adapted to its presence. In the winter months sea ice acts as a natural barrier to stormy weather, and thus protects coastal communities from the ravages of the sea. With decreasing sea ice cover, and the disappearance of multiyear ice in particular, coastal erosion has already worsened, with severe consequences for some communities in the North American Arctic. The presence and persistence of sea ice has also played an important role in subsistence hunting for animals such as seals. Uncertainty over sea ice distribution and thickness is a cause of concern for indigenous communities, which may face longer and more perilous journeys to the edge of the sea ice.

Intensifying resource extraction in both the maritime and terrestrial Arctic also has consequences for ecosystems and indigenous livelihoods, including fishing, reindeer herding, whaling, and sealing.

THE HISTORICAL BACKGROUND

World War II confirmed the strategic importance of the Arctic region. The Arctic convoys between the United Kingdom and the United States to the northern ports of the Soviet Union, including Murmansk, were a vital element in the Allied war effort. Between 1941 and 1945, seventy-eight convoys traversed the Arctic Ocean, delivering vital supplies to the Eastern Front. Harassed by German U-boats, eighty-five merchant vessels were sunk, along with sixteen Royal Naval warships. Norway became a major element in German naval strategy, and warships such as *Tirpitz* were based in the Norwegian fjords, ready to attack convoys and their armed protectors. Notwithstanding these German efforts, however, British escorts were able to resist repeated assaults in the Barents Sea and the Norwegian Sea.

At higher northern latitudes, the Norwegian territory of the Spitsbergen Islands featured as an active war theater. Allied soldiers were based there in 1941 in order to prevent German forces from occupying the islands and taking advantage of Soviet and Norwegian coal mines. Apart from the strategic resources of Spitsbergen, the collection of reliable weather data in the North Atlantic and Arctic Ocean was critical to Allied and German forces alike. Both sides not only wanted to collect such data but also to deny access to their adversaries. Reliable information on weather was essential to the routing of shipping convoys and for planning naval operations. Collection points included ships at sea, long-range aircraft, and a ring of weather stations dotted around Canada, Greenland, Iceland, Ireland, and Norway. In 1941 the British launched Operation Gauntlet and destroyed a weather station on Bear Island and another on Spitsbergen. However, the German forces retained other Spitsbergen-based weather stations, including Haudegen on Nordaustlandet, which operated from September 1944 to September 1945.

On the other side of the world, the Japanese attacked and occupied two of the Aleutian Islands, Attu and Kiska, at the southern edge of the Arctic, by way of diverting US forces away from what was intended to be a decisive engagement around Midway Atoll. During the Aleutian Islands campaign, American and Canadian forces attacked Japanese forces on Attu. Once the Japanese occupation had been repulsed, the US military committed itself to building weather stations and airfields and to upgrading the naval facilities in its most northerly territory. The Aleutians thus became a major transit stop for planes sent from the United States to the Soviet Union under the Lend-Lease Agreement. Strategically, both the United States and the Japanese recognized the value of the islands in terms of Pacific Ocean transportation routes, and US commanders considered that Japanese forces based on them might undertake assaults against military and civilian installations in the Pacific Northwest.

The onset of the Cold War swiftly led to the Arctic being incorporated into military planning by both sides. General Hap Arnold noted in 1946 that "if a third world war breaks out, its strategic centre will be the North Pole." Arnold urged North American citizens to study their globes in order to appreciate the new geostrategic realities—in particular how access to and control of the high latitudes were critical. Arnold was not alone, as both military and popular writers reflected on the newfound significance of the Arctic, in part because the flight paths over the Arctic represented the shortest distance whereby new generations of long-range bombers (and later missiles) could reach their intended targets.[12] The high latitudes were the new front line of an emerging Cold War geopolitical landscape and seascape.

During the Cold War, three developments were critical in transforming the Arctic's strategic significance. First, there was a recognition that the long-range bomber was not only annihilating distance but also highlighting the significance of attack corridors throughout the Arctic. Second, as a response to this recognition, new measures pertaining to early warning surveillance and aerial defense ensured that the Arctic coastal states would invest in the monitoring and surveillance of the High North. And third, the development of nuclear-powered icebreakers—and, more worryingly, nuclear submarines armed with sea-launched ballistic missiles—overturned the notion that the ice-infested seas posed formidable obstacles to naval operations.

The formation of the North Atlantic Treaty Organization (NATO) in April 1949 brought a number of Arctic littoral states—including Canada, Iceland, Greenland (an autonomous territory of Denmark), Norway, and the United States—into a new strategic partnership. The United States set up military bases across the High Arctic as part of a global strategy to contain the Soviet Union and its naval and aerial forces, especially those based in Murmansk on the Kola Peninsula. By the early 1950s surveillance of the North American Arctic was being upgraded with the initiation of the Distant Early Warning Line and the opening of Thule Air Base in northern Greenland. At this stage the focus was primarily on the danger posed by Soviet air power rather than the Soviet Northern Fleet.

US military personnel were also aware of the fact that a better understanding of polar ice and weather would benefit both air- and sea-based operational planning. The US Research and Development Board created a special panel on Arctic environments in the late 1940s. A whole network of research stations and institutes—such as the Arctic Research Laboratory in Alaska and the Office of Naval Research's Arctic Program—consolidated this trend toward developing new expertise on polar environments. The US Navy also had at its disposal the Hydrographic Office and the Underwater Sound Laboratory—and the latter was critical, given the manifold complications posed by shifting ice and the mixing of cold and warm waters in the polar convergence zone. The US Army established the Snow, Ice, and Permafrost Research Establishment (SIPRE) in 1949 to investigate glacial icesheets, and notably to aid military planning on the Greenland icesheet. In the late 1950s SIPRE researchers were instrumental in planning and implementing Project Iceworm, an audacious plan to construct missile facilities under the Greenland ice cap.

Throughout the Cold War, in the maritime domain, the US Navy's efforts to develop sonar capacities in ice-filled waters were a major technological challenge. The many relevant issues to be considered included the interrelationship between salinity and temperature, the din caused by polar storms, the distracting sounds of mammals such as seals and whales, the movement of ice (especially compression), and the changing distribution of sea ice throughout the seasons. The US Navy's Arctic Submarine Laboratory, located in the warmer climes of San Diego, was at the forefront of investigating submarine operations at high latitudes. Waldo Lyon, the director of the laboratory, was at the forefront of this research, even though some naval officers had initially expressed skepticism that the Arctic would ever be considered a theater of operations.

The period between the 1950s and 1980s was dominated by the rising significance of submarines rather than long-range bombers, which played an increasingly critical role in gathering intelligence, and in the conduct of war, if that proved necessary.[13] Naval strategists had to confront a series of profound geographical features, including the fact that the Arctic Ocean is a closed sea with only three major entry or exit points: the Bering Strait, the Canadian Archipelago, and the Norwegian Sea. Arctic ice also limits what naval forces can do in terms of operations and capabilities. Arctic maritime geography is also very varied, ranging from the comparatively shallow Barents Sea and Kara Sea to the depths of the central Arctic Ocean. Some areas of the Arctic, like the Barents Sea, are more icebound, though other bodies of water are comparatively ice free, such as the Northern Norwegian Sea.

Recognizing these simple geographical facts was one thing. It was quite another to develop the needed capacities to be able to operate in the harshest natural environment of the Cold War era.[14] Two basic problems had to be overcome: first, to design sufficiently robust submarines with adequate navigation (and accompanying knowledge of sea ice) to traverse under the ice pack; and second, to develop adequate surveillance capabilities so that, from the US point of view, they could discover, monitor, and if necessary destroy Soviet submarines operating in the icy waters of the Arctic. This was a sizable challenge given the nature of the region itself. A Soviet submarine, it was feared, could end up virtually undetected in Canada's Baffin Bay (or worse, Hudson Bay). From there, it was but a comparatively short distance for any ballistic missile to be targeted at the United States. Canada's archipelagic geography was a strategic nightmare, for which the only mitigation was actually the ice itself; the shallow waters of the Canadian Arctic were a difficult operating environment for submarines because of poor sound propagation.

The varied physical geography of the Arctic added considerable complexity to naval operations. The US–NATO strategy was primarily directed toward Northern Scandinavia and the Kola Peninsula, site of the headquarters of the Soviet Northern Fleet. Surveying and patrolling the Northern Norwegian Sea alongside the Greenland–Iceland–United Kingdom gap was a major element in NATO's naval planning, because the natural gap between Greenland, Iceland, and the United Kingdom meant that Soviet vessels had to travel through this region if they were to follow an Atlantic route to the United States. US and Allied ships and submarines were frequently stationed there to survey and monitor. Their patrolling was supplemented by a network of underwater listening devices called SOSUS (for SOund SUrveillance System), designed to collect sonic information on Soviet naval movements. This task was complicated by the fact that the northerly parts of both the Atlantic Ocean and Pacific Ocean were major commercial shipping arenas. Both the US and Soviet navies were eager to test each other's capabilities, and thus they plotted voyages designed to traverse ever closer to their adversary's naval bases and installations. The diesel-powered US submarine *Boarfish* was sent to reconnoiter the Chukchi Sea as early as 1947–48.

A major turning point in US naval strategy was the launching of the nuclear-powered submarine *Nautilus*, which reached the North Pole under water in 1958. This was followed, in March 1959, by the surfacing of the USS *Skate* at the same geographical point. These voyages demonstrated that nuclear submarines could operate in all seasons, and with greater understanding of the Arctic Ocean Basin it became increasingly feasible to detect and avoid icebergs and judge when and how to break surface ice—all matters of great interest to the US Office of Naval Research. This expanding corpus of geographical knowledge about the Arctic and the North Atlantic coincided with civilian mapping projects, funded by the Defense Research Development Board, that were designed to enhance understanding of the seabed floor and the oceans' temperature profile. As Jacob Hamblin has noted, "Reliable data would allow the US Navy to colonize this environment, i.e., control or master it in order to best navigate it in the next war."[15] But there were also limits to what this knowledge could offer. Shallow waters were always going to be dangerous for submarines, especially given numerous natural underwater choke points that an adversary could use to predict likely movement.

By the 1970s both NATO and the Soviets had developed submarine-launched ballistic missiles. If a Soviet ballistic missile were to be fired from a submarine in the Barents Sea, it would take little more than 30 minutes to hit a target in North America. Although missiles were helping to annihilate distance, in one sense, concern was also being expressed that a new generation of Soviet submarines might, under the cover of Arctic sea ice, travel further and penetrate into areas such as Baffin Bay. If a missile were to be released from somewhere in the Canadian archipelago, it might reach its target in as little as 15 or 20 minutes. Not that such a dangerous approach would be necessary. The Soviet *Typhoon* class of submarine, which features in the popular film *The Hunt for Red October,* carried twenty nuclear missiles of sufficient range that they could be fired from what were effectively home waters, icebound or not, off the Kola Peninsula. As Oran Young wrote in the mid-1980s, "The *Typhoon* is designed specifically for operations in ice-covered waters, but any modern SSBN [i.e., nuclear-powered missile submarine] can perform its mission in the Arctic Basin. There are numerous points under the polar ice pack where all modern submarines can break through the surface to fire their missiles."[16]

The final years of the Cold War were arguably the tensest for the Arctic. From the US perspective, the Soviet Northern Fleet represented a formidable foe, deploying well over half of Soviet nuclear submarines. With enhanced missile and navigational capabilities, the need to evade NATO acoustic devices in the open ocean was becoming increasingly redundant. In the mid-1980s, in the midst of the Reagan administration, the United States initiated further upgrading of its continent-wide surveillance systems and military infrastructure, including updating the Distant Early Warning line (the so-called North Warning System) and building two new radar stations in Iceland. At the same time, the US submarine *Parche* was involved in tapping the Soviet submarine cable system in the Barents Sea, with the explicit purpose of trying to improve intelligence about Soviet submarine strategy and readiness.

The US Navy's Maritime Strategy (first described in 1982) codified an approach premised on an early, forceful, and global deployment of naval power.[17] In the Arctic region, this would have involved US submarine forces penetrating the home waters of the Soviet Northern Fleet and searching and destroying Soviet nuclear-powered submarines before they had reached a position to attack North American and European targets. More generally, during the early to middle 1980s, the Northern Flank received renewed attention from NATO planners, with an emphasis on controlling sea lines of communication, especially in the Barents Sea and Norwegian Sea.

Engaging the Soviet Northern Fleet, however, represented a formidable military challenge. In the mid-1980s the fleet had nearly 150 submarines, including nearly 40 nuclear missile submarines (SSBNs). Even if the US submarines were being rapidly deployed to the Barents Sea, those SSBNs could be deployed under the sea ice and then lie motionless and hence virtually undetected. If NATO's attack submarines attempted to engage those vessels, they would face the difficult task of distinguishing between Soviet SSBNs and escorting submarines. If only a small proportion of the SSBNs remained, they could still carry out a counterattack that would be devastating to US cities. Like the Soviet Union before it, Russia today continues to invest heavily in research on permafrost and sea ice distribution and thickness, in large part because of the strategic importance of the northern hinterland of the Soviet Union and the NSR.

It was against this grim background that hundreds of billions of dollars (and rubles) were spent during the Cold War for the purpose of generating an enhanced understanding of the Arctic as a maritime domain. The result was the thorough militarization of this northerly environment, with implications that are still evident—from rusting military infrastructure and dumped materials across the North American and Russian Arctic to an enduring disposition to treat the Arctic as a highly strategic zone. This is one of the main reasons why the Arctic Council, when created in 1996, was not given a mandate to consider security-related questions. On a more positive note, however, investment in glaciology and research on permafrost and sea ice grew considerably during the Cold War, and helped to generate considerable expertise in cyrospheric environments.

CURRENT GEOPOLITICAL CIRCUMSTANCES

Although the term "Arctic" has been defined using a variety of physical and ecological parameters, it is widely acknowledged that there are a relatively small number of Arctic states. The five Arctic Ocean coastal states are Canada, Greenland, Norway, Russia, and the United States. There are three other states—Finland, Iceland, and Sweden—with territory above the Arctic Circle but without Arctic Ocean coastlines. The five coastal states have reaffirmed their role in the maritime Arctic via the Ilulissat Declaration agreed in May 2008:

> The Arctic Ocean stands at the threshold of significant changes. Climate change and the melting of ice have a potential impact on vulnerable ecosystems, the livelihoods of local inhabitants and indigenous communities, and the potential exploitation of natural resources.
>
> By virtue of their sovereignty, sovereign rights and jurisdiction in large areas of the Arctic Ocean, the five coastal states are in a unique position to address these possibilities and challenges. In this regard, we recall that an extensive international legal framework applies to the Arctic Ocean as discussed between our representatives at the meeting in Oslo on 15 and 16 October 2007 at the level of senior officials. Notably, the Law of the Sea provides for important rights and obligations concerning the delineation of the outer limits of the continental shelf, the protection of the marine environment, including ice-covered areas, freedom of navigation, marine scientific research, and other uses of the sea. We remain committed to this legal framework and to the orderly settlement of any possible overlapping claims.
>
> This framework provides a solid foundation for responsible management by the five coastal States and other users of this Ocean through national implementation and application of relevant provisions. We therefore see no need to develop a new comprehensive international legal regime to govern the Arctic Ocean. We will keep abreast of the developments in the Arctic Ocean and continue to implement appropriate measures.[18]

This declaration is highly significant because it noted the role of the Arctic five in shaping the environmental, political, and legal geographies of the maritime Arctic. The Greenland-based meeting that produced the declaration considered the Arctic Ocean, maritime protection, marine safety, and climate change. The declaration's reference to the "orderly settlement of any possible overlapping claims" is also noteworthy because it reaffirmed the importance of the Law of the Sea as the primary mechanism for resolving any current and future issues regarding maritime boundaries and outer continental shelf delimitation. The five parties met again in March 2010 in Canada in order to engage in further dialogue and to promote cooperation on these issues. In addition, the Arctic Ocean coastal states have maintained a dialogue with one another on other areas of mutual concern, including search-and-rescue operations and, most recently, planning for possible fishing activities in the central Arctic Ocean.

The Ilulissat Declaration, with its explicit focus on the five coastal states, serves as a reminder of those parties that were absent. Other interested and affected states and organizations in the Arctic region include Finland, Iceland, and Sweden on one hand, and indigenous groups on the other hand, such as the Inuit Circumpolar Council and the Sami Council (so-called permanent participants in the Arctic Council). Although these indigenous stakeholders are members of the Arctic Council, they are not party to any potential disputes involving sovereign rights in the Arctic Ocean, the delimitation of maritime boundaries, and extended continental shelves. However, this did not prevent some members of the Arctic Council from expressing their unhappiness that an apparent schism was opening up between the eight Arctic states, the permanent participants, and the five Arctic Ocean coastal states.

The 2008 declaration represents an important milestone in the transformation of Arctic geopolitics and governance. Most Arctic commentators have agreed that a 1987 speech by the Soviet leader Mikhail Gorbachev in the northern city of Murmansk was the major turning point in the Arctic's geopolitics. In his speech, Gorbachev called for the Arctic to be demilitarized and declared a zone of peace. As he noted, "The Soviet Union is in favour of a radical lowering of the level of military confrontation in the region. Let the North of the globe, the Arctic, become a zone of peace. Let the North Pole be a pole of peace. We suggest that all interested states start talks on the limitation and scaling down of military activity in the North as a whole, in both the Eastern and Western Hemispheres."[19]

In the following decade, Arctic parties helped to shift the region's balance from a highly militarized environment with limited international cooperation to one characterized by the development of nascent regional structures. These included the 1991 Arctic Environmental Protection Strategy, the 1996 Arctic Council, and the 1993 Barents Euro-Arctic Council, which was designed to reduce military tension in the European High North and increase transboundary cooperation between Russia and the Nordic countries.[20]

Within a decade of the Gorbachev speech, northern cooperation became more widespread and institutionalized, and the European Union–sponsored Northern Dimension program led to further investment in cross-border cooperation between the Nordic EU members and Russia.

The creation of the Arctic Council in 1996 was highly progressive, in the sense of involving Arctic states, organizations of indigenous peoples, and observer states such as France, the United Kingdom, and, later, Asian states such as China, India, Japan, Singapore, and South Korea. Although it is a soft law institution, it did unquestionably cement a more cooperative spirit among former Cold War adversaries. What was feared in the period between 2008 and 2010 was the possibility that the Arctic Council might split between the five Arctic coastal states and other members. Ultimately, what helped to avert such a schism was the further development of the Arctic Council, which came to new agreements on search-and-rescue and oil spill management involving all parties, and adopted a more consensual approach toward the participation of new observers such as China and India. The crisis over Ukraine has unsettled relations with Russia and led to fears that Arctic cooperation might suffer because of EU-US sanctions against Russia. Nevertheless, cooperation has continued in the Arctic Council's working groups and task forces. In 2015, under the US chairmanship, there is arguably renewed confidence that the Arctic Council is (and will remain) the most important intergovernmental forum for Arctic governance, and that Russian participation will endure.

Regional Stability and Rivalries

Despite the tone of some contemporary media reporting, in the Arctic there is no immediate prospect of unbridled rivalries leading to friction or conflict. This does not mean that there has not been concern expressed over the role of Russia by Western commentators, especially in the immediate aftermath of the planting of the Russian flag in the central Arctic Ocean in 2007. This jaundiced view of Russia as a disruptive geopolitical actor has gained further traction following the annexation of Crimea in 2014 and the ongoing military crisis in eastern Ukraine. Attention has been drawn to Russian investment in military facilities and capability in the Arctic, with new maps being constructed displaying the geographical distribution of Russian air bases, military deployment, and port facilities. Russian overflights in the North Atlantic and Scandinavia have also increased concern that the Russian government is flexing its military muscles. Notwithstanding concerns about

Russia's longer-term Arctic policies and strategies, especially under Vladimir Putin's leadership, there is also evidence that Russia is being cooperative when it comes to the Arctic Council, and that it is being supportive of international legal norms regarding the Law of the Sea and extended continental shelf submissions. An example of collaborative behavior is Russia's agreement with Norway in September 2010 over their unsettled maritime boundary in the Barents Sea. In August 2015 Russia resubmitted its materials regarding extended continental shelves off the Arctic coastline, following the rules governing such matters under Article 76 and 77 of the UN Convention on the Law of the Sea (UNCLOS).

Russia's Arctic policy is informed by a belief that the Arctic zone is a national strategic resource base that is vital to the country's future security and prosperity. The Russian government continues to regard the NSR as a major strategic concern, and it remains committed to limiting NATO's role in the Arctic region. Again, this does not mean that conflict is inevitable in the region. Rather, it is a reminder that Russia, like the other Arctic states, considers its northerly territories and maritime zones to be of strategic significance. Other Arctic states such as Norway remain eager to continue cold weather military exercises (e.g., Cold Response), despite Russian objections to NATO's approach close to their northern border, even if only for the purpose of training. Encouragingly, new initiatives such as the Arctic Security Forces Roundtable (ASFR, which was established in 2011) are providing forums for the region's militaries, and for observers such as the United Kingdom, in which to discuss issues of common concern, including search-and-rescue missions and maritime domain awareness. Russia, however, was not present at the 2015 meeting in Iceland, because security relations continue to be affected by the fallout from the crises in Crimea and Ukraine. As long as these conditions last, the ASFR may be more useful as a forum in which non-Russian partners can meet and discuss areas of common interest, such as the strategic implications of Russian military investment in the Arctic.

Maritime Territorial Disputes

The Northwest Passage

The Northwest Passage (NWP) has been a topic of fascination and interest for centuries. Long imagined and sought after, this elusive maritime passageway, which connects the North Atlantic to the North Pacific via the Canadian archipelago and the Bering Strait, can be more realistically described today as a series of potential transit routes. There are actually seven NWPs. After having been sought by naval officers and explorers for centuries, it was finally navigated by Roald Amundsen in 1903–6. While transiting the NWP, Amundsen also managed to carry out a full year's worth of scientific observations near the North Magnetic Pole, overwintering in the process for two seasons. Growing evidence of sea ice thinning has raised the specter (or enticing prospect, depending on one's perspective) of the NWP facilitating unencumbered movement through the high latitudes of the North American Arctic.

If increasingly unfettered movement did become a realistic possibility in the twenty-first century, then inevitably the NWP's contested international legal status would rise in prominence. The United States regards the NWP as an international strait, through which shipping enjoys transit passage rights, as defined by UNCLOS. Canadians have long considered the passage "internal waters," part of their territorial sea, and thus as subject to comprehensive Canadian regulation. Under such a legal regime, the Canadian authorities would have the right to impose fishing and environmental regulations, alongside other controls regarding shipping safety.

Although arguments continue regarding the NWP's international legal status, UNCLOS's Article 234 ("ice covered areas") does give coastal states such as Canada certain rights even beyond their territorial sea:

> Coastal States have the right to adopt and enforce nondiscriminatory laws and regulations for the prevention, reduction and control of marine pollution from vessels in ice-covered areas within the limits of the exclusive economic zone, *where* particularly severe climatic conditions and the presence of ice covering such areas for most of the year create obstructions or exceptional hazards to navigation, and pollution of the marine environment could cause major harm to or irreversible disturbance of the ecological balance. Such laws and regulations shall have due regard to navigation and the protection and preservation of the marine environment based on the best available scientific evidence [emphasis added].[21]

From Canada's perspective, this language has helped to cement its own position, as has the 1970 Arctic Waters Pollution Prevention Act, which asserts regulatory control by coastal states over a zone of 100 nautical miles.

However, Article 234 does not settle the NWP's legal status. The relationship between Article 234 and Part III of UNCLOS, concerning international straits, is not clear, and thus uncertainty prevails regarding the limits, under international law, for national legislation regarding navigation in ice-covered waters. The United States and the European Union maintain that the NWP is an international strait with an unfettered right to transit, and that Article 234 does not sufficiently clarify the rights of coastal states to regulate ice-covered waters.

The contending legal positions regarding the NWP were famously exposed by the voyage of the American oil tanker SS *Manhattan* in 1969. Starting on the eastern seaboard, the ship transited the passage via the Baffin Sea and Viscount Melville Sound. Thick sea ice impeded the ship's journey through McClure Strait, and a more southerly route to the south of Banks Island was selected. The *Manhattan's* eventual destination was Prudhoe Bay in Alaska. On its return, the Canadian icebreaker *John A. Macdonald* accompanied the *Manhattan* and helped to free it twelve times. Although the voyage was ultimately successful, it brought to the fore US-Canadian differences over the NWP's status. The voyage's official objective was to ascertain whether it might be possible (and indeed cheaper) to transport recently discovered oil in northern Alaska to European markets by ship. As it turned out, the oil companies decided that a trans-Alaska pipeline from Prudhoe Bay to Valdez, in the south of the state of Alaska, was commercially more appealing. Transiting oil across the NWP did not appear to be feasible or cost effective in the late 1960s and early 1970s, but this has become less true since then.

In 1985 the transit voyage of the US Coast Guard vessel SS *Polar Sea* again focused attention on the NWP's status. Although two members of the Canadian Coast Guard were on board the vessel as it transited through Canadian "internal waters," the US government made it clear that the vessel was exercising navigational and transit rights for which no permission was needed. And though the US government informed the Canadian authorities of its intention with regard to the ship's proposed voyage, it pointedly did not seek their consent.

Despite such public disagreements, since 1988 both the United States and Canada have operated under an agreement on Arctic cooperation whereby "the Government of the United States pledges that all navigation by US icebreakers within waters claimed by Canada to be internal will be undertaken with the consent of the Government of Canada."[22] This was important because if US Coast Guard vessels were carrying out oceanographic research, for instance, they would not be considered to be in transit.

These arguments regarding the NWP's international legal status were further heightened by the realization, in the summer of 2007, that ships might pass through Canadian waters without the apparent need for an icebreaker. This was a significant development, because hitherto the Canadian authorities had relied on the discouraging presence of sea ice to support their contention that there was no evidence of routine international usage. If sea ice no longer functions as a natural barrier to shipping, maritime traffic in the region is likely to increase. In August 2008 it was reported that the NWP was again open, making it possible for shipping to traverse between the Atlantic Ocean and Pacific Ocean. Such conditions have since become normal in the summer months. Although the NWP's accessibility should not be exaggerated, if only because such conditions pertain only to the summer season, it does highlight the possibility of further maritime traffic in the future using this transit route. To date, the vast majority of transits of the NWP have been made by either submarines, icebreakers, or ice-strengthened vessels, including voyages carrying tourists around the Canadian Archipelago and the High Arctic, and even to the North Pole.

For a strait to be defined as an international strait under international law, there are two fundamental requirements. First, there is a geographic test. The strait in question must connect two bodies of the high seas—in the case of the NWP, the Atlantic Ocean and the Pacific Ocean. Second, the strait must demonstrate functional usage. It is not sufficient to claim potential usage. There must be clear evidence of navigation and transit history. Canada contends that there have not been a sufficient number of vessels transiting the NWP without the permission of the Canadian authorities. In 2009, however, a US national security presidential directive and homeland security presidential directive, promulgated in the last days of the George W. Bush administration, reaffirmed that "freedom of the seas is a top national priority. The Northwest Passage is a strait used for international navigation, and the NSR includes straits used for international navigation; the regime of transit passage applies to passage through those straits. Preserving the rights and duties relating to navigation and overflight in the Arctic region supports our ability to exercise these rights throughout the world, including through strategic straits."[23]

In practice, notwithstanding forty years of debate, Canada and the United States have agreed to disagree with regard to the NWP's status. The issue continues to be of considerable importance within Canadian politics, and the Harper administration has been active in promoting Canada's military presence in the NWP region. In July 2007 Prime Minister Stephen Harper announced the establishment of a deepwater port in the far North, and he was quoted as noting that "Canada has a choice when it comes to defending our sovereignty over the Arctic. We either use it or lose it. And make no mistake, this Government intends to use it. Because Canada's Arctic is central to our national identity as a northern nation. It is part of our history. And it represents the tremendous potential of the future."[24]

What remains an intriguing possibility is whether Article 234 and its provisions might become less relevant in a warming world, where sea ice may no longer be quite so present. The key phrase in Article 234 might be "most of the year." It is not obvious how its provisions would apply if sea ice were to diminish for six months during a year, rather than for two or three.

The Svalbard Fisheries Protection Zone

The Barents Sea has been a major element in Norwegian–Russian relations, and before that in relations between Norway and the Soviet Union, particularly during the Cold War. Geographically, this maritime area was the primary transit route for the Soviet Northern Fleet to and from the Atlantic Ocean and Arctic Ocean. Moreover, in terms of resources, the Barents contains both living and nonliving resources such as fish, oil, and natural gas. At present, there remains a series of outstanding disputes over the common maritime boundaries of the Barents Sea, and over the legal status of the Svalbard Fisheries Protection Zone, which was established by Norway in 1977. In the case of the former, Norway argues that the maritime zones of the two countries should follow the meridian line from the mainland border. Russia holds that the boundary should be based on the line of longitude extending from the border to the North Pole. The end result of this schism has been to showcase the contested nature of the Barents Sea, most especially in the so-called gray zone, to the immediate north of the Norwegian/Russian border.

In recent times the Svalbard Fisheries Protection Zone has given rise to considerable political friction between Norway and Russia. Regulating fisheries activities in the Arctic is complicated by the physical characteristics of its ecosystems. As Geir Hønneland notes,

> the management of fisheries in the Arctic regions is subject to climatic and biological conditions. The ecosystems of Arctic waters are characterised by short and simple food chains with a low number of species, but large populations. . . . Living marine resources are extremely vulnerable to any degradation of their environment and the impact of human activities. At the same time, the polar marine ecosystems are among the most productive in the world since cold water is rich in the nutrients essential to marine life. . . .

In general the location of these regions far from population centres renders them accessible than most other areas where fishing is conducted.[25]

Although most fishery plans around the world seek to combine scientifically informed management and regulation with enforcement measures, this is always more problematic in regions where sovereign authority is disputed.

The protection zone around the Svalbard archipelago is a case in point. At the heart of the dispute lies a fundamental divergence in opinion between Norway and Russia over the 1920 Svalbard Treaty. Norway holds full and absolute authority over the Svalbard Archipelago; as a consequence, Norway contends that it can declare a fisheries protection zone, whereas the Russian authorities dispute this claim. The most dramatic example of the Norwegian-Russian contretemps over the zone involved the Russian trawler *Elektron* in October 2005.[26] This ship was apprehended by the Norwegian Coast Guard, which accused it of fishing illegally. With two coast guard inspectors on board, the vessel tried to escape the Norwegian authorities and head for Russian territorial waters.[27] It became a cause célèbre and provoked howls of outrage from Russian media and political commentators. The Russian Foreign Ministry issued a protest note, and the Northern Fleet deployed a destroyer for the purpose of protecting Russian fishing vessels operating in the Svalbard Fisheries Protection Zone. Although the situation was eventually resolved peacefully, it did highlight the political, legal, and resource stakes in the Barents Sea.

The Norwegian authorities, mindful that others besides Russia reject the legitimacy of its claims with respect to the protection zone, rarely penalize trawlers infringing the conservation measures designed to restrict illegal, unregulated, and unreported (IUU) fishing. However, in the last decade, as fears have grown that IUU fishing is undermining the stability of fish stocks, the Norwegian coastguard has become more assertive in the pursuit of suspected violators. In 2001 the Russian trawler *Chernigov* was arrested, and the vessel's master was charged with violating fishing regulations applicable to the zone. This was a pivotal intervention because it was the first time that a Russian vessel was prosecuted by the Norwegian authorities based in Tromso.

The *Elektron* incident was different, however, because it involved a lengthy pursuit in the Barents Sea, with the captain explicitly rejecting Norwegian claims that Russian trawlers could be detained in the Svalbard Fisheries Protection Zone if suspected of IUU fishing. Unlike the *Chernigov*, the *Elektron* refused to follow the Norwegian coastguard vessel to Tromso, and instead it bore away southeast toward the Kola Peninsula. The Norwegian vessel KV *Tromso* chased the trawler, and the pursuit continued into the so-called Barents Sea Loop Hole and the Russian exclusive economic zone. Four days later, the pursuit was called off when the Russian vessel entered Russian territorial waters, even though the two Norwegian officials were still on board. The two men were later transferred to another ship and returned to Norway. Eventually, the Russian authorities, following Norwegian evidence of IUU fishing, penalized the captain of the trawler for illegal fishing. Kidnapping charges were dismissed.

The incident, although peacefully resolved, did provoke a lively debate in Russia over the country's economic interests, the legal status of the Barents Sea, and the role of the Northern Fleet in protecting Russian trawlers. Russia's continued nonrecognition of Norway's fisheries protection zone around the Svalbard Archipelago has not changed from the late 1970s. However, it was clear from the *Elektron* incident that key stakeholders within the Russian government—including the Foreign Ministry, the FSB Border Service, and the Defense Ministry—were not inclined to advocate a more aggressive role for the Northern Fleet in protecting Russian economic interests in the Barents Sea. As many as 100 Russian vessels were involved in fishing for cod, shrimp, and capelin within the zone. Notwithstanding that activity, Russian officials chose not to escalate the incident. One reason may have been that the *Elektron* was not seized by the Norwegian authorities, so the Russians were able to punish the vessel's owner without formally changing their position of nonrecognition of the zone.

The joint management of living resources in the Barents Sea has witnessed cooperation between Norway and Russia, even in the disputed Svalbard Fisheries Protection Zone. The two countries have established a Joint Fisheries Commission and have worked together to respond to IUU fishing. Indeed, one of the striking aspects of the *Elektron* incident was both sides' willingness to avoid not only inflammatory political language but also the use of excessive military force on both the part of the Norwegian pursuers and any counterresponse by the Northern Fleet. Both countries were quick to declare the incident a dispute between the Norwegian Coast Guard and a Russian trawler. The issuance of a fine for IUU fishing confirmed that the matter would be treated as a criminal rather than national security issue.

In September 2010 Russia and Norway signed an agreement pertaining to their joint boundary over the Barents Sea. The agreement will enable a maritime delimitation line to be drawn, resolving claims over 175,000 square kilometers of disputed maritime space. The agreement also provides for further cooperation with respect to fisheries and hydrocarbon exploitation. This has been seen as an important step in Norwegian–Russian confidence building, and as facilitating further joint cooperation in oil and gas exploitation, fishing, and shipping.

CURRENT MARITIME OPERATIONS AND ISSUES

The debate over current and future maritime operations in the Arctic is being informed, in large part, by climate change and predictions that Arctic ice is getting thinner or disappearing entirely. The polar ice pack, though inhibiting trade and commerce, has also provided the Arctic coastal states with a buffer against others using their sea routes and potentially exploiting their resources. In September 2009 two German commercial ships, accompanied by Russian icebreakers, sailed through the NSR. This route shortened their journey from the Atlantic to the Pacific by about 4,000 kilometers. With some scientists predicting that ice-free summers will become increasingly the norm, coastal and geographically proximate states have necessarily begun a process of strategic and commercial reassessment, on matters ranging from the mitigation of environmental damage to the provision of appropriate insurance, search-and-rescue capabilities, and support infrastructure.[28]

Still lacking are legally binding standards for Arctic shipping. The Arctic Maritime Shipping Assessment Report, prepared by the Arctic Council in 2009, declared the lack of mandatory regulations for ships operating in ice-covered waters to be one of the major still-unsolved safety issues.[29] In addition, a lack of proper coastal infrastructure and pressure to develop alternative shipping lanes due to pressure on existing lanes, such as the Panama and Suez canals, are issues that still need to be resolved. There are hopes, however, that the Polar Code, adopted by the International Maritime Organization in November 2014, will contribute to resolving these difficulties when it enters into effect starting January 1, 2017.[30]

National Strategies

In recent years the Arctic region has attracted the attention of all five coastal states, and this attention in turn has led these countries to produce new strategic assessments. In each case, there have been calls to invest in new shipping assets, develop infrastructure, and in general enhance the region presence of their respective nation. Arguably, the most striking assessment has been that of Russia, which has reaffirmed the Arctic as a region of the utmost strategic importance. This is not surprising, given that Russia has the largest Arctic territories and that about 20 percent of its gross domestic product is generated in the High North, chiefly from the extraction of national resources. Russia has made it clear that it will upgrade its icebreaker fleet, maintain investment in the mapping of the Arctic Ocean, and enhance its overflight patrolling. Russia has resumed training sorties by strategic bombers over the Arctic, an arguably more substantial gesture than the famous planting of a Russian flag on the bottom of the Arctic Ocean.

In March 2009 the Russian Federation's Security Council released its "Foundations of the Russian Federation National Policy in the Arctic Until 2020 and Beyond."[31] This document asserts that the Russian Federation's Arctic Zone is the "strategic resource base" for Russia's future economic development. The NSR is reaffirmed as strategically vital to securing the Arctic as a source of future resource-based strength. To achieve this objective the Arctic zone will need to be protected, and the document notes the need to form a dedicated Arctic group of troops and equipment, comprising elements from the Northern and Pacific fleets, which will also undergo necessary modernization. Russia is not alone in thinking along these lines. Since 2007 NATO has conducted a large-scale annual exercise called Cold Response, during which conflict over natural resources in the Arctic is a common scenario.

Despite periodic gestures of intransigence or even belligerence, there is also plenty of evidence that the Russians have been following the procedures established by the Commission on the Limits of the Continental Shelf (CLCS) for submitting materials related to extended continental shelves. At the same time, Russian observers have complained that growing NATO activity in the Arctic is a cause for concern, given that the four other coastal states are NATO members.

The Arctic is also a major area of policy concern for Canada. It has the second-largest Arctic coastline, and its government has committed itself to investing in infrastructure and presence in the region. Prime Minister Harper set the tone following the warm summer of 2007, declaring that Canada had to "use it or lose it" when it came to defending its sovereignty. In the same year, plans were unveiled that detailed the acquisition of eight offshore patrol vessels, the establishment of an Arctic training base at Resolute, and a deepwater shipping facility at Nanisvik. Although the global economic downturn put a dampener on these investment plans, these efforts have since resumed. It is clear that enhancing Canada's military presence in the Arctic can be expected to remain a high priority.

Other Arctic coastal states have also renewed their commitment to the region. In March 2009 the Stoltenberg government in Oslo published its own northern strategy, which placed due emphasis on the importance of the Arctic to Norway. While emphasizing the importance of environmental and sociocultural factors, including the fate of indigenous populations such as the Sami, the Norwegian government also announced the transfer of the Norwegian Operational Command Headquarters, formerly at Stavanger, to new facilities outside the Arctic city of Bodo. Another major plank of the Norwegian Arctic strategy is cooperation with Russia on cross-border issues such as migration and environmental management, alongside energy development. Norwegian involvement and investment in the Shtokman gas fields is one such manifestation. Finally, Norway and Iceland have been at the forefront of highlighting a role for NATO in the Arctic.

Other Arctic countries—including Denmark, Finland, Iceland, and Sweden—have also released their own Arctic strategies, which tend to share a common commitment to articulating their national interests while emphasizing their commitment to cooperation and peaceful coexistence via international bodies like the Arctic Council. Observer participants in the council—such as the United Kingdom, France, and Germany—have released their own policy frameworks and statements, and it is now increasingly common to read and hear similar statements from Asian observers—such as China, South Korea, and Singapore. All these countries profess a shared interest in the maritime Arctic, despite their very different physical connections, legal rights, ecological connections, and economic-political interests. Given the centrality of the seaborne trade to the world economy, such interest is no more than realistic.

Prospects for Cooperation or Conflict

Notwithstanding bellicose warnings by both Russian and Western observers in recent years, the general tenor of the debate over the changing strategic situation in the Arctic has been characterized by a spirit of cooperation, especially via the Arctic Council, and as manifest by continuing efforts to clarify relevant international legal norms and processes. This does not mean that there are not potential flashpoints or areas for future conflict. There are three such areas that should be considered briefly. First, there are a number of unresolved territorial claims in the Arctic, and though there is no evidence to suggest that conflict might erupt, there are possibilities. No one expects the United States and Canada to fight over access to the Northwest Passage or resource exploitation in the Beaufort Sea. In practice, it is only Russia's commitment to the peaceful management of such conflicts that remains open to question.

Second, it is possible that the Arctic Council might bifurcate between the five coastal states and other members over questions of maritime security and resource management. The establishment of a new cooperation regime between the five coastal states has been considered to be highly divisive. Representatives of the five states met for the first time in Ilulissat, Greenland, in May 2008, at the so-called Arctic Ocean Conference, to discuss international legal mechanisms, maritime safety, environmental protection, and shipping routes. The conference issued a declaration in which the five Arctic coastal states reaffirmed their commitment to the existing international legal framework. The noncoastal Arctic states, as well as the representatives of indigenous Arctic peoples, were excluded from this meeting, however; and in March 2010 the five states met again in Canada to reaffirm their new cooperation regime. US secretary of state Hillary Clinton raised the stakes by formally criticizing the decision of the Canadian hosts to exclude others, such as Iceland and indigenous groups, from the March meeting. Although no one expects conflict, it does raise difficult issues about the future role of noncoastal states, not to mention more remote parties like China, the United Kingdom, and the European Union. Their position within the Arctic Council is a source of ongoing tension. In May 2013, for example, the European Union's application for observer status in the Arctic Council was deferred, having already been rejected in 2009. It was deferred again in 2015, in large part because Russia was expected to refuse to entertain the application, following the imposition of sanctions against the country in retaliation for its activities in Ukraine. Having overcome its dispute with Canada over an export ban on seal products, it might have been conceivable to imagine the EU as a permanent observer, if the crisis in Ukraine had not erupted. The differentiation between coastal and noncoastal participants always contains the possibility for discord, which may be heightened by changing environmental or economic conditions. One way in which this will be tested is in seeing how interested parties, both coastal and noncoastal, address the prospect of potential fishing in the central Arctic Ocean. Although unlikely in the near term, the area beyond the exclusive economic zones of the five coastal states is international waters, whose exploitation and regulation will necessitate the involvement of interested parties, such as China, the EU member countries, and South Korea.

Finally, the role of NATO in the Arctic might become a source of tension between the four NATO coastal states and Russia. In a statement following the Strasbourg/Kehl Summit in April 2009, it was noted that "developments in the High North have generated increased international attention. We welcome the initiatives of Iceland in hosting a NATO seminar and raising interest of Allies in safety- and security-related developments in the High North, including climate change."[32] Notwithstanding the lack of an official position on its role in the Arctic, the alliance continues to conduct its annual exercise, Operation Cold Response, which routinely involves naval and air units and upward of 10,000 personnel from more than a dozen countries. NATO officials have suggested that an exchange of information and a regular dialogue with the Russian authorities might be initiated in the NATO–Russia Council. Areas of common concern include search-and-rescue capabilities and disaster management. As noted above, however, the ASFR has proven a useful mechanism for information exchange and confidence building in the region. But, as noted, Russian nonparticipation has been a source of concern, and as a consequence, the ASFR's long-term efficacy may be called into question.

Resources and Outer Continental Shelf Submissions

One of the most important regional issues is the question of the Arctic's hydrocarbon resource potential. The US Geological Survey has estimated that areas north of the Arctic Circle have 90 billion barrels of undiscovered, technically recoverable oil (and 44 billion barrels of natural gas liquids) in twenty-five geologically defined areas that are thought to have potential for petroleum production. This represents 13 percent of the undiscovered oil in the world.[33] More than half the undiscovered oil resources are estimated to be located in three geologic areas: Arctic Alaska, the Amerasia Basin, and the East Greenland Rift Basins Province. It is further estimated that approximately 84 percent of the undiscovered oil and gas lies offshore, within the exclusive economic zones of the five Arctic Ocean coastal states. In its assessment of the recoverability of undiscovered oil and gas resources, the US Geological Survey did not consider economic factors such as the effects of permanent sea ice or oceanic water depth.

It also goes without saying that climate change in the Arctic will exert a profound influence on access to these resources. Improvements in shipping and pipeline-based technology are opening up the prospect of further development of hydrocarbon exploitation in the High North. The Norwegians are leading the field in this area. Ice-strengthened vessels are already moving liquefied natural gas from offshore Arctic Norway to markets in Southern Europe and North America. A major export facility is to be found at the Snow White gas liquefaction plant, which is linked via an underground pipeline on the seabed to a gas field in the Barents Sea.

The growing interest in the Arctic's hydrocarbon potential helps explain the interest of all five coastal states in mapping and surveying the Arctic, for the purpose of claiming an extended or outer continental shelf. Such claims, if approved by the CLCS, would convey sovereign rights to resources on or below the seabed. Norway, Russia, Canada, and Denmark are all members of the CLCS, which operates under the auspices of UNCLOS. Each country has launched its own mapping projects in order to articulate sovereign rights to extended sections of the Arctic seabed. The United States also has a mapping project, though it is not a formal party to the CLCS.

One sees, then, a growing trend on the part of coastal states to collect geological and oceanographic material on the seabed by way of extending sovereign rights over larger areas of the Arctic Ocean. Claims with respect to the continental shelf may extend up to 350 nautical miles from the coastline. As a consequence, the central Arctic Ocean—including underwater features such as the Lomonosov Ridge and the Mendeleyev Ridge—has been the subject of a number of submissions to the CLCS, whose general stance has been to urge interested parties to resolve their differences via negotiation. Depending on the outcome of these negotiations, the Arctic's maritime jurisdiction will involve a tapestry of coastal state jurisdictions and, potentially, an area of the central Arctic Ocean seabed that is under the authority of the International Seabed Authority.

What is likely to happen is that once the CLCS has released recommendations, there will be a series of negotiations whereby all parties attempt to settle the delimitation of extended continental shelves. The CLCS does not in fact have the legal capacity to settle remaining disputes unilaterally. Although journalists may write of a "scramble for resources" and a "new Great Game," the reality is that the interested parties will need to negotiate on the matter of sovereign rights in the central Arctic Ocean. The agreement between Norway and Russia in September 2010 on the delimitation of maritime boundaries for the Barents Sea provides grounds for optimism.

Canada, Denmark, and Russia have invested considerable time and money in preparing and submitting their materials to the CLCS. All three countries are expected to argue that their sovereign rights extend over large areas of the

Arctic seabed, including the North Pole. Norway already settled its outer continental shelves in 2009, and the United States cannot participate in this process because it did not ratify UNCLOS. Denmark's submission in 2014 and Russia's resubmission in 2015 have brought to the fore these two countries' competing claims that the Lomonosov Ridge is an extension to their respective continental shelves. Canada's submission also maintains that its sovereign rights extend to the central Arctic Ocean seabed as well. The CLCS will eventually issue what are termed "recommendations," and it is expected that the three countries will need to act collectively to resolve the delimitation of their respective outer continental shelves, and thus their sovereign rights over the seabed. Once these matters are settled, any remaining areas will fall under the jurisdiction of the International Seabed Authority as part of the global commons.

IMPLICATIONS FOR US MARITIME STRATEGY

When compared with the other Arctic coastal states, the United States has arguably been the least active in advancing policy development. The 2009 Arctic Regions Policy, released in the final days of the George W. Bush administration, provides some guidance on policy drivers and likely developments. The preamble notes that the United States is an "Arctic nation," and that the country has a number of interests to take into consideration, including the impact of climate change, the region's resource potential, existing governance arrangements like the Arctic Council, and homeland security and defense. The invocation of homeland security, which is clearly a reflection of the post–September 11, 2001, policymaking environment, may prove to be an important innovation. Moreover, it marked a policy break from previous administrations that tended to treat the Arctic and Antarctic in roughly parallel terms. This is no longer the case.

The US *National Strategy for the Arctic Region*, which was released in 2013, continued to feature security as the first of America's Arctic interests, alongside responsible environmental stewardship and the strengthening of international cooperation.[34] At a minimum, it is safe to say that American policy toward the Arctic will continue to reflect unresolved tensions among these priorities. One of the most significant arises from the United States' nonratification of UNCLOS. Adherence to the treaty would entitle the United States to submit materials to the CLCS pertaining to the extended continental shelf and would extend sovereign rights off the coast of Alaska. These things are not possible at present, though the United States has worked on an extended continental shelf project, and will presumably seek to craft a policy that conforms to UNCLOS's requirements, as it has in other areas of maritime governance.

During the past decade, the US Navy has displayed increasing interest in the Arctic, which holds significant implications for maritime strategy. Here, too, the impact of climate change and changing ice conditions has been the key driver. One indication of this shift can be found in a series of symposiums cosponsored by the US Naval Ice Center and the US Arctic Research Commission. Held at the US Naval Academy in Annapolis, the symposiums have focused on the impact of diminishing ice in the Arctic for naval and maritime operations. The latest was held in July 2013, and like its predecessors was predicated on the assumption that the extent of Arctic sea ice is declining at an accelerating rate. Participants were asked to consider potential naval missions, including freedom of navigation, legal enforcement activities, the protection of natural resources, and homeland defense.[35]

Driving the various "missions" and accompanying scenarios is the goal of enhancing the Arctic's accessibility in the coming decades. In 2007 the former US ambassador to Canada, Paul Cellucci, speculated that an ice-free Arctic might afford terrorist groups the means to transfer weapons of mass destruction. As a consequence, Cellucci argued that the United States should support Canadian sovereignty over the Northwest Passage, as a way of ensuring its security. Other commentators—including the Canadian Arctic expert, Michael Byers—have noted how challenges ranging from illegal immigration to shipping accidents and, most dramatically, terrorist activity have helped to resecuritize the Arctic in the post-9/11 era.[36]

US strategy regarding the maritime Arctic remains a work in progress. What is clear is that Alaska retains a military presence alongside the US Coast Guard. Although the Arctic no longer attracts a major US submarine presence, it is thought that at least one submarine does still traverse Arctic waters every year. In terms of ice-breaking capacity, as of 2015 the United States possessed only three icebreakers capable of operating in Arctic waters, and the coast guard has struggled to find the budget necessary to expand it fleet.[37] The US Coast Guard has been cooperating with its Canadian counterparts in mapping the Arctic seabed, and the USCG Cutter *Healy* has played a leading role in this effort.

The longer-term implications for US maritime strategy in the Arctic are as follows. First, the role of energy security is a key determinant. The hydrocarbon potential of Alaska continues to be seen as a necessary corrective to further dependence on overseas supplies, even given rapidly improving unconventional recovery techniques like fracking.[38] Second, the United States will need to decide how and to what extent to involve itself in the Arctic Council and to promote cooperation among the five coastal states. The March 2010 meeting of the Arctic five was strained because of US unhappiness that the Canadians had not invited other members of the Arctic Council and the permanent participants. Third, the economic exploitation of the Arctic in almost any form poses the risk of maritime accidents and environmental disasters in an exceptionally fragile ecosystem, and also one in which remediation efforts are likely to prove difficult.

In his recent assessment of US Arctic policy, the political geographer Phil Steinberg detects an interesting tension.[39] On one hand, the Arctic is conceptualized as a maritime region, which is no different from any other with which the United States, as a global maritime nation, might be concerned—hence the United States' reluctance to offer any concession to Canada's argument regarding the "internal waters" of the Northwest Passage. Even if the United States were sympathetic to their close political ally, there would be a concern about setting a global precedent. On the other hand, through its possession of Alaska, the United States considers itself an Arctic nation. The 2013 *National Strategy for the Arctic Region* was surely promulgated in part to make readers aware of that simple fact.

With the onset of the United States' chairmanship of the Arctic Council (2015–17), it is widely expected that, under the leadership of special representative Admiral Robert Papp, the United States will further develop its Arctic interests. In constrast to its Canadian neighbors, the United States has shown a willingness to work within the Arctic Council but also to act independently to bring interested parties together to talk about areas of mutual concern, including marine management, climate change, and the Arctic region's connections with other areas of global interest. But the United States has also acted to sustain and protect its economic and strategic interests, including approving the Shell Oil Company's highly controversial plans to drill in the waters north of Alaska.

CONCLUSION

Oran Young coined the phrase "the Age of the Arctic" in the mid-1980s in an attempt to highlight the region's growing salience for international affairs. Although it has perhaps taken a little longer than he may have expected for this sobriquet to be adopted in substance, it is undeniable that civilian and military attention has risen sharply. In the next fifty years the Arctic may well become an effectively ice-free sea. If that happens, the region will almost certainly witness exponential growth in maritime traffic, enhanced fishing activity as fish stocks migrate northward to milder waters, increased mineral exploration activity both onshore and offshore, and perhaps increased activity in the forestry and agricultural sectors ashore. Changes in ice cover thickness and distribution have already been held to be responsible for disrupting the lives of coastal communities throughout the Arctic. Melting sea ice is already having implications for community infrastructure, as the Arctic coastline is exposed to the erosive consequences of winter storms. Traditional subsistence lifestyles, including hunting and fishing, appear more vulnerable as indigenous peoples must cope with uncertain ice patterns and the disrupted migration patterns of the animals on which they depend for sustenance.

The ongoing claims to extended continental shelves and related maritime resources, including the future prospects for fishing in the central Arctic Ocean, alongside debates about the transoceanic accessibility of the Arctic for trade, seem certain to make the Arctic a focus of popular and formal geopolitical speculation for years to come. Sea ice thinning, which is at the root of all these changes, has also had the effect of dramatizing their seriousness and extent. Repeated warnings concerning the thinning of Arctic sea ice have contributed to what has become an increasingly far-reaching debate about the Arctic's accessibility—environmentally, economically, and strategically. Although impulses toward conciliation and cooperation have prevailed so far, the debate itself is far from over.

NOTES

1. C. Ebinger and E. Zametakis, "The Geopolitics of Arctic Melt," *International Affairs* 85 (2009): 1215–32, at 1215.

2. Nicholas Crane, *Mercator: The Man Who Mapped a Planet* (New York: Henry Holt, 2003).

3. Andrew Lambert, *The Gates of Hell: Sir John Franklin's Tragic Quest for the North West Passage* (New Haven, CT: Yale University Press, 2009).

4. Michael F. Robinson, *The Coldest Crucible: Arctic Exploration and American Culture* (Chicago: University of Chicago Press, 2010), chap. 4.

5. Muyin Wang and James E. Overland, "A Sea Ice Free Summer Arctic within 30 Years: An Update from CMIP5 Models," *Geophysical Research Letters* 39, no. 18 (September 2012), http://dx.doi.org/10.1029/2012GL052868.

6. The NSR stretches approximately 2,800 kilometers along the Russian Arctic coast, from Novaya Zemlya to the Bering Strait.

7. Laurence C. Smith and Scott R. Stephenson, "New Trans-Arctic Shipping Routes Navigable by Mid-Century," *Proceedings of the National Academy of Sciences of the United States* 110 (2013): 1191–1995.

8. Klaus Dodds, "A Polar Mediterranean? Accessibility, Resources and Sovereignty in the Arctic Ocean," *Global Policy* 1 (2010): 303–13.

9. Henry Pollack, *A World without Ice* (New York: Penguin, 2010), 120.

10. Ibid.

11. Ibid., 122.

12. Arnold is quoted by Steven Call, *Selling Air Power: American Aviation and American Popular Culture after World War II* (College Station: Texas A&M University Press, 2009).

13. Shepherd M. Jenks, "Navigating under the North Pole Icecap," *US Naval Institute Proceedings* 84 (1958): 62–67.

14. John Edwards Caswell, *Arctic Frontiers: United States Explorations in the Far North* (Norman: University of Oklahoma Press, 1956).

15. Jacob Darwin Hamblin, "Mastery of Landscapes and Seascapes: Science at the Strategic Poles during the International Geophysical Year," in *Extremes: Oceanography's Adventures at the Poles*, ed. Keith R. Benson and Helen M. Rozwadowski (Sagamore Beach: Science History Publications, 2007), 204.

16. Oran R. Young, "The Age of the Arctic," *Foreign Affairs* 61 (Winter 1985–86): 161–62.

17. See the first among the documents collected by John B. Hattendorf, ed., *US Naval Strategy in the 1980s*, Newport Paper 33 (Newport, RI: Naval War College Press, 2008), http://fas.org/irp/doddir/navy/strategy1980s.pdf.

18. Klaus Dodds, "The Ilulissat Declaration (2008): The Arctic States, 'Law of the Sea,' and Arctic Ocean," *SAIS Review* 33 (2014): 45–55.

19. See http://www.arctic.or.kr/files/pdf/m2/m22/1/m22_1_eng.pdf.

20. The Arctic Environmental Protection Strategy was designed to promote the monitoring, assessment, protection, emergency preparedness/response, and conservation of the Arctic. The subsequent eight permanent members of the Arctic Council signed it, but it is also important to note that it is not a treaty and is nonbinding on the signatories.

21. The inclusion of the word "where" has been particularly controversial because it raises the question of applicability and the area concerned.

22. "Agreement between the Government of Canada and the Government of the United States of America on Arctic Cooperation," http://www.treaty-accord.gc.ca/text-texte.aspx?id=101701.

23. National Security Presidential Directive 66, January 9, 2009, http://fas.org/irp/offdocs/nspd/nspd-66.htm.

24. Office of the Prime Minister, news release, July 9, 2007, http://www.pm.gc.ca/eng/news/2007/07/09/prime-minister-stephen-harper-announces-new-arctic-offshore-patrol-ships.

25. Geir Hønneland, "Fisheries in the Svalbard Zone: Legality, Legitimacy and Compliance," in *The Law of the Sea and Polar Maritime Delimitation and Jurisdiction*, ed. Alex G. Oude Elferink and Donald R. Rothwell (Utrecht: Martinus Nijhoff), 317–35.

26. This is not the first time that the zone's legality has been contentious. In August 1994 it formed the basis of a dispute between Iceland and Norway. Norway did show a

willingness to use force against Icelandic vessels, and in one case fired two nonexplosive shells into the hull of the trawler *Hagangur II*. The latter was accused of fishing without an approved quota.

27. The decision to flee to Russian territorial waters was understandable, given that the coastal state's right to pursue ("hot pursuit," under UNCLOS Article 111) ceases when the pursued ship enters the territorial waters of its own or a third-party state.

28. See, e.g., "US Navy Predicts Summer Ice Free Arctic by 2016," *The Guardian*, December 9, 2013, http://www.theguardian.com/environment/earth-insight/2013 /dec/09/us-navy-arctic-sea-ice-2016-melt.

29. See http://www.arctic.noaa.gov/detect/documents/AMSA_2009_Report_2nd _print.pdf. This judgment is reiterated in the follow-on report, "Status on Implementation of the AMSA 2009 Report Recommendations," May 2013, http://www .innovation.ca/sites/default/files/Rome2013/files/Arctic%20Marine%20Shipping%20 Assessment,%20Arctic%20Council,%202013.pdf.

30. The terms of the code, which will enter into force in 2017, are summarized on the International Maritime Organization's website, http://www.imo.org/MediaCentre /HotTopics/polar/Pages/default.aspx. Cf. Eric Haun, "Environmental Groups: IMO Polar Code Too Weak," *MarineLink.com*, November 21, 2014, http://www.marinelink .com/news/environmental-groups381260.aspx.

31. Security Council of the Russian Federation, "Foundations of the Russian Federation National Policy in the Arctic Until 2020 and Beyond," http://icr.arcticportal.org /index.php?option=com_content&view=article&id=1791%253afou.

32. Quoted by Robert Czulda and Robert Los, *NATO: Towards the Challenges of a Contemporary World 2013* (Warsaw: International Relations Research Institute, 2013), 200.

33. The only comprehensive assessment dates from 2008; see http://www.usgs.gov /newsroom/article.asp?ID=1980#.VVffuWAki68. More recent subregional assessments can be found at http://energy.usgs.gov/RegionalStudies/Arctic.aspx.

34. White House, *The National Strategy for the Arctic Region* (Washington, DC: White House, 2013), https://www.whitehouse.gov/sites/default/files/docs/nat_arctic _strategy.pdf.

35. The program of the most recent symposium is at http://www.star.nesdis.noaa .gov/star/Ice2013.php.

36. Michael Byers, *Who Owns the Arctic? Understanding Sovereignty Disputes in the North* (Vancouver: Douglas & McIntyre, 2009).

37. These efforts are described on the website of the US Coast Guard's Acquisitions Directorate, http://www.uscg.mil/acquisition/icebreaker/.

38. See "Arctic Drilling 2015: Shell Advances Plans to Drill in the Alaskan Arctic Despite Low Oil Prices, Environmental Concerns," *International Business Times*, May 13, 2015, http://www.ibtimes.com/arctic-drilling-2015-shell-advances-plans-drill -alaskan-arctic-despite-low-oil-prices-1918968.

39. P. Steinberg, "Maintaining Hegemony at a Distance: Ambivalence in US Arctic Policy," in *Polar Geopolitics: Knowledges, Legal Regimes and Resources*, ed. R. Powell and K. Dodds (Cheltenham, UK: Edward Elgar, 2014), 113–30.

CHAPTER 7

The Indian Ocean

JAMES A. RUSSELL

When intrepid Portuguese mariners finally rounded the Cape of Good Hope in significant numbers late in the fifteenth century, they discovered two ocean-going vessels plying the waters of the Indian Ocean: sturdy Chinese junks fastened together with belts of iron, and various models of what were described as stitched vessels constructed with planks held together by twine connected through a series of bored holes.[1] Versions of these vessels supported a thriving and complex system of seaborne trade that ranged from the East Coast of Africa to the Arabian Peninsula, the Red Sea, the Persian Gulf, the Makran Coast, the Indian subcontinent, Burma, Sumatra, Indochina, and the Chinese mainland.

This system of seaborne trade formed part of a trading network comprising various shipping routes and overland caravans that transported goods throughout Persia, Central Asia, Arabia, Mesopotamia, and Anatolia. These routes serviced consumers and suppliers in Asia and Europe. After the arrival of the Portuguese in the Indian Ocean, a succession of European maritime powers sought control over the Indian Ocean's bustling and vibrant trade. The centuries-old trading system that connected East and West in this body of water in no small measure helped create the globalized system of trade and interdependence that is a defining feature of the modern world.

If these mariners from an earlier era had found themselves in today's Indian Ocean, they undoubtedly would be astonished at the size of today's container ships and the mammoth oil tankers plying its waters.[2] Of particular importance, however, these mariners might not have found the range and diversity of today's Indian Ocean maritime activity all that extraordinary. The Indian Ocean became a truly global maritime crossroads more than two thousand years ago, and it continues in this role today. Understanding the context of this historic continuum is important. Although littoral empires surrounding this great body of water rose and fell during this period, sustained maritime interaction remained mostly uninterrupted. Moreover, a series of external powers seeking to control trade and project power in the area also came and went during the period. These powers managed maritime security in the Indian Ocean through direct naval presence, in combination with a series of formal and informal relationships with regional states.

The resilience of the Indian Ocean's trading system over the centuries is one of the defining features of this extraordinary body of water. Although external powers may have sought to control trade in this ocean's vast waters, these powers never sought to systemically disrupt it. The calculus of all states using the ocean has been that it was not in their interest to disrupt this vast and complex maritime domain. That basic calculus continues to this day, when the livelihoods of a burgeoning number of both state and nonstate stakeholders are increasingly dependent on a peaceful and orderly maritime environment. If there is an oceanic area that provides an example of the evolution of a collectively policed global commons, the Indian Ocean is it. Whether this environment can continue in perpetuity remains uncertain, but past history suggests an enduring logic that has discouraged states from seeking to disrupt an economic system upon which their livelihood depends. This logic also suggests a certain hopeful future in which otherwise competing states will likely refuse to let their quarrels on land stand in the way of their overwhelmingly peaceful interactions at sea.

This chapter analyzes twenty-first-century maritime strategy and security in the Indian Ocean, the historical context for today's security challenges, and the future challenges posed for the maritime strategies of states that depend on this body of water for seaborne trade. The chapter describes the critical characteristics of the geographic domain, its importance in global strategic and political affairs, the involvement of global navies on its waters, and attempts by maritime powers to police its vast areas and critical choke points.

THE OCEAN'S GEOGRAPHIC CHARACTERISTICS

The Indian Ocean covers an estimated 68.5 million square kilometers. It is bounded on the eastern rim by Africa; on the northeast by the Arabian Peninsula; on the north by India and Pakistan; on the northwest by Indonesia and Malaysia; and on the southwestern corner by Australia. It is the world's third-largest ocean and constitutes an estimated 20 percent of the water on the Earth's surface. Nearly 2 billion people live in the eighteen member states of what is called the Indian Ocean rim, which constitutes between 25 and 30 percent of the world's population.[3] Twenty-three states directly border this ocean or are in it, with that number rising to thirty-three if the Red Sea and the Persian Gulf are included.

This ocean contains a number of maritime chokepoints through which shipping traffic must pass to service both regional and global markets: the 55-kilometer-wide Strait of Hormuz at the western end of the Persian Gulf; the 30-kilometer-wide Bab el Mandeb, which is located at the southeastern tip of the Arabian Peninsula; the Strait of Malacca (which is approximately 800 kilometers in length and reaches its narrowest point of 2.8 kilometers in width in the Phillips Channel near Singapore), which connects the Indian Ocean to the Pacific; the Lombok Strait (which is 60 kilometers long and varies in width from between 18 and 40 kilometers), which connects the Indian Ocean to the Java Sea; the 50–80-kilometer-wide Palk Strait, which sits between India and the island of Sri Lanka; and the 465-kilometer-wide Mozambique Channel, which is located between the island of Madagascar and the east coast of Africa.

The Indian Ocean contains a number of islands, both on its periphery and in its interior. The island of Madagascar sits at the southwestern edge of the ocean. Directly to its north and east are the Comoros Islands and the Seychelles, the Zanzibar archipelago, and the islands of Pemba and Socotra further north. The island of Diego Garcia lies 1,600 kilometers to the south of India and is jointly used by the United States and the United Kingdom as a military base to support operations in the Persian Gulf and the Indian Ocean. The island served as an important staging area for US military operations in the Persian Gulf during the 1990s, and it continues to support US operations throughout the Gulf and South Asia. The Indian Ocean's eastern edge is framed by islands in the Indonesian archipelago.

THE OCEAN'S GEOSTRATEGIC IMPORTANCE

It is difficult to overstate the role played by the Indian Ocean in the global economy and its importance to maintaining international peace and stability. An estimated one-half of the world's container ships regularly traverse this ocean, along with one-third of its bulk cargo traffic and two-thirds of its oil supplies. The ocean is a critical link in the world's global trading system, and sustained disruption of this traffic would have catastrophic global consequences.

The Indian Ocean contains the world's two most important maritime choke points: the Strait of Hormuz and the Strait of Malacca. The global economy depends on seaborne trade through both these straits for energy and general commerce. During 2013 the US Energy Information Administration estimated that 17 million barrels of oil (up from 15.7 million barrels in 2009), contained in fourteen tankers, passed daily through the Strait of Hormuz. Oil exported through the strait represented 35 percent of all seaborne traded oil in 2013. The US Energy Information Administration estimates that 85 percent of the oil transiting through the Strait of Hormuz reaches consumers in Asia. The largest consumers of Gulf oil in Asia are India, China, Japan, and South Korea. In 2013, approximately 15.2 million barrels of day passed through the Strait of Malacca; and 3.8 million barrels passed through the Bab el-Mandab.[4] The amount of oil transiting through these straits will increase dramatically as the world's thirst for oil continues to grow, from 85.7 million barrels per day in 2008 to an estimated 112 million barrels per day by 2035.[5] China's demand for oil is projected to increase from 7.8 million barrels per day in 2008 to nearly 17 million barrels per day by 2035. India is projected to increase its consumption from 3 million barrels per day in 2008 to 7.5 million barrels per day by 2035.[6] Each of these states, as well as other states in Asia, will depend overwhelmingly on imported oil that must come from tankers traveling through the Indian Ocean.

Oil- and energy-related shipping traffic, however is a relatively minor part of the ocean's overall maritime activity if measured by actual numbers of vessels. The International Maritime Organization estimates that 50,000 ships annually transit the Strait of Malacca and 33,000 transit the Gulf of Aden en route to and from the Bab el-Mandab. The Indian Navy estimated in 2007 that more than 100,000 vessels annually transited the ocean.[7]

The economic downturn of 2008 prompted what is believed to be the first contraction in global output since the 1930s. Although significant by historical standards, this contraction of 2.7 percent (in 2009) slowed but did not systemically disrupt global shipping of twenty-foot-equivalent container units (TEUs).[8] The United Nations reported slower growth in demand for seaborne trade, falling from 4.5 percent in 2007 to 3.6 percent in 2008. Despite these conditions, demand for container port traffic grew by an estimated 4 percent in 2008 to reach 508 million TEUs and has continued to increase during the subsequent economic recovery. Although the recent economic slowdown has introduced some additional uncertainty into projections of continuously sustained global economic growth, the Indian Ocean is certain to remain a vital transit area. In 2007 the United Nations reported that the ocean had become the world's busiest TEU trade route, with traffic totaling 27.7 million TEUs.[9] The ocean contains a number of the world's busiest TEU throughput terminals, which in and of themselves represent critical nodes in the global economy. Singapore is currently the second-largest container port handler in the world, handling nearly 33 million TEUs in 2013. Dubai is the world's ninth-largest container port, throughputting 13.6 million TEUs during the same period.[10] India has undertaken an aggressive plan to expand its port capacity.[11] Saudi Arabia is also expected to dramatically expand its TEU capacity in Jeddah on the Red Sea. These throughput terminals will further expand and enhance the Indian Ocean's role in global seaborne trade, upon which the world will increasingly depend.

As highlighted in the previous paragraphs, the Indian Ocean and its maritime choke points collectively represent a busy global highway. This traffic, however, is an indicator of a broad, globally based strategic shift that is expected to unfold over the next quarter century. The economies of states bordering the Indian Ocean in South Asia, and of the states in East Asia that depend on its waters for seaborne trade, are projected to grow at dramatically faster rates than the economies of today's developed states in Western Europe or North America. The growth of South and East Asian states is part of a complex global phenomenon that represents a dramatic and unprecedented (at least in recent history) transfer of wealth from West to East. The US National Intelligence Council identifies this phenomenon as one of the most important systemic drivers of an evolving global order that will see China and India build their economic and political power as the world shifts to a multipolar power structure no longer dominated by the United States.[12] According to the National Intelligence Council, India and China will surpass the gross domestic product of all other economies except the United States and Japan by 2025. In 2010 China passed Japan to become the world's second-largest economy; experts predict that it will pass the United States in 2030.[13] The maritime domain of the Indian Ocean will play a central role as an enabler of this systemic change—a process that will almost certainly affect intraregional political and military relationships and the relationships of regional states with outside powers. The United States is clearly aware of this systemic shift in the global power structure and of the growing strategic importance of the Indian Ocean in the decades to come.[14] In recognition of this importance, the United States has openly stated its intent to keep "credible combat power" continuously deployed in the Indian Ocean (and elsewhere) for the foreseeable future.[15]

THE HISTORICAL BACKGROUND

The arrival of Portuguese mariners in the Indian Ocean in the fifteenth century represented the beginning of an era of sustained involvement by outside powers and rivalry that in some respects continues to this day. After rounding the Cape of Good Hope in 1504 in force, Portugal proceeded during the next ten years to establish a series of forts that rimmed the Indian Ocean all the way to Goa and the Malabar Coast of southwestern India. These coastal forts provided Portugal with the means to seize control over the Indian Ocean's maritime trade routes to and from the Indian subcontinent from the Arabs who had controlled the area's seaborne trade for centuries.[16] By the end of the fifteenth century, challenges to Portugal's naval position emerged from Holland and England. By the middle of the century, Portugal lost its strongholds in India, Oman, and East Africa; and by the end of the century, it had been supplanted by England, the Netherlands, and France as the dominant external maritime power in the Indian Ocean. By the early nineteenth century, England had cemented its position in India, and the Royal Navy firmly controlled the main trade routes with the Indian subcontinent. The nineteenth century saw several French and British naval actions in the Indian Ocean, in which the French were eliminated as a naval rival with the surrender of the Mauritius naval base in 1810.[17] In the late eighteenth and early nineteenth centuries, Persian Gulf–based pirates operating out of Ras al-Khaimah and the Trucial Coast became a persistent nuisance and forced the Royal Navy and the British East India Company to convoy merchant shipping in the area. By 1809 the problem had gotten so bad that a punitive expedition was launched from India against the Gulf pirates, successfully destroying many of their vessels.[18] In what was to later become a model for England's regional role, the captains of the vessels in this action were directed to focus only upon "destruction of these pirate vessels" and were specifically instructed not to become involved in local politics on land.[19] In 1819 Britain launched another successful expedition against Gulf pirates that further formalized Britain's role as maritime policeman and that again signaled a policy of noninterference in the internal political affairs of the Gulf tribes. The Arab sheiks of the western Gulf finally agreed to renounce piracy in the General Treaty of Peace, which was signed in 1820. The sheiks in the eastern Gulf signed similar treaties in 1834 and 1835. This system of security endured mostly uninterrupted for the next 150-odd years, until the British withdrawal east of Suez in 1971, and arguably it continues in existence to this today, with the United States replacing Britain as the dominant external maritime power. Up until the invasion of Iraq in 2003, it could be said that the United States also generally emphasized a policy of noninterference in internal political affairs on land.

Perhaps the most serious challenge to the Indian Ocean's maritime system emerged during World War II. The ocean remained under British control during World War II—despite the initial superiority of the Japanese Navy—and the trading system continued to operate as it had before the war. But all this was thrown into question in 1942. Amid British fears of a full-scale invasion of India in the spring of 1942 after the fall of Singapore, a force of Japanese aircraft carriers commanded by Admiral Chuichi Nagumo attacked the British bases of Colombo and Trincomalee on the island of Ceylon (now Sri Lanka). Another task force commanded by Vice Admiral Jisaburo Ozawa attacked merchant shipping in the Bay of Bengal, but subsequently withdrew after sinking eighteen merchant vessels. The attacks on Ceylon in March and April 1942 damaged the ports and airfields, but the bulk of Britain's Indian Ocean fleet, commanded by Vice Admiral James Somerville, successfully avoided the naval battle sought by the Nagumo and lived to fight another day. The raid on Ceylon and the foray to disrupt shipping in the Bay of Bengal represented the high-water mark of Japan's naval expansion into the Indian Ocean during the war, and must be seen as the most serious threat to this maritime domain in recent history. Although Japanese submarines mounted periodic operations in the Mozambique Channel, allied shipping was never severely disrupted. In the end, the raid was just that—an episodic event—and for the rest of the war, the Japanese Navy never systemically challenged British naval ascendance in the Indian Ocean. After the Doolittle bombing raid on Japan in April 1942 and the rebuff of the Japanese advance on Port Moresby in the Battle of the Coral Sea on May 7–8, 1942, Japanese naval operations decisively shifted to the Pacific theater, much to the relief of the British Royal Navy. Any intentions of Japan to then reenter the Indian

Ocean quickly evaporated after its crushing defeat at the Battle of Midway in June 1942.[20] Maintaining control over the Indian Ocean during World War II played an important role in the Allied victory. It permitted the Allies to maintain control over the Middle East's oil fields and to resupply Britain's forces in Egypt, which were critical to the defeat of Germany in North Africa. It also facilitated the allied resupplying of Russia through Iran, which totaled 5 million tons of war matériel.

With the emergence of the Cold War, coupled with the gradual decline of Britain's naval power, the US Navy slowly but surely supplanted the British Navy in the Indian Ocean and the Persian Gulf as the dominant external naval power. As the United States gradually lost its position as a major exporter of oil (a position that new extractive techniques have lately allowed it to regain), it became clear that Gulf region producers would become the dominant suppliers for world oil markets. In the decades after the end of World War II, the US Navy slowly built out a logistical infrastructure in and around the Persian Gulf and the Indian Ocean in Bahrain, Aden, Saudi Arabia, Ethiopia, and Ceylon. During the late 1940s and 1950s, American naval operations around the world became critically dependent on Gulf-based oil supplies delivered by chartered oil tankers. In 1949, in recognition of the growing importance of the Gulf and the Indian Ocean to American interests, the United States formed a regional military command called the Middle East Force headquartered in Bahrain.[21]

Despite its growing involvement in Saudi Arabia and Iran during the 1950s and 1960s, the US Navy remained under what it regarded as a British-administered regional security umbrella. In 1966 the newly elected Labour government in Britain announced plans to dramatically reduce the country's military presence in the Indian Ocean and the Persian Gulf as part of a plan to reduce the defense budget and realign Britain's global defense posture. In November 1967, following an unsuccessful counterinsurgency campaign, Britain hastily abandoned its base in the colony of Aden located at the mouth of the Bab el-Mandab.[22] In 1971 Britain formally announced its decision to withdraw east of Suez and closed its military facilities in Mauritius, the Maldives, and the airfield located on Masirah Island off the coast of Oman. Britain retained its military base on the Diego Garcia atoll.

The response of regional states to the British withdrawal varied. The newly independent Gulf Trucial sheikdoms initially floated an unsuccessful proposal to themselves fund the continued presence of the Royal Navy. At the eastern edge of the Indian Ocean, the states of Australia, New Zealand, Britain, Singapore, and Malaysia formed the Five-Power Defense Arrangements (FPDA), in which each state agreed to consult with the other in the event of aggression against Malaysia or Singapore.[23] The FPDA continues in force to this day, and the participating states routinely hold both ground and naval exercises and annual multilateral meetings pursuant to the group's initial purpose. As of this writing, the FPDA had established an integrated air defense system coordinated out of Butterworth Air Base, a former Royal Air Force base now operated by the Royal Malaysian Air Force in the state of Penang.

As it became bogged down in Vietnam, the United States at first resisted adopting the role taken on by the British in the Indian Ocean and the Persian Gulf. Indeed, the 1970s remained a decade where outside naval powers exercised little overt influence in the Indian Ocean. Alone among the Western powers, France retained an active naval base on the island of Réunion, which is located 500 miles east of Madagascar. While maintaining a small naval presence in Bahrain and a jointly administered US–UK base at Diego Garcia, the United States instead sought to build up regional powers such as Iran and Saudi Arabia to protect its interests. Under the so-called Nixon Doctrine, the United States sought to arm, train, and equip regional defense partners as a substitute for a direct military presence.[24] Of particular importance, maritime interactions in the Indian Ocean continued uninterrupted in this decade, as they had done before, despite conflict in the littoral areas surrounding the ocean.

During the 1970s, as the United States sought to retreat from direct global commitments, the Soviet Union maintained a modest naval presence in the Indian Ocean, averaging ten surface combatant and support vessels continuously deployed on an annual basis. During the period, it built up a network of bases bordering the Indian Ocean in Somalia, Ethiopia, and Aden.[25] It also cultivated a burgeoning military relationship with India. At the time, the Soviet presence was not seen by the United States as a particularly threatening posture. Moreover, the navies of the littoral states bordering the Indian Ocean remained undeveloped. During the 1970s the Indian Ocean clearly was seen by the United States as a less important theater of operations than either the Pacific Ocean or the Atlantic Ocean.[26]

In 1971, in an effort to control the superpower involvement in the Indian Ocean, the Non-Aligned Movement successfully pushed Resolution 2832 through the United Nations General Assembly, declaring that the Indian Ocean was a zone of peace. This resolution called for the elimination of all military bases and the removal of any nuclear weapons from the ocean. It called for the establishment of "a system of universal collective security without military alliances and strengthening international security through regional co-operation" to limit the prospect of military confrontation and to permit the free right of passage by vessels of all nations using the ocean.[27]

Although the superpowers declined to endorse the resolution, during 1977 and 1978 the United States and the Soviet Union conducted naval arms limitation talks aimed at reducing their respective naval forces in the Indian Ocean. After agreeing on a draft treaty outlining limitations on their naval forces, the United States abandoned the talks due to Soviet military assistance to Ethiopia.[28]

Events in the late 1970s and early 1980s eventually forced the US Navy to assume much of the responsibility in the Indian Ocean and the Gulf that had been performed by the Royal Navy since the late eighteenth century. Both regional events and the superpowers' Cold War rivalry played critical roles in shifting the United States' regional posture toward one of naval superiority in the Indian Ocean. The 1979 Iranian Revolution and the takeover of the US Embassy in Tehran in November of that year kicked off what was to become an undeclared war between the United States and Iran that saw the states exchange fire both directly and through proxies. The unsuccessful hostage rescue mission in April 1980 mounted by the United States highlighted the lack of infrastructure to support forward regional military operations. In December 1979 the Soviet Union invaded Afghanistan, a move portrayed by many at the time as the USSR's thrust toward obtaining its long-sought warm-water port on the Indian Ocean and the Persian Gulf. In September 1980, seeking to take advantage of the turmoil created by the Iranian Revolution and to settle a festering territorial dispute on the Shatt al-Arab waterway, Iraq invaded Iran. The debilitating nine-year war would see a million casualties on each side and the first battlefield use of chemical agents since World War I.[29]

These events combined to force a change in the United States' strategic and maritime posture in the Indian Ocean and the Persian Gulf. In his State of the Union Address in January 1980, President Jimmy Carter declared: "An attempt by any outside force to gain control of the Persian Gulf region will be regarded as an assault on the vital interests of the United States of America, and such an assault will be repelled by any means necessary, including military force."[30] This statement set in motion a series of actions that saw the United States formally commit to defending its interests in the Gulf and Indian Ocean. The Reagan administration subsequently adopted a more aggressive global maritime posture that sought to expand the US Navy's presence around the world, including in the Indian Ocean, both as a means to counter the Soviet Union and to project American power more comprehensively.[31] The growing emphasis on Indian Ocean maritime operations was emphasized in the fiscal year 1987 Posture Statement by then–navy secretary John Lehman, who stated: "We no longer depend on West Asia and the Gulf for our vital energy needs.

Oil from this area now forms less than 5 percent of our total oil imports. Today, the United States has an Indian Ocean orientation at least equal to our involvement with Europe in war. We plan to deploy two Carrier Battle Groups and one Battle Ship Group to operate in the Indian Ocean." The United States has maintained at least one carrier battle group in and around this body of water ever since. These commitments subsequently became enabled through a tried-and-true template used throughout the Cold War that consisted of a number of critical elements: (1) bilateral agreements with states that committed the United States to the defense of these countries; (2) access to host nation military facilities and agreement in principle to preposition military equipment; (3) routinized security relationships built around joint military exercises, training, and arms sales; and (4) provisions addressing the legal status of US military personnel stationed in these countries.

These events prompted the United States to develop security relationships with a variety of the littoral states bordering the Indian Ocean in the Gulf region and South Asia. In 1980 the United States concluded a facilities-access agreement with Oman—the first of a number of similar agreements with states in the Gulf region. The United States also improved facilities at Diego Garcia and concluded agreements for the use of facilities in Mombasa, Kenya, and Berbera, Somalia. Under the auspices of the United States–Oman agreement, American equipment and military units were stationed at Thumrait and Masirah, and these units proved important to Operation Desert Shield, which was launched in the fall of 1990 to bolster the defense of the Arabian Peninsula after Iraq's invasion of Kuwait.[32] The US relationship with Pakistan also gathered momentum as the United States started to supply mujahedeen groups resisting the Soviet occupation of Afghanistan.

At home, the United States developed a number of programs and organizations designed to execute its security commitments in the Persian Gulf and Indian Ocean. In March 1980 President Carter established the Rapid Deployment Joint Task Force to start military planning devoted to defending American interests in the Gulf. In January 1983 President Reagan formed the Central Command to coordinate military activities in the Gulf region and South Asia. In parallel, the United States created the maritime pre-positioning ships program so it could station equipment close to areas of potential involvement by US ground forces. Having these ships served to reduce the amount of time it would take to stand up a ground force nearly 8,000 miles away from the United States. A squadron of these ships, with equipment for a combat brigade to operate ashore for thirty days (comprising five vessels), would become permanently stationed at the joint US–UK base on Diego Garcia. During the 1990s the United States eventually based two brigades' worth of equipment ashore in the Gulf in Kuwait and Qatar. This ground-based equipment could be quickly joined up with the maritime-based equipment to form a heavy mechanized division that would counter any ground threat to the Arabian Peninsula.[33]

During the 1980s the United States gradually expanded its regional military involvement in the Persian Gulf and Indian Ocean due to the instability created during the Iran-Iraq War. The superpowers' rivalry also played an important role in guiding the thinking of the United States during the period. Moreover, the Soviet Navy expanded its naval presence in the Indian Ocean in the 1980s, constructing a series of naval bases on the Horn of Africa and in Aden on the Arabian Peninsula. The USSR also pursued an aggressive arms relationship with India.[34] Although the superpowers' rivalry manifested itself in a series of competing relationships with the littoral powers surrounding the Indian Ocean, this competition never led to a disruption of seaborne trade.

The Soviet presence in the Indian Ocean proved relatively short-lived, ending in 1991, and the US/Soviet naval rivalry was never a contest among equals. For all the bluster of the Reagan era proclaiming the general rise of Soviet military power, the Soviet Navy could never have been considered on an equal footing with the US Navy. The superiority of the US Navy and its allied partners led to the emergence of a series of coalition naval operations that started policing the Indian Ocean and its surrounding waters. By the late 1980s a coalition maritime presence of more than thirty naval vessels gradually took shape, made up of the navies of the United States, Italy, France, England, the Netherlands, Australia, and West Germany. These navies operated collaboratively from the mid-1980s onward in response to a variety of maritime threats in Indian Ocean–related areas. In 1984 nineteen commercial vessels struck mines in the Red Sea—prompting an international effort to clear its waters. Even Soviet naval vessels were involved in the countermine operations.[35] Although a culprit was never officially identified, many held Libya responsible for laying the mines.

In the Persian Gulf, a variety of incidents prompted greater maritime involvement by the United States and other naval powers. Iraq began attacks against Iranian export terminals and Iranian shipping virtually at the outset of the Iran-Iraq War in the fall of 1980. In May 1982 Iraqi Air Force planes struck the first oil tanker in the war, the Turkish ship *Atlas I*.[36] In 1984 Iraq stepped up its air attacks against Iranian oil installations, in part to counter reverses experienced in the ground war. Iraq mounted a series of air attacks against Iran's oil export terminal at Kharg Island, and Iran responded with attacks on

Kuwaiti vessels to retaliate for what it believed to be that country's help to Iraq during the war. Iran was actually unable to directly target Iraqi oil exports, because those exports were proceeding via overland pipelines through Turkey and Saudi Arabia. By the end of 1986 Iran and Iraq had, combined, damaged 269 vessels transiting the Gulf—a substantial figure, though still representing less than 1 percent of the waterway's shipping traffic.[37]

In December 1986 Kuwait forwarded a request to the United States to reflag eleven oil tankers and thereby assume protection for these ships as they transited the Gulf's treacherous shipping lanes. Citing the need to forestall Soviet influence, the United States agreed to this request.[38] Iran responded by laying mines in Gulf shipping lanes and by starting to construct deployment sites along the Strait of Hormuz for the Silkworm antiship missiles that it had bought from the Chinese. By mid-1987 at least five tankers had struck Iranian mines laid in the channel leading to Kuwait's oil terminal at Al-Ahmadi. Iran struck the US-reflagged Kuwaiti tanker in October 1987 with a Silkworm antiship missile. The United States retaliated by blowing up an Iranian oil platform. Throughout 1987 the United States and Iran remained in a state of tension, which reached a high point when the USS *Samuel Roberts* struck an Iranian mine on April 14, 1988, blowing a 30-foot hole in the vessel's port side. Following this incident, on April 18–19, the United States launched Operation Praying Mantis, in which it destroyed three oil platforms and sank or damaged two Iranian Navy frigates. On April 29, the United States extended the scope of its protection from Kuwaiti shipping to include all neutral shipping in the Gulf. Some argue that this expansion in the scope of protection laid the groundwork for the tragic shooting down of Iran Air Flight 655 on July 13, 1988, by the USS *Vincennes*.

The Iran-Iraq War saw the US Navy eventually move into the maritime role that had once been performed by the British Royal Navy in protecting shipping in and around the Persian Gulf. Of particular importance, however, the United States was not the only navy escorting ships in the Gulf during this period. The Royal Navy, operating under what it called the Armilla Patrol, was still active; it escorted 342 ships through the Strait of Hormuz in the first half of 1988 alone, after having escorted 405 ships in 1987.[39] As noted above, during this period the Gulf had attracted the attention of the navies from a variety of regional states as well as those of outside powers. This pattern of informal but collective maritime interactions gathered further momentum in the aftermath of Iraq's invasion of Kuwait on August 2, 1990.

Following the invasion, the United Nations Security Council passed a series of resolutions demanding that Iraq withdraw from Kuwait. Of particular relevance for maritime operations, Security Council Resolution 661, passed on August 6, 1990, placed Iraq under a trade embargo. The enforcement of this embargo was then enabled by Resolution 665, which asked member states to "cooperate as may be necessary to ensure compliance" with the trade embargo.[40] By the middle of August, coalition naval vessels had begun enforcement of the embargo by conducting what became known as maritime interception operations. The first actual boarding of vessels occurred on August 16, and two Iraqi oil tankers were prevented from exiting the Strait of Hormuz on August 18. In October 1990 the US aircraft carrier *Independence* entered the Gulf—the first aircraft carrier in these waters since the 1970s. This marked the beginning of an era for the US Navy that would see an aircraft carrier continuously present in and around the Gulf waters. During the post-1990 period, the US Navy clearly became the dominant maritime power in the Indian Ocean. The American naval ascendance was further reinforced by the end of the Cold War and the disintegration of the Soviet Union and the subsequent withdrawal of the Russian Navy from the Indian Ocean. During the 1990s US aircraft carriers patrolled Gulf waters and were regular visitors at the Jebel Ali berthing pier just south of Dubai in the United Arab Emirates.

Under the auspices of what became known as the Multinational Interdiction Force, the coalition stood up a naval presence that at various points reached sixty vessels from fifteen countries conducting patrols and vessel boardings in the Gulf, the Arabian Sea, and the Red Sea.[41] In 1995, to facilitate these operations, the United States assumed responsibility for establishing a shore-based command-and-control infrastructure at the Fifth Fleet headquarters in Manama, Bahrain. Each state providing ships to the Multinational Interdiction Force used their own rules of engagement but gradually adopted a common set of best practices in conducting these operations. Over the course of the twelve-year operation, naval forces queried 42,000 ships, did 3,000 boardings, and diverted 2,200 ships for in-port inspections. Coalition naval operations patrolled an estimated 250,000 square miles of sea lanes in and around the Red Sea, the Gulf of Oman, the Persian Gulf, the Gulf of Aden, and the Eastern Mediterranean. In addition to surface operations, air patrols of P-3 Orion aircraft, Royal Air Force Nimrods, and French Atlantiques ranged over the Gulf and Red Sea areas. The organizational relationships and activities undertaken in these extensive operations provided a template for the range of maritime activities conducted by global navies that continues to this day in the western Indian Ocean.

RECENT OPERATIONS

Most recently, the presence of American and international navies in the Gulf and Indian Ocean has been focused largely on maritime security operations as exercised through a variety of combined task force commands that include the naval forces of up to two different countries. Coalition and US forces conduct extensive and ongoing maritime security operations (MSOs), acting as police forces in the maritime environment. MSOs complement the counterterrorism and security efforts of the region's nations and seek to disrupt violent extremists' use of the maritime environment as a venue for an attack or to transport personnel, weapons, or other matériel. The Coalition Maritime Force conducts MSOs in international waters from the Strait of Hormuz to the Suez Canal, and from Pakistan to Kenya. MSOs include a full range of activities—ranging from assisting mariners in distress, to undertaking interaction patrols, to conducting visiting, boarding, and search-and-seizure operations, to engaging regional and coalition navies. These operations today are conducted by three combined task forces (CTFs).

CTF 150 operates in the Gulf of Aden, the Gulf of Oman, the Arabian Sea, the Red Sea, and the Indian Ocean. Command of this task force rotates among the states contributing naval forces to it: Australia, Canada, Denmark, France, Germany, Italy, South Korea, the Netherlands, New Zealand, Pakistan, Portugal, Singapore, Spain, Turkey, the United Kingdom, and the United States. CTF 151, a counterpiracy task force, was established to create a lawful maritime order and develop security in the maritime environment. It operates in the Gulf of Aden and in the Somali Basin. This task force coordinates with navies from around the world, including NATO, the European Union, and the navies of many other states. As with CTF 150, command rotates periodically among the two dozen states that participate. CTF 152 operates in the Arabian Gulf in coordination with the six countries of the Gulf Cooperation Council—Saudi Arabia, Bahrain, Oman, Qatar, Kuwait, and the United Arab Emirates. This task force has been commanded by various officers of the various member states.

A number of other formally constituted naval task forces have also conducted counterpiracy and relief operations in and around the Indian Ocean. In 2008, for instance, the European Union launched EU NAVFOR Somalia Operation Atalanta, to conduct counterpiracy operations off the West African coast. The mission of the task force is to protect chartered vessels of the World Food Program, protect merchant vessels, and combat piracy, using force if necessary. Through early 2010 this task force had escorted 308 vessels, including the African Union's military mission to Somalia, and had overseen the delivery of almost 1 million tons of food and other aid.[42]

The creation of the EU naval task force occurred nearly simultaneously, with a parallel naval task force established by NATO, which started operations in October 2008 in response to the United Nation's request to protection the World Food Program's vessels delivering humanitarian assistance to Somalia. NATO subsequently expanded this naval mission to include general counterpiracy tasks. These operations, which are coordinated by Standing NATO Maritime Group 1, typically include between four and six naval vessels commanded by the Allied Maritime Component Command in Northwood, the United Kingdom. In January 2009 NATO established the Contact Group on Piracy Off the Coast of Somalia to facilitate the exchange of information between states coordinating their antipiracy activities.[43] This group meets routinely at the United Nations and in the region to coordinate naval operations off the Horn of Africa and Somalia.

In August 2008 these formal and informal naval task groups agreed to the creation of a Maritime Security Patrol Area in the Gulf of Aden to serve as the focus of naval escort operations. Within this area the groups also established eastbound and westbound Internationally Recommended Transit Zones to separate the inbound and outbound traffic and to make Yemeni fishermen aware of the transit zones.

It is particularly important that these formally constituted task forces are complemented by a number of other navies around the world; thus Russia, China, and India have all deployed naval forces to the Gulf of Aden to escort ships and conduct antipiracy operations. Cooperation between the more formal task forces and additional navies that have deployed forces to the Gulf of Aden (including China, Russia, and India) is facilitated through the Shared Awareness and De-confliction Working Group, or SHADE. Formed in December 2008, this group routinely meets at the Fifth Fleet headquarters in Manama to coordinate their operations and reports to the Contact Group for Piracy off the Coast of Somalia.[44] Communications between task force and non–task force members is enabled through an unclassified, internet-based information-sharing forum. This internet network—called Fleet Exercise Web, or FEXWEB—is hosted by the European Union's naval forces command in Northwood. The network is based on a shared awareness of the maritime environment and on the shared procedures for convoying duties and responsibilities of the states that are contributing ships and other assets to the collective effort. As an example of states' varied contributions to these patrols, in

2009 Japan deployed two P-3C maritime patrol aircraft to Djibouti to conduct patrols of the waterways leading up to the Bab el Mandab. These patrols provide information on suspected pirate activity to the European Union's anti-piracy task force as well as to the CTF 151 patrols off the coast of Somalia.[45]

The evolution of naval operations in the Gulf followed logically from the maritime interception operations (MIOs) launched after the United Nations placed Iraq under a trade embargo under UN Security Council Resolution 661, and then called for the enforcement by coalition naval forces in Resolution 665. During the 1990s the Navy established the infrastructure in Bahrain to assume command responsibilities for MIOs, which involved the navies of more than a dozen countries. MIO-directed naval vessels conducted thousands of boardings a year in the Persian Gulf and the Indian Ocean. Naval forces conducting MIO operations have transitioned seamlessly to the new CTFs—performing essentially the same missions and same operations as they did during the preceding decade. These operations have been largely prosecuted by a collection of global navies—many of which are now bound together with encrypted data links that provide joint e-mail and intelligence, as well as a common situational awareness of the maritime domain. The command of these task forces is rotated among the participating navies on a routine basis—to include the navies of Pakistan, Saudi Arabia, the United Arab Emirates, France, Great Britain, and others.

These MIOs have coincided with the rhetorical embrace of the maritime security mission by the world's major navies. As noted in August 2008 by the chief of India's Naval Staff, Admiral Sureesh Mehta, cooperation in maritime security may become a new naval norm in the foreseeable future:

> Globalization imperatives have given impetus for concerted and cooperative effort of maritime forces in securing the maritime highways. Cooperative efforts of the littoral countries of the Malacca Strait [have] led to a dramatic decrease in incidents of piracy and armed robbery. On the Western flank of the region, the efforts of the multi-national Task Force 150 are underway to keep maritime crime in check. Similarly deserving of praise are Australia's, South Africa's and India's efforts towards capacity-building and capability-enhancement. An increasing number of navies around the world, including the Indian Navy[,] views "Constructive Engagement" as the answer to common maritime challenges.[46]

Admiral Mehta's statements are entirely consistent with the US Navy's global strategy, as enunciated in *A Cooperative Strategy for 21st-Century*

Seapower, which declares that "no one nation has the resources required to provide safety and security throughout the entire maritime domain. Increasingly, governments, nongovernmental organizations, international organizations, and the private sector will form partnerships of common interest to counter these emerging threats."[47]

These norms are shaping the unfolding of a parallel series of organizations aimed at coordinating the diverse range of cooperative maritime activities. Just as important as the formal coalition naval command arrangements are the series of additional framing international partnerships that form yet another link in the complex web of international maritime cooperation in the Indian Ocean. In 2004 the International Maritime Organization successfully concluded agreement among sixteen states to coordinate antipiracy operations in the straits of Malacca and Singapore. The Regional Cooperation Agreement on Combating Piracy and Armed Robbery against Ships in Asia facilitates information sharing and agreement on a code of conduct to guide members in their antipiracy efforts. In January 2009 the International Maritime Organization successfully replicated this template with an agreement called the Djibouti Code of Conduct that committed the seventeen signatory states to improve communications between states; enhance the antipiracy capabilities to deter, arrest, and prosecute pirates; improve maritime situational awareness; and build the capacities of local coast guards.[48]

THREATS TO MARITIME SECURITY

Although broadly based around several policing functions, the constructive engagement of the maritime powers in the Indian Ocean is perhaps best illustrated by their cooperation against pirates operating off the coast of Somalia and the Horn of Africa who threaten ships transiting the Bab el-Mandab.[49] There are some well-publicized threats to international shipping—though it must be said that even at their worst, these threats are remarkably low, statistically speaking, and pose no more than an episodic threat to the global seaborne highways. Nevertheless, it is striking that pirate attacks in the Gulf of Aden, off the Somali coast, and elsewhere in the Indian Ocean, after having increased steadily during the first decade of the twenty-first century, have now been brought substantially under control, owing in large part to the high level of international cooperation at sea that the pirate threat inspired.[50]

Terrorist groups also seek to disrupt the maritime domain of the Indian Ocean, but thankfully they have experienced less success than the Somali pirates. Perhaps the most notoriously destructive of these efforts was the October 2002 attack by Islamic extremists affiliated with al-Qaeda on the French oil tanker *Limburg*. After the *Limburg* had transited through the Bab el-Mandab, an explosives-filled small boat rammed the tanker and blew a hole in its side, killing one crew member. Some 90,000 barrels of oil leaked into the Gulf of Aden. The attack on the *Limburg* followed two similarly executed attacks against US naval vessels in Aden: an unsuccessful attack on the USS *Sullivan* in January 2000, in which the boat carrying the explosives sank; and the successful attack on the USS *Cole* in November 2000 that killed 19 sailors and disabled the ship. In July 2010 an al-Qaeda affiliated terrorist group called the Abdullah Azzam Brigades apparently rammed the Japanese oil tanker *M. Star* as it passed through the Strait of Hormuz. The attack dented the ship's port side and injured one crewman.[51]

Other episodic and mostly unsuccessful attacks have been mounted by Islamic terrorist groups. In April 2004 extremists affiliated with the Zarqawi network in Iraq attacked the Khaw al-Amaya and Basra oil terminals, killing two sailors and one US Coast Guard crew member. This attack shut down the terminal for two days, resulting in Iraq's losing an estimated $40 million in oil revenues. In August 2005 terrorists launched a rocket attack against the USS *Ashland* and USS *Kearsage* while they were docked in the Jordanian port of Aqaba.

Alongside these episodic threats stands the seemingly more remote, but infinitely more consequential, prospect of interstate conflict, which is believed by some to constitute a significant potential threat to the Indian Ocean's maritime environment. An interstate war among the ocean's littoral states could affect the maritime domain if the antagonists sought to close one of the critical chokepoints. Clearly, the ongoing standoff between Iran and the international community over its nuclear program in combination with its hostility toward the United States and Israel constitute one such potential threat. It remains unclear whether the recently concluded agreement to restrain Iran's nuclear program will eventually reduce these tensions. Some argue that, as part of hostilities stemming from a conflict involving these antagonists, that Iran could seek to close the Strait of Hormuz, a maritime choke point bordering the Indian Ocean through which between 15 and 17 million barrels of oil a day pass. Such an action would clearly disrupt maritime activities in and around the strait and the Arabian Sea, though for how long is hard to say. In any event, an Iranian attempt to close the strait—however unlikely—has long been regarded as the most serious near-term maritime threat that a single state could pose in the region.

Geostrategic rivalry may present another future challenge. As the United States has drawn down its involvement in Iraq and Afghanistan, some have suggested that the Indian Ocean may become the focus of a three-way competition for global power and influence between India, China, and the United States.[52] China and India have been historic adversaries, whereas China and the United States have become rivals for global influence, economically if not militarily. In this strategic triangle, the United States has focused on building political and security partnerships with both states.[53] Of these, the political partnership with India—the world's largest democracy—is likely to be more comfortable for the United States than cooperation with China's communist leadership. Proponents of realpolitik argue that, even without reference to circumstantial details, these kinds of interactions must inevitably lead to frictions that could spill over into the Indian Ocean's maritime domain.[54]

Of particular concern to both India and the United States are the naval support facilities that China has established in the Maldives, Bangladesh, Sri Lanka, Oman, Pakistan, and Myanmar. Dubbed the string of pearls, these bases have undoubtedly been established to support China's growing naval presence in the Indian Ocean.[55] And this presence, it is argued, is in turn meant to protect China's sea lines of communication ranging around the rim of the Indian Ocean that connect the country with vital markets for energy and commerce throughout the area. China will increasingly depend on imported oil to continue its economic growth, and, it is argued, it is preparing to use force if necessary to ensure its access to the oil and natural gas that will drive its continued economic expansion.[56] Some Indian commentators have opined that this activity is part of a Chinese strategy to encircle India and become the dominant maritime power in the region.[57] By 2020, some argue, China plans to deploy naval forces consisting of aircraft carriers, nuclear-powered submarines, and supporting destroyers and frigates into the Indian Ocean.[58]

The occurrence of a large-scale war among developed states over energy supplies (or some other casus belli) would certainly constitute a profound challenge to the ocean's system of maritime security.[59] Even in such a scenario of large-scale war between the developed states, however, it is worth noting that disruption of the Indian Ocean's maritime domain would require ships capable of long-range blue-water operations. The number of navies in the world today capable of extended operations is limited to a relatively small number of states: the United States, the large European nations, China, Russia, and India. These navies would face significant challenges in disrupting maritime traffic given the scale and magnitude of the ocean's seaborne commerce.

IMPLICATIONS FOR MARITIME STRATEGY

Maritime security and stability in the Indian Ocean are provided through the myriad formal and informal organizations that are all helping to police the ocean's waters.[60] As was noted at the outset of this chapter, the Indian Ocean today in some respects constitutes the quintessential globally policed environment, as envisioned by the authors of the United Nations charter. Although weak or failing states certainly pose threats to stability on land, it is difficult to see this instability disrupting the maritime domain. At present no state seeks domination or control over the Indian Ocean's waters. Instead, maritime security in the region is supported by many stakeholders, undergirded by the international community's acceptance of the norm of nonviolence on the high seas. As of this writing, there is no imminent systemic threat that could disrupt this vast maritime domain. The most significant threat in recent years has come from piracy surrounding the Horn of Africa and the coast of Somalia, to which the world's major navies, representing its most important trading nations, have responded vigorously and effectively. That the world has made such a concerted effort to solve such a small problem is in itself a testament to the benign maritime security environment in the Indian Ocean.

Just as important, the navies of the world that have been contributing to these efforts seem particularly willing to perform these policing functions in both formal and informal command and organizational structures. Operations in the maritime domain, built as they are on common best practices exercised by the world's navies, are particularly amenable to informally structured, task-centered organizations. It is clear that these cooperative maritime operations, which have a lineage dating back at least to the 1980s, have built a certain momentum and fostered the cooperation seen in today's Indian Ocean. There is no reason to believe that these cooperative efforts will somehow falter, propelled as they are by the inexorable logic that has promoted cooperation. All states have an undeniable and vital stake in the orderly functioning of the Indian Ocean's maritime environment, and under present conditions none could plausibly expect to gain from its disruption.

There are a number of uncertainties that will determine whether this logic continues to produce the array of globally administered maritime policing operations in the Indian Ocean. First and most important is the role of the US Navy, which, over the last forty years, has helped foster international participation in an array of cooperative seagoing operations that started in the Iran-Iraq War and have evolved into the combined task force operations conducted out of the Fifth Fleet's headquarters in Bahrain. The US Navy has been the glue for these various operations, providing shore-based command-and-control systems and administrative support to various task forces. It has also helped to develop the naval capacities of its partners in the region through its security cooperation programs. As long as the United States continues to support the development of the system of global maritime security, as proclaimed in the strategy documents that have followed the publication of *A Cooperative Strategy for 21st-Century Seapower* in 2007, this system will in all likelihood continue to grow and flourish in the Indian Ocean. The opposite is also true, however. If political, budgetary, or strategic circumstances were to cause American political and military leaders to deemphasize these activities, the system of cooperative maritime security would suffer. Without US leadership, maritime security in the Indian Ocean would certainly be less robust and effective than it is today.

A central issue facing maritime strategy and security in the Indian Ocean is the degree to which these myriad organizations could survive and function in the event of a war involving one or more of the region's major states. It is hard to see any other scenario that could systemically disrupt the Indian Ocean. Although Iran could certainly make life difficult in the Strait of Hormuz, it is difficult to see how it could keep the strait closed for an extended period. Clearly, the less formally structured of the maritime task forces would be the first to lose their coherence in such a scenario. The formally structured task groups, such as the CTFs and the EU and NATO operations, would have more staying power, but would be placed under operational stresses that would accrue from a generalized conflict that could reduce the national importance of counterpiracy operations.

Although there are certain fragilities in the Indian Ocean's system of maritime security, it is nonetheless difficult to envision realistic scenarios in which this system would fall apart. The ocean's place in the system of globally based maritime commerce resembles that of a supertanker, whose direction can be changed but whose forward momentum makes the vessel almost impossible to stop. This suggests that the future will indeed be like the past, as the Indian Ocean continues in its now well-established role as a peaceful maritime highway.

NOTES

1. W. H. Moreland, "The Ships of the Arabian Sea about AD 1500," *Journal of the Royal Asiatic Society of Great Britain and Ireland*, No. 1 (January 1939) 63–74.

2. For details on the activities of Portuguese vessels in the Indian Ocean in the fifteenth century, see Peter Boxhall, "Portuguese Seafarers in the Indian Ocean," *Asian Affairs* 23, no. 3 (November 1992): 322–30.

3. These are the states making up the Indian Ocean Rim Association for Regional Cooperation and Development. See the information paper on this association by Sasidaran Gopalan and Ramkishen S. Rajan, http://ramkishenrajan.gmu.edu/pdfs/publications/other_policy_briefs_and_opeds/2009/IOR.pdf.

4. US Energy Information Administration, *World Oil Transit Chokepoints* (Washington, DC: US Government Printing Office, 2014), http://www.eia.gov/beta/international/regions-topics.cfm?RegionTopicID=WOTC.

5. US Energy Information Administration, *International Energy Outlook 2011* (Washington, DC: US Government Printing Office, 2011), http://www.eia.gov/pressroom/presentations/howard_09192011.pdf.

6. Ibid., appendix A, 162.

7. Integrated Headquarters of the Indian Ministry of Defence (Navy), *Freedom to Use the Seas: India's Maritime Military Strategy* (New Delhi: Ministry of Defence, 2007), 44, http://www.irfc-nausena.nic.in/irfc/ezine/maritime_strat.pdf/Q2.

8. United Nations Conference on Trade and Development, *Review of Maritime Transport 2009: Report by the UNCTAD Secretariat* (Geneva: United Nations Conference on Trade and Development, 2009).

9. United Nations Conference on Trade and Development, *Review of Maritime Transport 2008: Report by the UNCTAD Secretariat*, United Nations (Geneva: United Nations Conference on Trade and Development, 2008), 23–24.

10. These figures were drawn from American Association of Port Authorities, "World Port Rankings 2013," http://aapa.files.cms-plus.com/Statistics/WORLD%20PORT%20RANKINGS%2020081.pdf.

11. "India to Construct Ports for Bigger Vessels," *The Hindu*, June 29, 2010, www.thehindu.com/business/Industry/article492144.ece.

12. National Intelligence Council, *Global Trends 2025* (Washington, DC: US Government Printing Office, 2008), 7.

13. David Barboza, "China Passes Japan as Second-Largest Economy," *New York Times*, August 15, 2010.

14. These views were encapsulated by Hillary Clinton (US secretary of state), "America's Pacific Century," *Foreign Policy*, 11 October 2011, www.foreignpolicy.com/articles/2011/10/11/americas_pacific_century. Also see Robert Kaplan, *Monsoon: The Indian Ocean and the Future of American Power* (New York: Random House, 2010); and Andrew S. Erickson, Walter C. Ladwig III, and Justin D. Mikolay, "Diego Garcia and the United States' Emerging Indian Ocean Strategy," *Asian Security* 6, no. 3 (2010): 214–37.

15. US Department of the Navy, *A Cooperative Strategy for 21st-Century Seapower* (Washington, DC: US Government Printing Office, 2007), 9.

16. Boxhall, "Portuguese Seafarers." Also see Michael Pearson, *The Indian Ocean* (London: Routledge, 2003); K. N. Chaudhuri, *Trade and Civilization in the Indian Ocean: An Economic History from the Rise of Islam to 1750* (Cambridge: Cambridge University Press, 1985); Emrys Chew, *Crouching Tiger, Hidden Dragon: The Indian Ocean and the Maritime Balance of Power in Historical Perspective*, Working Paper 144 (Singapore: S. Rajaratnam School of International Studies, 2007).

17. For additional detail, see Elmer Belmont Potter, ed., *Seapower: A Naval History* (Annapolis, MD: Naval Institute Press, 1960).

18. This was by no means a new problem. See Patricia Risso, "Cross-Cultural Perceptions of Piracy: Maritime Violence in the Western Indian Ocean and Persian Gulf Region during a Long 18th Century," *Journal of World History* 12, no. 2 (Fall 2001): 293–319.

19. This is as quoted by J. F. Standish, "British Maritime Policy in the Persian Gulf," *Middle Eastern Studies* 3, no. 4 (July 1967): 327.

20. Paul S. Dull, *The Battle History of the Imperial Japanese Navy* (Annapolis, MD: Naval Institute Press, 1978); and Stephen W. Roskill, *The War at Sea Vol. II: The Period of Balance* (London: Her Majesty's Stationery Office, 1956).

21. The early years of the US Navy's presence in Bahrain are chronicled by David Winkler, *Amirs, Admirals & Desert Sailors* (Annapolis, MD: Naval Institute Press, 2007).

22. For the details, see Peter Hinchcliffe, John T. Ducker, and Maria Holt, *Without Glory in Arabia: The British Retreat from Aden* (London: I. B. Tauris, 2007).

23. The texts of the agreements can be found at www.austlii.edu.au/au/other/dfat /treaties/1971/21.html. Good recent treatments of the accords are those by Carlyle A. Thayer, "The Five-Power Defence Arrangements: The Quiet Achiever," *Security Challenges* 3, no. 1 (February 2007): 79–96, http://www.securitychallenges.org.au /ArticlePDFs/vol3no1Thayer.pdf; and Ralf Emmers, *The Role of the Five-Power Defence Arrangements in the Southeast Asian Security Architecture*, Working Paper 5 (Singapore: S. Rajaratnam School of International Studies, 2010), www.rsis.edu.sg/publications /WorkingPapers/WP195.pdfQ3.

24. One of the best summaries of this period is given by Michael A. Palmer, *Guardians of the Gulf* (New York: Free Press, 1992).

25. Albert E. Graham, "Soviet Strategy and Policy in the Indian Ocean," in *Naval Power in Soviet Policy*, vol. 2, ed. Paul J. Murphy (Washington, DC: US Government Printing Office, 1978); Bruce W. Watson, *Red Navy at Sea: Soviet Naval Operation on the High Seas 1956–1980* (Boulder, CO: Westview Press, 1980); Walter K. Andersen, "Emerging Security Issues in the Indian Ocean: An American Perspective," in *Super-power Rivalry in the Indian Ocean: Indian and American Perspectives*, ed. Selig. S. Harrison and K. Subrahmanyam (New York: Oxford University Press, 1989), 12–83.

26. Alvin J. Cottrell and Walter F. Hahn, *Naval Race or Arms Control in the Indian Ocean* (New York: National Strategy Information Center, 1978).

27. For background on this period, see Inder Khosla, "Indian Ocean as a Zone of Peace," *International Studies* 21 (1981): 417–43; For a good summary of the role that the deterioration that superpower relations played in the Indian Ocean in the late 1970s, see Chandra Kumar, "The Indian Ocean: Arc of Crisis or Zone of Peace?" *International Affairs* 60, no. 2 (Spring 1984): 233–46.

28. The background for this is given by Walter K. Andersen and Leo Rose, "Superpowers in the Indian Ocean: Goals and Objectives," in *The Indian Ocean as a Zone of Peace*, International Peace Academy Report 24 (New York: United Nations, 1986), 1–48.

29. Dilip Hiro, *The Longest War: The Iran–Iraq Military Conflict* (London: Routledge, 1991).

30. See www.jimmycarterlibrary.org/documents/speeches/su80jec.phtml.

31. William M. Arkin and David Chappell, "Forward Offensive Strategy: Raising the Stakes in the Pacific," *World Policy Journal* 2, no. 3 (Summer 1985): 481–500.

32. The background for this is given by Joseph A. Kechician, *Oman and the World: Emergence of an Independent Foreign Policy* (Santa Monica, CA: RAND Corporation, 1995).

33. US Department of Defense, *United States Security Strategy for the Middle East* (Washington, DC: US Government Printing Office, 1995).

34. Rasul B. Rais, *The Indian Ocean and the Superpowers* (New York: Barnes & Noble, 1987).

35. The details of this are given by William E. Smith and Phillip Finnegan, "Terrorism: Scouring the Red Sea Floor," *Time Magazine*, August 27, 1984, www.time.com /time/magazine/article/0,9171,926817,00.html.

36. This is as summarized by Stephen Andrew Kelley, "Better Lucky Than Good: Operation Earnest Will as Gunboat Diplomacy" (master's thesis, Naval Postgraduate School, Monterey, CA, June 2007), 19–33.

37. This is comprehensively covered by Martin S. Navais and E. R. Hooten, *Tanker War: The Assault on Merchant Shipping during the Iran–Iraq Crisis* (London: I. B. Tauris, 1996).

38. See the statement by Michael H. Armacost, undersecretary of state for political affairs, before the US Senate Foreign Relations Committee, June 16, 1987; released as Current Policy 978 by the Bureau of Public Affairs of the US Department of State.

39. Hansard 1803–2005, June 15, 1988, on Armilla Patrol, http://hansard.millbank systems.com/lords/1988/jun/15/armilla-patrol.

40. The texts of the UN Security Council resolutions can be found at www.fas.org /news/un/iraq/sres/sres0665.htm.

41. The background for this is given by Norman Friedman, "Sailing in the Sand: The US Navy's Role in the Gulf War," in *The Eagle and the Desert: Looking Back on US Involvement in the Persian Gulf War*, ed. William Head and Earl H. Tiford Jr. (Westport, CT: Praeger, 1996), 251–66. Also see US Department of Defense, *Conduct of the Persian Gulf War: Final Report to the Congress* (Washington, DC: US Government Printing Office, 1992), http://www.tjsl.edu/slomansonb/9.7_Conduct_PGW_I.pdf.

42. See http://eunavfor.eu/key-facts-and-figures.

43. NATO, "Counter-Piracy: Operation Ocean Shield," Public Diplomacy Division Press and Media Section, Media Operations Centre, NATO Headquarters, www.nato .int/nato_static/assets/pdf/pdf_2010_01/20100204_20100128-Fact_Sheet_Counter piracy.pdf.

44. The thirty-first quarterly meeting, in March 2014, brought together ninety delegates from thirty-three countries; see http://combinedmaritimeforces.com/2014 /03/13/31st-shade-conference-held-in-bahrain/.

45. This was detailed in a presentation by Michio Harada, director of the Maritime Security Policy Division of the Japanese Ministry of Foreign Affairs, at the Naval Postgraduate School, June 11, 2010.

46. Admiral Sureesh Mehta, chief of Indian Naval Staff, "Changing Roles of Navies in the Contemporary World Order, with Specific Reference to the Indian Navy," speech before the Institute for Defence Studies and Analysis, New Delhi, August 13, 2008, http://www.idsa.in/jds/3_2_2009_ChangingRolesofNavies_smehta.html.

47. US Department of the Navy, *Cooperative Strategy*, 7.

48. For the details of the International Maritime Organization's meeting, see www .imo.org/OurWork/Security/PIU/Pages/DCCMeeting.aspx.

49. This is comprehensively covered by Lauren Ploch, Christopher M. Blanchard, Ronald O'Rourke, R. Chuck Mason, and Rawle O. King, "Piracy off the Horn of Africa," Congressional Research Service, Report R40528, Washington, DC, April 19, 2010.

50. See the most recent report by the International Chamber of Commerce's International Maritime Bureau, January 2015, http://www.hellenicshippingnews.com/wp-content/uploads/2015/01/2014-Annual-IMB-Piracy-Report-ABRIDGED.pdf. For an assessment of US counterpiracy operations off the coast of Somalia, during the period when the threat was at its worst, see Lesley Anne Warner, "Pieces of Eight: An Assessment of US Counterpiracy Options in the Horn of Africa," *Naval War College Review* 63, no. 2 (Spring 2010): 61–87.

51. For the details, see Robert F. Worth, "Tanker Damage Caused by Attack, Inquiry Finds," *New York Times*, August 7, 2010.

52. This is as argued by Kaplan, *Monsoon*.

53. The idea of such a strategic triangle is discussed by James R. Holmes and Toshi Yoshihara, "China and the United States in the Indian Ocean: An Emerging Strategic Triangle?" *Naval War College Review* 61, no. 3 (Summer 2008). The authors downplay the prospect that this triangle will disrupt maritime interactions in the Indian Ocean. Also see Bronson Percival, "Growing Chinese and Indian Naval Power: US Recalibration and Coalition Building," in *Southeast Asia and the Rise of Chinese and Indian Naval Power: Between Rising Naval Powers*, ed. Sam Bateman and Joshua Ho (London: Routledge, 2012), 36–47.

54. Realists assert that states will inevitably collide as they vie for power and influence in the international system as they continuously seek to balance and counterbalance their rivals. For different variations in this argument, see Hans Morgenthau, *Politics among Nations* (New York: Alfred A. Knopf, 1948); Kenneth N. Waltz, *Theory of International Politics* (Reading, MA: Addison-Wesley, 1979); John J. Mearsheimer, *The Tragedy of Great Power Politics* (New York: W. W. Norton, 2001); and Stephen M. Walt, *The Origins of Alliances* (Ithaca, NY: Cornell University Press, 1990).

55. Christopher J. Pehrson, *String of Pearls: Meeting the Challenge of China's Rising Power across the Asian Littoral* (Carlisle, PA: US Army War College Strategic Studies Institute, 2006).

56. Ibid.

57. These views are summarized by Captain Sameer Saxena, Indian Navy, "One Ocean, Two Shades: Perceptions about the Indian Ocean," *Journal of National Security Studies*, Fall 2011, 25, www.usnwc.edu/Lucent/OpenPdf.aspx?id=101&Title=Evolution. For background on India's push to develop a blue-water navy, see David Scott, "India's Drive for a 'Blue Water' Navy," *Journal of Military and Strategic Studies* 10, no. 2 (Winter 2007–8), www.jmss.org/jmss/index.php/jmss/article/download/90/100.

58. Chauduri, *Trade*.

59. This scenario is addressed by Daniel Moran and James A. Russell, eds., *Energy Security and Global Politics: The Militarization of Resource Management* (New York: Routledge, 2009).

60. This is as argued by Lee Cordner, "Progressing Maritime Security Cooperation in the Indian Ocean," *Naval War College Review* 64, no. 4 (Autumn 2011): 68–88.

PART III

Architecture

CHAPTER 8

The Warship since the End of the Cold War

LARRIE D. FERREIRO

WHAT IS A WARSHIP IN THE POST-COLD WAR ERA?

A warship is the most visible expression of a nation's maritime strategy, the physical manifestation of its ability to exercise power away from its own shores. This exercise of power may take several forms: military, economic, and political. A warship is unique in a nation's overall arsenal, in that it embodies all three. A tank, a fighter, and a destroyer may all bring military force to bear on an objective. But only a warship is routinely used in the economic projection of power, either in the protection of sea lines of communication (SLOCs) or in denying an adversary maritime access. Ground combat vehicles, by contrast, do not regularly accompany eighteen-wheel freight haulers across borders; nor, barring extraordinary circumstances, do fighters interdict passenger or cargo jets. And of course if a nation's army were to pay a visit to a neighboring country, it would be seen as an act of aggression, whereas warships routinely show the flag in foreign ports, exerting political and diplomatic influence simply by their presence. Under international law, a warship is considered a mobile parcel of sovereign national territory.[1]

A warship is also different from other military platforms in more elemental ways. Although it is no longer the most complex or even the most expensive system in a nation's arsenal (these honors now belong to military aircraft), it is fundamentally distinct from a fighter, bomber, tank, or helicopter. Like the other platforms, a modern warship is just one node in a complex system of systems comprising naval, air, and land forces, an operational model that long predates the network-centric concept of war fighting. Unlike the other platforms, however, a warship can also be a self-sufficient unit capable of independently carrying out multiple missions on extended deployment, compared with an individual tank or fighter, which performs a single (or at most dual) task measured in hours or a few days, and which must operate within a larger organization to carry out multimission, long-term operations. In fact, a medium-sized warship such as a destroyer more closely resembles an entire army battalion or aviation squadron than an individual tank or aircraft. Table 8.1 shows a comparison between a NATO-type destroyer and a notional Western army battalion, which is generally the lowest administrative element organized around a specific set of tasks and capable of self-sufficient, long-term deployment. As this chapter argues, it is the warship's inherent multitasking flexibility that makes it uniquely effective throughout the extended cycles of maritime strategy.

A warship is defined by the *Oxford English Dictionary* as "a ship armed and manned for war." Many other sources use similar language to describe a weapons-carrying vessel. In this chapter I argue that this definition is no longer useful in the post–Cold War era. The lines between traditional combatants and other naval vessels are becoming blurred as their roles evolve and, in some cases, merge; the Danish flexible support ship *Absalon*, the New Zealand multirole vessel *Canterbury*, and the Dutch Joint Support Ship are some recent examples that combine elements of sealift and fleet command.

Table 8.1 A Comparison of a NATO-Type Destroyer and a Notional Western Battalion

Aspect	Destroyer	Battalion (task-organized)
Commanding officer	O-5 (commander)	O-5 (lieutenant colonel)
Crew/troops	150–350	300–500
Guns	1–2 medium-caliber 300–1,200 rounds	30–40 medium/heavy tanks 900–1,600 rounds
Land attack	8–90 land attack missiles	6–9 howitzers (support element)
Antiair defense	Short- and medium-range	Short-range (support element)
Helicopter	1–2 (organic)	3–8 (support element)
Deployment time	30 days (typical)	30 days (typical)

Sources: Organization of the US Army, *Pamphlet 10–1* (Washington DC: US Department of the Army, 2004); author's synthesis of information from *Jane's Fighting Ships*, 1989–2009.

Therefore, in this chapter I employ a more expansive definition of my own: a ship equipped to carry out the means of war, project a nation's influence and protect its interests, which encompasses traditional warships (submarines, destroyers, aircraft carriers, etc.), as well as mine warfare vessels, patrol and coast guard ships, and logistics support vessels (including naval auxiliaries) that carry fuel, cargo, troops, and supplies to fleets and theaters of operation on both land and sea.

This chapter describes the modern post–Cold War warship; or, more accurately, it provides a snapshot of the warship's continuous evolution, taken at a point twenty years after the fall of the Berlin Wall, as the broad outlines of post–Cold War world are beginning to emerge. That they will continue to evolve is, of course, certain. The global forces that are shaping the warship's future are discussed throughout this book and are not repeated here. I argue that national strategic and technological responses to these forces require ever more flexible warships, capable of carrying out a wider range of missions; and that such flexibility has driven the post–Cold War warship to become (1) increasingly expeditionary in nature, meaning that it will need to carry a wider range of systems and payloads in order to project force over longer distances and for greater durations; (2) larger and designed with open architectures, both for the flexibility to carry a wider range of systems and payloads across increasing distances and periods of endurance, as well as ensuring that they will continue to function over the life of the vessel as these systems are upgraded and replaced; and (3) progressively more expensive in real terms, in spite of efforts to rein in costs, due to the escalating complexity of systems and the growth of requirements and standards.

This chapter is international in scope, examining a globally representative cross section of fourteen navies from every continent and of every scale. It begins with the naval policies and doctrines that emerged in the aftermath of the Cold War, and examines how national fleets have adapted to new conditions in the two decades following the fall of the Berlin Wall. Fleets and ships always respond to such far-reaching political change, but they are also the product of other influences. Maritime industries and technology are all shaped by market and governmental forces over which navies often have little direct control. This forms the second section of the chapter. The final section weaves these two threads—strategic imperatives and national infrastructure—into an examination of the post–Cold War warship and the implications for its future development.

STRATEGY: FROM THE SEA TO THE SHORE

The end of the Cold War in 1989 caused every nation on Earth to rethink its national strategy, in many cases requiring a wholesale rewriting of existing policies and doctrine.[2] During the Cold War, the actions of many nations were often defined within a very simple framework: Did they more greatly benefit the American sphere of influence or the Soviet one? The stunningly rapid demise of the Soviet Union, and the equally rapid gravitation of former Soviet Bloc nations toward Western structures like NATO, created a single, overarching sphere of influence consisting of the vast majority of nations now striving for unfettered global commerce. At the same time, each nation had to confront its own distinct strategic priorities outside the old clash-of-the-superpowers framework. Nowhere were these changes more noticeable than in the rapid evolution of maritime doctrines. In this section I briefly describe the naval postures adopted by representative nations around the globe in the immediate aftermath of the Cold War, using published doctrines and analyses as well as a quantitative evaluation of how their naval strength evolved in the period from 1989 to 2009. These data are summarized in table 8.2, which gives basic information on the evolution of selected fleets in the immediate aftermath of the Cold War.[3] I then synthesize how the broad trends that became apparent during this period may shape future warship development.

The United States, the world's lone remaining superpower, articulated its post–Cold War naval strategy in two white papers issued in 1992 and 1994, titled respectively ". . . From the Sea" and "Forward . . . From the Sea." Together, these documents clarified the shift away from countering the massive Soviet Navy and toward engaging in smaller-scale operations in the littoral regions and projecting power ashore in land-based conflicts. In fact, these were precisely the kinds of missions that the US Navy had already been performing throughout the Cold War, so the demise of the Soviet Union did not augur any major naval restructuring in the manner that the air force and army underwent.[4] As table 8.2 shows, although fleet numbers diminished by roughly half in the twenty years after the Berlin Wall fell, the proportion of submarines, surface combatants, and the like remained roughly constant. Even so, the average size of vessels grew by almost 40 percent, a trend that, for reasons that are considered further below, is likely to continue.

The shift to extended deployment in the littorals required a rethinking of doctrine. During the Cold War, mine warfare (MIW) and antisubmarine warfare (ASW) were focused on the protection of SLOCs and moving forces

Table 8.2 The Evolution of Naval Strength for Selected Countries, 1989–2009

Country and Force Type	1989		1999		2009	
	Number	Displacement	Number	Displacement	Number	Displacement
Australia						
Submarine	6	2,300	6	3,500	6	3,500
Expeditionary	1	5,700	4	6,000	5	18,000
Surface combatant	14	3,600	14	3,900	15	4,300
Ocean patrol / coast guard	None		None		2	6,900
Mine warfare	3	200	6	700	6	700
Logistics	2	8,500	2	32,000	2	32,000
Fleet total	26	89,000	32	167,000	36	238,000
Chile						
Submarine	4	2,000	4	2,000	4	1,500
Expeditionary	5	1,200	5	2,400	5	2,600
Surface combatant	11	5,200	6	4,600	8	3,900
Ocean patrol / coast guard	1	3,000	6	500	6	1,000
Logistics	6	8,800	3	10,000	3	10,000
Fleet total	27	127,000	24	82,000	26	86,000
China						
Submarine	46	3,900	84	2,400	68	3,000
Expeditionary	75	2,000	56	2,000	86	3,100
Surface combatant	54	2,600	62	2,600	78	3,100
Ocean patrol / coast guard	None		None		6	2,000
Mine warfare	24	600	41	700	21	700
Logistics	66	3,000	70	3,400	126	3,600
Fleet total	265	690,000	313	743,000	385	1,209,000
Denmark						
Submarine	4	500	6	500	None	
Expeditionary	None		None		2	6,300
Surface combatant	7	2,000	7	2,700	10	3,500
Ocean patrol / coast guard	16	400	16	700	12	700
Logistics	3	1,000	1	500	1	500
Fleet total	30	22,000	30	35,000	25	57,000

Table 8.2 The Evolution of Naval Strength for Selected Countries, 1989–2009 (*continued*)

Country and Force Type	1989		1999		2009	
	Number	Displacement	Number	Displacement	Number	Displacement
France						
Submarine	27	3,700	12	5,700	10	7,300
Expeditionary	12	10,000	12	11,2000	11	18,500
Surface combatant	42	2,800	31	3,300	35	4,700
Ocean patrol / coast guard	12	600	22	1,300	21	2,000
Mine warfare	10	500	13	600	13	600
Logistics	17	12,500	8	10,900	8	14,600
Fleet total	120	561,000	98	431,000	98	593,000
India						
Submarine	15	2,600	19	2,700	22	2,400
Expeditionary	11	5,800	11	4,5000	14	11,500
Surface combatant	30	2,600	34	3,200	41	3,900
Ocean patrol / coast guard	6	1,300	21	1,500	32	2,000
Mine warfare	12	800	12	800	10	800
Logistics	8	5,700	10	9,000	12	12,500
Fleet total	82	246,000	107	340,000	131	597,000
Japan						
Submarine	17	2,500	18	2,700	22	3,600
Expeditionary	6	1,800	8	6,6000	5	15,600
Surface combatant	63	2,900	62	3,800	53	5,400
Ocean patrol / coast guard	78	1,800	95	1,600	57	2,200
Mine warfare	37	600	34	1,000	37	1,000
Logistics	6	5,700	6	3,700	7	15,700
Fleet total	207	395,000	223	546,000	181	718,000
Singapore						
Submarine	None		4	1,200	6	1,300
Expeditionary	5	4,100	5	8,000	4	8,500
Surface combatant	6	600	6	600	12	2,600
Ocean patrol / coast guard	None		12	500	12	500
Mine warfare	2	400	4	400	4	500
Fleet total	13	26,000	31	56,000	38	73,000

Country and Force Type	1989		1999		2009	
	Number	Displacement	Number	Displacement	Number	Displacement
South Africa						
Submarine	3	1,000	2	1,000	3	1,600
Surface combatant	2	2,100	None		4	3,600
Mine warfare	8	400	6	400	3	400
Logistics	3	20,000	2	17,000	1	12,500
Fleet total	15	50,000	10	38,000	11	32,000
South Korea						
Submarine	3	200	9	1,300	14	1,300
Expeditionary	15	2,100	13	3,600	7	6,300
Surface combatant	30	2,200	46	1,900	49	2,600
Ocean patrol / coast guard	3	3,000	6	3,000	12	3,000
Mine warfare	9	400	16	600	10	900
Logistics	6	2,700	4	6,700	3	9,200
Fleet total	66	123,000	94	200,000	95	263,000
Spain						
Submarine	8	1,400	6	1,200	8	2,100
Expeditionary	7	11,700	6	10,200	6	15,000
Surface combatant	23	3,300	17	3,200	12	4,800
Ocean patrol / coast guard	4	1,000	7	1,500	18	1,800
Mine warfare	12	500	9	500	6	500
Logistics	7	4,400	7	5,600	6	10,500
Fleet total	61	209,000	52	177,000	56	264,000
United Kingdom						
Submarine	37	4,300	16	7,800	17	8,200
Expeditionary	11	13,000	8	18,200	6	42,400
Surface combatant	57	4,000	38	4,400	31	5,100
Ocean patrol / coast guard	11	1,600	7	1,300	7	2,000
Mine warfare	49	700	25	600	16	600
Logistics	19	27,000	23	25,200	21	24,200
Fleet total	184	1,100,000	117	913,000	98	1,087,000

Table 8.2 The Evolution of Naval Strength for Selected Countries, 1989–2009 (*continued*)

Country and Force Type	1989		1999		2009	
	Number	Displacement	Number	Displacement	Number	Displacement
United States of America						
Submarine	162	7,200	66	8,100	77	10,200
Expeditionary	95	29,000	67	36,500	62	36,200
Surface combatant	251	6,500	123	7,700	118	7,900
Ocean patrol / coast guard	38	1,400	55	1,600	49	2,400
Mine warfare	30	900	27	1,800	14	1,400
Logistics	159	34,000	123	37,600	98	46,800
Fleet total	735	11,053,000	461	8,687,000	418	8,700,000
USSR (1989); Russia plus other former Soviet Union (1999, 2009)						
Submarine	372	5,800	89	8,700	75	9,400
Expeditionary	97	9,200	32	6,300	29	6,300
Surface combatant	376	3,700	124	3,400	77	3,900
Ocean patrol / coast guard	134	900	36	1,000	43	2,000
Mine warfare	323	500	72	500	59	600
Logistics	358	18,000	43	9,000	48	10,500
Fleet total	1,660	6,600,000	396	1,824,000	331	1,751,000
Russia only			364	1,776,000	290	1,697,000

Sources: Jane's Fighting Ships, 1988–89, 1999–2000, and 2008–9. Displacement figures are the average for each ship type, in tons, except for the fleet total. Submarines include strategic, attack, and patrol submarines. Expeditionary ships include aircraft and helicopter carriers plus amphibious assault ships. Surface combatants include cruisers, destroyers, frigates, and corvettes. Ocean patrol / coast guard and mine warfare ships exclude inshore and limited-capability coastwise craft such as fast-attack craft, as their numbers sometimes overwhelm the fleet count. China, for example, had 857 fast-attack craft in its fleet in 1989. Logistics ships include fleet logistics ships (e.g., underway replenishment) as well as expeditionary cargo and troop transport vessels.

into enemy bastions, with dedicated ships providing a protective bubble around each. In the post–Cold War era, these threats shifted into the littoral theater, so new doctrine pointed to the need for a fleet-based, organic capability with MIW and ASW that could move with (or even ahead of) the naval force, as embodied, for instance, in the littoral combat ship (LCS) concept. Post–Cold War maritime strategy also redirected attention to a type of amphibious warfare known as ship-to-objective maneuvering, in which an armed force bypasses vulnerable beachheads to strike directly at critical inland targets; also to the need for ships, such as the joint high-speed vessel, to deploy rapidly, even without developed shore infrastructure; and for at-sea basing of troops and equipment in order to securely support its forces ashore.[5]

In 2007 the US Navy, US Marine Corps, and US Coast Guard issued a revised general statement of their strategic approach, which explained how they would also work with international partners to deter war and maintain global order. *A Cooperative Strategy for 21st Century Seapower* firmly established the commitment to protect global commerce as part of the core mission of America's sea services. It also elevated humanitarian assistance and disaster response to core capabilities. The *Cooperative Strategy* also noted that only a full-scale maritime partnership between nations can ensure that all of America's strategic imperatives are met.[6] More recent developments have added texture to this maritime strategic posture, including the elevation of the sea-based Aegis Ballistic Missile Defense (BMD) system to the primary means of countering future ballistic missile threats, and the Arctic Roadmap, which outlines a near-term strategy to address the opening of the Arctic region to shipping and industrial activities like mining.[7]

Russia

During the Cold War the former Soviet Navy was built to support the Red Army, by denying NATO forces access to the European theater and protecting the Soviet Union's maritime bastions. These missions required massive submarine and surface combatant fleets that could surge at short notice to strike Western convoys and battle groups. Even the late–Cold War aircraft carriers were primarily intended to support surface naval action. Ships were manned by large numbers of conscripts, and the operational tempo was far less intense than in NATO navies, whose crews were increasingly all-volunteer professionals.

After the new Russian Federation was founded in 1991, its military underwent a ten-year free fall. As table 8.2 shows, the navy discarded eight out of every ten ships. In 2000–2001 the Russian government signed new military and maritime doctrines (updated in 2009) that reflected the much-reduced role of the armed forces. They were now defensive in nature, and thus were primarily intended to defeat both internal and external threats to Russia's sovereignty, with the navy focused on the security of Russian territorial waters (including the Arctic) and the protection of its maritime approaches. This was reflected in the fleet's makeup, which saw a proportional diminution of the logistics force in favor of more patrol and coast guard vessels, an expeditionary capability limited to regional deployment, and the loss of much of its fledgling aircraft carrier fleet. Russia aimed to modernize its military by professionalizing its personnel and buying equipment from abroad, originally contracting with France for a pair of *Mistral*-class landing helicopter dock (LHD)–type amphibious ships equipped with large flight decks and well docks before the contract was canceled in 2015, due to political concerns.[8] The other former Soviet navies (Ukraine, Latvia, etc.) have since slowly built up their capabilities, primarily in coastal and mine warfare.

The United Kingdom

The British Ministry of Defence immediately reexamined the roles of Britain's armed forces in the post–Cold War world, beginning with the 1990 *Options for Change*, through the decisive 1998 *Strategic Defense Review* and a pair of policy statements in 2003–4, the two-volume *Delivering Security in a Changing World*. Its maritime vision, *British Maritime Doctrine (BR 1806)*, was also revised and updated several times.[9] Together, they marked a shift away from a NATO-centered strategy—in particular, supporting ASW and MIW operations to protect North Atlantic SLOCs—and toward a robust and sustainable expeditionary capability for projecting force landward, either independently or as part of a coalition.

This expeditionary focus was immediately visible in the rapid evolution of the British fleet. The submarine force shed its diesel boats to become all-nuclear, and added the capability to carry and employ land-attack cruise missiles. It replaced its three light aircraft carriers with two large carriers that embark the short takeoff / vertical landing (STOVL) F-35 Strike Fighter, and added several large amphibious ships (including amphibious logistics support ships) and a dedicated helicopter carrier. Dedicated mine warfare ships were phased out in favor of MIW systems deployed on other ships. The net result has been that, though the number of ships was halved in the aftermath of the Cold War—that is, the period 1991–2009—their average size almost doubled, so the British navy's aggregate tonnage remained almost constant.

China

During the Cold War, China's Navy, like that of the USSR, was principally focused on supporting its ground forces; the Chinese Navy was then, and remains, under the control of the People's Liberation Army. Army and navy missions have thus tended to evolve together. In 1985, well before the end of the Cold War, China's military posture shifted from defense against a Soviet attack to limited wars around its borders. Its maritime strategy consequently shifted from coastal to offshore defense, and has been evolving on that basis ever since. The specific goals and objectives of this strategy have been the subject of intense scrutiny and debate. China regularly publishes white papers on its national defense, the latest in 2015.[10] These papers have been rather general and somewhat vague, so a host of assessments by Western analysts have attempted to fill in the gaps. Although no clear consensus has emerged, the broad outlines appear to be that, though the navy has continued to emphasize sea denial missions to prevent Western forces from interfering in a Taiwan scenario, its focus has shifted to military operations other than war, toward extending China's regional influence in the Pacific Ocean and Indian Ocean, and protecting its vital flow of imports (especially oil) from interruptions. These trends all became apparent in the early years of this century.

China long relied on Russian-built or -designed ships and equipment for its fleet. After 1989 it developed a greater indigenous capability to design and produce these systems. As table 8.2 shows, these efforts focused on building up and modernizing its surface combatant and submarine forces. Its coastal defense fleet of fast-attack craft and torpedo boats shrank drastically, but also became more integrated with shore-based networks that included ballistic and cruise missile systems. Its logistics and expeditionary capabilities, though becoming more extensive, remained limited to local operations. Long-range power projection remained limited, though a step toward remedying this was taken in 2012, with the commissioning of China's first aircraft carrier, *Liaoning*.[11]

Japan and South Korea

Japan and South Korea emerged from the Cold War with remarkably similar defense and security structures (even their defense white papers are almost mirror images). Both were (and remain) strongly allied with the United States, and they are primarily focused on the potential threat from North Korea, while keeping a wary eye on other regional powers, notably China. Both have worked to develop their abilities to operate out of area, in conjunction with international peacekeeping forces.[12] Japan's navy—along with its notably robust coast guard, which controls its extensive maritime territory— grew steadily in tonnage and capability, augmenting its expeditionary forces with helicopter-carrying LHD-type ships and equipping its Aegis-equipped destroyers with BMD capability. South Korea's navy, about half the size of Japan's, has a similar makeup, including Aegis-equipped destroyers and LHD-type ships deploying helicopters. Both navies built submarines equipped with conventional air-independent propulsion (AIP), designed to give them a longer submerged patrol capability.

India

As shown in table 8.2, the Indian navy almost doubled in size in every domain in the twenty years following the end of the Cold War. The aim was to secure India's regional primacy, a policy that has been compared with the emergence of a Monroe Doctrine for the Indian Ocean basin. The goals of the navy and coast guard were initially codified in a 2007 strategic document, *Freedom to Use the Seas*, which declared India's determination to deter conflict, ensure maritime domain awareness, guarantee the free flow of goods, project and sustain power within the region for extended periods, and participate in UN operations.[13] The navy's modernization programs aimed to replace its heavily Russian infrastructure with ships and equipment designed and built indigenously or under license from other nations like France. The Ministry of Defence took over the state-owned Hindustan Shipyard in 2009, and has focused its efforts on warship building in order to speed up the process.[14] The diesel boats in its submarine force have given way to new models with AIP, and nuclear boats, including India's first class of ballistic missile subs. Its expeditionary capabilities grew rapidly with the purchase of a Russian aircraft carrier, the construction of an indigenously built aircraft carrier, and plans for four new amphibious ships.[15] It also expanded its coast guard fleet in the wake of a series of terrorist attacks.[16]

France

The demise of the Soviet Union did not dramatically alter France's military posture, which had traditionally placed sovereign national interests, including protection of its overseas territories, well ahead of alliance obligations. The 20 percent reduction in its fleet numbers after 1989 was thus proportionally smaller than that of the other major naval powers. The first post–Cold War *livre blanc* (white paper), issued in 1994, established the creation of an all-professional military and laid the groundwork for augmenting its force projection capability.[17] The 2007 *livre blanc* reinforced the requirements for long-distance force projection, especially in the Indian and Pacific oceans.[18] As a consequence, the total fleet tonnage of the French fleet actually increased, by virtue of being made up of a smaller number of much larger ships, capable of operating on distant stations. The submarine force shed its conventionally powered boats in favor of an all-nuclear fleet. Meanwhile, patrol vessels and amphibious ships increased in size and number. Focus shifted away from NATO to the European Union, in particular to addressing the need for a pan-European defense industrial policy. This new emphasis became apparent in France's ship and equipment programs—for example, the *Horizon* and multimission frigates jointly developed with Italy, and the Principal Anti-Air Missile System systems, jointly developed with Italy and the United Kingdom.

Spain and Australia

During the Cold War Spain's navy was built around providing NATO with ASW and MIW defenses against Soviet forces, although it had some expeditionary capability as well. Australia's navy gradually lost its expeditionary role and instead concentrated on countering the Soviet threat. These two nations emerged from the Cold War with a renewed focus on power projection, or, as the Spanish navy puts it, on "projecting stability" in a globally connected world. The connection between the two navies has gone beyond comparable strategic goals. In 2007 the Spanish naval shipbuilder Navantia won the contract to build up Australia's navy with ships based on Spanish designs, including Aegis-capable destroyers and amphibious ships supporting STOVL aircraft. Both nations augmented their ocean patrol and logistics capabilities in similar fashion.[19]

Chile, Denmark, Singapore, and South Africa

The navies of Chile, Denmark, Singapore, and South Africa are all smaller than those discussed so far. Each has had a somewhat different maritime focus. The Chilean Navy, like many South American navies, spent much of the Cold War in the uncomfortable role of providing ASW support to US forces, using second-hand vessels and equipment. After the Cold War it moved toward a more diversified three-vector strategy: the defense of maritime sovereignty, enforcement of maritime laws, and participation in international operations. Although it still has a sizable second-hand fleet, it has developed many of its own mission systems and is building new patrol ships. The Danish Navy reduced its numbers and rationalized its missions. It shed its submarine fleet and consolidated many activities into fewer but larger vessels, most notably in the *Absalon* class of flexible support ships, which have proved their worth in antipiracy operations. Singapore's post–Cold War navy, centered on six frigates built under license from France, has been deployed mainly against seaborne terrorist threats and for the protection of shipping in its strategically vital straits and territorial waters. Its small but capable amphibious fleet participated in both military and humanitarian international operations around the Indian Ocean region. South Africa's navy was also constructed around a fleet of frigates (built in Germany) with a largely sea-control mission, including protection of the vital shipping route around the Cape of Good Hope.[20]

General Strategic Trends

Several trends emerged from this global portrait of the world's navies, as they adapted to the collapse of what had been a preponderant global threat:

- Increased expeditionary role: More navies were tasked to project power overseas and ashore, and to control the littorals, in wartime as well as for other missions such as disaster response. This has translated into a greater number of aviation ships (helicopter and aircraft carriers) and ships with amphibious assault capability (well-dock ships). Many navies, especially medium-sized ones, have turned to LHD-type ships to provide both capabilities. Land-attack missiles, which would have had little or no application against the Soviets, have been deployed on many surface combatants and submarines.
- The changing nature of expeditionary warfare: Controlling the littorals has meant that fleets must have their own ASW and MIW capabilities, requiring either faster ships to move ahead of the fleet or the deployment of these systems aboard fleet vessels. The increasing emphasis on expeditionary operations has also led to increased seaborne logistics capabilities, to maintain fleets and forces ashore for extended periods.

- Increased threats to merchant shipping, homeland, and territorial waters: Navies and coast guards have deployed to wider and more distant areas of the oceans (including the Arctic) to control and protect vital commerce routes, economic zones, and maritime approaches. This is likely to mean more extensive requirements for surveillance of operational regions.

- Expanded cooperation: The end of the bipolar Cold War shifted the focus from conflict to cooperation, beyond traditional alliances like NATO; notable examples are the multinational Combined Task Forces 150 and 151 arrayed against piracy and terrorism around the Horn of Africa, as discussed by James Russell in chapter 7 of this volume. Many nations have collaborated in the development of new warships and major systems—for example, the joint frigate and antiaircraft warfare programs between France, Italy, and the United Kingdom. Such cooperation between navies has required a high level of professionalization, another notable trend as nations end conscription in favor of all-volunteer forces.

- Emergence of sea-based BMD: The mobile nature of warships allows them to quickly deploy to specific regions as required by the threat. This has made sea-based BMD an increasingly important component of many nations' arsenals, a trend that is likely to continue.

INFRASTRUCTURE: MARITIME TECHNOLOGY AND INDUSTRY

As stated above, the modern warship is neither the most complex nor the most expensive weapon system in a nation's arsenal. The cost to design, develop, and test a modern fighter plane can be an order of magnitude greater than that for a frigate or destroyer. Since 1989 the United States has regularly spent about three times more on its aviation assets than it has on ships and submarines.[21] Table 8.3 shows that, twenty years after the end of the Cold War, the cost associated with developing modern military aircraft dwarfed that of warships, a trend that seems certain to continue:

The industrial base for military aircraft has become much larger than for warships, and it employs a more highly skilled workforce. In the United States, the aircraft manufacturing sector at the dawn of the twenty-first century employed more than twice as many as the shipbuilding sector, with a 60 percent higher wage structure and almost three times the productivity

Table 8.3 Warship Class versus Military Aircraft Costs

Ship Type, Number, or Aspect of Costs	UK Type 23	UK Typhoon	US DDG 51	US F22
Ship type	Frigate	Fighter	Destroyer	Fighter
No. of units	16	620	62	187
Development costs	$0.7 billion	$24 billion	$3 billion	$28 billion
Procurement costs	$4.3 billion	$23 billion	$60 billion	$34 billion
Total	$5.0 billion	$47 billion	$63 billion	$62 billion

Sources: For UK data, acknowledgments to Michael Pryce, University of Manchester Business School (from Hansard and National Audit Office). Note that the *Typhoon* fighter is a multinational program. For US data: Jeff Drezner, *Are Ships Different? Policies and Procedures for the Acquisition of Ship Programs* (Santa Monica, CA: RAND Corporation, 2011); and US Department of Defense, selected acquisition reports.

levels.[22] In other words, warship programs were, and continue to be, seen as much lower on the domestic priority list than the procurement of military aircraft, and thus they have normally received less political backing.

Navies have long faced a conflict between cost and performance. It is, in fact, very difficult to design a "cheap" warship, and has been since the Age of Sail. An illustrative example of this tension was the development of the British Type-23 frigate in the early 1980s. The original requirement, as outlined in 1981, was for a relatively inexpensive, lightly armed and protected ASW platform suited to North Atlantic convoy defense. As the design process continued, additional requirements were added, in particular after the experience of the Falklands War (1982) showed the need for higher survivability standards and a medium-caliber gun for shore bombardment. The result was a robust, multimission combatant far more capable, and more expensive, than originally envisioned.[23]

In this section I examine the principal post–Cold War trends in maritime infrastructure as they relate to the warship—specifically, the technology of its two primary components, the hull and mission systems, and the shipbuilders and systems integrators that develop and produce these components. "Hull systems" in this context means the structure and machinery that keep a ship afloat and provide power and propulsion. "Mission systems" are the weapons, sensors, and embarked vehicles and aircraft. A continuing theme in this post–Cold War evolution is the emphasis on reducing the construction and operational costs of warships. At the same time, advances in computers, sensors, and communications have reshaped the means whereby warships carry out their missions.

Hull Systems

The end of the Cold War led many navies to seek new ways to balance costs and effectiveness. A report by the NATO Naval Group on Ship Design, "Ways to Reduce Costs of Ships," examined this dilemma in detail. Requirements, whether customer driven or statutory, were the single largest factor in cost growth. Rising standards for safety, environmental protection, and habitability all contributed to increasing costs. One of the most onerous requirements at all times is for high speed (nowadays, above 30 knots for an oceangoing warship), which dramatically increases production and life-cycle costs, because the size of the propulsion plant and fuel consumption increase exponentially with speed. The NATO group also examined the impact of commercial or military standards and practices for design and construction. Military standards might demand higher levels of survivability and lower radar detection signatures, but these were found to add almost 40 percent to hull production costs, and 25 percent to maintenance over the life cycle of a ship.[24] Thus there emerged a strong push to adopt commercial practices in warships.

One commercial-type practice that found favor with many navies was to make the ship more voluminous in order to cut down on construction costs. Warships have historically been designed "tight" (i.e., with close tolerances between hull systems and mission systems) to keep weight down. However, because the majority of modern shipbuilding costs are not in material (steel is comparatively cheap) but in engineering and construction labor, enlarging the hull for a given payload has been proven to simplify the layout and fitting of cables, pipes, and so on, and to shorten the design and construction schedule. The Japanese Navy purposely built its *Kongo*-class destroyer, a near-sister to the American *Arleigh Burke*–class of guided-missile destroyers (which, in NATO parlance, are known as DDGs), with a much larger hull in order to simplify construction. The Dutch navy realized a 50 percent reduction in hull engineering costs, and 20 percent in steel production costs, by enlarging the *De Zeven Provinciën*–class air defense ships, compared with their predecessors. Studies of submarines have shown comparable cost savings due to increasing the hull volume. Larger hulls provide military benefits as well, allowing greater flexibility to add, remove, repair, and modify mission systems over the ship's lifetime (which can span thirty to forty years), which reduces life-cycle costs.[25]

Another commercial practice increasingly favored by navies is the use of classification societies (like Lloyd's Register and the American Bureau of

Shipping) to establish and maintain naval standards and practices. Before the end of the Cold War, most navies maintained a strong in-house engineering workforce to design, build, and maintain their ships and systems. When fleet numbers suddenly dropped, so did that workforce. For example, from 1990 to 2006 the number of US Navy design engineers and shipbuilding inspectors was reduced by half.[26] Classification societies had developed and maintained commercial shipbuilding rules for more than a century, and thus they were the natural choice to supplement this diminished naval capability. Since 1989 many major navies have worked hand in hand with their national classifications societies. Thus, for example, the British Navy came to rely on Lloyd's Register, the US Navy on the American Bureau of Shipping, and the French Navy on Bureau Veritas, both to develop unique military standards for warships, and to provide life-cycle inspection services for these vessels.[27]

In the post–Cold War era the military ceased to dominate technological developments in the West, as it had since World War II. In the 1980s, during the height of the Cold War, the US Department of Defense accounted for a quarter of all domestic research and development (R&D) performed in the United States. By 2005 it accounted for about 12 percent. The military has even less impact in other nations; by 2007 it accounted for under 5 percent of R&D spending in the European Union, and for less than 1 percent in Japan.[28] Defense procurement agencies thus turned to commercially developed technologies to provide state-of-the-art capability for military systems. For example, even complex vessels like passenger liners operate with very small crews, using automation to reduce the engineering and navigational workload. Post–Cold War navies have adopted such capabilities (e.g., automated fire suppression systems and unmanned machinery spaces) to trim crew sizes and reduce operational costs.

Navies also began employing commercial propulsion technology, which is increasingly based on electric transmission systems, to a much greater extent than during the Cold War. For example, the British Type-45 destroyer *Daring* and the US DDG 1000, *Zumwalt*-class destroyers have integrated electric plants. The amphibious ships *Mistral* (French) and *Johan de Witt* (Dutch) both employed podded propulsors (which combined propulsion with steering) derived from commercial systems. Commercially developed waterjets powered the South African *Valour*-class frigates, first laid down in 2001, as well as the US Navy's joint high-speed vessel (2004) and LCS (2008). The latter two were both based on commercial fast ferry designs.

Some platform technologies are specific to the military and have no commercial industrial base, and therefore must be developed with in-house resources, either within defense laboratories or by specialized industries under government contract. For surface warships, integrated survivability, including signature management (radar cross section, infrared, acoustic, etc.), is generally the highest-priority technology domain. This includes the ability to analyze current and emerging threats; balance the requirements for signature management; trade off countermeasures and defensive systems; balance vulnerability with recoverability; and finally develop, test, and manufacture the various systems and technologies.[29] For submarines the need to operate underwater for long periods became far more widespread after 1989. Nations such as the United States, Britain, France, Russia, and China have long maintained a strong nuclear industrial base that allows their submarine forces to deploy for extended periods. Many other navies have now begun investing significant R&D and industrial resources to develop AIP systems (fuel cells, closed-cycle diesel and steam engines, Stirling engines, etc.) that significantly extend the submerged cruising range of nonnuclear submarines. Thus, the individual expense of each of these technologies is matched by the significant government investment needed to maintain a national research and production capability across the entire domain.

Mission Systems

The mission systems of a warship (weapons, sensors, and vehicles) account for more than half the total cost. The latitude to reduce these costs is far more limited than for hull systems, except if operational requirements are changed.[30] In fact, the trend for the past half century has been just the opposite. The increasing number and complexity of modern combat systems have been major factors in the inexorable rise in the costs of warships. These same factors are responsible for the similar rate of cost growth in military aircraft.[31]

The trend toward enhancing mission systems as force multipliers, offering greater capability to the fleet with the same (or even a reduced) number of warships, thus antedates the end of the Cold War, and has accelerated since. Major areas of emphasis for the improvement of mission systems include providing greater flexibility to adapt to rapidly evolving (and often unexpected) threats and requirements; increased data collection and dissemination, so as to rapidly comprehend the dynamics of a changing operational environment; and greater use of autonomous vehicles to extend data collection and bring the fight closer to the enemy, while minimizing risk to ships and crew. These three trends, taken together, defined the still-evolving network-centric concept of operations, which has placed less importance on individual platforms and more on interconnected systems that share information and distribute capabilities across the battle force.

The most potent example of mission systems' flexibility is found in the aircraft carrier, which in its various guises is just over a century old. The ship, as the name indicates, is simply the carrier. Its mission systems are the aircraft themselves, which can be changed depending on the task. For example, ASW squadrons aboard many Cold War–era carriers have since been largely decommissioned or reconfigured for reconnaissance and strike missions. Well-dock amphibious ships are also able to carry different types of vehicles and craft depending upon the mission. Such ships have increasingly been configured around large internal payload hangars (up to 40 percent of the total volume of the ship), which accommodate a wide range of modularized systems housed in commercial, International Standards Organization–compliant shipping containers that can be rapidly swapped out for changing missions—another example of the influence of commercial practices on post–Cold War navies.

In addition to containerization, other forms of modularization afford improved weapon systems flexibility.[32] The German MEKO (*MEhrzweck-KOmbination*, i.e., multipurpose) and Danish STANFLEX systems have both featured plug-and-play modules, which are configured to fit standardized openings in the hull and deckhouse. Such modules can carry a variety of weapons and sensors, including guns, missile launchers, and radar. Other examples include the US Mk 41 and Mk 57 vertical launch systems, which allow surface warships to carry any required mix of BMD, antiaircraft warfare, ASW, and strike missiles; and the next-generation Flexible Payload Modules, which provide submarines with capabilities for strike missiles, unmanned vehicles, and force insertion. Command-and-control systems, which increasingly employ commercially developed hardware and operating systems, now use open software architecture and common consoles to achieve mission flexibility and ease of upgrading.

Warships have increasingly been designed to be data collection platforms, as reflected in the enormous proliferation of sensors—radar, electro-optical systems, communication antennas, electronic countermeasures, and so on— that dominate the topsides. Requirements for topside "real estate" have often dictated the physical layout of surface combatants, because every sensor and antenna must be located so as to minimize physical and electromagnetic interference. The hull and deckhouse of the US DDG 51 (and its variants in many nations) have been built around the powerful Aegis air defense radar installations to ensure that each of the four planar arrays has a clear sweep around its quadrant of the horizon. The European Principal Anti-Air Missile System requires specific separation between its major antennas and a minimum height above sea level. These requirements in turn drove the length and beam requirements of the UK Type-45 destroyer and the *Horizon*-class combatants of France and Italy. The interconnectivity and bandwidth needed to achieve "net-centricity" have strained the limited topside space available to fit communications antennas, leading several defense research organizations to pioneer integrated, multifunction masts and radio apertures to minimize the shipboard impact.

During the Cold War, long-range guided weapons (shells, missiles, torpedoes) vastly extended the lethal range of a battle fleet. Long-range reconnaissance, however, was largely carried out by manned aircraft and submarines. The fall of the Berlin Wall coincided with the proliferation of miniaturized computers that have allowed powerful sensors, processors, and digital transceivers to be packaged and deployed on smaller-scale robotic vehicles. These have come to operate with increasing autonomy, for far longer times on station, and in areas inaccessible to deeper-draft warships. The trend toward shifting sensors and weapons from individual ships to multiple autonomous vehicles is still nascent in the second decade of the twenty-first century, but seems certain to have a substantial impact on warships in the years ahead. At one stroke these vehicles extend the range and persistent coverage of a fleet, while minimizing the risk to ships and crew. The most-cited historical precedent for this shift is the early development of the aircraft carrier, which moved surveillance and strike capability from the area within a 10-mile horizon to the tens of thousands of square miles that multiple aircraft could cover. And in the span of just a few years, the aircraft themselves evolved from wood-and-baling-wire reconnaissance planes into robust fighters and bombers.

An early example of where such developments may lead has been provided by the American LCS, whose unofficial motto is "Get connected, get modular, get off-board, get unmanned."[33] The ships are designed, among other things, to conduct MIW. Unlike previous MIW ships, for example, the LCS vessels do not themselves have onboard mine-hunting sonars and sweep gear. Rather, these are deployed aboard unmanned vehicles that the LCS launches, controls, and recovers. The French and British navies have explored similar capabilities with (respectively) the ESPADON and FAST mine warfare demonstrator projects. All these programs have relied on small craft with limited sensor payloads and capabilities (e.g., line-of-sight control for certain units). Follow-on programs, such as the US carrier-based X-47B unmanned combat aerial vehicle, have shown promise for achieving far greater autonomy while carrying larger sensor and weapon payloads. There seems to be little doubt that navies will increasingly rely on autonomous vehicles to carry out a wide range of missions.

Shipbuilders and Systems Integrators

Long before the end of the Cold War, the naval shipbuilding industry was being reshaped by economic forces beyond the control of any navy. In the period just after World War II, it was common for warships to be built in a combination of government-owned naval shipyards and commercially owned shipyards. By the 1970s most Western nations were moving toward exclusive reliance on commercially owned yards, while the job of integrating radars, sonars, and missile systems was taken on by large defense firms with roots in the aerospace industry.

By the time the Cold War came to an end, merchant shipbuilding was rapidly gravitating toward Asia, leaving many European and American shipyards ever more dependent on naval work. By 2005 the shipyards of South Korea, Japan, and China were the largest on the planet, producing 80 percent of the world's merchant tonnage.[34] This single fact explains why these nations are able to systematically build both warships and merchant vessels in the same shipyards, while the majority of other nations have again become reliant upon specialized naval shipyards, albeit in private hands, to build their warships. The economics of these two approaches stand in stark contrast.

An illustrative example of the first approach is found in Japan's Mitsui Engineering and Shipbuilding Company. Mitsui's primary business is the construction of bulk carriers and tankers, which are low-cost, high-volume products. But it also uses the same production facilities to build a comparatively small number of high-cost, complex warships, such as amphibious ships and destroyers. The advantage of this approach is that overhead costs (facilities, staff, etc.) are spread over a wider base, and production costs are kept lower via a continuous learning curve.[35] It also allows a more rapid adoption of commercial technologies into naval shipbuilding.

Apart from the major shipbuilding states of Asia, most other nations have found it increasingly difficult to combine warship and merchant shipbuilding when both are low-volume activities. The pace of warship construction is much slower than for merchant ships and requires more specialized systems integration. Many American and European naval shipyards that have adapted to warship production have also created permanent corporate partnerships with mission systems integrators. Three of the dominant naval shipbuilders in the United States are owned by General Dynamics, while BAE Systems and Thales own major stakes in European warship yards. This approach has had the advantage of spreading the overhead costs for mission systems to other sectors, such as aerospace; but this has come at the expense of ship platform costs. Very few naval-specialized yards have been able to break into the fast-paced, low-cost merchant shipbuilding market, which has prevented them from spreading facility and staffing expenses across a larger order book.[36]

Several nations have attempted to control naval shipbuilding costs by placing more warship orders with merchant shipyards, so as to benefit from commercial building practices and technologies. Such shipbuilders have normally teamed up with a mission systems integrator to deliver a completed warship. This approach has had only mixed success so far. For example, in 2000 the Spanish government combined its naval and merchant shipbuilders into a single entity, only to separate them again five years later due to legal concerns. The same year, the French navy ordered a pair of *Mistral*-class LHDs from the cruise-ship builder Alstom (now STX), with a follow-on order in 2008. The Danish Navy contracted in 2001 with the Odense Steel Shipyard, which specialized in container ships, to build its *Absalon*-class support ship, but the yard closed in 2012. In the United States mid-tier shipyards specializing in small merchant vessels have built the LCS, but in the process they have repeatedly experienced significant cost overruns. And, as noted above, the Indian Ministry of Defence recently took over the state-owned Hindustan Shipyard, effectively displacing commercial contracts in order to speed up warship construction.[37]

General Infrastructure Trends

Collectively, post–Cold War developments in hull and mission systems, combined with a rapidly evolving shipbuilding industry, can today be recognized as the basis for a number of ongoing trends:

- Cheap warships are not simple: Improving standards (safety, environmental protection, etc.) and increased mission systems complexity will continue to push the overall costs of warships higher.
- Bigger is better: For a given payload, more voluminous warships can save hull construction and maintenance costs as well as ease through-life upgrades.

- Leveraging commercial practice: As both the defense workforce and military R&D shrink, navies will increasingly employ classification societies and adopt industry-standard technologies and practices for warship design and construction.
- Proliferation of sensors and antennas: Warships will continue to have more, and more varied, types of data-gathering sensors, and means of sharing data with the network.
- Inherent flexibility: Containerization, modularization, and open architecture are the means by which warships will quickly adapt to changing roles and missions.
- Rapid evolution of unmanned autonomous vehicles: The current generation of small, limited-role vehicles will rapidly evolve into larger, more capable craft that will carry out an increasingly large part of a warship's functions, and allow missions such as MIW to be distributed among multirole ships rather than dedicated platforms.
- Growing specialization in naval shipbuilding: With the notable exceptions of South Korea, Japan, and China, nations will increasingly rely upon naval-specialized shipyards (often owned by or partnered with mission systems integrators) to build their warships. There will, however, be continued efforts to expand warship building into merchant-oriented shipyards to better realize the benefits of commercial practice.

IMPLICATIONS

Emerging trends in strategy and infrastructure, taken together, underscore the fact that the warship of the future is likely to become ever more flexible in nature, employing an increasingly diverse portfolio of operational concepts and technologies to carry out a wider range of missions, both autonomously and in conjunction with other forces. These trends will of course vary by navy and nation, but they are useful as broad predictors for longer-term policy considerations.

More Expeditionary Missions

Navies have increasingly been tasked with carrying out missions in the far abroad, whether to project military power ashore, perform constabulary duties on the high seas, or assist in humanitarian operations. There is no reason to think this trend will not continue. Such operations require extensive aviation and amphibious capabilities, pointing to an increase in multipurpose vessels like LHDs or support ships that combine elements of command and logistics.

The fluid nature of such expeditionary roles (and the uncertainty of where future conflicts may lie) requires mission flexibility, in both the near and far terms. A future warship might need to quickly pivot from carrying out antipiracy operations to assisting tsunami victims, as well as to adapt and upgrade its mission capabilities in response to rapidly evolving threats and requirements. This mission flexibility will increasingly be provided by off-board vehicles, both manned and unmanned, that are launched and retrieved from warships.

Warships of all types will travel further and stay on station for much longer periods than previously. Nonnuclear submarines, for example, are becoming powered by AIP systems to extend submerged range and time on station. As with nuclear boats, they are increasingly equipped for strike operations and force insertion. Coast guards and ocean patrols are carrying out longer-range operations to protect and secure economic resources, and are deploying much further abroad on international missions like disaster relief. A recent development—sea-based ballistic missile defense—carries with it the need to maintain extended patrols at sea. "Expeditionary" also implies a more robust logistics force to maintain deployed forces both at sea and ashore, including the possibility of positioning troops and equipment in mobile seaborne bases.

Larger Ships, with Open Architectures

The trend toward longer-range missions and more time on station calls for larger warships, not only for more fuel, supplies, and improved habitability but also to improve operability—bigger ships are more seaworthy. This trend is also a function of the demand to accommodate more, and more varied, types of data-gathering sensors (radar, electro-optical, etc.) communications antennas, and weapons (e.g., vertical launch systems), all of which will continue to drive up topside "real estate" requirements. For a given payload, bigger warships afford several additional advantages—the increased volume reduces hull engineering, construction, and maintenance costs, and eases life-cycle upgrades as missions and requirements change. There is no reason to think that the warships of the future will not be expected to operate for thirty to forty years, like those of the recent past.

Open architectures—including combat systems modularity, open software architecture, and common consoles—also provide mission flexibility and ease of upgrading. The growing use of off-board vehicles to carry out missions has provided an additional level of flexibility, and will allow missions such as MIW to be distributed among multirole ships rather than dedicated platforms. These trends will tend to drive warship designs to feature large, open hangars, and mission spaces that can accommodate a varied mix of mission contain-ers, vehicles, and stores, all of which will also tend to increase warship size.

The primary trade-offs for larger warships are that their size can limit operations in confined waters, and that it becomes exponentially more expen-sive to push them at higher speeds. However, as naval fleets and task groups become increasingly interconnected, more missions can be expected to be carried out by deployed assets like helicopters and unmanned vehicles. The specific utility of shallow draft and high speed has perhaps been overestimated in the past, and will need to be very carefully weighed against the mission flex-ibility afforded by size.

More Expensive Ships

Warships will continue to become costlier in real terms, a trend that dates back to (at least) the last decade of the nineteenth century, when the design requirements for modern battleships solidified. Although this may seem an obvious conclusion, the past half century has witnessed any number of overly optimistic predictions that advanced technologies or novel operational con-cepts will somehow result in cheaper warships. Adopting commercial prac-tices for shipbuilding, together with reduced manning (which new technology has facilitated), can help bend the cost curve downward, but not sufficiently to reverse what is likely to be a general upward trend, driven by the increas-ing range and complexity of mission systems, combined with rising standards (e.g., for safety and habitability).

This growth in warship costs is often viewed with great alarm and fre-quent finger-pointing, despite the fact that much more highly priced sectors of the defense budget, notably military aviation, have experienced the same degree of cost growth, and for many of the same reasons. It is also important to note that for many nations, fixed costs for naval R&D and shipbuilding are no longer spread across merchant order books but rather are shared among an increasingly small pool of warships, also driving up the unit cost. Where and how such tendencies will change is difficult to foresee. But their continuance at present seems certain.

As noted at the beginning of this chapter, the modern warship is an inherently flexible, multimission platform that is comparable to an entire army battalion or aviation squadron. Unlike a single aircraft or a tank, even a medium-sized vessel can independently carry out missions far afield from its home port for long periods of time; then, without even returning to base, it can be quickly integrated into a multinational force in order to take on completely different tasks. A warship is at once a weapon of war, a guardian of economic security, and a diplomatic tool. As it continues to evolve, the inherent flexibility that it affords will make it ever more central to the exercise of a nation's power—both military and nonmilitary—along the long, slow cycles of maritime strategy.

NOTES

I thank the following individuals for their insights: David Andrews, Mark Arena, Irv Blickstein, Alain Bovis, Joseph Carnevale, Bernard Cole, Jeffrey Drezner, Norman Friedman, John Hattendorf, Philip Koenig, Eric Labs, Ronald O'Rourke, Michael Pryce, John Schank, Philip Sims, Peter Swartz, Alexandre Sheldon-Duplaix, Stan Weeks, and Paul Wrobel. Any errors in facts or analyses are mine alone.

1. United Nations Convention on the Law of the Sea (1994), Article 95 and Article 96.

2. Among works that treat maritime strategy in the post–Cold War era, see especially Colin S. Gray, *The Leverage of Sea Power* (New York: Simon & Schuster, 1992); Eric Grove and Peter Hore, eds., *Dimensions of Sea Power* (Hull: University of Hull Press, 1998); Norman Friedman, *Seapower as Strategy: Navies and National Interests* (Annapolis, MD: Naval Institute Press, 2001); and Geoffrey Till, *Seapower: A Guide for the Twenty-First Century* (London: Frank Cass, 2004).

3. Up-to-date information on all the countries shown in table 8.2 can be found on the *Jane's* website, http://www.janes.com (subscription required), or in the successive annual volumes of *Jane's Fighting Ships*.

4. The white papers ". . . From the Sea" and "Forward . . . From the Sea" are concisely explained by Friedman, *Seapower*, 219–32. On the evolution of US naval strategy during the Cold War, see Peter M. Swartz and E. D. McGrady, *A Deep Legacy: Smaller-Scale Contingencies and the Forces That Shape the Navy* (Alexandria, VA: Center for Naval Analyses, 1998); and John Hattendorf and Peter Swartz, eds., *US Naval Strategy in the 1980s* (Newport, RI: Naval War College Press, 2008).

5. On sea basing, see Geoffrey Till, *Naval Transformation, Ground Forces, and the Expeditionary Impulse: The Sea-Basing Debate* (Carlisle, PA: US Army War College Strategic Studies Institute, 2006).

6. "A Cooperative Strategy for 21st Century Seapower," October 2007, http://ise.gov/sites/default/files/Maritime_Strategy.pdf.

7. On sea-based ballistic missile defense, see "White House Scraps Bush's Approach to Missile Shield," *New York Times*, September 17, 2009; "Navy Arctic Roadmap," http://www.navy.mil/docs/USN_arctic_roadmap.pdf; and Klaus Dodd's discussion of the Arctic in chapter 6 of this volume.

8. On Russia's military doctrines for 2000, see "Russia's Military Doctrine," www.armscontrol.org/act/2000_05/dc3ma00; and on these doctrines for 2009, see "Strategja: Nacional'noj bezopasnosti Rossijskoj Federacii do 2020 goda" [Strategy: The national security of the Russian Federation until 2020], www.scrf.gov.ru/documents/99.html. On Russia's naval doctrine, see "Morskaja doktrina Rossijskoj Federacii na period do 2020 goda" [Maritime doctrine of the Russian Federation for the period until 2020], *Nezavisimoe voennoe obozrenie* [Independent Military Review], August 3, 2001. For an overview of the development of these doctrines, see Anne Aldis and Roger N. McDermott, *Russian Military Reform, 1992–2002* (New York: Routledge, 2003), 171–76. See also "Russia Intent on Mistral Purchase," *Jane's Defence Weekly*, February 17, 2010, 6.

9. See *Delivering Security in a Changing World, Volume 1: White Paper*, and *Volume 2: Future Capabilities* (Norwich, UK: Crown Copyright, 2003–4); and British Maritime Doctrine BR 1806 (Norwich, UK: Crown Copyright, 2004). The most recent version, for 2011, is at https://www.gov.uk/government/uploads/system/uploads/attachment_data/file/33699/20110816JDP0_10_BMD.pdf.

10. China's defense white papers since 1995 are all available in English at http://eng.mod.gov.cn/Database/WhitePapers/.

11. *Liaoning* is a refurbished *Kuznetsov*-class Soviet carrier, originally laid down in 1988. It is officially classified by the Chinese as a training vessel.

12. Japan Ministry of Defense, "Defense of Japan 2009," www.mod.go.jp/e/publ/w_paper/2009.html; South Korea, "Defense White Paper 2008," www.mnd.go.kr/mndEng/DefensePolicy/Whitepaper/index.jsp. Broad strategic analyses for the region are given by Duk-Ki Kim, *Naval Strategy in Northeast Asia* (London: Frank Cass, 2000); and Toshi Yoshihara and James R. Holmes, eds., *Asia Looks Seaward* (London: Praeger, 2000).

13. Integrated Headquarters of the Indian Ministry of Defence (Navy), *Freedom to Use the Seas: India's Maritime Military Strategy* (New Delhi: Ministry of Defence, 2007). This statement was further elaborated by the Indian Ministry of Defence (Navy), *Indian Maritime Doctrine INBR-8* (New Delhi: Indian Ministry of Defence, 2009). For an analysis of India's maritime power, see Ravi Vohra and Devbrat Chakraborty, eds., *Maritime Dimensions of a New World Order* (New Delhi: National Maritime Foundation, 2007); James R. Holmes, Andrew C. Winner, and Toshi Yoshihara, *Indian Naval Strategy in the Twenty-First Century* (New York: Routledge, 2009); and Harsh V. Pant, ed., *The Rise of the Indian Navy: Internal Vulnerabilities, External Challenges* (Farnham, UK: Ashgate, 2012).

14. "On National Security Interests, Govt Moves Hindustan Shipyard to Defence Ministry," *Times of India*, December 24, 2009, http://timesofindia.indiatimes.com/india/On-national-security-interests-Govt-moves-Hindustan-Shipyard-to-Defence-ministry/articleshow/5373703.cms.

15. Although India declared its intention to purchase four "landing platform dock" ships in 2009, financing did not become available until 2013. See "Indian Navy

to Build Four Landing Platform Docks (LPDs)," *The Hindu*, December 14, 2009, http://indiandefance.blogspot.com/2009/12/indian-navy-to-build-four-landing.html; and Vivek Raghuvanshi, "India to Construct 4 LPDs," *Defense News*, December 21, 2013, http://archive.defensenews.com/article/20131212/DEFREG03/312120012/India -Construct-4-LPDs.

16. "India to Boost Coast Guard's Size, Resources," *Defense News*, October 28, 2009.

17. High-level strategic pronouncements by the French Navy have been relatively rare. The 1994 white paper was only its second, the first having appeared in 1972. The most recent, as of this writing, was published in 2013. There is a brief comparative discussion, with links to all of them (in French), at http://www.vie-publique.fr/focus /defense-securite-quatre-livres-blancs-1972-2013.html.

18. French Ministry of Defence, *Défense et Sécurité nationale: Le Livre Blanc* (Paris: Odile Jacob, 2008).

19. For Spanish defense policy, see Spanish Ministry of Defence, *Revisión Estratégica de la Defensa* (Madrid: Spanish Ministry of Defence, 2005), 54; for Australian defense policy, see Australian Ministry of Defence, *Defending Australia in the Asia Pacific Century: Force 2030* (Canberra: Australian Ministry of Defence, 2009).

20. On Chile, see Armada de Chile, *Doctrina Marítima: El Poder Marítimo* (Valparaiso: Armada de Chile, 2009). On Denmark, see Danish Ministry of Defence, "Danish Defence Agreement 2005–2009," http://www.fmn.dk/eng/allabout/Docu ments/Implementeringsnotatet6.pdf. On Singapore, see National Security Coordination Centre, *The Fight against Terror: Singapore's National Security Strategy* (Singapore: National Security Coordination Centre, 2004). And on South Africa, see "South Africa Defence Review 1998," www.dod.mil.za/documents/documents.htm.

21. This is as judged by the combined totals across R&D, procurement, and maintenance from annual national defense budget estimates, the most recent of which (for 2016) is at http://comptroller.defense.gov/Portals/45/Documents/defbudget/fy2016 /FY16_Green_Book.pdf.

22. US Department of Commerce, *National Security Assessment of the US Shipbuilding and Repair Industry* (Washington, DC: US Government Printing Office, 2001), xv.

23. See David Andrews and David Brown, "Cheap Warships Are Not Simple," in *Proceedings of SNAME Symposium on Ship Costs and Energy* (Alexandria, VA: Society of Naval Architects and Marine Engineers, 1982); and Lindsay Bryson, "The Procurement of a Warship," *RINA Transactions*, 1984.

24. NATO, "Ways to Reduce Costs of Ships," Allied Naval Engineering Publication, NATO Naval Group 6 on Ship Design, November 1995, A2–A4.

25. Ungtae Lee, "Improving the Parametric Method of Cost Estimating Relationships of Naval Ships" (master's thesis, Massachusetts Institute of Technology, Cambridge, 2014); Benjamin P. Grant, "Density as a Cost Driver in Submarine Design and Procurement" (master's thesis, Naval Postgraduate School, Monterey, CA, 2008).

26. Statements before the Armed Services Committee of the US House of Representatives, by Delores Etter et al., February 8, 2007, and by Sean Stackley and Kevin McCoy, July 30, 2009.

27. Glenn Ashe et al., "Naval Ship Design," in *Proceedings of the 16th International Ship and Offshore Structures Conference*, ed. P. A. Frieze and R. Ajit Shenoi (Southampton, UK: School of Engineering Sciences at University of Southampton, 2006).

28. US Congressional Budget Office, *Federal Support for Research and Development* (Washington DC: US Congressional Budget Office, 2007), 2, 5.

29. UK Ministry of Defence, *Defence Technology Strategy for the Demands of the 21st Century* (London: UK Ministry of Defence, 2005), 137–39.

30. NATO, "Ways to Reduce Costs of Ships," A7–A9.

31. Mark V. Arena et al., *Why Has the Cost of Navy Ships Risen?* (Santa Monica, CA: RAND Corporation, 2006); Mark V. Arena et al., *Why Has the Cost of Fixed-Wing Aircraft Risen?* (Santa Monica, CA: RAND Corporation, 2008).

32. Note that modularization is distinct from modular construction, which is the technique universally employed by major shipyards to build and outfit an entire section of a vessel, usually in an enclosed factory setting, before it is lifted into the building dock and joined to other modular sections.

33. Robert Work, *Naval Transformation and the Littoral Combat Ship* (Washington, DC: Center for Strategic and Budgetary Assessments, 2004), 75–77, http://www.google .com/url?sa=t&rct=j&q=&esrc=s&source=web&cd=1&cad=rja&uact=8&ved=0C B0QFjAAahUKEwjO7sz-rovIAhWCFj4KHSFBA30&url=http%3A%2F%2Fwww .csbaonline.org%2Fwp-content%2Fuploads%2F2011%2F03%2F2004.02.18-Littoral -Combat-Ship.pdf&usg=AFQjCNGTt9XUwFsEVP9uS1MZm_cwlmMo8w&sig2=vfkd NqSpfgMiPq3aHUIzMA.

34. James Brooks, "Korea Reigns in Shipbuilding, for Now," *New York Times*, January 6, 2005. See also "The Asian Shipbuilding Market," *Ship and Shore* 5 (2011), http://www .shipandoffshore.net/fileadmin/user_upload/puplicationen/Shipandoffshore/2011-05 /The_Asian_shipbuilding_market.pdf; and "Asian Shipyards: The Deeper the Better," *Economist*, November 13, 2013.

35. John Birkler et al., *Differences between Military and Commercial Shipbuilding* (Santa Monica, CA: RAND Corporation, 2005), 89.

36. US Government Accountability Office, *High Levels of Knowledge at Key Points Differentiate Commercial Shipbuilding from Navy Shipbuilding*, GAO Report 09–322 (Washington DC: US Government Accountability Office, 2009), http://www.gao.gov /assets/290/289531.pdf.

37. "India to Boost Coast Guard's Size, Resources."

CHAPTER 9

The Influence of Law on Maritime Strategy

STEVEN HAINES

The law has a much greater influence on military operations today than it did in the relatively recent past. Admiral Ian Forbes, the last-ever NATO supreme Allied commander Atlantic, has commented that the law had become a progressively more influential feature during his four decades in uniform.[1] The end of the Cold War, in particular the two years from 1989 to 1991, seemed to him to represent a watershed. The Iraqi invasion of Kuwait, followed by the coalition response, together with the beginning of the Balkan wars, signaled the end of the period of Cold War predictability for Western armed forces. The law had not been a significant consideration for the admiral preceding those events. After them, it became a constant concern.[2] Military lawyers have accordingly become an essential presence on Western military staffs. Although they are not usually deployed at the unit level, they certainly are deployed at higher tactical and the operational levels. This fact can lead to the assumption that the law is having an increasing influence on all aspects of the use and application of force, including at the strategic level and the development of strategy. James Kraska, for example, has argued that legal issues have shaped the diplomatic space to such an extent that they now may be seen as the principal impetus behind the development of the 2007 US maritime strategy, *A Cooperative Strategy for 21st-Century Seapower*.[3]

Is the increasing influence of law on the tactical level necessarily indicative of a similar degree of influence at the strategic level? Interestingly, Geoffrey

Till, who discusses maritime strategy during the Cold War in chapter 3 of this volume, makes little reference to the law in the recent edition of his authoritative text on sea power.[4] He devoted no chapter to the subject, and a glance at his index reveals only two references to the law: to the Law of the Sea in general, and to the United Nations Convention on the Law of the Sea (UNCLOS) in particular. Colin Gray, one of the most perceptive contemporary writers on strategy, tends to altogether avoid any mention of the law.[5] Historically, Till and Gray are in distinguished company.[6] Clausewitz famously dismissed the influence of law on war,[7] and one finds little on the subject in the pages of Mahan.[8]

The aim of this chapter is to look beyond the law's undoubtedly increasing influence at the tactical level and to assess the extent of its strategic influence. Is contemporary maritime strategy affected at all by the law, and, if so, to what extent? Given the starkly contrasting views of Kraska and Gray in particular, this is a question well worth exploring.

"Strategy" can, of course, mean many things. In its broadest sense it applies to all elements of a state's power—political, economic, and military—and their use to advance and defend its interests. Core interests have to do with ensuring political independence and territorial integrity, but they are accompanied by wider interests that benefit the state and both enhance its position internationally and serve the security needs and aspirations of its people. All three elements of a state's power need to be applied in pursuit of these objectives, and it makes most strategic sense for them to be interrelated and their application coordinated—although this is easier said than done. The overarching strategy that this approach implies is often referred to as "grand" strategy, which in its maritime dimensions is the concern of this volume.

The more traditional meaning of strategy, however, is that which focuses on the calculated use of military force. This is distinguished from grand strategy by the use of the term "military strategy," which pertains to the manner in which military force is applied, as well as the development of military forces appropriate to the state's needs and purposes over time. The military dimensions of maritime strategy pose distinctive concerns, both financially and operationally. Given the costs of developing modern naval forces, the length of procurement cycles, and the time scales within which major weapons systems remain in service, armed forces need to be developed against a backdrop of long-term strategic expectations. The author himself served as a junior officer in a guided missile destroyer in the early 1970s, the design for which had first been conceived in the early 1950s. That ship left Royal Navy service in the mid-1980s, following distinguished service in the Falklands War, only to get a new lease on life with the Chilean Navy, which deployed it operationally into the 1990s.[9] Much later in his career, while a member of the Naval Staff in the British Ministry of Defence (MoD) in 1997, he wrote the doctrinal justification for the Royal Navy's future carriers.[10] These are likely still to be in operational service in the second half of this century. From initial conception to final decommissioning, a major warship project can easily have a life stretching over half a century.

The more significant platforms and weapons systems possessed by the major military powers tend to be more than short-term features of the strategic environment. Although some other features are considerably more enduring—the physical geography of the planet, for example—others can change quite rapidly, as the global economy fluctuates, for example, and as political developments catch us unawares. The characteristics of the contemporary strategic environment are many and various. All need to be taken into account when developing strategy. One dimension of this environment is legal.

At the time of the 2001 terrorist attacks on New York and Washington, the British MoD approached strategic analysis by breaking the problem down into seven interactive but nevertheless discrete dimensions: political, economic, social and cultural, physical, technical, military, and legal.[11] Although this chapter focuses on only one of these, all must be acknowledged as having an influence on strategy. Indeed, the legal dimension is itself greatly influenced by the other six, particularly but not exclusively by politics. With this caveat stated, what follows concentrates on the law.

THE LEGAL DIMENSION
OF THE STRATEGIC ENVIRONMENT

Today, the legal dimension is very different from what it was around the middle of the twentieth century, and profoundly different from that which prevailed in the nineteenth century, when Clausewitz and Mahan posited their ideas about, respectively, war and naval power. Although one should certainly not dismiss either of those two intellectual giants out of hand (as some do), one needs to be conscious of the extent to which both were products of their time and were writing against a strategic backdrop that was quite different from what we are familiar with today. A gulf separates the role of law in the nineteenth century and the influence of law today.

The nature of international law in the modern, or Westphalian, state system has invariably been a product of the tension between natural law and positivism. Periods when the former has prevailed display a preponderance of top-down influence; sovereigns are obliged to comply with various norms having their origins in some higher order (either God or human reason). Legal positivism, in contrast, suggests a bottom-up process, with the law consisting only of precepts by which sovereigns have themselves agreed to be bound.[12] The nineteenth century witnessed the apogee of legal positivism, with the demands of balance-of-power politics largely eclipsing notions of natural or divine justice.

The reputed father of international law, the Dutchman Hugo Grotius, was a natural lawyer. In the seventeenth century, when he wrote both *De Jure Belli ac Pacis* and *Mare Liberum*, natural law was dominant. His rational approach to justice allowed for the Christian doctrine of just war to maintain its relevance despite its origins in theology. In the same way, the notion that God had created the oceans for all (justifying the belief that the high seas should be free for all to use) was redrawn against a backdrop of rationality. By the nineteenth century, however, the development of the modern state and the strategic imperatives associated with the balance of power between the states of Europe had caused such notions as just war and the God-given freedom of the seas to be regarded as little more than naive sentimentalism. Norms governing recourse to force had all but disappeared, and the high seas remained free only because the dominant maritime power of the day (Britain) regarded free movement on the oceans as in its best interests. In the event that war broke out, if the rules concerning the conduct of hostilities (*jus in bello*) existed at all, they did so only because mutual compliance was perceived to be in the best interests of the belligerents.[13] What Clausewitz said about the law's almost total lack of influence on war was an accurate reflection of contemporary reality, at least in relation to war on land.

At sea, the situation was not so absolute, primarily because the conduct of war on the high seas demanded a degree of restraint with respect to the treatment of neutral shipping. Belligerents were obliged to recognize the rights of neutrals because failure to do so risked turning neutral states into additional hostile powers. The pragmatic need to recognize the rights of neutrals, while ensuring their compliance with their obligations not to assist opposing belligerents, gave rise to rules governing the carriage of goods supported by the customary distinction between legitimate and contraband cargoes. Legitimate trade by both neutrals and belligerents was allowed to proceed, subject to the belligerent right to visit and search. Belligerents were expected to respect the integrity of neutral territorial waters, customarily assumed to consist of a zone extending no more than 3 nautical miles from the shore. Neutrals, for their part, were obliged to respect a legitimate blockade of a belligerent coast. Both belligerent and neutral ships carrying contraband were subject to seizure, and the extensive jurisprudence of prize courts was an important legal feature of maritime warfare at that time.[14]

Such pragmatic provisions aside, however, war at sea was subject to little in the way of legally based restrictions. The high seas were free for all to use, as Grotius had argued, but what belligerents and neutrals did or did not do there had very little to do with either natural justice or divine providence. Neutrals had the right to be spared the violence of war, but the legitimacy of war as a feature of the international system was not questioned. At the end of the nineteenth century, when Mahan was articulating his theory of sea power, it would have been surprising if he had devoted significant space to the influence of the law on naval strategy.

Nevertheless, by then the reemergence of natural law thinking was already in evidence. The character of war was changing as a result of technological developments that rendered armed conflict more bloody than it had previously been. This had the effect of resurrecting an interest in *jus in bello*. Henry Dunant's shocked reaction to the aftermath of the Battle of Solferino in 1859 led to the founding of the International Committee of the Red Cross and the negotiation of the first Geneva Convention in 1864. Although the convention was principally concerned with the human consequences of war on land, the move to mitigate war's worst effects spilled over into the realm of maritime warfare, which became a major focus of the Second Hague Peace Conference in 1907. Eight of the thirteen conventions negotiated at the conference were about the conduct of war at sea.[15]

It required the even more appalling carnage of World War I to regenerate interest in *jus ad bellum*. The Paris Peace Conference of 1919 marked the beginning of formal attempts to restrict the purpose of war. This was followed, less than a decade later, by the negotiation of the 1928 Kellogg-Briand Pact, which sought to outlaw war as a routine instrument of policy. Although this was itself followed by the outbreak of World War II in 1939, the humanitarian impulse survived, and was a key influence on the drafting of the UN Charter in 1945. The charter may be described as essentially a modern reaffirmation of the natural law doctrine of just war.

The determination to delegitimize recourse to war, and to mitigate its worst effects when it does occur, has contributed to a fundamental shift in the nature of international law. Apart from the law governing the use of force and the conduct of war, the most striking legal consequence of the worst effects of World War II has been the raising of individual human rights together with the correlative obligations placed on states to respect them. Although World War II was the catalyst for the emergence of international human rights law, its influence at first spread only gradually.[16] By the late 1960s, however, the belief that international law was about more than the rights and obligations of states, and included rights and obligations at the individual human level, was taking hold. Human rights law, though it may not be immediately associated with the conduct of maritime operations, is having an increasing influence at the tactical level, in particular in the context of law enforcement.

Concurrent with the development of human rights law, a significant change was taking place within the international system that would have a major impact on a body of law of obvious relevance to maritime operations. The dismantling of the European-based empires in the 1950s and 1960s contributed substantially to the trebling of UN membership. By the late 1960s an association of nonaligned states called the Group of 77 had come to dominate the proceedings of the UN General Assembly, and became profoundly influential in calling for a radical review of the Law of the Sea.

The Third UN Conference on the Law of the Sea (UNCLOS III) dominated maritime affairs during the 1970s and into the 1980s. Politically, it was a product of the tension between the newly independent coastal states of the developing world (which sought to enhance their position at the expense of major maritime interests) and the major maritime powers (which sought, and secured, the preservation of high seas freedoms and rights of navigation). Economically, ocean resources, especially those on the continental shelf, were becoming more easily exploitable, and hence more valuable economically. The ownership of ocean resources, previously free for the taking, had become an issue. The resulting ocean regime, established in law through UNCLOS III, has been an important development in contemporary international law. Despite certain continuing disputes, the compromise package deal at the heart of UNCLOS has so far proved remarkably stable, in a world where power is no longer distributed as it once was.

The reemergence of an influential *jus ad bellum*, the creation of an increasingly substantial human rights element within international law, and the substantial increase in international regulation, not least in relation to the oceans, have all shaped the contemporary strategic environment in myriad ways. At the same time, however, the international system remains dominated by the interests of sovereign states, and laws governing their relations remain central to its functioning. Despite claims by some that states are rapidly losing their relevance, and by others that international law is no more than a chimera, the evidence of the vigorous health of both is there for all to see. Statehood remains the central aspiration of political communities seeking independence and international legitimacy. At the same time, international law continues to advance in both scope and influence. Treaty law is proliferating, and there is an increasing tendency for the requirements of compliance and enforcement to be met.

The nature of international law has changed markedly during the past century, and particularly in the last fifty years. It has done so because other key dimensions of the strategic environment have shifted and created the conditions for this change to occur. For the future, much will depend on political developments; but if globalization intensifies, if international institutions and organizations continue to develop in the way they have recently, and if the world's most advanced societies can avoid the sort of rivalry that has led to great power conflict in the past, then the prospect for the rule of law in international affairs is bright. What might all this mean for maritime strategy?

USING AND DEVELOPING MARITIME FORCE

Maritime forces can do many things. They can wage war, they can enforce law, and they can help people in distress. This breadth of utility is well captured in the three categories of operations long used by the British navy in formulating its maritime doctrine, within which it distinguishes roles that are described as either military, constabulary, or benign.[17] These roles imply different legal bases for mounting operations. The military application of naval power implies one in which combat is either used or threatened as a persuasive backdrop to diplomacy. It suggests an application of force governed by the Law of Armed Conflict (LOAC), whereby the decision to apply lethal or destructive force would be based on the identity of the potential target irrespective of its actions. In an armed conflict, an enemy's warships are always legitimate targets, regardless of where they might be or what they might be doing at the moment of the attack—unless, of course, they are either in neutral waters or are in the act of surrendering.[18] In contrast, the constabulary application of force has to do with law enforcement, especially within coastal states' maritime domains, but including high seas operations to maintain good order at sea and enforce UN mandates.[19] Constabulary operations imply the minimum level of force necessary to enforce the law, with lethal force only being used in extreme instances, including in self-defense.[20] Even in self-defense, the use of force would need to be both proportionate and necessary. In the conduct of constabulary operations (in contrast to operations under LOAC), it is the target's actions rather than its identity that are significant in determining the legitimacy of attack. Finally, benign operations are those in which the application of force is intended and expected to be largely irrelevant, because the mission is to provide emergency assistance, humanitarian relief, search-and-rescue services, or something similar.[21]

Some smaller navies, whose roles and force structures are more akin to those of a coast guard, may have a clearly promulgated "strategic" role to play in their state's contingency planning for natural disasters, especially if their geographic location is in a zone of high risk. For them, the ability to mount benign operations may be an important reason for their existence—and, hence, a central element of their national maritime strategy. Nevertheless, the ability to mount a benign operation is in most cases a by-product of a navy's ability to do other things of a military or constabulary nature, both of which imply an ability to apply force. For the most part, navies exist to conduct military and constabulary operations—some mainly the former, some mainly the latter, and often a combination of both.

The full range of military operations can be conveniently divided into three. The first aims at achieving sea control for one's own purposes or pursuing sea denial to restrict the options of one's enemy. In their ultimate form, sea control operations are about maritime forces clashing with opposing maritime forces—navies against navies—and, in the joint maritime context, will include achieving air superiority in relation to the maritime environment. They need not involve combat, however.[22] The important objective is to provide a secure and conducive environment for other activities. Sea control operations are invariably necessary, unless a maritime force exercises total command of the sea (which is not likely).[23]

The second type of military operation has to do with a maritime force projecting power ashore, either in its own right or in support of land forces. Power projection can involve such actions as the landing of an amphibious force, the provision of naval fire support (including with sea launched cruise missiles), or of air support. These days, these sorts of operations are frequently associated with the term "littoral operations."

The final traditional military purpose for navies has been to wage economic warfare at sea. This has involved the interdiction of shipping on the high seas to prevent the passage of contraband. It has also involved the mounting of a belligerent blockade of the enemy coast to prevent goods entering enemy ports and sustaining its war effort.

The four principal purposes of naval forces are, therefore, the three military objectives—sea control, power projection, and economic warfare—together with the conduct of constabulary (or law enforcement) operations. Any sound naval strategy will be predicated on the ability to conduct at least two of these, with the more capable maritime powers able to conduct all four. Sea control, which is invariably necessary, should never be an end in itself. It is a vital enabler in creating the conditions for the successful delivery of the other three.[24] All four types of operation are subject to legal restraint. War-fighting or combat operations in the context of an armed conflict (sea control, power projection, and economic warfare) will be governed by LOAC applicable at sea, while constabulary operations will be governed principally by minimum use of force and human rights considerations. There is much that can be said about the legal framework for operations under all four of these headings.

The LOAC applicable at sea has been subject to very little formal review, and none since the middle of the twentieth century.[25] The Law of the Sea, as embodied most authoritatively in UNCLOS and additional agreements pursuant to it, does not deal with armed conflict at all, so none of the major maritime developments arising from its negotiations were conceived as altering the conduct of navies during armed conflict.[26] Some of UNCLOS's provisions may do so, nonetheless, particularly the extension of coastal state jurisdiction to the full range of maritime zones. LOAC regulates relations between belligerents and neutrals, including the maritime domains of the latter. These were extended by UNCLOS in ways that will certainly affect the operations of belligerents. This was one of the factors that prompted the Institute for International Humanitarian Law in San Remo to launch an informal review, which resulted in the 1995 publication of the *San Remo Manual*.[27] Although the *San Remo Manual* has no formal legal status (it is neither a treaty nor a universally accepted codification of customary law), it has nevertheless become for many the first point of reference on the subject. When Britain's official *LOAC Manual* was being drafted, for example, the *San Remo Manual* was being used as the first draft of the chapter dealing with maritime warfare (although the final published version differed in detail from it).[28] For sea control operations and power projection in armed conflicts, the wider body of LOAC also applies, with maritime forces projecting power ashore obliged to comply with LOAC applicable to land operations. In the case of economic warfare at sea, however, the *San Remo Manual* continues to rely heavily on traditional principles of neutral and belligerent rights and obligations as they existed before and during World War II. It is worth saying something about this.

The economic warfare provisions of LOAC applicable at sea were developed in the context of great power war, and were influenced by state practice in the two world wars of the twentieth century. The economic activities of opposing belligerents came to be regarded as a legitimate target for action, in particular those activities that were likely to contribute to a belligerent's ability to prosecute war. The two main methods by which economic warfare has traditionally been waged at sea are, first, the control of shipping on the high seas to ensure that contraband goods would not reach the opposing belligerent, and, second, the imposition of blockade adjacent to the enemy's coast.

A classic example of the former was the operation mounted against British shipping by the German pocket battleship *Graf Spee* in the first three months of war in 1939.[29] It sought out British shipping in the southern Indian and Atlantic oceans, stopped any vessel encountered, removed its crew, and then sank it. Although the strategic decision by Nazi Germany to wage an aggressive war was itself unlawful (Germany having been party to the Kellog-Briand Pact of 1928), the *Graf Spee* was essentially compliant with LOAC. Opposing tactical commanders are not responsible for the strategic decisions of their states' leadership, and are not criminally liable as long as they themselves comply with LOAC.[30] Captain Langsdorf of the *Graf Spee* was generally regarded as an honorable officer by his British Merchant Navy victims. His suicide, following his decision to scuttle the *Graf Spee* in the Plate River estuary, did nothing to harm his reputation.

It has been the better part of a century since the *Graf Spee* was seizing and sinking British merchantmen in the South Atlantic and Indian oceans. The *San Remo Manual* contains virtually the same rules that then governed war at sea. Under its terms, it would apparently not be unlawful to mount such operations today. The principal reason, one suggests, why such actions remain apparently lawful is that operations of that sort have not been repeated since. As a consequence, they have attracted neither the international attention nor the opprobrium that would almost certainly attach to any state that sent its warships out today to deliberately interdict and sink enemy merchant vessels. International law develops through state practice and, in the absence of relevant practice, customary law will be slow to change or may not change at all. The active resumption of such practice might, however, have the effect of changing the law against it more rapidly, through either a formal ban or customary abandonment. International opinion is now mobilized more readily than it once was, and normative standards are determined as much by engaged publics as they are by legal officials advising statesmen.

The other method of waging economic warfare—belligerent blockade—has occurred since World War II, including in the period since the end of the Cold War, although not to the degree necessary to prompt either formal change in the law or confirmation of its customary legitimacy. It has been employed by Israel, most recently starting in January 2009 off the coast off Gaza. It was also considered, but not applied, in the context of NATO's intervention over Kosovo in 1999. Both examples raise serious questions about the current acceptability of a blockade as a method of warfare.

In the NATO case, blockade was considered in response to a fear that Serbia would be supported through the Adriatic port of Bar in Montenegro. Because NATO was acting without a UN mandate, there was no possibility that a Security Council resolution authorizing a maritime economic embargo operation would be approved. Consideration was given to putting a belligerent blockade in place, on the basis that NATO was at war with Serbia. There was a marked reluctance in NATO capitals to pursue this option, however, because this would have formally confirmed that a state of war existed (blockade is, by definition, an act of war). Although governments were apparently comfortable with the reality that a state of "armed conflict" existed, this was not viewed as synonymous with "war," and a blockade was, for that reason, considered a step too far. A vain attempt was made to put in place an embargo regime by consent, but this would have been largely pointless because the states likely to provide support to Serbia were not going to give their consent. In the end, the matter was resolved before it became critical, when Serbia acquiesced to the deployment into Kosovo of NATO ground forces.[31]

In the case of the Gaza blockade, the legality of Israel's actions remains in doubt because of the ambiguous status of Gaza itself. Israel maintains that it is in a state of international armed conflict with the "hostile entity" of Gaza. Few support this position. Notwithstanding *jus ad bellum* concerns, at the tactical level the blockade was conducted largely within customary law and in accordance with the terms outlined in the *San Remo Manual*.[32] For this reason, Israel cannot be accused unequivocally of acting unlawfully in its tactical handling of the incident at sea that occurred in May 2010, when Turkish-flagged vessels (neutrals) attempted to beat the blockade. That said, the Israeli action provoked widespread international condemnation. Although it would be going too far to claim that the international public response to this incident substantially undermines the legitimacy of blockade as a method of warfare, it has certainly done nothing to endorse it.

As a result of both these experiences, the very least one can say of blockade is that it is today seriously controversial. Although it is mentioned in the

UN Charter as a legitimate method of warfare when applying military sanctions under Article 42, such an action has never been expressly authorized. In this context it is important to stress that a blockade under Article 42 is very different in its legal basis from maritime economic embargo operations, such as might be authorized under Article 41. Tactically, they look similar, and navies undertaking embargo operations will appear to be using similar procedures to stop, board, and search vessels to those they would employ for blockade. In law, however, they are emphatically not the same, and they imply different bases for the application of force.[33]

From a political point of view, and bearing in mind the extent to which the legal dimension of the strategic environment has shifted since World War II, it seems unlikely that traditional economic warfare will be a serious option for the foreseeable future—unless, that is, the international system succumbs to the sort of great power rivalry and conflict in which such warfare originally emerged. International opinion today is unlikely to look favorably on *guerre de course*, or to accept attacks on ships as an inevitable part of war at sea. It is a truism that shipping and trade are international enterprises. In the last half century, moreover, the shipping industry has itself become markedly more diverse in terms of the ownership and manning of merchant ships, not to mention the ownership, point of departure, and eventual destination of the diverse cargoes they carry. In a rapidly globalizing world, in which the economic and commercial approach to the purchase and supply of goods (including those that are strategically vital) is characterized by the phrase "just enough, just in time," the consequences of the disruption of oceanic trade are likely to be severe. All these considerations may undermine the likelihood that economic warfare at sea will continue to be regarded as an acceptable method of warfare. It is perhaps telling that, though a belligerent blockade, as traditionally understood, is still mentioned in British maritime doctrine, no substantial mention is given to *guerre de course* operations against either an enemy or a neutral merchant ship.[34] The Royal Navy, for one, is apparently not expecting to mount such operations in the future.

Moving on now to constabulary operations, these are essentially about law enforcement and the maintenance of good order at sea. It is, of course, possible that a constabulary operation might precipitate an escalation that crosses the threshold of armed conflict. Nevertheless, fundamentally, constabulary operations are not about war fighting. The majority of these take place in the maritime domains of coastal states, where operations are conducted to enforce law arising out of the coastal state's own jurisdiction. From a situation as recently as 1945, in which the maritime domain of a coastal state extended to a mere 3 nautical miles offshore, we have moved to a radically new position in which territorial waters have moved out to 12 nautical miles, with a contiguous zone a further 12 miles beyond that limit, and finally an exclusive economic zone (EEZ) that stretches out to 200 nautical miles. In addition, the current legal regime governing the continental shelf provides for jurisdiction extending as far as 350 nautical miles from shore, or to 100 nautical miles beyond the 2,500-meter isobath, whichever is the more distant.[35] The extension of sovereign interest and control, represented by the creation of the EEZ and the current regime governing the continental shelf, has enormously increased the jurisdictional reach of coastal states and has generated a substantial range of constabulary responsibilities and law enforcement requirements as a consequence. In some states the responsibility for much of this enforcement and maintenance of good order falls on a designated coast guard. In others, navies perform the law enforcement function. In yet others, there is a multiagency distribution of responsibility, including customs, excise and quarantine operations, fishery protection, drug interdiction, and maritime counterterrorism. No matter how the tasks are allotted, the need to maintain the integrity of the maritime domain will form part of a sound maritime strategy, with coast guards and other relevant civil agencies appropriately regarded as an element of coastal states' maritime forces.

Constabulary operations are also increasingly being conducted on the high seas. Counterpiracy operations and counterterrorism are particularly high-profile examples of late. The need to respond to good order requirements by taking law enforcement operations onto the high seas has prompted a number of international agreements, the purpose of which is to circumvent the legal restrictions imposed by exclusive flag state jurisdiction. Examples include the International Convention for the Suppression of Unlawful Acts against the Safety of Navigation, and the Vienna Convention against Illicit Traffic in Narcotic Drugs and Psychotropic Substances, both concluded in 1988.[36] Although the Proliferation Security Initiative, launched by President George Bush on a visit to Krakow in Poland in 2003, is not a treaty and has no binding international legal status, it has a similar effect in relation to vessels flagged to those states that are participants (almost 100 to date).[37] The UN Security Council has also authorized a number of operations whose effects also extend to the high seas, principally maritime embargo operations in support of economic sanctions under Article 41 of the UN Charter. The author himself served on the first of these, mounted by the Royal Navy off the Mozambique port of Beira in the late 1960s and early 1970s, following the illegal declaration of independence by the white minority government in Salisbury (now Harare), the objective being to enforce sanctions against Rhodesia (now Zimbabwe).[38] Subsequent operations under UN auspices have been undertaken in the Adriatic, the Persian Gulf, and, most recently, off the coast of Libya.

The demands of maintaining good order at sea beyond territorial limits have not yet undermined, in any fundamental legal sense, the notion of exclusive flag state jurisdiction on the high seas. Nevertheless, one can discern the beginnings of a process that might in time lead to this. The principal significance of regulation on the high seas has to do with its legal potential, therefore, rather than its legal impact to date. There is a discernible trend, however, and one that is entirely consistent with the growing tendency for global regulation. The reaction to the attacks on New York and Washington in 2001 has even resulted in the United States—a traditionally strong supporter of high seas freedoms—countenancing restrictive operations on the high seas. Issues like piracy (particularly that by Somalian pirate gangs, which have ranged far out into the Indian Ocean), and irregular migration by sea (both forced and economic), have added to an international public perception that the high seas need to be properly regulated and patrolled. It is not difficult to imagine demands of this sort increasing in years to come, posing a threat to the juridical status of the high seas. Where this might lead is difficult to predict; but that the constabulary function has expanded in recent years is unmistakable.

DOES THE LAW INFLUENCE STRATEGY?

What does all this mean for maritime strategy? It should by now be obvious that the influence of the law at the tactical level has much increased since World War II. Although the oceans, as a strategic environment, have long been subject to a greater degree of international legal influence than the land, the recent and general increase in the influence of law on all military operations has tended to create a sense of legal balance between the two. This overall increase in the influence of law on warfare, in the last two decades in particular, can lead to an understandable assumption that the law is having a much greater influence at the strategic level. But is this actually the case?

As noted above, maritime strategic decisions are about the actual employment of the maritime forces currently at the disposal of the state, or about the shaping and development of forces for the future. The law tells us what maritime forces can legitimately be used for today, and an understanding of how the law is developing provides us with guidance on how maritime forces may legitimately be used in the future. Today, they may be employed on military tasks that are supportive of strategic aims permitted under the terms of the UN Charter. The deployment of maritime forces, merely to maintain a general presence, even a potentially ominous one, is not unlawful, as long as the territorial limits of other states are respected. Such a maritime presence might serve to reinforce a state's powers of diplomatic or political persuasion, serving to either deter or compel, as the case may be. Strategic defense is generally governed by Article 51 of the UN Charter, and needs to be both necessary and proportionate in relation to the nature of the threat being faced. Put in simple terms, a state's assessment of the strategic environment will suggest the range and type of maritime forces it needs to deploy to counter a given threat to its territorial integrity, political independence, or wider interests. The first two of these—territorial integrity and political independence—are spelled out in Article 51. Although wider interests are not mentioned as such, the basic right of self-defense applies in all circumstances. If, for example, the security of a state's merchant shipping is threatened on the high seas by the actions of other states or by nonstate entities (pirate gangs or terrorist groups, for example), applying force in defense of those interests would be legitimate as long as the action could be demonstrated to be both necessary and proportionate. There is nothing currently in the law forbidding states from protecting their wider interests, including oceanic trade, and nothing suggests that the law is developing in ways that will forbid them from doing so in the future.

Beyond self-defense and the legitimate protection of interests, however, the use of force must be authorized by the UN Security Council. Strategic aggression is not the legitimate or morally neutral option it once was. Nevertheless, this certainly does not imply that maritime forces must be restricted to those capable of purely defensive actions, for three important reasons.

First, to achieve effective strategic defense, it would be necessary for any military force (on land, on the sea, or in the air) to go onto the operational or tactical offensive. A strategically defensive objective will almost certainly require offensive tactical action if it is to be achieved. This amounts to no more than common sense, and is reflected in any reputable collection of so-called principles of war. The British conduct of the Falklands War was a good example of tactically offensive action taken in pursuit of a strategically defensive objective.

Second, offensive capability is a necessary feature of effective strategic deterrence. Although the word "deterrence" has been associated particularly with nuclear forces, it obviously has a much broader meaning that includes all the forces that a state deploys to deter others taking action against it. It is commonplace today, in a strategic environment that seems to be characterized by the prevalence of noninternational armed conflict and asymmetric threats, to downplay the possibilities of war between economically and technologically advanced adversaries—what were once called great powers. It would be irresponsible, however, to dismiss such a possibility altogether. The maintenance of an effective offensive capability is central to the deterrence of violence within the international system.

Third, the UN Security Council may authorize military sanctions and enforcement action under Article 42 of the UN Charter. The charter is a document that acknowledges the importance of coercion. As originally conceived, the UN would itself have had the military capability to deliver coercive force. Because the provision of dedicated standing forces at the UN's disposal failed to materialize, it falls to its member states to provide the organization with the military wherewithal to perform coercive measures. This would include taking preemptive action against rogue states judged to be imminently dangerous to others. Unilateral preemptive action against nonimminent threats would be unlawful, but such threats that were judged by the UN Security Council to represent a threat to peace and security could be dealt with legitimately under a UN mandate. Of course, in implementing a UN mandate, forces may very well have to go onto the offensive at all levels, including strategically.

There is certainly no legal bar to the deployment or development of an effective offensive capability at sea, no more than on land. It remains a legitimate strategic choice. The law is, however, permissive rather than influential. It places no legal obligation on states to possess an offensive capability. The only potential legal restriction identified above is that relating to economic warfare at sea. This may no longer be a wholly legitimate use of force, and the deployment or development of capabilities with *guerre de course* specifically in mind might come under the restricting influence of the law. Since the interdiction of merchant shipping would most likely be conducted by warships designed with other objectives in mind, however, legal restrictions on such activities, were they to be codified, would be unlikely to have any significant influence on naval force structures.

Turning to constabulary tasks, these are by definition about the law, its enforcement, and the maintenance of good order at sea. In the sense that they are a legal imperative, it is a truism that the strategic decision to deploy maritime forces for such purposes is influenced by the law. Indeed, one might suggest that the deployment of forces capable of enforcing the law at sea is a legal obligation related to a state's right to assert claims of maritime jurisdiction under UNCLOS.[39] For the major maritime powers, the constabulary tasks they undertake will frequently fall to naval units whose principal intended purpose is to conduct military tasks. For smaller maritime powers, meaning those principally focused on territorial defense and good order offshore, constabulary tasking may be the principal raison d'être for their navies, which may be coast guards in all but name. Maritime strategy is not the exclusive preserve of the most powerful, and a relatively small coastal state's decision to focus on maritime domain management, including the enforcement of a fisheries regime for its EEZ, for example, could represent the principal focus of its maritime strategy. In such cases, strategic force development decisions will certainly be influenced by the law. Strategic decisions would be about purchasing a force of vessels for EEZ patrolling, the most appropriate types of vessels depending on the nature of the constabulary task, and about the optimal deployment of that force to meet the demands of regime enforcement in the zone. For a coastal state with no blue-water aspirations, the influence of the law on its strategy may well be profound.

CONCLUSION

Maritime strategy today is surely influenced by the law. Nevertheless, that influence is far from being an important driver of all strategic decisions. This is the case whether we are concerned with the operational deployment of maritime forces or with their development over time. The main exception is posed by the application of maritime forces by smaller coastal states, whose main focus may be on maritime domain security and the preservation of good order at sea. For the larger maritime powers, and certainly for the largest of them all, the direct influence of the law on the development of strategy is likely to remain less significant than other, principally political, considerations. In the main the law affects the tactical conduct of operations rather than the strategic decision to mount them. If the law is strategically influential, it tends to be permissively so, rather than imposing either obligations or restrictions.

To offer a final example: When decisions were made in a great many capitals to deploy naval forces into the Indian Ocean and the Gulf of Aden as a reaction to Somali-based piracy, many observers presumably assumed that such operations would be relatively straightforward from a political and legal point of view. Piracy has long been an international crime subject to universal jurisdiction, so there should have been few problems of a legal nature. But straightforward it certainly has not been. It is one thing saying that something is an international crime subject to universal jurisdiction, but quite another to put in place an effective and defensible process for its investigation, prosecution, and punishment. The legal difficulties have been complex and frustrating for naval commanders faced with detained pirates onboard their ships. Issues to do with the human rights of those taken prisoner, and their transfer to a jurisdiction capable of prosecuting them, have taxed legal advisers at all levels. Transfer to the domestic jurisdiction of the warship's flag state has often been resisted because the domestic law of the state has no provisions for the effective prosecution of pirates, or because its asylum laws may result in either convicted or acquitted pirates seeking to remain in the prosecuting state rather than return to Somalia on completion of due process. So far, there has not been a legal challenge on human rights grounds to the rendition of prisoners for trial in the region (principally to Kenyan jurisdiction), but it would not be surprising if there were. Two or three centuries ago, a naval commander would have simply hung a pirate from the yardarm of his ship without any requirement to seek legal advice before doing so. The law has come a long way since then, and it seems reasonable to assume that its influence will continue to grow.

Naval planners and maritime strategists thus need to be aware of the developing nature of the law. The strategic environment is becoming much more networked, globalized, and ordered, and the law has become significantly more influential than it was in the middle of the twentieth century, when so many of the foundational documents of today's international legal regime, including the UN Charter, were codified. The legal norms that have developed since then have shown no sign of getting simpler with the passage of time.

NOTES

I am extremely grateful to my former Geneva colleague, Graeme Hurd, who kindly read through an early draft of this chapter, and to Daniel Moran, whose editorial influence included valuable suggestions that improved the final text. As usual, any faults in the text remain my own.

1. Admiral Ian Forbes, "Military Operations and the Law: An Operator's Perspective," opening speech to the Second Annual Senior Officers' Security and Law Conference, Geneva Centre for Security Policy, Geneva, June 14–17, 2010; text in the author's possession.

2. That is not to say that Forbes was suggesting that law was not taken into account; but for commanders operating at the tactical level, there was a general assumption that the law was covered through rules of engagement and adherence to the basic rules in the Geneva Conventions during armed conflict.

3. James Kraska, "Grasping the Influence of Law on Sea Power," *Naval War College Review* 63, no. 3 (Summer 2009): 113–35, at 114.

4. Geoffrey Till, *Seapower: A Guide for the Twenty-First Century*, 2nd ed. (Abingdon, UK: Routledge, 2009).

5. For Gray's latest and his most mature thinking on strategy, see Colin Gray, *The Strategy Bridge: Theory for Practice* (Oxford: Oxford University Press, 2010).

6. Despite this, it should be stressed that Till is by no means dismissive of the law's relevance in the maritime context, and his apparently cursory treatment of it in his text *Seapower* may be misleading in that respect. The same cannot be said for Gray's decision not to dwell on the law. He is a committed Clausewitzian, and it would have been surprising if he had dwelt on the law.

7. Carl von Clausewitz, *On War*, ed. and trans. Michael Howard and Peter Paret (Princeton, NJ: Princeton University Press), 87.

8. Mahan's writings were many, but his groundbreaking work was undoubtedly *The Influence of Sea Power upon History, 1660 to 1783*, which was published in 1890. It was the first of a trilogy, the other two being a work on the French Revolution and French Empire, which was published in 1892, and one on the War of 1812, which was published in 1905.

9. The ship was HMS *Antrim*, a *County*-class guided missile destroyer.

10. Commander S. Haines, Royal Navy, "The Utility of the Future Aircraft Carrier (CV[F])," Directorate of Naval Staff Duties, UK Ministry of Defence, Ref. D /DNSD/8/36/8b, of 12 August 1997; unclassified paper retained in the author's possession.

11. See British Ministry of Defence, *British Defence Doctrine*, 2nd ed. (London: British Ministry of Defence, 2001), 2:1–3. The author wrote this document, and established the seven dimensions of the strategic environment used in the strategic analysis published as *Strategic Trends* (London: British Ministry of Defence, 2003). The seven dimensions are no longer formally used by the MoD, but the author continues to use them for his own approach to strategic analysis.

12. See the treatment of natural and positive law approaches given by Jules Coleman and Scott J. Shapiro, eds., *The Oxford Handbook of Jurisprudence and Philosophy of Law* (Oxford: Oxford University Press, 2002), esp. 1–165.

13. *Jus in bello* is variously referred to as the Law of War, the Law of Armed Conflict, or International Humanitarian Law, all of which are synonymous. The term "Law of Armed Conflict" (LOAC) is used throughout this chapter.

14. For an excellent treatment of the prize law process, see Richard Hill, *The Prizes of War: The Naval Prize System in the Napoleonic Wars 1793–1815* (Stroud, UK: Sutton Publishing, in association with Royal Naval Museum Publications, 1998).

15. Hague Conventions 6 through 13 are concerned with various aspects of naval warfare, including the status of merchant ships, the laying of submarine mines, the right of capture, and the rights and duties of neutral powers in naval war. The conventions can be found at http://avalon.law.yale.edu/subject_menus/lawwar.asp.

16. An important marker of the growing influence exercised by the International Court of Justice was its comment that states could no longer act with impunity within their borders, especially in relation to *erga omnes* (universal) obligations, including human rights. Barcelona Traction Case, *ICJ Reports 1970*, 3, http://www.icj-cij.org /docket/index.php?p1=3&p2=3&case=50&p3=4.

17. These categories were first promulgated in BR1806 *The Fundamentals of British Maritime Doctrine* (London: Her Majesty's Stationery Office, 1995), 34–36, and were

further developed in *BR1806 British Maritime Doctrine,* 2nd ed. (London: Her Majesty's Stationery Office, 1999), 51–67, and were described in *BR1806 British Maritime Doctrine,* 3rd ed. (London: Her Majesty's Stationery Office, 2004), 57–58. *BR1806* has since been replaced by Joint Doctrine Publication 0–10, *British Maritime Doctrine* (2011), https://www.gov.uk/government/uploads/system/uploads/attachment_data /file/33699/20110816JDP0_10_BMD.pdf.

18. Political controversy generated by the sinking of the Argentine cruiser *General Belgrano* during the Falklands War was the result of ignorance of the LOAC applicable at sea, most especially on the part of critics of Margaret Thatcher's decision to authorize the necessary change in rules of engagement. The *Belgrano* was a legitimate military target, whatever it was up to at the time it was sunk. In recent years, however, a view has evolved that an enemy vessel should only be targeted if it is in the region of the armed conflict. According to this view, a British warship encountering an Argentine warship in the Indian Ocean at the time of the conflict would not have been free to target it. Although there is some sense in this suggestion, consistent with the view that conflicts should be geographically limited, such an approach does not reflect any legal obligation. Enemy vessels encountering each other anywhere on the high seas would be free in law to regard each other as legitimate targets (although their own rules of engagement may not allow them to do so for policy reasons).

19. The term "maritime domain" is used to describe the collection of jurisdictional zones claimed by a coastal state. See Steven Haines, *Centrepiece 15: Britain's Maritime Domain: Zones of Jurisdiction* (Aberdeen: Centre for Defence Studies, 1990); and Steven Haines, "Military Aid to Civil Authorities in Britain's Maritime Domain" (PhD thesis, University of Aberdeen, 1993). "Domain" strictly implies some degree of legal authority or control over the area defined. When writing the second edition of *British Maritime Doctrine* (see note 18 above), he used the term in that way, including a definition at p. 218. The phrase has since migrated into US Navy usage and has been distorted to signify the world's oceans in their entirety, in which sense it is frequently used—e.g., in such expressions as "maritime domain awareness." Sadly, this distortion has now migrated back to Britain, and the term, coined for a very specific descriptive purpose, is now generally misleading. However, this author continues to use it in the way he originally intended it to be used.

20. Different jurisdictions have different approaches to what constitutes legitimate self-defense, with some (e.g., the United States) including the protection of property, and others (e.g., the United Kingdom) restricting it to the defense of persons whom one has a right or duty to protect.

21. This is notwithstanding the possibility that benign humanitarian aid operations may well be conducted in insecure theaters of operations, necessitating other operations of a military or constabulary nature, to run in parallel in order to provide a secure space for humanitarian action.

22. A powerful navy, especially one like the US Navy today or the Royal Navy in the nineteenth century, may well be able to control a substantial maritime region simply by appearing in force within it.

23. Sea command does not imply total control of the world's oceans but command of what would undoubtedly be a substantial region. E.g., a navy might exercise sea command in the Mediterranean, without doing so concurrently in the Pacific.

24. The categorization of maritime powers or, more specifically, navies, has been well dealt with by Eric Grove, who has proposed a hierarchy of nine levels, with complete major global power projection navies at Level 1 (only the US Navy falls into this level at present) down to token navies at Level 9. See Eric Grove, *The Future of Seapower* (London: Routledge, 1990), 236–40.

25. The most recent treaty dealing with warfare at sea is the Second Geneva Convention of 1949, for the Amelioration of the Conditions of Wounded, Sick, and Shipwrecked Members of the Armed Forces at Sea; but this is about the victims of war, not about how navies should fight, or about the means and methods they should use when doing so. The most recent formal law dealing with these issues is the Hague Conventions concluded more than a century ago.

26. Traditionally, the Law of the Sea was part of the Law of Peace; and for that reason, it was distinct from the Law of War.

27. Louise Doswald-Beck, ed., *San Remo Manual of the Law of Armed Conflict Applicable at Sea* (Cambridge: Cambridge University Press, 1995).

28. MoD, *Manual of the Law of Armed Conflict* (Oxford: Oxford University Press, 2004). This author chaired the manual's Editorial Board and was also one of the authors of its maritime warfare chapter. I described the extent to which that chapter differed from the *San Remo Manual* in Steven Haines, "The United Kingdom's Manual of the Law of Armed Conflict and the San Remo Manual: Maritime Rules Compared," in *Israel Yearbook on Human Rights 36* (Leiden: Martinus Nijhoff, 2006), 89–118.

29. For accounts of the *Graf Spee*'s operations, see Steven Roskill, *The War at Sea 1939–1945, Volume 1: The Defensive* (London: Her Majesty's Stationery Office, 1954), 112–21; D. P. O'Connell, *The Influence of Law on Seapower* (Manchester: Manchester University Press, 1975), 27–39; and, most recently, Eric Grove, *The Price of Disobedience: The Battle of the River Plate Reconsidered* (Stroud, UK: Sutton, 2000).

30. To quote Christopher Greenwood: "Once hostilities have begun, the rules of international humanitarian law apply with equal force to both sides in the conflict, irrespective of who is the aggressor"; Christopher Greenwood, "Historical Developments and Legal Basis," in *The Handbook of International Humanitarian Law*, 2nd edition, ed. Dieter Fleck (Oxford: Oxford University Press, 2008), 10.

31. The author, who was serving in the MoD at the time of Operation Allied Force, was asked by the director of naval operations for his view about how to deal with vessels bound for Bar. He raised the legal option of belligerent blockade, as did others.

32. There is some dispute as to whether or not interdiction operations can commence before a declared blockade runner has entered the defined blockade zone. Article 17 of the *Declaration of London* states that "neutral vessels may not be captured for breach of blockade except within the area of operations of the warships detailed to render the blockade effective." See Natalino Ronzitti, ed., *The Law of Naval Warfare: A Collection of Agreements and Documents with Commentaries* (Boston: Martinus Nijhoff, 1988), 231; and C. John Colombos, *International Law of the Sea*, 6th ed. (London: Longmans, 1967), 727–28. In fact, the *Declaration of London*, though signed by ten major powers, never entered into force through lack of ratification. Arguably, practice since then has negated Article 17. D. P. O'Connell, *The International Law of the Sea* (Oxford: Clarendon Press, 1984), 2:1157, makes the point that "the breaking of the blockade must occur within the forbidden area of sea, *or be so intended*" (emphasis added), thus suggesting

that a preemptive interdiction would be permitted. O'Connell goes on to stress, however, that the capture and condemnation of a neutral vessel may only be permitted as it engages in the act of breaching the cordon, i.e., entering the blockade zone. A reading of both O'Connell and Colombos seems to suggest that anticipatory interdiction would not be lawful in the case of neutral vessels. A. R. Thomas and James C. Duncan, eds., *Annotated Supplement to the Commander's Handbook on the Law of Naval Operations*, US Naval War College International Law Study 73 (Newport, RI: US Naval War College, 1999), 390–98, takes the opposite position, favoring anticipatory interdiction of vessels once they have left their ports of departure.

33. Article 41 of the UN Charter deals with the imposition of diplomatic and economic sanctions. A common method of enforcing economic sanctions is to use maritime forces to conduct an embargo operation. Article 42, in contrast, deals with military sanctions, and blockade is a method of coercion mentioned in that context. An embargo operation under Article 41 would be a constabulary operation, whereas a blockade mounted under Article 42 would be a military operation. An important distinction between them is that, under Article 41, the use of force would need to be restricted to the minimum necessary to enforce the economic sanctions, while under Article 42 naval forces imposing blockade would be using force under LOAC conditions.

34. In the 1st edition of *British Maritime Doctrine*, operations against enemy merchant shipping are hinted at under "Operations against Enemy Forces" (p. 95); but they are oddly listed under "sea control" operations in table 5.1 (p. 105) rather than under an "economic warfare" heading, which is omitted. Mention of action against enemy merchant shipping was omitted from the second edition; nor is there mention of operations against neutral shipping to check for contraband. There has been no significant shift in this position in the third edition. The author, who contributed to all three editions (having particular responsibility for writing the second), was conscious of no dissent from the other members of the editorial board, which included representatives of all the relevant Naval Staff directorates as well as Fleet Headquarters.

35. See UNCLOS Article 3, on the territorial sea; Article 33, on the contiguous zone; Article 57, on the exclusive economic zone; and Article 76, on the continental shelf.

36. The Convention for the Suppression of Unlawful Acts, together with its 2005 Protocol, can be found at http://www.un.org/en/sc/ctc/docs/conventions/Conv8 .pdf. The Vienna Convention against Illicit Traffic is at http://www.unodc.org/pdf /convention_1988_en.pdf.

37. For a recent summary of the Proliferation Security Initiative, see US National Institute for Public Policy, *The Proliferations Security Initiative: A Model for Future International Collaboration* (Fairfax, VA: National Institute Press, 2009).

38. UN Security Council Resolution 221, April 9, 1966.

39. E.g., Article 61 of UNCLOS obliges coastal states to ensure, through "proper conservation and management measures that the maintenance of the living resources in the exclusive economic zone is not endangered by over exploitation." This obligation would not be met unless the state deployed fisheries enforcement aircraft and vessels to enforce fisheries law.

CHAPTER 10

Mahan Revisited

Globalization, Resource Dependency, and Maritime Security in the Twenty-First Century

MICHAEL T. KLARE

At the end of 2004 the George W. Bush administration adopted National Security Presidential Directive 41 (NSPD-41), which designates the "Maritime Domain" as a theater of strategic concern. According to the directive, this "domain" encompasses "all areas and things of, on, under, adjacent to, or bordering on" the seas and oceans. These areas are of vital concern, it is affirmed, because the oceans constitute an essential thoroughfare for international trade and resource flows, and also because they can be used to launch attacks on this trade or the territory of the United States and its allies. Under the 2004 directive, it became American policy "to take all necessary and appropriate actions . . . to enhance the security of and protect US interests in the Maritime Domain." To this end, all affected government agencies were enjoined to strengthen their relevant capabilities, and an interagency body, the Maritime Security Policy Coordinating Committee, was established to coordinate these endeavors.[1]

In accordance with NSPD-41, the three bodies most directly affected by the directive—the Navy, the Marine Corps, and the Coast Guard—undertook a comprehensive review of the changing strategic environment and adopted a common approach to maritime security. In a document titled *A Cooperative Strategy for 21st-Century Seapower*, published in 2007, the three services laid out the broad outlines of this new approach. Beginning, as does NSPD-41, with the assertion that unfettered maritime commerce is essential to US security and well-being, it identified the ways in which naval power can best be used to secure these interests: "Because the maritime domain . . . supports 90% of the world's trade, it carries the lifeblood of a global system that links every nation on Earth," the document noted. "As our security and prosperity are inextricably linked with those of others," it continued, "US maritime forces will be deployed to protect and sustain the peaceful global system comprised of interdependent networks of trade, finance, information, law, people, and governance."[2]

As a maritime power and a major trading nation, the United States has long placed great emphasis on maritime security and the protection of international commerce. Yet, in recent years, there has been a sharp increase of interest in maritime security affairs, as exemplified by the adoption of NSPD-41 and the *Cooperative Strategy*. Other nations with a significant seaborne trade have also shown a growing interest in maritime security. In 2007, for example, the Indian Navy released a strategic blueprint of its own, *Freedom to Use the Seas: India's Maritime Military Strategy*, which bears considerable resemblance to that adopted by the United States.[3] Brazil, which has recently acquired a significant strategic interest in the protection of its offshore oil fields, has also adopted a new military policy with a maritime focus.[4]

What accounts for this growing interest in maritime security affairs? The greatest factor, of course, is globalization, which has substantially increased the reliance of the world's major economies on international trade—and thus on the global flow of goods by sea. According to the International Monetary Fund, the share of the world's gross domestic product (GDP) accounted for by international trade rose from 41 percent in 1980 to 57 percent in 2005, at the same time that global GDP as a whole jumped from about $13 billion to $61 billion (in purchasing power valuation by country).[5] Some areas of the world have seen an even greater increase in reliance on trade. In East Asia, for example, the share of GDP accounted for by foreign trade rose from 47 percent in 1990 to 87 percent in 2006.[6] And greater reliance on imports and exports means greater reliance on the sea: "Over the past four decades, total seaborne trade has more than quadrupled," the three US maritime services noted in their 2007 document. "Ninety percent of world trade and two-thirds of its petroleum are transported by sea." As a result, the global sea lanes and supporting shore infrastructure represent "the lifelines of the modern global economy."[7]

For many countries, this reliance on foreign trade is compounded by a growing dependence on imported supplies of energy, notably oil and natural gas. In 2014 the United States relied on imported petroleum for about 27 percent of its total energy supply, despite the recent dramatic growth in domestic production from domestic shale deposits.[8] A significant share of this imported supply will need to come by tanker from troubled areas of Africa and the Middle East. China and the European Union are even more reliant on oil from these sources, and will become still more so in the future, placing greater emphasis on the security of vital sea lanes.[9]

Accompanying this growing reliance on foreign trade and imported energy is a conspicuous increase in threats to the safety of maritime commerce. These threats arise from several sources: terrorist and insurgent attacks on oil tankers and loading facilities; piracy and criminal assaults on merchant shipping; disputes over contested offshore resource zones; and deliberate attacks on merchant shipping by parties to war. The potential for increasing attacks of this sort was highlighted in *Global Trends 2025*, the long-term strategic assessment released by the US National Intelligence Council in 2008, and in its successor document, *Global Trends 2030*, in 2012.[10]

In response to these developments, the US government—and those of many other countries—has placed increased emphasis on "maritime security," or the protection of global seaborne commerce against interference and attack. This is the stated objective of NSPD-41 and similar documents adopted by other countries. Ideally, these endeavors could spur greater international cooperation in efforts to combat terrorism, piracy, and other such threats; as is argued here, however, there is a substantial risk that these efforts will instead provoke rivalry and competition among the major naval powers, increasing the risk of crisis and conflict at sea.

THE MAHANIAN DOCTRINE OF SEA POWER

The use of naval forces to ensure access to overseas resources and protect seaborne commerce is hardly a new concept. Many analysts and historians believe, for example, that it was Britain's overarching emphasis on the development and maintenance of superior naval power that was largely responsible for its rise and extended tenure as the greatest among the European imperial powers.[11] One of those analysts, the American naval officer and educator Alfred Thayer Mahan (1840–1914), drew on Britain's example in attempting to persuade US leaders of the signal importance of sea power in ensuring economic survival in the increasingly competitive and interdependent world of the late nineteenth century. In his classic text *The Influence of Sea Power Upon History, 1660–1783*, he wrote that Britain triumphed over its rivals in part through superior leadership, but mostly "by the superiority of her government using the tremendous weapon of her sea power. This made her rich, and in turn protected the trade by which she had her wealth. . . . Her power was everywhere that her ships could reach, and there was none to dispute the sea to her."[12]

For Mahan, who served for many years as president of the Naval War College in Newport, Rhode Island, it was essential that the United States learn from Britain's example and acquire a powerful navy of its own, so as to better protect its seaborne commerce. "As the practical object of this inquiry is to draw from the lessons of history inferences applicable to one's own country," he wrote in 1890, "it is proper now to ask how far the conditions of the United States involve serious danger, and call for action on the part of the government, in order to build again her sea power."[13] For Mahan, the answer to these questions was self-evident: The United States faced a growing challenge from other powers—many of which possessed far larger and more potent navies than it did—and so had no choice but to expand and modernize its own maritime capabilities. Believing, moreover, that the United States needed overseas colonies to bolster its foreign trade and facilitate its control of the seas, Mahan campaigned tirelessly for US military intervention in what became the Spanish-American War, and, following that struggle, the acquisition of Puerto Rico and the colonization of the Philippines.[14]

Among those who were strongly influenced by Mahan was the young Theodore Roosevelt, who from 1897 to 1898 served as assistant secretary of the Navy. It was at this time that Mahan's signature work, *The Influence of Sea Power upon History*, was published—and Roosevelt was an enthusiastic reader.[15] In his capacity as assistant secretary of the Navy, Roosevelt drew on Mahan's advice in advance planning for a war with Spain, which both assumed was inevitable.[16] After being elected president in 1901, Roosevelt implemented many of Mahan's recommendations for the expansion and modernization of US naval power. "A fervent believer in the Mahanian doctrine of sea power, Roosevelt paid particular attention to the US Navy as the first line of defense and a primary instrument of American foreign policy," Matthew Oyos wrote in *The Oxford Companion to American Military History*. "Roosevelt operated in effect as his own secretary of the Navy. A competitor in the international naval arms race of the day, he won congressional approval for sixteen battleships, including new, powerful dreadnaughts, and increased the naval budget by 60 percent."[17]

What Oyos calls the "Mahanian doctrine of sea power" has continued to dominate US military thinking since Theodore Roosevelt's day. Another follower of Mahan (and Theodore's fifth cousin), Franklin D. Roosevelt, continued the work of implementing this doctrine while himself serving as assistant secretary of the Navy (1913–20), and later as president. Roosevelt placed great reliance on naval power during World War II, both in projecting power to Europe and in wresting control of the Pacific from Japan. After World War II, the US Navy lost some of its preeminence as Cold War policies placed greater reliance on intercontinental missiles, long-range bombers, and Army forces in Europe. Nevertheless, it generally received strong support from Congress and continued to lead in the development of submarines and aircraft carriers.[18] Naval forces played a critical role in maintaining the trade embargo against Iraq from 1991 to 2003, in supporting US combat operations in Iraq and Afghanistan, and in sustaining global pressure against terrorist organizations like al-Qaeda and the so-called Islamic State of Iraq and Syria.

Now that American troops have withdrawn from Iraq and Afghanistan, we are likely to witness a significant shift in the overall orientation of US forces, from an emphasis on large-scale conventional combat to one on small-scale counterinsurgency and counterterrorism operations. In his budget statement of April 6, 2009, then–secretary of defense Robert Gates indicated that his highest priority for combat planning was to enhance US capabilities for counterinsurgency and low-intensity warfare—not full-scale conventional combat involving large numbers of troops, tanks, and armored vehicles. Thus he called for increased spending on pilotless Predator aircraft (aka "drones"), battlefield surveillance gear, and Special Operations capabilities, while postponing work on the Army's Future Combat Systems program, a multibillion dollar ensemble of armored vehicles.[19] This approach is likely to place greater reliance on air and naval forces, which can provide support to lightly armed special units and bring pressure to bear in distant trouble spots with less risk of entanglement in protracted ground wars. A very similar outlook was manifest in the Pentagon's most recent Quadrennial Defense Review, released in March 2014.[20]

The Navy has always touted its advantages in this respect, but it is doing so with even greater vigor now, as Congress's and the public's appetite for involvement in future Iraq-like conflicts is evaporating. "Permanent or prolonged basing of our military forces overseas often has unintended economic, social, or political repercussions," the *Cooperative Strategy* declares. Using language that Mahan would find congenial, it continues, "The sea is a vast maneuver space, where the presence of maritime forces can be adjusted as conditions dictate to enable flexible approaches to escalation, de-escalation and deterrence of conflicts."[21] Indeed, in many ways the Navy's new doctrine can be seen as a reassertion, in contemporary terms, of the Mahanian doctrine of sea power: "The security, prosperity, and vital interest of the United States are increasingly coupled to those of other nations. Covering three-quarters of the planet, the oceans make neighbors of people around the world. They enable us to help friends in need and to confront and defeat aggression far from our shores."[22]

THE ABIDING US RELIANCE ON IMPORTED RESOURCES

As suggested above, this growing emphasis on sea power is occurring against the backdrop of continued reliance, on the part of the United States and the developed world generally, on imported raw materials, and growing threats to the safety of maritime commerce. As time goes on, these are likely to prove even greater spurs to the resurgence of naval power.

The United States was once largely self-sufficient in energy—one of the few major powers in the fortunate position of being so—and its position in this regard has recently improved, owing to advancements in the extraction of oil from shale. Nevertheless, its long-term reliance on imported petroleum for part of its consumption is never likely to disappear. In May 2015, despite all recent improvements in domestic production, the United States was still importing more than 290 million barrels of crude oil and petroleum products per month, a figure little different from twenty years earlier.[23] Some of this oil is transported by pipeline from Canada, but most of it is carried by ship to American ports.

Soon after assuming office, President Barack Obama announced ambitious plans to diminish US reliance on imported petroleum. These include efforts to enhance the fuel efficiency of American motor vehicles and to increase the availability of alternative sources of energy, including advanced biofuels, wind power, and solar energy. "It will be the policy of my administration to reverse our dependence on foreign oil," he declared on January 26, 2009. But despite increased production from domestic sources, notably offshore fields in the Gulf of Mexico and oil-laden shale deposits, the United States will continue to rely on imported oil for a significant share of its energy supply in the years ahead, as so much of the nation's economy and transportation system is dependent on a continuous supply of petroleum-derived fuels and because so much of these must be obtained from foreign sources. Even in 2040, the United States will still rely on imported oil for approximately one-half of its total crude oil supply, according to the most recent projections from the Department of Energy.[24]

The Obama administration has also sought to increase the share of US crude supplies derived from producers in the Western Hemisphere—especially Brazil, Canada, and Mexico—but these suppliers are not likely to furnish enough oil to eliminate US reliance on extra-hemispheric sources. Mexico, once a major supplier of crude oil to the United States, is facing a significant decline in output as older fields are depleted. At the same time, Mexican domestic consumption is growing rapidly, so the country is projected to become a net importer of oil by 2020, if not before.[25] Although production in Brazil is likely to grow in the years ahead, domestic consumption is rising rapidly, so that the amount available for export will not be great.[26] Only Canada is expected to post a notable increase in exportable oil in the years ahead, but this will require continuing investment in the development of bitumen-rich tar sands (also called oil sands)—a thick, viscous substance that can only be converted into liquid fuel through costly and environmentally hazardous processing. Such investment cannot be assured; nor can a continued willingness to tolerate the resulting environmental costs.[27]

For all these reasons, the United States will continue to rely on oil imports from extra-hemispheric sources, primarily the Middle East and West Africa. This means greater reliance on energy supplies carried by tankers over long distances, in some cases traversing potentially pirate-infested or war-affected waterways, including the Persian Gulf, the Gulf of Guinea, the Red Sea, and the Strait of Malacca.

Like all industrialized nations, the United States is also highly dependent on imports of vital minerals that are not found in its territory or are produced at too modest a level to satisfy national requirements. True, the United States is unusually blessed, in that it harbors large reserves of iron, copper, uranium, and other key resources; but, even so, it must import significant quantities of other minerals, including bauxite (the source of aluminum), chromium, cobalt, nickel, tin, and the platinum group metals (PGMs).[28] Some of these can be obtained from Canada, Mexico, and other Western Hemisphere sources; but others—notably chromium, cobalt, and the PGMs—are largely found in Africa and Eurasia. As older reserves in the Western Hemisphere are depleted, an ever-increasing share of many critical minerals will need to be obtained from Africa and remote areas of Asia.[29] Virtually all these materials must be carried by ship, and so will face the same threats from piracy and conflict as will shipborne deliveries of oil.

What is true of the United States is equally true of other industrial powers: Except for Russia, which possesses vast supplies of energy and minerals, most industrialized countries will remain heavily dependent on imports of energy and other vital materials carried by ship from distant sources of supply. This is especially true for China, which many analysts believe will overtake the United States to become the world's leading economy by the middle of the twenty-first century.[30] Like the United States, China was once self-sufficient in oil and other key materials; but once it adopted economic reforms and began expanding at double-digit rates of growth, it quickly exceeded the output capacity of many domestic resource suppliers, and so became highly dependent on imports. For example, China now obtains approximately 60 percent of its petroleum supply from foreign suppliers, and it is projected to rely on imports for about 75 percent of its oil supply in 2040.[31] China is also highly dependent on imports for its supply of many key industrial minerals, including copper, cobalt, and iron ore. And, as India's economy grows, it too will rely on ever-increasing imports of energy and industrial imports obtained from overseas sources of supply.[32]

GROWING THREATS TO MARITIME SECURITY

At a time of growing international reliance on seaborne deliveries of vital raw materials, the threats to such commerce appear to be increasing. Although long evident to students of international security affairs, this phenomenon received international attention in November 2008, when Somali pirates hijacked the *Sirius Star*, a Saudi supertanker carrying more than $100 million worth of crude oil, while it was sailing a few hundred miles off the Kenyan coast. The hijacking of the *Sirius Star* received worldwide coverage, highlighting the growing audacity of pirates operating from war-torn Somalia.[33] The threat posed by piracy was accorded even greater attention in April 2009, when Somali pirates hijacked an American-flagged vessel, the *Maersk Alabama*. But piracy is only one of the threats to maritime commerce. Others include terrorism, the spillover effects of local and regional wars, and offshore territorial disputes.

By all accounts, the frequency and sophistication of piracy attacks worldwide—including in the Gulf of Aden, the Gulf of Guinea, offshore Indonesia, and waters along the east coast of Africa—is growing.[34] "A dramatic increase in activity by Somali pirates led to a near doubling in the number of ships attacked during the year's first quarter compared with the same period in

2008," the International Maritime Bureau (IMB) reported on April 21, 2009, shortly after the hijacking of the *Maersk Alabama*. Although rigorous efforts by the international community to suppress piracy have proven effective in curbing the frequency of armed incidents off the east coast of Africa, the IMB continues to warn of significant dangers in many areas, especially in the Gulf of Guinea and the South China Sea.[35]

The pirates are also becoming increasingly sophisticated, using well-honed tactics and a primitive but effective intelligence gathering system. "Today's pirates and criminals are usually well organized and well equipped with advanced communications, weapons, and high-speed craft," notes *The National Strategy for Maritime Security*, an interagency response to NSPD-41.[36] The IMB's Piracy Reporting Center has also indicated that pirate bands in Somalia rely on "mother ships"—innocent-looking fishing trawlers and tugboats—to identify and track prospective targets. Pirates based on such ships look for slow-moving vessels like oil tankers that are difficult to maneuver; once a ship is spotted, the prospective hijackers jump into small, fast-moving skiffs and attempt to board the slower target ships and capture their crews.[37]

Of even greater concern than piracy is the prospect of stepped-up terrorist assaults on oil tankers and oil-loading facilities.[38] This prospect first arose in October 2002, when a small boat filled with explosives came alongside the French oil tanker *Limburg* in waters off Yemen and detonated, blowing a hole in the hull and spilling 100,000 barrels of burning oil into the surrounding waters.[39] This attack, widely attributed to al-Qaeda, was seen as the opening salvo in a campaign to punish and weaken the West by attacking the exposed conduits of the global oil supply system.[40] Indeed, in a subsequent message disseminated by sympathetic internet sites, Osama bin Laden implored his followers in the Middle East to "do your best to prevent [the Western powers] from stealing our oil. Focus your operations on it, especially in Iraq and the Gulf."[41]

Whether inspired by these words or not, terrorists linked to al-Qaeda conducted an even more audacious attack on February 23, 2006, breaking through the outer perimeter of the Abqaiq oil-processing facility on Saudi Arabia's Persian Gulf coast and detonating two explosive-laden vehicles inside the Kingdom's most important energy installation, potentially jeopardizing the export of 6.8 million barrels per day, or about 8 percent of world consumption. Although the attack was foiled before the attackers could get close to the installation's most vital facilities, it exposed the vulnerability of the global oil transportation system and the degree to which such facilities have become targets of terrorist attacks.[42] Since then, the Saudis have undertaken enormous efforts to prevent future attacks, vastly increasing their security efforts at major oil installations and arresting hundreds of suspected sympathizers with al-Qaeda.[43]

Maritime shipping can also come under attack due to the spillover of local or regional conflicts. In southern Nigeria, for example, the ongoing conflict on the Niger Delta has spread into offshore areas of the Gulf of Guinea. Essentially, this conflict pits impoverished peoples of the Delta against the central government in Abuja, with distribution of oil revenues the central issue in contention. Historically, the vast majority of Nigeria's vast oil wealth has been pocketed by elites in the capital, with very little of it being redirected to inhabitants of the Delta, where most of the oil is produced. This, quite predictably, has provoked hostility from Delta residents, who in many cases have seen their livelihoods endangered by the adverse environmental consequences of protracted oil production.[44] Increasingly, this hostility has taken a violent form, entailing attacks on oil facilities and the kidnapping of oil company personnel. Several armed groups, including the Movement for the Emancipation of the Niger Delta (MEND), have engaged in such activities.[45] For the most part, these attacks have occurred on land, but on June 19, 2008, militants from MEND seized Royal Dutch Shell Oil's main offshore oil facility in the Gulf of Guinea, temporarily halting production of some 225,000 barrels per day, or approximately one-tenth of Nigeria's daily output.[46] "The location for today's attack was deliberately chosen to remove any notion that offshore oil exploration is far from our reach," the group declared in an e-mail message, telling foreign oil firms to remove all expatriate oil workers from Nigeria.[47]

It is likely that future conflicts in major producing regions will also pose a threat to the safe flow of crude oil by sea. Of greatest worry, perhaps, is the possibility of a clash between the United States and Iran arising from US concerns over Tehran's apparent determination to acquire nuclear weapons. During the Bush administration, it was common for senior officials to warn of military action in the Persian Gulf area as a response to Iranian intransigence in the nuclear dispute and other issues of concern to Washington. During a May 2007 visit to US vessels engaged in naval maneuvers off Iran, for instance, Vice President Dick Cheney declared, "With two carrier strike groups in the Gulf, we're sending clear messages to friends and adversaries alike. We'll keep the sea lanes open. We'll stand with our friends in opposing extremism and strategic threats."[48]

Although, as of spring 2015, the Obama administration has made significant progress to resolve this dispute through diplomatic means, the president has also made it clear that he has not ruled out the use of force if all other efforts to prevent Iran's acquisition of nuclear munitions fail. In response to such statements, whether from President Obama or his predecessor, the Iranians have repeatedly stated that they will retaliate against any US attacks by attempting to block maritime commerce through the Strait of Hormuz, thereby precipitating a global economic crisis. "Naturally every country under attack by an enemy uses all its capacity and opportunities to confront the enemy," General Mohammad Ali Jafari, commander of Iran's Revolutionary Guards, told the newspaper *Jam-e-Jam* in June 2008. "Iran will definitely act to impose control on the Persian Gulf and Strait of Hormuz," causing oil prices to "rise very considerably."[49] Western analysts differ in their assessments of whether such a move by Iran would succeed for very long in the face of strong American countermeasures, but they could nevertheless result in a temporary blockage of approximately one-fourth of daily world oil deliveries.

The global commerce in oil and other vital materials could also be endangered by another form of maritime conflict: disputes over contested offshore territories that are believed to harbor valuable resources of one sort or another. Although interstate conflicts over disputed borders and territories on land have become relatively rare in recent years—the Eritrean/Ethiopian border war of 1998–990 representing one of the few exceptions—disputes over contested offshore territories have become more common. Typically, these have arisen in areas like the Caspian Sea, the Persian Gulf, the East China Sea, the South China Sea, and the Arctic Ocean, where the contested areas are thought to harbor valuable undersea reserves of oil and/or natural gas.[50]

On some occasions, these disputes have provoked armed clashes at sea, in some cases involving attacks on commercial shipping. In July 2001, for example, an Iranian gunboat threatened to fire on an oil-exploration vessel belonging to BP in an area of the Caspian Sea claimed by both Azerbaijan and Iran. The vessel, which had been operating under an exploration agreement granted by the former, fled the area.[51] Also, in the South China Sea, fishing boats and oil survey vessels belonging to the various claimants have been seized or harassed by the naval forces of other claimants. An especially serious incident of this sort occurred in May 2014, when China deployed a large flotilla of naval and coast guard vessels to fend off Vietnamese ships attempting to dislodge a Chinese drilling rig positioned in waters claimed by both countries.[52] Disputes of this sort could become more heated in the years ahead, as oil and gas reserves on land are progressively depleted and greater emphasis is placed on the exploitation of deposits located in offshore locations.

THE SECURITIZATION OF RESOURCE DEPENDENCY

In response to the persisting and inevitable US dependence on overseas supplies of vital materials, and the perception that deliveries of these supplies face a greater risk of obstruction, American policymakers have chosen to place greater reliance on the use of military means—especially the naval forces—to ensure their safety. In general terms, of course, the use of military force to protect America's maritime commerce is almost as old as the nation itself. When the Barbary Pirates menaced US shipping in the Mediterranean at the dawn of the nineteenth century, Congress responded by authorizing construction of the nation's first warships. As we have seen, Alfred Thayer Mahan also proselytized for a strong navy in order to protect American commerce. But the explicit link between US dependence on imported resources and the use of military force is of relatively recent derivation, arising largely from the nation's reliance on foreign petroleum.[53]

This link was first articulated at the highest level of policy on January 23, 1980, in President Jimmy Carter's State of the Union Address. Coming one year after the shah of Iran was overthrown by militant Islamic clerics loyal to the Ayatollah Khomeini, and one month after the Soviet invasion of Afghanistan, Carter's speech was viewed as a turning point in US relations to the Persian Gulf. "The region which is now threatened by Soviet troops in Afghanistan is of great strategic importance," Carter declared. "It contains more than two-thirds of the world's exportable oil. The Soviet effort to dominate Afghanistan has brought Soviet forces to within 300 miles of the Indian Ocean and close to the Strait of Hormuz, a waterway through which most of the world's oil must flow." If the free flow of oil through this vital passageway were to be impeded by the Soviets or anyone else, he continued, the economic well-being of the free world would be at risk. Under these circumstances, the United States had no choice but to guarantee the safety of this flow. "Let our position be absolutely clear," he declared. "An attempt by any outside force to gain control of the Persian Gulf region will be regarded as an assault on the vital interests of the United States of America, and such an assault will be repelled by any means necessary, including military force."[54]

Given that the United States had very few forces specifically earmarked for operations in the Gulf area at that time, the burden for implementation of this precept—since known as the Carter Doctrine—naturally fell chiefly on the Navy (and to a lesser extent the Air Force). "We've increased and strengthened our naval presence in the Indian Ocean," Carter declared on January 23, "and we are now making arrangements for key naval and air facilities to be used by our forces in the region of northeast Africa and the Persian Gulf." To bolster these moves, Carter also established a new ad hoc command organization with responsibility for US combat operations in the Gulf, the Rapid Deployment Joint Task Force (RDJTF). In 1983 President Reagan elevated the RDJTF to a full-scale regional command, the US Central Command (CENTCOM).[55] Today CENTCOM continues to bear responsibility for ensuring the free flow of oil from the Persian Gulf to ports around the world.

The task of protecting vital sea lanes has been shared by other regional commands, including the Pacific Command, which has responsibility for the Indian Ocean and the vulnerable waterways through and around Indonesia, and the European Command (EUCOM), which, until the establishment of the African Command in 2008, had responsibility for the Atlantic waters off Africa, including the Gulf of Guinea. Noting the growing importance of African oil to the United States and the various threats to maritime commerce in that region, EUCOM commander General James Jones indicated in 2003 that the carrier battle groups under his command would shorten their visits to the Mediterranean and "spend half the time going down the west coast of Africa."[56]

In December 2004 the protection of vital seaborne commerce was incorporated into a larger framework of "maritime security" under NSPD-41. As noted above, the directive called on the departments of Defense, State, Commerce, Energy, and Homeland Security, along with other affected agencies, to develop detailed plans for enhanced maritime security. Particular emphasis was placed on defense against terrorist attacks at sea and what was termed "maritime commerce security," or protection of the "global supply chain" against terrorists, criminals, and other hostile parties. A follow-up document, *The National Strategy for Maritime Security* (September 2005), provided further guidance on the development of these plans.

Consistent with these documents, the three maritime services issued their own policy template, the *Cooperative Strategy*, in October 2007. As indicated, it calls on America's three sea services to bolster their capabilities in several core areas, especially "sea control" and "maritime security." Sea control, described in the 2007 document as "the ability to operate freely at sea," is given particular emphasis, and expressly includes commercial, and not merely military, operations: "We will [not] permit an adversary to disrupt the global supply chain by attempting to block vital sea lines of communication and commerce. We will be able to impose local sea control wherever necessary, ideally in concert with friends and allies, but by ourselves if we must." Maritime security, as described in the document, covers the protection of seaborne trade against terrorism, piracy, drug trafficking, and other maritime perils.[57]

MARITIME SECURITY IN THE OBAMA ERA

As in other key areas of national policy, the Obama administration has taken a fresh look at military policy and the future roles of the armed forces. Such a reassessment would have been expected in any change of administrations, but was given added urgency by the global economic crisis, which has posed extraordinary constraints on the allocation of federal funds.

In his 2009 comments on the nation's security dilemma, Secretary of Defense Robert Gates insisted that it is no longer possible for this country to maintain capabilities and procure weapons for every conceivable military contingency. "This department must consistently demonstrate the commitment and leadership to stop programs that significantly exceed their budget or which spend limited tax dollars to buy more capability than the nation needs," he declared.[58] All the military services will be held accountable to this standard; and all, no doubt, will experience the loss of some cherished weapons programs. But at a time when funds are scarce and every government organization is being judged in terms of its contribution to the nation's well-being, the Navy is likely to emerge from this process of scrutiny in better shape than the other services because of its mobile nature and direct role in protecting the flow of vital resources to American ports.

For many of these reasons, the Navy and its sister maritime services are likely to see more direct involvement in combat operations than has been the case in recent years. This is so in part because of the American public's reluctance to get involved in more protracted ground wars like those in Iraq and Afghanistan and in part because of greater national concern over piracy, terrorism, and other threats to international commerce. In this new environment, naval forces (plus associated amphibious assault and aviation) can be used to signal American intentions through assertive show-of-force operations, conduct punitive attacks against menacing adversaries from offshore platforms, and protect vital merchant shipping—all at costs far below those required to maintain ground forces in distant locations like Iraq and Afghanistan. Naval forces are also best positioned to deal with the threat of piracy, as demonstrated by the daring rescue in April 2009 of Richard Phillips, captain of the *Maersk Alabama*. Following that event, President Obama declared that his administration was "resolved to halt the rise of piracy in that region"[59]—a task that has resulted in an expanded US naval presence in the Indian Ocean. As part of this effort, US naval vessels play a central role in the operations of Combined Task Force 151 (CTF-151), a multinational antipiracy force established in 2009 in accordance with several UN Security Council resolutions.

The Obama administration has also reaffirmed the US commitment to ensure the safety of the oil flow from the Persian Gulf to global markets. Although the United States is now importing less oil from this region due to the upsurge in domestic output, Washington views the safety of the oil flow as essential to global economic stability. "The United States of America is prepared to use all elements of our power, including military force, to secure our core interests in the region," Obama told the UN General Assembly on September 24, 2013. "We will ensure the free flow of energy from the region to the world. Although America is steadily reducing our own dependence on imported oil, the world still depends on the region's energy supply, and a severe disruption could destabilize the entire global economy."[60]

Similar concerns over the safety of maritime commerce can be seen in other countries. The Defense Department's annual report on Chinese military strength, *The Military Power of the People's Republic of China*, has repeatedly warned of Chinese plans to substantially modernize and expand its "blue-water" (deep-sea) navy in accordance with Beijing's growing concern over foreign resource dependence. These predictions appeared to be confirmed in April 2009, when China's Communist Party leadership announced a significant modernization of the country's navy, known as the People's Liberation Army Navy (PLAN). "The Party central leadership has demanded that the navy make preparedness for military struggle at sea a priority in national security strategy and military strategy," Admiral Wu Shengli was quoted as saying. "We must accelerate progress in developing key weapons equipment," he added, singling out large warships, long-distance stealth submarines, supersonic jet fighters, and high-accuracy long-range missiles. Wu, as a member of China's Central Military Commission (which overseas the nation's armed forces), is considered the authoritative voice on PLAN strategic planning.[61]

Other rising powers with a similar degree of reliance on imported resources are also expanding their naval capabilities. In May 2007, for example, the Indian Navy released its own strategic template, *Freedom to Use the Seas*. "Among other factors, India's economic resurgence is directly linked to her overseas trade and energy needs, most of which are transported by sea," the document notes. "The primary task of the Indian Navy towards national security is, therefore, to provide insulation from external interference, so that the vital tasks of fostering economic growth and undertaking developmental activities can take place in a secure environment."[62] Although limiting its scope of operations to the Indian Ocean area, the Indian Navy's blueprint calls for the enhancement of many of the same sort of capabilities that were highlighted in the US *Cooperative Strategy*. Another emerging power, Brazil, has recently announced plans to spend billions of dollars on the modernization of its own naval forces. As part of this plan, Brazil will undertake the construction of nuclear submarines with French technical assistance; once completed, the submarines will be used to help defend Brazil's vast territorial waters and its proliferating offshore oil wells.[63]

One would hope that these endeavors (and others like them now under way around the world) could lead to growing international cooperation in efforts to curb piracy, terrorism, ethnic strife, and regional conflict. In fact, the National Intelligence Council spoke of such a possibility in *Global Trends 2025*. "Growing concerns over maritime security may create opportunities for multinational cooperation in protecting critical sea lanes," the report indicated. The US National Intelligence Council warned, however, that the naval programs now under way combined with growing resource competition could have the opposite effect: "Mutual suspicions regarding the intentions behind naval build-ups by potential regional rivals or the establishment of alliances that exclude key players would . . . undermine efforts for international cooperation."[64]

Increased reliance on the use of military forces as a political instrument, to intimidate potential adversaries through "show-of-force" in a crisis or to conduct "police" operations of one sort or another, also carries with it the risk of clashes with the warships of other countries, by either intention or mishap. This could occur, for example, in the policing of trade embargoes or disputes over the location of offshore boundaries. The United States, for example, has stated that it will use force to prevent any power from obstructing the freedom of navigation through the South China Sea, even though China has said these waters are part of its national territory and its ships have the right to monitor and control shipping there.[65]

Just how quickly and easily such disputes can trigger a major crisis was suggested in March 2009, when a group of five Chinese vessels harassed the American surveillance ship *Impeccable* in the South China Sea, forcing it to leave the area. The American vessel reportedly was conducting an antisubmarine surveillance mission, involving the towing of sonar equipment, when it was surrounded by the Chinese flotilla, composed of a naval intelligence ship, two trawlers, a fisheries patrol boat, and an official oceanographic ship. The Chinese ships came within 25 feet of the *Impeccable* while it was sailing about 75 miles off the coast of Hainan Island, and ordered it to leave. When the American crew requested safe passage, Chinese sailors dropped pieces of wood in its path and tried to snag the cables towing the sonar lines. The *Impeccable* was operated by a civilian crew under contract to the Military Sealift Command and was not equipped with large-caliber weapons. It eventually used a water hose to douse the Chinese sailors and free a path for its escape.[66] Although no shots were fired in this encounter, and both sides agreed to treat it as an unfortunate misunderstanding, it is easy to imagine how some future incident of this sort, involving fully equipped warships, could lead to something far more serious.

Assuming, then, that the Obama administration does opt for a national security strategy that places greater reliance on naval power and a preference for the use of sea-based rather than ground forces, it will be necessary to pay greater attention to the risks of a new arms race at sea and of the potential escalation of unintended naval clashes at sea. History suggests that these risks will increase in direct proportion to the degree to which naval force and gunboat diplomacy become the preferred instruments of military policy—and how many countries choose to adopt this approach. This is not to say that reliance on sea power is necessarily less preferable than a strategy predicated on the frequent deployment of ground forces, only that the implications of naval-centric military policy, focused largely on the need to protect US access to foreign supplies of vital resources, deserves much closer attention than it has so far received.

NOTES

1. White House, "National Security Presidential Directive NSPD-41, Maritime Security," December 21, 2004, http://fas.org/irp/offdocs/nspd/nspd41.pdf; this document is also designated "Homeland Security Presidential Directive HSPD-13."

2. US Department of the Navy, *A Cooperative Strategy for 21st-Century Seapower* (Washington, DC: US Government Printing Office, 2007), 4, 6, http://web.archive.org/web/20090227115427/http://www.navy.mil/maritime/MaritimeStrategy.pdf.

3. Integrated Headquarters of the Indian Ministry of Defence (Navy), *Freedom to Use the Seas: India's Maritime Military Strategy* (New Delhi: Ministry of Defence, 2007), 10.

4. See Alexi Barrionuevo, "President of Brazil Unveils Plan to Upgrade Military," *New York Times*, December 19, 2008.

5. Martin Parkinson, "The Role of the G-20 in the Global Financial Architecture," address to the Lowy Institute and Monash Faculty of Business and Economics, Melbourne, October 9, 2006, 17g20.pa.go.kr/Documents/role_g20_global_fin_arch _091006.pdf.

6. World Bank, *World Development Indicators 2008* (Washington, DC: World Bank, 2008), 317, data.worldbank.org/sites/default/files/wdi08.pdf.

7. US Navy, *Cooperative Strategy*, 5.

8. US Energy Information Administration (hereafter, USEIA), http://www.eia.gov /tools/faqs/faq.cfm?id=32&t=6.

9. See Michael T. Klare, *Rising Powers, Shrinking Planet: The New Geopolitics of Energy* (New York: Metropolitan Books, 2008).

10. US National Intelligence Council, *Global Trends 2025: A World Transformed* (Washington, DC: US Government Printing Office, 2008), 66, dni.gov/files/documents /Newsroom/Reports%20and%20Pubs/2025_Global_Trends_Final_Report.pdf. Cf. the next edition of this document, *Global Trends 2030: Alternative Worlds* (2012), which identifies competition arising from the "food, water, energy nexus" as one of the "megatrends" that will drive global politics in the immediate future, http://www.dni .gov/files/documents/GlobalTrends_2030.pdf.

11. See, e.g., Paul Kennedy, *The Rise and Fall of the Great Powers* (New York: Random House, 1987), 31–139.

12. Alfred Thayer Mahan, *The Influence of Sea Power upon History, 1660–1783* (Charleston, SC: BiblioBazaar, n.d.), 358. This edition is a reprint of the original, which was published in 1890.

13. Ibid., 115.

14. For a collection of Mahan's political writings, see Alfred Thayer Mahan, *The Interest of America in Sea Power Present and Future* (Charleston, SC: BiblioBazaar, n.d.). For background on Mahan's life and political activities, see Warren Zimmerman, *First Great Triumph: How Five Americans Made Their Country a World Power* (New York: Farrar, Straus & Giroux, 2002), 83–122.

15. See Zimmerman, *First Great Triumph*, 100.

16. Ibid., 235, 237.

17. Matthew Oyos, "Theodore Roosevelt," in *The Oxford Companion to American Military History*, ed. John Whiteclay Chambers III (Oxford: Oxford University Press, 1999), 624.

18. See John Lehman, "Navy, US," in *Oxford Companion to American Military History*, ed. Chambers, 489–91.

19. "DoD News Briefing with Secretary Gates from the Pentagon," April 6, 2009, http://www.defense.gov/transcripts/transcript.aspx?transcriptid=4669.

20. US Department of Defense, *Quadrennial Defense Review Report* (Washington, DC:, US Government Printing Office, 2014), http://www.defense.gov/pubs/2014 _Quadrennial_Defense_Review.pdfQ4.

21. US Navy, *Cooperative Strategy*, 8.

22. Ibid.

23. USEIA, "Petroleum & Other Liquids: US Imports by Country of Origin," http:// www.eia.gov/dnav/pet/hist/LeafHandler.ashx?n=PET&s=MTTIMUS1&f=M.

24. USEIA, *Annual Energy Outlook 2014, with Projections to 2040*, table A11, http:// www.eia.gov/forecasts/aeo/pdf/0383(2014).pdf.

25. For background on Mexican oil production, see USEIA, "Mexico," Country Analysis Brief, April 24, 2014, http://www.eia.gov/beta/international/analysis.cfm?iso=MEX.

26. USEIA, "Brazil," Country Analysis Brief, October 1, 2013, http://www.eia.gov/beta/international/analysis.cfm?iso=BRA.

27. USEIA, "Canada," Country Analysis Brief, December 10, 2012, http://www.eia.gov/beta/international/analysis.cfm?iso=CAN.

28. In 2006, e.g., the United States relied on imports for 100 percent of its bauxite, 93 percent of its platinum group metals, 81 percent of its cobalt, 79 percent of its tin, 75 percent of its chromium, and 60 percent of its nickel. US Census Bureau, *Statistical Abstract of the United States 2008* (Washington, DC: US Government Printing Office, 2007), 561, table 869.

29. See Klare, *Rising Powers, Shrinking Planet*, 55–59.

30. See, e.g., Roger C. Altman, "The Great Crash, 2008," *Foreign Affairs*, January–February 2009, 11.

31. USEIA, *International Energy Outlook 2013*, 184, table A5, and 248, table G1, http://www.eia.gov/forecasts/ieo/pdf/0484(2013).pdf.

32. See Klare, *Rising Powers, Shrinking Planet*, 63–87.

33. See Chip Cummins, "Pirates Snatch a Supertanker, Its Crew and $100 Million in Oil," *Wall Street Journal*, November 18, 2008.

34. For a list and description of recent piracy incidents, see International Maritime Bureau, "Live Piracy & Armed Robbery Report 2015," and earlier versions, https://icc-ccs.org/piracy-reporting-centre/live-piracy-reportQ5.

35. International Maritime Bureau, "Piracy Attacks Almost Doubled in 2009 First Quarter," April 21, 2009, https://icc-ccs.org; International Maritime Bureau, "Live Piracy & Armed Robbery Report 2015."

36. White House, *The National Strategy for Maritime Security* (Washington, DC: White House, 2005), 5, http://georgewbush-whitehouse.archives.gov/homeland/maritime-security.html. See also Jeffrey Gettleman, "Long Scourge of Somali Seas, Pirates Provoke World Powers," *New York Times*, September 27, 2008; and Jeffrey Gettleman, "Pirates in Skiffs Still Outmaneuvering Warships off Somalia," *New York Times*, December 16, 2008.

37. See Cummins, "Pirates Snatch a Supertanker."

38. See US Government Accountability Office, *Maritime Security: Federal Efforts Needed to Address Challenges in Preventing and Responding to Terrorist Attacks on Energy Commodity Tankers* (Washington, DC: US Government Accountability Office, 2007).

39. Ibid., 25.

40. See, e.g., Heather Timmons, "Got Oil? Now, Try to Find Tankers to Carry It," *New York Times*, June 9, 2004. See also Justin Blum, "Terrorists Have Oil Industry in Cross Hairs," *Washington Post*, September 27, 2004.

41. From an audio taped address released on Islamic websites on December 16, 2004, as cited by David Cook, *Oil and Terrorism* (Houston: James A. Baker III Institute for Public Policy, 2008), 7.

42. See Bhushan Bahree and Chip Cummins, "Thwarted Attack at Saudi Facility Stirs Energy Fears," *Wall Street Journal*, February 25, 2006.

43. See Andrew England, "Saudis Set Up Force to Guard Oil Plants," *Financial Times*, August 27, 2007; and Rasheed Abou-Alsamh, "Saudis Arrest 208 in a Sweep to Head Off Terrorist Attacks," *New York Times*, November 29, 2007.

44. For the background on this, see USEIA, "Nigeria," Country Analysis Brief, April 2005.

45. For the background on this, see Last, "Nigeria's Oil Hope and Despair"; Lydia Polgreen, "Blood Flows with Oil in Poor Nigerian Villages," *New York Times*, January 1, 2006; and Lydia Polgreen, "Armed Group Shuts Down Part of Nigeria's Oil Output," *New York Times*, February 25, 2006.

46. Angela Henshall and Spencer Swartz, "Shell Reduces Nigerian Oil Output after Attack at Sea," *Wall Street Journal*, June 20, 2008.

47. This is as cited in "Nigeria Attack Stops Shell's Bonga Offshore Oil," Reuters, June 19, 2008, http://uk.reuters.com/article/2008/06/19/uk-nigeria-shell-attack -idUKL1961289220080619.

48. David E. Sanger, "Cheney, on Carrier, Warns Iran to Keep Sea Lanes Open," *New York Times*, May 12, 2007.

49. As cited by "Iran Threat to Close Oil Strait," *Sydney Morning Herald*, June 30, 2008, http://www.smh.com.au/news/world/iran-threat-to-close-oil -strait/2008/06/29/1214677845717.html.

50. See USEIA, "South China Sea," Country Analysis Brief, March 2008; also Michael T. Klare, *Resource Wars* (New York: Metropolitan Books, 2001), 109–37. On the East China Sea, see USEIA, "East China Sea," Country Analysis Brief, March 2008; and Klare, *Rising Powers, Shrinking Planet*, 221–24. On the Caspian Sea, see USEIA, "Caspian Sea," Country Analysis Brief, January 2007; and Klare, *Resource Wars*, 81–108.

51. "Iran Is Accused of Threatening Research Vessel in Caspian Sea," *New York Times*, July 25, 2001.

52. See USEIA, "South China Sea," February 7, 2013.

53. See Jane Perlez and Rick Gladstone, "China Flexes Its Muscles in Dispute with Vietnam," *New York Times*, May 9, 2014; and Michael T. Klare, *Blood and Oil: The Dangers and Consequences of America's Growing Dependency on Imported Petroleum* (New York: Metropolitan Books, 2004), 1–55.

54. See www.jimmycarterlibrary.org/documents/speeches/su80jec.phtml. For background on the Carter Doctrine, see Michael A. Palmer, *Guardians of the Gulf* (New York: Free Press, 1992), 101–11.

55. For background on CENTCOM, see Klare, *Blood and Oil*, 1–6, 13.

56. Quoted by Charles Cobb Jr., "Larger US Troop Presence May Be Needed in Africa, Says NATO Commander," *All Africa*, May 2, 2003, available at http://allafrica .comQ6.

57. US Navy, *Cooperative Strategy*, 13–14.

58. "DoD News Briefing with Secretary Gates from the Pentagon," April 6, 2009.

59. As quoted by Peter Baker, "Obama Vows to Stop Piracy's Rise off the Coast of Africa," *New York Times*, April 14, 2009.

60. White House, Office of the Press Secretary, "Remarks by President Obama in Address to the United Nations General Assembly," September 24, 2013, https:// www.whitehouse.gov/the-press-office/2013/09/24/remarks-president-obama -address-united-nations-general-assembly.

61. See "China's Navy Spells Out Long-Range Ambitions," Reuters, April 15, 2009, http:// www.reuters.com/article/2009/04/16/us-china-military-idUSTRE53F0G920090416.

62. Integrated Headquarters of the Indian Ministry of Defence (Navy), *Freedom to Use the Seas*, 10.

63. See Alexei Barrionuevo, "President of Brazil Unveils Plan to Upgrade Military," *New York Times*, December 19, 2008; and Alexei Barrionuevo, "Brazil Signs Arms Deal with France," *New York Times*, December 24, 2008.

64. National Intelligence Council, *Global Trends 2025*, 66.

65. See Klare, *Resource Wars*, 109–37.

66. See Thom Shanker, "China Harassed US Ship, the Pentagon Says," *New York Times*, March 10, 2009.

CHAPTER 11

Intelligence, Information, and the Leverage of Sea Power

JOHN FERRIS

This chapter assesses two pairs of overlapping yet distinct topics: the relationship that intelligence and information each has with navies and with sea power. Each of these matters is complex, and their interrelationship is even more so. All intelligence is information, but not all information is intelligence. Phrased in modern jargon, information is evidence found by open sources. It is not hidden, even if it is naturally difficult to acquire or to interpret. Intelligence is a form of information that can be collected only through special means, on matters that are deliberately concealed. Acquiring intelligence means breaching the barriers of concealment, as through the use of spies, or by employing means that the barriers cannot block, as by capturing the electronic emissions of radar sets. Once acquired, intelligence and information enter the same pool of evidence for action. Until 1914 systematically analyzed information mattered more to navies than did intelligence. Since then, they have become, and remain, equals.

Sea power is the ability of a state to achieve its political, economic, and military ends on and through the oceans, by means such as maintaining access to markets and transporting troops. It is a distinct domain of power, though always, and increasingly, integrated with power in other realms. Navies are close to the center of sea power, but not the only important part. Land-based forces affect sea power: Armies are needed to hold ports, and aircraft may strike ships. Such strategic connectivity now extends to space. Until recent times, navies were the institutions on Earth that required the greatest industrial base and used the most complex machines and systems of information processing. Air forces now rival navies in these spheres, whereas space systems may supersede them. In any case, compared with armies, navies are scarce and costly, which affects their role in power politics and war. Naval battles are rare, increasing the significance of the effect of ephemeral matters like surprise, chance, and intelligence in any engagement, because another clash is unlikely to modify the outcome soon. In peacetime, the main role of navies is to exercise strength and strategy over the long term, through presence or deterrence. The value of this aim declines in war yet still remains significant. A fleet in being will always weigh heavily in negotiations, and sea control can be either challenged or asserted, even in the presence of an undefeated foe.

The value and autonomy of sea power, navies, and naval intelligence change frequently. The story of naval intelligence usually focuses on sources and methods, ignoring the broader context of power and strategy. This view is mistaken. Intelligence and information are means to guide action, whereas sea power is a lever. The actions they enable vary, depending upon the nature of naval forces, the ends and means of maritime strategy in a given period, state interests, international order, markets, and resources. The relationships among these factors have thus far fallen into three ages, with each one resting on a distinct foundation of nautical techniques, technology, and knowledge. The first age occurred when seagoing navies initially emerged, during the millennia starting in 2500 BCE. The second arose slowly between 1200 and 1600, as sailors unified the world's oceans and applied new modes of information and data processing to sea power. The third developed between 1815 and 1900, driven by changes in communications, command, and knowledge. And a fourth age may be in sight.

The role of naval intelligence in these epochs has never been examined as a topic in its own right. The best-known examples—how intelligence affected operations between 1914 and 1918 and between 1939 and 1945—are important, but they are exceptional relative to war in the more distant past, and not necessarily binding for the future. Battles, moreover, are just one matter affected by the relationship between intelligence and information on one hand, and navies and sea power on the other hand. To focus on combat alone is to overlook other functions of this relationship, and the illumination provided by older strategic experiences, as against recent operational ones. All these issues must be considered in order to comprehend the relationship between intelligence and sea power in the past, and to understand how it is changing underneath our feet.

INTELLIGENCE AND INFORMATION
IN THE FIRST AGE OF SEA POWER

Between 2500 BCE and 1400 CE, sea power emerged separately in many bodies of water, mostly narrow ones, with raiding and trading as its primary functions.[1] Sea power was a distinct domain, but navies normally were an adjunct to armies. Only in the Mediterranean Sea—and, less so, in the rivers and waters of east Asia—did navies routinely fight each other. Judging from the surviving references, and the inferences to be drawn from them, navies needed information more than they did intelligence, and found both of them hard to master. Sources were constrained. Agents and deserters occasionally proved useful, probably more than we know, but scouting and observation were the predominant sources of naval information. They offered little to strategy, but much to stratagems. The greatest effect, fundamental in import, was negative. The inability to determine enemy intentions and dispositions prevented navies from undertaking the classic functions of sea power. Its offensive elements were powerful, but its defensive ones were weak. Fleets might blockade a port, never a coast. They could damage trade but not destroy it. Navies enabled one to ship troops and invade coasts, and perhaps intercept enemy vessels trying to do so, yet as long as the foe had a fleet, it never could be prevented from using the seas or raiding one's territory or ships.

Information and intelligence offered little help to the deployment of navies, but they did shape battle, through their interaction with ignorance, surprise, and admiralship. Fleets—operating in narrow seas, often on the coast, and moving via stereotyped routes—fought mostly by mutual consent, with fair foreknowledge on both sides. Even so, perhaps only half of recorded battles were set-piece engagements with both sides prepared as they wished, which was a smaller proportion than was true on land. Surprise framed the rest. In its accidental form, stemming from the limits to information and intelligence on both sides, encounter battles were common. This condition multiplied the significance of skill, initiative, and flukes, as fleets moved suddenly from order of sail to line of battle. Thus, off Cape Bon in 468 CE, when the Vandal navy sighted the combined fleet of the Eastern and Western Roman empires, it struck before they could organize, using windward advantage to throw fire ships against vessels caught on the coast, destroying them and the last chance to salvage their state.[2] Surprise in its intentional form, by one party against another, reinforced the power of calculation. Ambush might annihilate a fleet, especially when it rested on shore, as was essential each night for classical navies on campaign. Through this means, in 405 BCE, Sparta shattered

Athens's fleet, and its independence, at Aegospotami in the Dardanelles. In 318 BCE on the Bosphorous, Antigonus the One-Eyed wrecked the navy of his Diadochi rivals, hastening their end. In 1161 CE the southern Song navy saved its state by twice ambushing and wrecking larger Jin forces as they advanced in narrow waters.

Tactical information was essential to intentional surprise. Intelligence alone could penetrate the secrecy about some combination of intentions and capabilities. It was rare, but it could shape battles as much as ever. Off Cyprus in 306 BCE, Demetrius Poliorcetes achieved the epitome of naval intelligence for perhaps the first time in history, exploiting news of a surprise attack against his fleet in order to ambush an ambusher, suddenly attacking its order of sail with his line of battle. Themistocles at Salamis in 479 BCE, and Huang Gui at Red Cliffs in 208 CE, lured larger enemies to disaster through deception, by leading foes to think they were ready to betray their allies, and so to enter an ambush. Surprise also emerged when technology was married to security, by developing edges in weaponry and hiding them from the enemy before action. Such matters were decisive in a large minority of battles, as when Romans deployed boarding bridges against Carthaginians, Rhodians threw fire pots against Seleucids, Song used catapult-launched explosives against the Jin, and Byzantines wielded Greek fire against Arabs.

Wherever they sailed, ancient mariners collected geographical, strategic, political, and economic information—and sometimes more. Carthage, Pharaonic Egypt, and Achaemenid Persia sponsored exploration on the coasts of Africa, while Asian sailors developed the monsoon route across the Indian Ocean. Carthage, and monsoon mariners, pursued monopolies on the knowledge of trading routes. Carthage and Rhodes combined their naval and commercial policies, a mercantilist strategy, using sea power to dominate markets. Most ancient states with great navies did not do so. They were not sea powers, merely landlubbers with warships. Exploration was dominated not by navies but by merchants, or by stateless people, like the greatest of the ancient sailors, the Polynesians and Norsemen. Navigation was the nautical action most supported by multiple sources of information, including memory, situational awareness, and mnemonic devices, observing the position of stars and the sun, the shapes of coastlines, and the color of water.

Navigation was also supported by tools. Sailors deep in unknown seas released birds to watch where they flew, indicating the presence of land—the earliest example of airborne reconnaissance for ships. The cast-lead, drawing data from the seabed, was the most sophisticated instrument applied to navigation, until the compass. In about 500 BCE, sailors in the Mediterranean

Sea began to produce *periplous*; this term refers both to ship's logs and to sailing directions. *Peripli* were the first known application of information processing to sea power. In words, they described navigational features, or the imports and exports associated with various locales. They guided voyages through dead reckoning across open water, by discussions of prevailing winds, sailing times, and distances. *Peripli* may have been augmented by charts of stars and coastlines, though the evidence on that matter is unclear. They were the possession of merchants, publicly available rather than secret, which was generally true of navigational knowledge as a whole. Notably, exploration and navigational technique among advanced states and merchants stalled in about 200 BCE. Ancient geographers knew how to apply mathematics to maps, combining visual representations of coastlines and degrees of latitude, but these techniques were not applied to navigation. Ancient peoples had no need for such steps. Old methods met their demands.

INTELLIGENCE AND INFORMATION IN THE SECOND AGE OF SEA POWER

Between 1200 and 1500, by improving old techniques and adding new tools, sailors moved toward processing not just information but also data, representing things through numerals or vectors. Starting in the 1100s, Chinese sailors navigated with the compass. Between 1405 and 1433, they were the first to apply it, along with charts and mnemonic devices, to oceanic voyages, in known waters, on the monsoon route. In about 1200, European sailors adopted the compass and married it to a revived form of the Portolan charts, called "rutters," which provided sailing and commercial descriptions. Nautical maps, inscribed with compass bearings and scales, so as to determine the distances between points, emerged as a genre distinct from rutters, removing the description of locales while representing a great area in one view.[3] These developments occurred when mariners worked within known waters, but subsequently supported exploration. From 1450, Iberian and Italian explorers opened the oceans by compass and dead reckoning, and recorded their discoveries on rutters and logs. In order to exploit these opportunities, their successors adapted instruments that astronomers had used for centuries, astrolabes and quadrants, to measure the altitude of the sun or stars above the horizon, so fixing latitude, which was inscribed on rutters. These data, compass bearings, and recorded distance, were collated on the master charts of oceans, which states maintained for strategic purposes.

During the 1500s states and entrepreneurs linked exploration, colonies, mercantilism, science, technology, and intelligence. As they united the oceans and the continents, mariners became the greatest sources of geographical, strategic, political, and economic information ever known. Sea power became a larger, more autonomous, domain. Navies rose in moment.[4] The seas were dominated by navies from one region, but not one polity. Every Atlantic Ocean state with a navy acted like a sea power, pursuing mercantilist policies and developing separate colonial systems. Modes of navigation became mathematized, directed by state and science. Governments sponsored training and technical developments for navigation and, later, scientific research on related matters such as longitude and magnetic declination. For the same reasons, and the first time, a source and a form of intelligence, geospatial representation— that is, maps and strategic geography—became mathematized and governed through data processing, a pattern that would become common after 1914.[5] Data fundamental to fortifications and strategy, drawn from open sources but processed methodically, were applied to topography and hydrography. This material also became securitized. Rutters and master charts became state secrets. Maps became great tools of statecraft; few copies were made, and those were often hidden even from the commanders who needed them.[6]

States collected and assessed information more than ever before, and intelligence too. Spies and code-breakers became central to power politics, but their product was hard to use for operations on land, and even harder to use at sea, where intelligence was uniquely compartmentalized, with strategic effect. Thus Elizabeth I had a great security and intelligence system. Yet it did not provide certain warning of an attack by the Spanish Armada in 1588, simply advance notice that one might happen in time to allow whatever response England could afford. Nor did this agency aid operations when the campaign began. Britain's first sure news of Spanish plans and tactics came when Francis Drake interrogated the captain of a ship taken in battle when the Armada entered the English Channel; also by observation—intelligence through combat.[7] As sea power expanded across the world, sources of naval information, intelligence, and communications remained static, augmented solely by the telescope, which extended observation only at the tactical level. The main source remained observation, characterized by the lookout on the mainmast, augmented by reports from prisoners, deserters, spies, friendly or neutral merchants, and captured documents. Old problems grew in scale precisely as—and because—sea power did.

Multiple sources of information served operations and strategy better than ever, but not intelligence, which was no more common than before. Better information aided strategy in new ways, but not tactics. In peacetime, news on the order of battle—the numbers, weapons, and characteristics of warships at various locales—was plentiful, through simple observation at sea or ashore, though one easily might miss or misconstrue data on how they would be used, on matters that turned quantities into capabilities. Mistaken judgments stemming from such technological and tactical issues (occasionally turned into intentional surprise by one side, as when Korean "turtle ships" with armor plates and artillery devastated Japanese junks in the 1590s) characterized naval battles during the transition from galleys to sail of the line, between 1530 and 1680. They declined over the next 180 years, when individual warships stayed in service for generations and worked in known ways. Material on operational matters in war, however, was hard to gather. Limits to signals made warships at sea difficult to locate, once beyond sight of land. Fleets were ignorant of anything outside the visual range of their furthest-flung vessels, perhaps fifteen miles by day and four at night. Not being able to communicate with ships beyond sight prevented the centralized collection, collation, and dissemination of information, or the use of resources, by an admiral or an admiralty. So did the scale of maritime empires; one-way communication between Europe and the Americas took ten weeks, and between Europe and India ten months. During the Napoleonic wars, whenever the British naval commander in the West Indies acquired certain knowledge of enemy forces in the region, he immediately dispatched the news to the Admiralty. Typically, the packet boat took a month to arrive. Uncertainty and inefficiency shaped the use of navies more than they did armies. A stronger power was exposed to pinpricks from inferior forces, creating opportunities and vulnerabilities in every form of oceanic struggle. The sea was easy to use for your purposes, but hard to deny to an enemy. Any force at sea, merchantman or fleet, was on its own; although, equally, once away from the coasts, a fog of ignorance shielded the vulnerable or valuable. Thus the greatest targets on the oceans, the silver galleons sailing from Mexico to Manila and the treasure fleets sailing from Havana to Cádiz, were intercepted and captured just four times each in 230 years, and then only when in coastal waters. Intended or accidental interception on the high seas was rare for fleets, but common for ships. The offensive and defensive functions of sea power worked as in antiquity, but in a greater area.[8]

Almost all naval battles still happened on the coasts, but now the coasts stretched around the world. The proportions of set-piece and encounter battles, and of accidental and intended instances of surprise, remained as in antiquity, but ambush altered in nature. It turned away from technology and toward strategy and tactics, from the intended exploitation of secret weapons toward attacks on ports, or lurking at the landfalls between continents. As they sailed into battle, fleets tried to confuse the enemy by hiding, until the last moment, how they intended to assault its formation. The vulnerability to surprise, to instantaneous assault on bad terms, combined with combat stress and the effect of smoke on visiblity, forced fleets to focus on the ability to react immediately and to avoid fragmentation. All these developments favored rigid styles of command.

The best navy of the period exemplified these problems and solutions. Between 1690 and 1898 the difficulty of finding enemies or forcing them to battle made the Royal Navy (RN) play for safety at sea, keeping most of its warships in home waters, so as to block the gravest danger, that a strong enemy suddenly might dominate those seas. This necessity weakened its sea power elsewhere, at some cost in wars between 1742 and 1763, and at a high cost in 1783, when it was a proximate cause for Britain's loss of the thirteen American colonies. Whenever pursuing an unknown enemy in open waters, the RN was driven to rely on frigates for reconnaissance, or a cordon system, ships sailing line-abreast but miles apart. During the Dutch Wars, whenever an enemy fleet was sighted, every squadron was ordered to send a frigate to join all those observing that force,

> so nigh as they can conveniently, the better to gain knowledge what they are, and of what quality; how many fireships and others; and what posture their fleet is in; which being done, the frigates are to speak together, and conclude on the report they are to give; and, accordingly, to repair to their respective squadrons and commanders in chief; and not to engage (if the enemy's ships exceed them in number), unless it appear to them on the place that they have an advantage.[9]

Thus, reconnaissance forces rather than commanders were to build and disseminate a "common operating picture" for fleets, and to determine whether battle could occur.[10] Fighting instructions, intended to maintain cohesion of command, restricted the initiative of officers.

Between 1792 and 1814, conversely, the RN broke from these restrictions, as its relative quality reached rare heights, and it found a particular solution to the problems of strategic intelligence and signals, and of denying an enemy the use of the seas. The RN's combat superiority and ability to endure a close blockade let it freeze the enemy in ports, which were known locations. Close blockades held great value for intelligence, where they were almost the functional equivalent of Room 40 (as the RN's code-breakers were known) during World War I. These circumstances maximized the RN's ability to use intelligence from all other sources, peering into ports, questioning neutral or friendly merchants, reading captured enemy shore and naval signal books, or simply reading newspapers. Whenever the enemy broke out, however, intelligence became as difficult as ever, forcing even Horatio Nelson into bizarre evolutions. Then the best source of intelligence was his sea log, a record of daily situational awareness, built up over thirty years of service, which let him predict meteorological and nautical conditions across the waves with rare accuracy, as he followed the faint spoor of his prey across the Mediterranean in 1798 and the Atlantic in 1804; just as his preferred deployment was to make his order of sail also his line of battle, allowing instantaneous assault when the enemy was found, its effect multiplied by initiative unleashed to his subordinates.[11]

INTELLIGENCE AND INFORMATION IN THE THIRD AGE OF SEA POWER

After 1815 an integrated political and economic system emerged around the world, resting on sea power, liberalism, industrialization, communication, and colonialism. Britain, the first sea power to master the oceans, used its navy to establish rules for this order, allowing all states and firms access to a maritime commons, which it policed through presence and deterrence. Other powers accepted British hegemony, which rested on power and persuasion, for a century. But then, between 1900 and 1945, they challenged these rules, and Britain's status within them. Yet this system survived these challenges, the collapse of colonialism, and the transition in dominance between two liberal powers, Britain and the United States. At sea, the order remained constant, however much its center moved, and power shifted on land.

Industrialization reshaped navies. It enabled constant changes in warships and weaponry, making the preservation or the penetration of technological secrets more important than ever. Technology always had mattered to navies, but less so to naval intelligence. Until 1670 technological surprise often shaped battle, reflecting failure in intelligence, whereas from then until 1840, designs and weapons remained stable, negating the need for it. After 1850 intelligence confronted new problems: the need to follow revolutions in warships and weapons, to gauge their impact on power, to steal foreign secrets and protect one's own. So to hasten industrialization in undeveloped countries, states and firms often cooperated to acquire advanced technology, essentially through open sources—purchases of equipment, the licensing of patents, and joint ventures.[12] The significance of acquiring intelligence on naval technology, and the secrecy surrounding it, rose steadily. In this process, closed societies had advantages over open ones, while the leaders in technology had more to protect, and to lose. Though open sources remained predominant, espionage increasingly joined the fray, with Japan taking the lead until 1941, to be succeeded by the USSR. Mistakes were common, but generally, navies understood the design characteristics of foreign equipment fairly well. The greater problem was the relationship between technology and tactics—to tell how weapons and warships actually would perform in war, well enough not to suffer surprise on fundamental matters. Given the range of issues and the ease of error, rarely could one side make major and lasting gains through technological intelligence, especially because enemies struck back.

These matters became a secondary factor in sea power and were perhaps most important in 1941, when the Imperial Japanese Navy's equipment rested on Western technology, while British and American intelligence could not determine the characteristics of Japanese warships, aircraft, and torpedoes, along with admirals and tactics. These failures were fundamental to the power of the Japanese Navy, and to the surprise that gave it an advantage as the Pacific War began, though the effect vanished within a year.[13] They stemmed from Japan's easy access to foreign technology and its ability to prevent observation of its forces, augmented by ethnocentrism, which led foreigners to think that the Japanese could not develop original technology or tactics. Yet contrary to conventional views, racism was scarcely a source for these errors. They emerged from national stereotyping, a mode of thought common among analysts and admirals, both then and now.[14]

Meanwhile, industrialization caused two revolutions in communications, which transformed both sea power and the world. Starting in 1840 the telegraph stitched the Earth together, enabling data to circulate with unprecedented quantity and speed. Though old problems of communication at sea remained, they vanished with the rise of radio. Starting in 1898, ships at sea could report their news instantly to others far away. Admiralties could give information and orders to fleets in real time, reducing uncertainty, ignorance, and inefficiency. Suddenly, and for the first time, fleets could exploit knowledge and techniques that previously had been land bound, like General Staffs and code-breaking. Two new sources made intelligence fundamental to sea power, though no one fully appreciated this fact before 1914. Signals intelligence and aircraft reconnaissance eased ambushes and enabled counter-ambushes. These solutions in depth and breadth to age-old problems of intelligence and communication bolstered the strengths of sea power, especially functions that had been hard to practice, like denying an enemy the use of the seas or conducting controlled oceanic operations, including interception by fleets. Intelligence was essential to the exercise of the classic principles of sea power, which truly became possible only in about 1900. Intelligence enabled command of the seas to become a reality, instead of words. Intelligence rose and ignorance declined among the ephemeral matters shaping battles. The power of intelligence, added to calculation, changed the nature of admiralship, and battle. Surprise characterized battle at sea, more than on land. Intended surprise became more common than ever before, as did the accidental version, though for a new reason: The complexity of naval technology made it hard to predict how kit would interact with tactics in battle. These developments were complicated by another: the rigidity of command adopted by admirals, as they sought to control fleets of unprecedented size and complexity, through brittle and fragile communication systems, and to combine a culture of reconnaissance, decision, and battle based on the ability to see with another resting on reports about matters one could not observe but only take on trust.[15]

When these events occurred, Britain dominated both the seas and signals intelligence. All lines led to London. Before 1914 the RN also made better use of these possibilities than any other fleet. It processed maritime information with unprecedented sophistication, but understood the emerging power of intelligence less well.[16] After World War I began, however, luck and ability enabled Britain to read German naval codes. In information and intelligence, the RN possessed one-sided power over its foes but found these advantages hard to apply. The Admiralty tried to use signals intelligence hundreds of times between 1914 and 1918, almost always without success—spectacularly at Jutland, and routinely against U-boats.[17] Aircraft were too slow and their ordnance was too primitive to deliver the killing blows guided by the signals intelligence of the day. If one gauged effect through operations alone, Room 40 would be a failure—more British than German warships sank in the battles it enabled; but Britain had battleships to burn and the reward was above the battle. At the strategic level, intelligence, security, and deception were fundamental to the war at sea. Simple procedures of security could achieve surprise for a fleet operation, but twenty-four hours' warning eliminated that edge—and Britain easily won the war of knowledge. For most days during the war, it knew what the German Navy was doing. This situation—combined with each side's fear that it might lose a fleet action, the Germans' unwillingness to fight except at an advantage, and the British superiority in warships—was fundamental to the war at sea, and thus to a stalemate in operations and the Teutonic defeat in strategy. Room 40 denied Germany the advantage of intelligence or surprise and wrecked its only (however faint) chance to win the naval war, a "whittling" strategy that aimed to provoke warships into ambushes. This strategy could work only if backed by intelligence. With intelligence weighted against it, these efforts enabled counter-ambushes. Intelligence strengthened the stronger navy, by removing the faint chance that German strategy could upset its weakness in sea power, less by multiplying force than by preventing its multiplication. The strategic outcome—that Britain avoided an ambush—mattered more than the tactical one: its difficulties with ambushing the ambusher. Control of the seas bolstered the bigger side, letting the Allies wield the world's resources as a weapon in Europe, and damaging the enemy's economy, with a blockade guided by the greatest systems of information processing and intelligence analysis yet seen.

The situation was more complex during World War II. Operational command and control were more fluid and powerful than twenty years before, while specialist intelligence bureaus rose in size and power. The Royal Navy declined in strength, but was augmented by the US Navy. Axis intelligence ranged from incompetent to good, but was mostly mediocre.[18] Allied services were mediocre to great, but mostly good. Initially, however, the side with superior intelligence and matériel misused its advantages. Good Axis agencies won the intelligence war in European waters during the period 1940–42. They backed an aggressive German naval campaign, supported an Italian strategy of sustaining a fleet in being, and shaped the destruction of numerous large British warships. Intelligence and information aided the success of U-boats against commerce. Yet at a strategic level, these successes, including the U-boat campaign, were minor, even counterproductive. Their pursuit broke the German navy and smothered the Italian one, which became locked in an equal, attritional exchange with Britain, which still had battleships to burn.[19] Britain won that war at sea because its sea power was greater. Ultra (the Allied code name for high-grade signals intelligence) merely contained its competition. That was all it had to do. Across the Pacific, operational conditions enabled signals intelligence of lesser technical quality than in Europe to achieve greater triumphs. Ratios of force to space were low. Naval forces were rarely in contact, and their dispositions were masked. Rarely has the initiative had such power. There was an unusual ability to concentrate against the enemy's weakness, to catch it by surprise, and to profit from knowledge of its intentions, especially for that most complex of operations, amphibious assaults. Failures in these areas were unusually costly. Ultra gave American power a razor edge, by showing how to force the enemy into disadvantageous battle, and to prevent it from returning the favor. Poor signals security and intelligence, imagery, and radar left Japan vulnerable to surprise and hastened its loss of the initiative. The United States won the Pacific War because of the quantity and quality of its forces, but intelligence let it win faster and more cheaply than it could have otherwise.

Intelligence affected sea power during the world wars more than any other campaigns in history, and not just in operations and strategy. Power and intelligence were concentrated at the tactical level through the rise of target acquisition systems for strike warfare—attack by long-range weapons directed at objects their users cannot see, guided by systems that locate targets and guide fire. Between 1914 and 1918 systems of C3I (command, control, communications, intelligence) and ISR (intelligence, surveillance, reconnaissance) filled the tactical needs of strike warfare for fleets, via distant gunfire and data processing. However labor intensive and convoluted, these systems combined the leading edges of technique and technology as well as ever. They also were stronger than the weapons they supported: guns, attacking armored targets, in many exchanges between enemies of equal capabilities. This outcome simply sharpened the process of attrition by both sides at once, changing the margins rather than the nature of operations. By 1940, however, revolutions had occurred in operations and in command-and-strike warfare, as admirals and forces, especially aircraft carriers, caught up with the opportunities enabled by C3I. Intelligence was turned into target acquisition, and operations into hard, rapid, accurate, and repetitive strikes, moving from the radius of guns to those of aircraft, and thus transforming key aspects of war. Signals intelligence, radio, radar, aircraft, and aircraft carriers created a new form of maritime war centered on strikes against soft targets— thin hulls or decks, rather than turrets. Over the next sixty years, these trends were multiplied by increases in the range and power of aircraft; in weapons, especially nuclear warheads and precision-guided munitions (PGMs); and in modes of information processing, particularly data links between ships and systems, which evolved into what is now called C4ISR (command, control, communications, computers, intelligence, surveillance, reconnaissance). Navies and air forces, working on the leading edge of information processing, developed net-centric command long before the internet existed.[20]

Sea power remained a pillar of Western strength during the Cold War, and helped the winning side to achieve its aims through dominance, presence, and deterrence, rather than combat. The enemy also was able. If the Cold War had gone hot during the 1970s, information about the US Navy's cryptographic systems provided by the Walker spy ring would have significantly aided the Soviet Navy.[21]

The period after the Cold War witnessed the culmination of three trends, which began in 1900: the increasing size and sophistication of intelligence services, and of strike forces; and the integration of power on land, sea, air, space, and cyber, into a greater sphere. These domains remained distinct, yet they were more interdependent than before. The seas mattered as much as ever to power politics, and more to economics. Sea power lost autonomy, but increased its reach. In war, weapons based on land would drive fleets from the coasts, while navies could strike further ashore than ever before. In peacetime, naval presence on the seas exerted influence inland. Strikes, space, and cyberspace reconfigured the instruments of sea power. New relationships emerged between information, intelligence, navies, and sea power. Some things changed, others remained the same.

INTELLIGENCE, INFORMATION, NAVIES, AND SEA POWER

The seas are one—a commons—as Mahan explained, open to all but ordered by sea power. Navies are a rich man's weapon, dependent on industry and wealth. Fleets, which are expensive to build and maintain, vanish without a regular program of shipbuilding. Usually, navies die in the dockyard, not in battle. Sea power is the child of wealth and resolve. Few states have maintained large navies for long, and these have commanded the seas as armies rarely have the land. Although not inevitable, hegemony at sea has been the norm since the eighteenth century. Sea powers have been few. Even spoilers (the Germans before 1914, the Soviets in the 1970s) have been uncommon. Most states and sailors are free riders. For a hegemonic sea power, all bilateral relationships shape the whole. The global nature of maritime strategy means that one problem may trigger a cascade. Like sharks, challengers cluster around signs of blood in the water.

Navies produce, consume, and act on intelligence, which focuses on the narrowest of technical issues and the broadest of political ones. Intelligence is not power, but a means to guide its use. Intelligence does not make decisions; people do. Intelligence is instrumental: It cannot be understood apart from the aims and means of actors. It provides the basis for rational action, reduces friction and uncertainty, and maximizes the efficiency of the use of one's resources while minimizing those of one's opponent—but in the context of a balance between the capabilities and characteristics of all actors. The value of intelligence is not constant; it varies with competitions and competitors. Until 1900 merely to acquire information at sea, much less intelligence, was hard—far harder than on land. Ignorance and uncertainty shaped the actions of navies more than they did those of armies. In the twentieth century developments in C3I reversed this situation. In the two world wars and the Cold War, secret and technical means—centered on technological issues, weapons, operational intentions, and capabilities and order of battle—provided the intelligence that mattered. Yet these characteristics may not hold true tomorrow. Their effect on our ideas about naval intelligence, however, distorts our ability to see changes in means, or needs, as they emerge.

Judging by doctrine, buzzwords, and investments, Western navies today think of intelligence essentially in technical and operational terms, isolated from strategy. They are good at the technicalities of C4ISR, but they overlook key problems and solutions. Today American and allied navies, the coalition sustaining the maritime order, stand strong, while sea power underwrites the world system. But this power may erode and new centers of sea power may arise, while the experience of the last hegemonic sea power to lose maritime supremacy, Britain between 1919 and 1941, demonstrates that even a country that gets most things right and outbuilds its competitors can still lose, merely by making mistakes. Nonetheless, unless Western states are foolish, probably no challenge to their dominance of the oceans, or the liberal system that governs the waves, will emerge before the middle of the present century. Thereafter, the picture will become more clouded. In readying for these eventualities, sailors and statesmen must watch for the evolution of trends in power, politics, and the instruments of sea power; and also for tipping points, moments when revolutions strike systems. They must consider questions like: Are we approaching a new age of sea power? How will it interact with the first ages of power in space and cyberspace? What will be the world order and its relationship to sea power? What changes will occur in navies, or naval intelligence, or the competitions they shape? Those issues will shape the role of sea power—as a lever for national interests, the maintenance of international order, policing, coercion, deterrence, or war—and of intelligence as a means to these ends.

These conditions define the priorities and problems for intelligence. For the foreseeable future, naval intelligence will not center on operations; however, like the battle fleet it serves, power must be retained in this area. Technical concerns may well change as much in the next twenty years as during the two decades following the collapse of the Soviet Union, a period described by Larry Ferreiro in chapter 8 of this volume. Even more, intelligence must achieve these ends while addressing current problems of order and watching for storms on the horizon—especially in strategy, technology, sources, and the links between domains of power. This process will be complicated by contradictions in the trends driving these matters, and the uncertainties that opportunity costs always introduce into policy and preparations.

PRESERVING PRESENCE

Terms like "presence" and "policing" describe standard roles for sea power, two issues that are distinct in theory but overlap in practice. The first matter, policing the maritime commons, is a principal means to exercise the functions of sea power in peacetime. Through this practice, sea powers pursue national interests and collective goods, and find that this exercise strengthens the muscles. In conditions of international anarchy, the power of the policing determines that of the maritime order that it enforces. This strength also gives sea powers the last word on law at sea. The second matter—using maritime power to shape events on the coasts, or inland—has acquired the title "stability, security, transition, and reconstruction" (SSTR).[22] Intelligence can help navies to address both these matters, which rarely involve clashes with large or advanced foes. The means are powerful, but the problems are complex. Often, they arise in areas where states have collapsed, actors are unknown, and policy is difficult to determine, while Western knowledge and sources are poor. One matter fundamental to maritime order, the rise of piracy in the Indian Ocean between 2005 and 2011, illustrates these problems. The issue is not simply force or knowledge, because navies easily could locate and destroy any pirate vessels at sea, or their bases; it is the lack of clarity about policy, and hence about the aims and use of force. Pirates were easier to handle when, once sighted, they were attacked and, once captured, they swung from the yardarm. Nor is this the worst problem at hand. Whenever Western navies engage failed states, guerrilla wars, and humanitarian crises, they will face the same problems as armies do.

Yet for the foreseeable future, Western navies can handle any matters of maritime order that they choose to address. To a lesser extent, they also can address problems of SSTR; but they should be wary, tackling only a few issues at any time, while seeking to pass those responsibilities to other entities. The requirements of SSTR and sea power conflict as much as they coincide.

Deterrence and presence are easier to exert when fleets stand on the horizon than beached ashore. SSTR is possible at present because Western navies have much power and few threats. But this situation may change. Just as ships built to fight the Cold War have proven poorly suited to SSTR, so fleets designed for policing may not match the call of combat. Similar problems might emerge for naval intelligence. In SSTR the main sources of intelligence are not naval but a mixture of materials from strategic and local levels, produced by agencies beyond the rule of admiralties. This situation raises problems of coordination. Even if sailors do collect intelligence relevant to the problems of SSTR, this intelligence will not pertain to warships or their operations but to societies. Nautical knowledge will offer little help in interpreting such material, and may receive little benefit from it. For the purposes of assessment, intelligence must delineate issues and assist in the execution of policy, which includes noting the limited value of sea power as a solution to some problems. As in other areas of military and naval practice, intelligence systems that work in SSTR may be poorly suited to perform other tasks. Such problems are manageable, with care. These missions need not harm intelligence or navies, provided their limitations are kept in mind.

KNOWING NAVAL POWER

In peacetime, assessing capabilities requires comparing what forces a rival has or is building with those you possess. It involves computations of the quality of organizations, and of technical and tactical matters—how forces and weapons actually will work against each other in war. Navies find accurate comparisons of capabilities even harder to make than armies do, because of the greater complexity of the weapons systems on which they rely, and the scarcity of the best source of evidence. Combat between land and air forces is common enough, even outside the context of a major war, offering participants and observers ample evidence for deduction. Naval battles are rare. Air forces share this characteristic to some extent; but relatively speaking, navies rely more on small numbers of the most complex machines, and fight less often, while maritime combat involves interactions among a greater range of weapons systems. In these regards, space power may prove more similar to sea power than to air power, and replace it as the strategic environment in which capabilities are the most difficult to assess.

Many problems dog judgments about naval power. States may not complete the building programs they declare, or they may hide their technical characteristics. One gauges not just foreign kit but also ideas about how it will work against yours, the classic problem of net assessment. Your views of yourself—and of sea power, operations, and warships—shape the data you try to collect and your assessment of them. To know the characteristics of any weapon is not easy, but it is nevertheless easier than knowing how it will matter in action. Technical and tactical developments may not work as you or your enemy expect, perhaps through the subsequent effects of changes in other material, as when the rise in the power of airplanes and their ordnance imposed a stiff and unexpected discount on the power of gun-firing battle-ships. Alterations to any part of a weapons system can revolutionize the work-ing of the whole, the tactics they shape, and the forces they serve, in ways no one may appreciate until the test.

Assessment involves the expertise of technical and operational authorities, not only intelligence, and it inevitably drags politics into the base of analysis. Even if you understand enemy programs perfectly, your assessment of technical and tactical matters must rely partly on guesswork about aims and intentions. Such assessments are always uncertain. The less accurate they are, the more they expose you to an ambush, or to error, to tipping points in power and surprise in war. Far more than with armies or air forces, one cannot know the technical and tactical capabilities of another navy until you fight it. These problems matter less, the stronger you are compared with your rivals.

Naval programs, especially for building the greatest of warships, have long lead times. Even when based upon the best intelligence and information available at the time, such long gestation periods (and even longer service lives) present the obvious danger of trapping oneself too early in aging technology or of starting programs too late to meet necessity. Threats take time to emerge, but one cannot easily recover from any failure to match them. Tipping points are not advertised in advance. In order to be secure, navies must recognize the emergence of potential dangers and respond long before they are obvious, and before their technical and tactical characteristics are entirely clear. Technological espionage and its security will matter more than ever as the pace of innovation increases. Yet for warnings, one cannot rely only, or primarily, on intelligence about the intentions and capabilities of rivals. The fundamental need is wisdom: a thirst for knowledge coupled with a low threshold of alarm, enough to avoid complacency on one hand, and the seductions of worst-case scenarios on the other hand. Only excellent intelligence can warn the complacent not to contemplate best cases. Good intelligence can help wise leaders distinguish worse cases from the worst ones.

It is tempting, and perhaps natural, to suppose that the characteristics of any navy can be extrapolated into the future, primarily though bean counting of current forces and construction, projection of past quality, and the watching of doctrine or declaration. At best, such calculations rest on worse cases. Intelligence cannot solve these problems—its limits are part of them. Intelligence can outline what other navies want to do, as against what they will do, given their limits and your reaction; yet it is open to error on details, especially because it encourages one to react and respond before a rival completes an action. Sailors and civilians, moreover, differ over all the problems that make sea power a distinct domain, and navies differ from other services in many crucial respects—lead times, judgments about threats, and unspoken assumptions about hegemony and challenges—to which must be added the need for steady and costly programs in the absence of clear menace. These circumstances politicize intelligence: the exaggeration of present dangers, and thus the impetus to start a program that admirals imagine will be needed against all comers a decade ahead; or attempts by politicians to economize by deferring construction, which may be justified by best-case logic. These practices pose greater obstacles for navies than for other forms of peacetime military policy.

SEA POWER AND INTELLIGENCE: A NEW AGE?

A leading sea power takes its dominance for granted. It cannot see why anyone should dislike a status that seems so convenient, is used so responsibly, and supports so many free riders. Yet any state that wishes to challenge a sea power on any matter will resent this dominance, even if there seems little reason to fear Poseidon's wrath. Why should any rival be granted the last word at sea? How better to prevent a sea power from exerting its weight on land than by pressing it on the water? Most states with navies seek not dominance but only a means to project strength, while constraining a hegemonic sea power—sometimes, merely to catch the latter's attention. Normally, friction marks relations between sea powers. Absent common enemies, interests, or ideology, the only friendly navies are weak ones. Friction shaped the simplest transfers of sea power on record—between the Netherlands and England in 1689–1715, and between the United States and Britain during the period 1918–42, even though they were eased because both sides developed close bonds while fighting deadly threats. The present cooperation between Western navies stems from common foes, a shared commitment to a liberal international system, and the shared recognition of a clear leader. If these things were to change, so might that coalition. The loss of friends shapes power as much as the rise of challengers.

In coming generations, the requirements of Asian nations for access to raw materials and markets, coupled with the Western dominance of the sea lanes connecting producers and consumers, will inevitably cause friction. Although some of these states may not seek to become sea powers, merely land powers with navies, others may present concerted challenges at sea, complicating the assessment of quality and the preparation of forces. The greatest present danger, Sino-American competition, involves problems of mutual miscomprehension in net assessments, stemming not just from differences in interests but also from the faith in legalism, progress, technology, and management common to liberal states, and from differences in perceptions between a hegemonic sea power and a challenger. Both American and Chinese leaders are certain to view their actions as defensive, and any challenge to their interests as one to virtue. Such a shared but conflicting outlook can give rise to high-risk incidents, in the belief that teaching lessons to neighbors is a good thing that they can control. These attitudes will drive any crisis between these powers in dangerous directions, and not necessarily in those directions that either intends. True success for a Western sea power would be to deter any Chinese challenge at sea through strength and persuasion, though such an outcome might simply deflect energies elsewhere. China may not attack America's sea power directly, as Germany did Britain's, thus exposing its own geopolitical and economic weaknesses. Rather, it may seek to transform the struggle through an asymmetric strategy, which might work well in the waters around Asia. China can more easily regain Taiwan through politics than warships.

Uncertainties also are emerging about the nature of navies, which present increasingly obscure targets for intelligence assessment. Given the absence of a recent maritime war, key points about combat remain obscure, though sea exercises and air battles have provided some lessons. One cannot simply assume that by 2050, operational intelligence will work as it did in 1945, or operations either—that, for instance, sea power will continue to center on "capital ships," whose dominant form is now the aircraft carrier. The rise in power of PGMs, C4ISR, and increasingly granular connectivity via "cyberspace," will change, and may transform, what navies know, and how they are able to act on that knowledge. Space-based weapons and submarines may rule the waves. Equally, given the reductions in the sizes of armies and air forces, PGMs and C4ISR might enable navies to affect land power more than ever before. Western states may dominate these areas as much, or as little, as they do sea power, because all utilize the most advanced technology, and rest on the same base of will and resources. It is unlikely that sea power will be swallowed up by the land, but these spheres will increasingly overlap. By 2050 aircraft carriers and manned combat aircraft may be obsolete, and surface navies may be secondary elements in sea power, more like a coast guard than the Grand Fleet. Understanding these developments is the central requirement for naval intelligence, and naval policy, over coming generations.

How far naval intelligence will remain a distinct domain is unclear. Sources outside the control of navies will meet many of their needs, even as the value of naval means of collecting intelligence and information rises for other consumers. Naval intelligence is likely to become even less self-contained and controlled than before 1989. Beyond narrow spheres—operations, technical and tactical matters, and strikes—naval intelligence may be dominated by open sources, and by secret ones generated by nonnaval bodies. The significance of strikes, and of the sources that service them, will expand, but both matters may cease to be primarily naval in nature. Open sources might dominate SSTR, where the best secret sources will be like those needed for counterinsurgency, social and political rather than military. At the strategic level, the dominant sources, both open and secret, may not be naval. And of course the politics of naval intelligence are liable to become confused as it ceases to be a specialist tool, working for navies alone.

The study of intelligence points to its own limits, as problem or solution. The best response to the deficiencies of intelligence at sea is to be strong, all the time, which creates problems for policy. In order to avoid surprise and to achieve victory in war, hegemonic navies must maintain a healthy superiority in peace, which has the bonus of deterring threats. Thus, during its heyday between 1715 and 1929, the Royal Navy generally relied on some version of a two-power standard. No single state could endanger Britain, only a coalition, its numerical strength divided by political fractures. A challenger finds the projected target for its naval strength even harder to define. Only when a dominant sea power backs down to a challenge can a challenger know that it is strong enough to mount one. Challengers, like Germany and the USSR, routinely spend much to build a second-best fleet, only to find it of third-rate value. The security dilemma governs the seas in unusual ways—a hegemonic sea power cannot be sure it is secure, unless its rivals know they are insecure, and accept inferiority. In naval competitions, optimality is an illusion or an accident. The only safe reaction is overreaction, however counterinstinctual to believers in arms races. Navies constantly face the problem of being far too strong, or just too weak. Stronger is better. The trick for a hegemonic sea power is to find ways to make its rule palatable to all, through mutually profitable ground rules, combined with an entry cost for competition so high as to deter all but the most determined challengers, who become easy to identify. The key challenges for naval intelligence are to distinguish reasonable worse cases from worst ones; and to define the level of superiority needed to deter serious challenges, preferably without sparking one.

NOTES

1. This analysis draws particularly from Gregory P. Gilbert, *Ancient Egyptian Sea Power and the Origin of Maritime Forces*, Foundations of International Thinking on Sea Power 1 (Canberra: Sea Power Centre, 2008); Philip De Souza, *Piracy in the Graeco-Roman World* (Cambridge: Cambridge University Press, 2002); Lionel Casson, *The Ancient Mariners*, 2nd rev. ed. (Princeton, NJ: Princeton University Press, 1991); Susan Rose, ed., *The Naval Miscellany, Volume 7* (Farnham, UK: Ashgate, 2008); and Susan Rose, *Medieval Naval Warfare, 1000–1500* (New York: Routledge, 2002). Perhaps the best work on ancient Chinese sea power is by Joseph Needham, *Science and Civilization in China, Volume 4, Part 3: Civil Engineering and Nautics* (Cambridge: Cambridge University Press, 1971).

2. Peter Heather, *The Fall of the Roman Empire: A New History of Rome and the Barbarians* (Oxford: Oxford University Press, 2005), 402–5.

3. J. B. Harley and David Woodward, eds., *The History of Cartography, Volume 1: Cartography in Prehistoric, Ancient, and Medieval Europe and the Mediterranean* (Chicago: University of Chicago Press, 1987); John Blake, *Sea Chart: The Illustrated History of Nautical Maps and Navigational Charts* (London: Conway Maritime Press, 2004).

4. John Guilmartin, *Gunpowder and Galleys: Changing Technology and Mediterranean Warfare at Sea in the 16th Century*, rev. ed. (Annapolis, MD: Naval Institute Press, 2003); Jan Glete, *Navies and Nations: Warships, Navies and State Building in Europe and America, 1500–1860* (London: Coronet Books, 1993).

5. David Woodward, ed., *The History of Cartography, Volume 3: Cartography in the European Renaissance* (Chicago: University of Chicago Press, 2007); Maria Portuondo, *Secret Science: Spanish Cosmography and the New World* (Chicago: University of Chicago Press, 2009).

6. Josef W. Konvitz, *Cartography in France: Science, Engineering, and Statecraft* (Chicago: University of Chicago Press, 1987); David Buisseret, ed., *Monarchs, Ministers, and Maps: The Emergence of Cartography as a Tool of Government in Early Modern Europe* (Chicago: University of Chicago Press, 1992).

7. Geoffrey Parker, "The Worst-Kept Secret in Europe? The European Intelligence Community and the Spanish Armada of 1588," in *Go Spy the Land: Military Intelligence in History*, ed. Keith Neilson and B. J. C. McKercher (Westport, CT: Praeger, 1992).

8. For useful accounts, cf. J. D. Alsop, "British Intelligence for the North Atlantic Theatre in the War of Spanish Succession," *Mariner's Mirror* 77, no. 2 (May 1991): 113–18;

and Ethan R. Bennett, "Fidelity & Zeal: The Earl of Sandwich, Naval Intelligence, and the Salvation of Britain, 1763–1779," *The Historian* 70, no. 4 (Winter 2008): 669–96.

9. "Instructions for the Better Ordering His Majesty's Fleet in Fighting," in *Memorials of the Professional Life and Times of Sir William Penn, Knt., Admiral and General of the Fleet . . . from 1644 to 1670*, 2 vols., ed. Granville Penn (London: James Duncan, 1833), 2:605.

10. Julian Corbett, ed., *Fighting Instructions, 1530–1816*, Publications of the Navy Records Society 29 (London: Navy Records Society, 1905).

11. Ibid.; Steven Maffeo, *Most Secret and Confidential: Intelligence in the Age of Nelson* (Annapolis, MD: Naval Institute Press, 2000); Andrew Lambert, *Nelson: Britannia's God of War* (London: Faber, 2004).

12. Alexandre Sheldon-Duplaix, "French Naval Intelligence during the Second Empire: Charles Pigeard Reporting on British and American Shipbuilding, (1865–69)," *Mariner's Mirror* 94, no. 4 (2008): 406–19; John Ferris, "A British 'Unofficial' Aviation Mission and Japanese Naval Developments, 1919–1929," *Journal of Strategic Studies* 5, no. 3 (September 1982): 416–39.

13. Douglas Ford, *The Elusive Enemy: US Naval Intelligence and the Imperial Japanese Fleet* (Annapolis, MD: Naval Institute Press, 2011).

14. Christopher Bell, "The Royal Navy, War Planning, and Intelligence between the Wars," in *Intelligence and Statecraft: The Use of and Limits of Intelligence in International Society, 1870–1970*, ed. Peter Jackson and Jennifer S. Siegel (Westport, CT: Praeger, 2005); and Greg Kennedy, "Anglo-American Strategic Relations and Intelligence Assessments of Japanese Air Power 1934–1941," *Journal of Military History* 74, no. 3 (July 2010): 737–73.

15. For one navy's experiences, cf. Andrew Gordon, *The Rules of the Game: Jutland and British Naval Command* (London: John Murray, 1996).

16. John Ferris, "Before Room 40: The British Empire and Signals Intelligence, 1989–1914," *Journal of Strategic Studies* 12, no. 4 (December 1989); Nicholas Lambert, "Transformation and Technology in the Fisher Era: the Impact of the Communications Revolution," *Journal of Strategic Studies* 27, no. 2 (June 2004): 243–72; Nicholas Lambert, "Strategic Command and Control for Maneuver Warfare: Creation of the Royal Navy's 'War Room' System, 1905–1915," *Journal of Military History* 69, no. 2 (April 2005): 369–410.

17. Patrick Beesley, *Room 40: British Naval Intelligence, 1914–18* (London: Hamish Hamilton, 1982).

18. Marcus Faulkner, "The Kriegsmarine, Signals Intelligence, and the Development of the B Dienst Before the Second World War," *Intelligence and National Security* 25, no. 4 (August 2010): 521–46.

19. David Syrett, *The Defeat of the German U-Boats* (Columbia: University of South Carolina Press, 1994); W. J. R. Gardner, *Decoding History, The Battle of the Atlantic and Ultra* (Annapolis, MD: Naval Institute Press, 2002).

20. Norman Friedman, *British Destroyers: From Earliest Days to the Second World War* (Annapolis, MD: Naval Institute Press, 2009); John Ferris, "Achieving Air Ascendancy: Challenge and Response in British Air Defence, 1915–1940," in *Air Power History: Turning Points from Kitty Hawk to Kosovo*, ed. Sebastian Cox and Peter Gray (London: Frank Cass, 2002), 21–50.

21. Christopher A. Ford and David Rosenberg, *The Admirals' Advantage: US Navy Operational Intelligence in World War II and the Cold War* (Annapolis, MD: Naval Institute Press, 2005).

22. James J. Wirtz and Jeffrey A. Larsen, eds., *Naval Peacekeeping and Humanitarian Operations: Stability from the Sea* (London: Routledge, 2009).

Conclusion

Maritime Strategy and the Next World Order

DANIEL MORAN

There is only one sea.

—Juan Sebastian del Cano, 1521

Strategy is about the future. In this it is not special; human beings spend most of their time thinking about the future, or trying to. Strictly speaking, it is impossible to think about the future because the future does not exist. Whatever we know, we know it about the past. The one thing we know about the future, or believe we do, is that it will be different. This is a distinctly modern outlook, insofar as it looks beyond the day-to-day realities of life, whose transience has always been apparent. All traditional societies have been marked by a strong confidence that, as far as the broader shape of things goes, the past is a reliable guide to the future. Traditional societies are organized to ensure that this is so. At the other extreme, modern times have been marked by such profound and pervasive experiences of change—rooted in technology and economics, but extending to all forms of social interaction and cultural expression—that we are today as confident that the future will be different as our ancestors were sure that it would not. I do not know what kinds of answers the contributors to this volume might offer if they were asked to describe what maritime strategy or global order will be like in twenty, fifty, or a hundred years; but I am confident that the least likely answer would be that they will be the same as they are today.

This situation should, in turn, force us to think carefully about the past, the raw material from which all ideas about the future must arise. Conventional wisdom in this matter is not reassuring. Hindsight, we are told, is twenty-twenty, a claim that is usually made (oddly) by way of expressing annoyance; and in any case no one really believes this, at least not about matters of real importance. The lessons of the past, whatever they are, do not leap from the page. They must be learned, and failure to learn them is bad. But living in the past is also bad, and fighting the last war especially so—because, as we know for sure, the future will be different. Historians, who make their living thinking about the past, tend to be unhelpful about the future. They like to think that nothing ever happens for the first time. But they also know that nothing ever happens again. Thinking about the future, if seriously intended, must find its way in whatever space remains between these paradoxical propositions.

In attempting to do a brief thought experiment about where maritime strategy may be headed, then, one must at least be mindful, as Ernst Gombrich once said, that "anyone who can handle a needle convincingly can make us see a thread that is not there."[1] One purpose of this volume has been to consider the threads from which the future of maritime strategy will most likely be woven. In tugging them forward in time, it makes sense to take care not to break them, even if some stretching may be required.

The strongest thread connecting the past and the future is undoubtedly the shape of the current global order as a whole. This volume has not included a theoretical discussion of the concept of order because in theoretical terms it is not especially interesting—any arrangement that is not random must display some degree of order, after all. The book's contributors have thus sought to consider the practical implications of global order as a real feature of modern economic and political life, for which purpose the important word is not "order" but "global." The claim that global order is bound up with humanity's increasingly intensive and proficient use of the sea is empirical, not theoretical. The Age of Discovery was less about finding things that were unknown than about connecting things that had been separate.

The biggest discovery of all, as reported by Magellan's master navigator, Juan del Cano, was that there was only one sea.[2] This remarkable, unitary feature of planetary geography encouraged people to conceive of economic and political relations in terms of (ostensibly) universal values that transcended the inherited norms and practices of historically separate communities, and the regional systems of trade (and war) in which they had always been embedded.[3]

The preponderant role of the marketplace in shaping the present global order has been so prominent a theme of this volume that it scarcely requires further discussion. If one wishes to pose challenging questions about the future, the possibility that the norms and values of the market might be displaced by something else is a good place to start. What might cause such displacement is anyone's guess. The triumph of the market has obviously depended on its capacity to facilitate economic growth, a process that may prove self-limiting for any number of reasons—resource constraints, environmental externalities, and the debilitating effects of persisting inequality are all prominent concerns nowadays. But the real future may turn on something else entirely. How the sea might figure in a world whose highest value is not economic growth but, for the sake of argument, ecological stability, is difficult to foresee. There is no obvious reason why the preservation of peace and good order at sea would be a lower priority in such a world. War is as bad for the environment as it is for business. The imponderable question is how far the preservation of peace at sea would matter, if the relative leverage afforded by the synergy between seaborne trade and naval power were to diminish. It is at this point, at the latest, that needle and thread part company.

More ominous, perhaps, are the anxieties that such a transition would provoke. Even if one can imagine an orderly future based on systemic values other than those that prevail at present, it is hard to imagine getting there without passing through a vale of tears reminiscent of the world wars. Such apprehension is apparent in the increasingly common practice of comparing China today with Germany before 1914.[4] The basic proposition—that a powerful nation-state's dissatisfaction with its place in the general scheme of things can prove dangerously destabilizing—is fair enough, though also fairly common. This being the case, it is not clear what, apart from illustrative drama, this particular analogy adds to the general argument. Economic growth has always created costs that are inequitably and inefficiently distributed, and the losers in this process generally get their say eventually.[5] The central question remains the same: How far the normative position and instrumental value of war today resemble what they were a century ago. This is, by definition, a matter on which history cannot provide a conclusive answer, however instructive it may be as a cautionary tale.

Most of those who argue that maritime strategy in the future will be shaped by Chinese ambition do so by way of advocating a policy of increased defense spending and robust conventional deterrence by the United States and its allies. To the extent that this argument draws strength from the events that preceded the outbreak of World War I, it turns on the possibility that, if Britain had adopted a more determined stance in opposition to Germany, Germany's leaders might not have miscalculated so badly in embarking on war. And on this issue, at least, the historical record does shed some light. In relative terms, American naval strength today far exceeds that of Great Britain at the turn of the twentieth century. One recent study has concluded that about 30 percent of all the naval combat power in the world was in British hands in 1900, and that this power was approximately double that of Britain's nearest rival, which was France. In contrast, the United States today commands about half of all the naval power that exists, and this power is about five times that of America's nearest rival, which is Russia, and ten times that of China. In naval terms, China is not a "peer competitor" of the United States; it is a peer of France.[6] This situation leads to two general conclusions. First, decisions on the margin about what kinds of naval forces the United States wishes to possess will not materially alter the balance of conventional deterrence with China anytime soon. Second, both China and the United States would do well to develop their navies with reference to broader interests, however defined, rather than each other.

That being said, the fact remains that it is hard to say how far choices about naval force structure will continue to define maritime strategy in its most elemental form: the use of force at sea. This is primarily a question of which emerging technologies offer the greatest future payoff—a matter so perplexing that it is less a question of which needle really has the thread than of which needle to follow in the first place. It is striking, for instance, that at a time when the future of aircraft carriers has become a matter of concern in the United States, the acquisition of such vessels has become a priority for a number of countries in Asia.[7] To American eyes, carriers are beginning to look awfully vulnerable to a variety of "anti-access" weapons—ranging from naval mines and antiship missiles to railguns and lasers—whose shared purpose is to force hostile warships to stay so far from shore that they cannot influence events on land. To Asian eyes, these emerging perils do not yet detract from the operational flexibility—and, arguably, political prestige—that carriers afford.

No one can say with confidence where the future balance between these trends will lie. It seems likely that the twenty-first century will see an increasingly large share of the sea controlled from the land. This probability is also reflected in emerging legal norms, which have deemed sovereign control, to varying degrees, to extend further and further from shore. But how much these developments will reduce the strategic significance of warships is hard to say. A shift of the tactical balance in favor of defensive, anti-access weapons, whether operated from sea or shore, would undoubtedly alter the manner in which maritime strategy is exercised; but whether it would reduce or strengthen its salience as a prop to global order is a matter of speculation.

Submarines represent something of an exception to this rule, and an important one. Their continued ability to operate undetected beneath the surface is owed less to human ingenuity than to the laws of physics, which have bestowed upon seawater a great capacity to dissipate the energy a submarine generates. The fact that submerged submarines are so difficult to find has lent them special significance in the nuclear arena, where they have helped to guarantee that any nuclear attack will meet with remorseless retaliation. If submarines were to become as easily detectable as, say, frigates, the destabilizing effect on nuclear deterrence would be difficult to reverse. However remote such a prospect may seem, it is not impossible. The sensitivity of astronomical radio telescopes has improved ten-thousand-fold in the last fifty years. There is no reason to think the ocean's depths will remain impenetrable forever.

It is worth recalling, finally, that the institutional and financial require-ments for exercising sea power on a scale that matters to global order have tended to moderate the disruptive consequences of new technology, and will almost certainly continue to do so. Technological mastery does not change hands overnight, a reality that the long service lives of warships reinforce. Twenty years is a long time for strategic planners, but not for naval architects. A fair share of the warships that will be floating on the sea in twenty years are there now, or in the procurement pipeline waiting to be laid down. To that extent, the capital-intensive requirements of maritime strategy make the future a little less mysterious than it might otherwise appear.

New technology may sometimes empower a war's weaker side at sea—as the submarine and the torpedo empowered Germany in 1914—but such effects have tended to fall short of what is required to determine strategic outcomes. Almost anything can be accomplished at sea in the short term—the closing of a strait, the blocking of a harbor, the sinking of a ship taken unawares. Strategic success, as this volume has emphasized, only becomes manifest with the passage of time. Among the requirements for the effective exercise of maritime strategy, a deep confidence that time is on your side may be among the most important. For those who do not believe this, the exercise of sea power holds many perils. For those who do, it remains a formidable resource.

NOTES

1. Ernst Gombrich, *Art and Illusion: A Study in the Psychology of Pictorial Representation* (Princeton, NJ: Princeton University Press, 1960), 206.

2. J. H. Parry, *The Discovery of the Sea* (Cambridge, MA: Harvard University Press, 1981), xi–xvi.

3. The universality of the values on which global order has rested have always been contested—in the past, when they were presumed to foster the natural ascendancy of the West; and more recently, when a similar presumption has attached to the efficiency and equity of market outcomes. Among recent work on the first theme, see Duncan Bell, ed., *Victorian Visions of Global Order: Empire and International Relations in Nineteenth-Century Political Thought* (Cambridge: Cambridge University Press, 2007); and on the second theme, see Ronald Findlay and Kevin H. O'Rourke, *Power and Plenty: Trade, War, and the World Economy in the Second Millennium* (Princeton, NJ: Princeton University Press, 2007).

4. See, e.g., Richard N. Rosecrance and Steven E. Miller, eds., *The Next Great War? The Roots of World War I and the Risk of US–China Conflict* (Cambridge, MA: MIT Press, 2014); and Christopher Coker, *The Improbable War: China, The United States, and the Logic of Great Power Conflict* (Oxford: Oxford University Press, 2015).

5. See Harold James, *The Creation and Destruction of Value: The Globalization Cycle* (Cambridge, MA: Harvard University Press, 2009).

6. Brian Crisher and Mark Souva, "Power at Sea: A Naval Power Dataset, 1865–2011," *International Interactions* 40, no 4 (2014), 602–29, figure 1, http://www.briancrisher.net /naval-data-project/. Crisher and Souva disregard nuclear weapons in their estimate of naval combat power.

7. See Christian P. Richer, "The Carrier Arms Race in East and South Asia" (master's thesis, Naval Postgraduate School, 2014), http://calhoun.nps.edu/bitstream /handle/10945/43987/14Sep_Richer_Christian.pdf?sequence=1; and, more generally, Geoffrey Till, *Asia's Naval Expansion: An Arms Race in the Making?* (London: International Institute for Strategic Studies, 2012).

Contributors

Klaus Dodds is professor of geopolitics at Royal Holloway, University of London.

Larrie D. Ferreiro is director of research and professor of systems engineering, science, and technology management at the Defense Acquisition University in Fort Belvoir, Virginia.

John Ferris is professor of history at the University of Calgary.

Steven Haines is the Vice Chancellor's Research Professor in Public International Law at the University of Greenwich and research associate at the Centre for Rising Powers at the University of Cambridge.

Michael T. Klare is the Five College Professor of Peace and World Security Studies, a joint appointment at Amherst College, Hampshire College, Mount Holyoke College, Smith College, and the University of Massachusetts Amherst.

Andrew Lambert is Laughton Professor of Naval History in the Department of War Studies of King's College London.

Daniel Moran is professor of international history at the Naval Postgraduate School, Monterey, California.

Alessio Patalano is a lecturer in war studies and director of the Asian Security and Warfare Research Group at the Department of War Studies of King's College London.

James A. Russell is associate professor of Middle Eastern politics at the Naval Postgraduate School in Monterey, California.

Giuseppe Schivardi is a captain in the Italian Navy, and former director of the research center of the Italian Naval Staff College in Venice.

Geoffrey Till is emeritus professor of maritime studies in the Defense Studies Department of King's College London.

Index